Megan

Tasting
the **Word** of
God

Commentaries on the
Daily Lectionary

New City Press
Hyde Park, New York

Published in the United States by New City Press
202 Comforter Blvd., Hyde Park, NY 12538
www.newcitypress.com
©2010 Megan McKenna

Cover design by Durva Correia

Library of Congress Cataloging-in-Publication Data:

McKenna, Megan.
  Tasting the Word of God / by Megan McKenna.
    p. cm.
  Includes bibliographical references.
  ISBN 978-1-56548-355-2 (v.1 : pbk. : alk. paper) — ISBN 978-1-56548-356-9
(v.2 : pbk. : alk. paper) 1. Church year meditations. 2. Catholic Church—
Prayers and devotions. 3. Bible—Meditations. 4. Catholic Church. Lectionary
for Mass (U.S.). 5. Common lectionary (1992) I. Title.
  BX2170.C55M425 2010
  242'.3—dc22   2010025965

Printed in the United States of America

Contents

WEEKDAYS IN ORDINARY TIME

PROPER OF SAINTS

CONTENTS

INTRODUCTION

Is not my word like fire, says the Lord, like a hammer shattering rocks?

- Jeremiah 23:29

There are so many descriptions of what the Word of God is like, both in the Older Testament of the Jewish people and in the New Testament. And these descriptions also tell us what the Word of God is supposed to be doing to us, and calling forth within us when we listen and take heed of this holy Word of God. The Word of God was first and foremost (and still should be) meant to be read aloud, in community so that others could listen, watch, be attentive together and then call each other to conversion and to actually putting into practice this Word of God on a daily basis. The Word of God is formational, a discipline, a practice, a way of sitting at the feet of a master, as disciple among other disciples, confirming and exhorting, comforting and transforming, and the source of not only our personal relationships with God and one another, but our relationship as the Body of Christ as the beloved children of God born of the Spirit, with Jesus to the honor of the Father—all of us dwelling in the Trinity together.

To listen to the Word of God daily in the liturgy of the Church or with a small community of believers gathered as Church provides a very different experience than hearing the Word within the context of the Sunday liturgy that of its nature is more universal to the Church's life, more pastoral for the parish and community's life and more a witness to what the Church is supposed to be in the world as witness and presence. The daily readings [and liturgy] must deal with a tension between extremes: that of becoming purely a personal devotion for those attending and the temptation to become another mini-celebration of the Sunday Eucharist among a few that can often begin to think that "they" really are the 'church' rather than the larger universal Body of Christ. And it is for these reasons that the daily readings of the Word of God must be approached, listened to and absorbed, even reflected upon and preached with another focus, another intent, or another purpose. The descriptions of the Word of God in the Scriptures can serve as places of reference and sources of how to listen and how to become the Word that we proclaim.

In Jeremiah's description there are two powerful forces that are used to describe the Word of God—fire and a hammer shattering rocks! Neither of them are very comforting. Both are demanding and provocative as images. Fire—we like to think of fire as warming, comforting, light in darkness, a place of protection from what is 'out there', cooking food making it more edible and giving it richer flavor and taste. And all of these can be images of what the Word of God on a daily basis can be—but because fire is paired with a hammer shattering rock, it must give us pause. Fire also burns, reduces to ashes, destroys utterly, inflicts terrible pain, purifies, cauterizes, cleans and takes from us material possessions, and our lives and the lives of others. It can be on a personal scale—an accident, house-burning or over a stove, in a forest when one is not prepared for the wind—or it can be on a massive scale, an explosion, a weapon, nuclear power, bombs, accidents at power plants, fires sparked by lightning or carelessness. The Word of God on a daily basis can be like that too—and should be—because as the beloved children of God, we are called to constant conversion, a lifestyle of change and transformation—until we become the words we proclaim, words of God in the world, speaking by our presence and actions to others. This is the basis of evangelization—being living breathing words of God for others.

What is like to think of the Word of God like a hammer shattering rock? Again, this is no easy image. It is relentless, never ending, even to getting to the first break off of stone. It is brutal, exhausting, demanding, reminding us constantly of hardness of heart, of our own stubbornness and how we are heavy stones, rocks that are often burdens to others. We can build walls with our religion and spiritualities—that divide, and separate rather than protect, and forget to leave openings and spaces for others to enter or leave. We are often stumbling blocks for others and stand in the way of the coming of the kingdom of justice, mercy and peace in the world. In Mark's gospel we are told the story of Jesus turning on Peter and the disciples who don't want to hear what he is saying or accept what it might mean for Jesus and for them—the reality of the cross. "Then Peter took him aside and began to rebuke him. At this he [Jesus] turned around and, looking at his disciples, rebuked Peter and said, "Get behind me, Satan. You are thinking not as God does, but as human beings do." (Mk 8:32b-33) Peter, the rock, is also Peter the stumbling block, the spokesman for all the disciples' reluctance and refusal to listen to Jesus. It is interesting to note that the word 'listen' means to obey and the word 'Satan' means the hinderer—or the stumbling block or the one who is like rock that needs a hammer to work on it to become once again a building block for the kingdom of Jesus in the world.

Thomas Merton, a Trappist monk wrote in one of his Journals these words:

"The Word" [of God] is 'a flood that breaks the dam." This from a Babylonian source, but in the Spirit of the Old Testament…but basic. One senses this in our community to some extent. Uneasiness, anguish, dis-ease, because something is building up to break the dam and this 'word' is inscrutably different from the comforting platitudes of the Superiors. But this sense pervades all of society—is resisted by those who erect their word into a dam and are determined to 'hold' it at any price. Journals 6:165, The Merton Institute, Advent Daily Reflection, Saturday, December 19, online.

This short passage reflects both sides of the Word of God being 'a flood that breaks the dam'….an image closely aligned to that of the hammer shattering rock—describing us, those who listen to the Word over and over again, and those who resist and reject the

Word, making our own dams and hammers of our words. The Word of God was originally written by the inspired authors for people who already believed in Jesus as the Word of God and who called themselves disciples of the Way of Jesus but were having difficulty living up to their Baptismal promises in their daily life, in history, politically, economically, personally and in public. They needed to constantly be reminded of what they had professed to be—the beloved children of God the Father, the brothers and sisters of Jesus, the dwelling places of the Spirit of Truth and the Body of Christ in the world as witness. The Word must speak to individuals, to small communities, to parishes and to the Church at large. Continual hearing of the Word of God in daily liturgies must incorporate this process and power in what is said as commentary and reflection, short as it must be, of necessity.

And there are other images. On a more personal level, in an earlier chapter of Jeremiah, this is what he has to say, speaking directly to God about God's word.

> You duped me, O Lord, and I let myself be duped; you were too strong for me, and you triumphed.
> All the day I am an object of laugher, everyone mocks me.
> Whenever I speak, I must cry out, violence and outrage is my message;
> The Word of the Lord has brought me derision and reproach all the day.
> I say to myself, I will not mention him, I will speak in his name no more,
> But then it becomes like fire burning in my heart, imprisoned in my bones; I grow weary holding it in, I cannot endure it.
>
> *- Jeremiah 20:7-9*

Now we can comfort ourselves, or even excuse ourselves with the thought that Jeremiah was a prophet—and we are not. But in reality, by our baptisms and confirmation we are all called to be prophetic, and as members of the Body of Christ to speak the truth on behalf of justice, peace, no violence, the poor and outcast and to uncover the kingdom of God among us and build it up into a dwelling place for all the needy of the world. The Word of God is always about our brothers and sisters—all the other people in the world, perhaps even more than it is about us as individuals. It is always about our relationship with others that are the primary places of revelation about the state of our relationships with God. We, like Jeremiah often, can wax eloquent about the state of our own souls and lives, but we don't often do as well in compassion and justice for others. We are summoned daily in the Word of God 'to speak in his name' but do we?

But Jeremiah and the other prophets know the Word of God *as a fountain of living water, as the source of joy and happiness of his heart that he devoured* [Jer 16:16] and as the source of anyone who is just and trusts in the Lord, *'like a tree planted by the waters that stretches out its roots to the stream; It fears not the heat when it comes, its leaves stay green; in the year of drought it shows no distress, but still bears fruit.'* [Jer 17:7-8] The Word of Lord taken in daily is the source of development, growth, maturity and fruit for others—no matter the season. It is the mainstay of faithfulness, of daily devotion and practice and it can be refreshment and courage to persevere (what is needed as a prerequisite to serve others). It stretches us and keeps us healthy, reminding us that we live so as to serve God in worship by serving others in their need, bearing with one another's burdens and easing one another's way as we walk together before God, with God and dwell within God.

The prophet Isaiah uses an image of the Word of God that is strong and connects us to all of earth, the weather, time and to the will and work of God. It comes immediately after an impassioned plea to repent, to call on and seek God while God is close, and to turn to God for mercy for God is generous and forgiving. The piece tells us much about God and about God's word.

> For my thoughts are not your thoughts, nor are your ways my ways, says the Lord. As high as the heavens are above the earth, so high are my ways above your ways and my thoughts above your thoughts.
> For just as from the heavens the rain and the snow come down and do not return there tell they have watered the earth making it fertile and fruitful,

Giving seed to him who sows and bread to the one who
eats,
*So shall my word be that goes forth from my mouth; it shall
not return to me void, but shall do my will, achieving the end
for which I sent it.* [Isaiah 55:8-11]

God's Word is meant to become a reality in the world, and in our
lives personally and with others. It is not just for reflection, comfort,
praying with and singing—it is to come true in our lives. When
we listen to the daily readings of the lectionary which often follow
paragraph upon paragraph in a particular text, we must make sure
that there is something pragmatic, practical and specific that we can
do, either alone, or with others so that God's word does indeed 'not
return to me void, but shall do my will.' Daily listening to the Word
of God must penetrate deeply into our thoughts and be expressed in
our ways of living and relating with others—do we seek the mercy
of God and reflect our God in the mercy we share with others. God's
Word often reveals God—especially in the words of the prophets
and in the mouth of Jesus who describes his Father in all his words,
his parables, stories and preaching and in what he does, who he
takes into his company and who he befriends. This must form part
of our response to the Word of God if daily reflections are to retain
integrity.

There are innumerable other images of God—the famous line
in one of Paul's letters: *"The Word is a double-edged sword that cuts
through bone..."* [Hebrews 4:12], and in many of the prophets we
are told to 'eat the scroll' and become the words we speak to others.
We must become the message. The readings of liturgy, the breaking
open of the Word are intimately connected to the breaking of the
bread, the sharing and the eating of the Eucharist. The Word tells
us what we are to become and we chew on the Word, and then eat
so that we might have the strength, the courage and the sources to
obey the Word that we have heard and seek to take to heart.

Daily reflections must be short, precise, pointed. These com-
mentaries are like drops of water, bits of fire, one hammer slam,
one sword slice, a flicker of flame, an insight, a taste of courage

or comfort. There is a saying in New Mexico and many parts of the southwestern deserts of the United States when it rains—for only for short moments. It is said that 'God is spitting at us.' In some ways that is what these reflections are for the daily readings of the Lectionary. Take a word, a phrase, a sentence at most— from the readings and comment on it, spin it out pastorally, pragmatically—how to live this today and make it come true. Ask them for a word, only one that struck them—and listen as the words are spoken—no explanations, just the Word of the Lord, literally that spoke to them and allow a few minutes (3 or 4) for all to sit and absorb what they have heard. Take one line and repeat it 3 or 4 times so that all can hear it and learn it by heart. In daily readings and reflections, brevity and depth let the Word act upon us, calling us to deeper integrity, knowledge of God and summons us to become what we proclaim—the Word of God, enfleshed in Jesus, by the power of the Spirit to the glory of the Father—now hopefully enfleshed in us.

- Megan McKenna

PROPER OF SEASONS

ADVENT and CHRISTMAS

FIRST WEEK OF ADVENT

Monday

FIRST READING   **I.** Is 4:2–6

                                            II. Is 2:1–5

Responsorial Psalm   Ps 122:1–2, 3–4, 4–5, 6–7, 8–9

GOSPEL   Mt 8:5–11

✺ "I am not worthy to have you come under my roof. Just give an order and my boy will be healed." A statement of obedience, of knowing whose authority you live under and what authority is most true and powerful. This is a military man who knows that before the face of Jesus, his authority is nothing. Who do we obey? Who do we belong to? When Jesus says: "Do this." Do we actually move to comply? Jesus wills to heal us, not only of illness. He wills to take our divided hearts and turn them whole-heartedly to the service of life and those in need. Come, Lord Jesus, come!

✺ Advent is the time of dreams, old and traditional yet ever de-sired and hoped for by the peoples of the earth. We are sum-moned to climb the mountain of the Lord and be instructed in the ways of God. These ways are of peace, nonviolence, food for all, living with wisdom and no war. Is it a dream? Or is it the will of God that we have all wandered far from in our sin and arrogance? God invites all of us to come and sit at the feast in His kingdom. Are we obedient and faithful to Jesus' words, knowing the power of God in Jesus?

✺ Now is the time for visions. These are the priorities of God— are they ours too? Are we the holy ones of God? Have we been purged and cleansed? Do we live with the knowledge that God is our shelter, our protection, and is always present with us as a refuge and cover from turmoil? Do we treat the earth so that it is luster and splendor revealing God for everyone?

What is our attitude towards Jesus the Christ—is it like that of the centurion, an outsider who comes with such respect and honor for Jesus' power that he knows just Jesus' Word is enough to heal and give life, releasing from paralysis and even from a distance? Does God find faith like this in us who cherish his Word and seek its power to convert and heal our own broken lives in Church and the world?

Tuesday

FIRST READING   Is 11:1–10
Responsorial Psalm   Ps 72:1–2, 7–8, 12–13, 17
GOSPEL   Lk 10:21–24

Jesus prays, teaching us. First we are to praise the will of our Father and to remember that all that is given to us comes from God's goodness. And we only know the Father by the kindness and revelation of Jesus and only know Jesus by the Father's disclosure. In our baptisms the Trinity dwells with us and the Spirit teaches us how to pray—in words, beyond words, into the silence of presence, knowledge and obedience. How fortunate we are to know what kings and prophets longed for. Today may we live in gratitude for the gift of the indwelling presence of the Holy Ones seeking to make us one with all people, one with Them.

The one sent by God is blessed with the fullness of the Spirit and gifts that are used for judging the poor with justice and care for the land's afflicted. His presence brings peace among enemies, and the power of the child of God to lead and guide them together: this peace is knowledge of God that will be like a signal flare for the entire world. Jesus is the beloved child of God, and we are all God's beloved children in baptism. And our God seeks to reveal hidden mysteries and knowledge of the Father, Son and Spirit to us—are we listening and seeing what is given to us?

Our God comes: he is the one who bears the Spirit of the Lord upon him, filled with the gifts of the Spirit (shared with us in baptism). He comes with justice, with the words of truth and he decides for the afflicted of the world. Do we? If so, then there will be healing of divisions, the coming together of enemies and the climate and care for peace among all peoples, nations, religions. A child will guide them—the child of God whose dwelling place is glorious because it is one of reconciliation and peace for all.

Jesus prays in gratitude for the fulfillment of this prophecy not only in his own person as the beloved child of God, but in the lives of all of us who have been made children of God by baptism and by Jesus' Word, life, death and resurrection. This dwelling place is with God, the Father, the Son and the Spirit—this is home. This is peace upon the earth and if we dwell in God, then we must make Jesus' prayer and words come true in the world. Have we been taught by the word of God, or are we still blind and deaf to God's prayer?

Wednesday

FIRST READING   Is 25:6–10
Responsorial Psalm   Ps 23:1–3, 3–4, 5, 6
GOSPEL   Mt 15:29–37

The dreams of God always include feasting and communion among all peoples, rejoicing together and forgiveness. This is the marvel of God's salvation—we are rescued from death and evil that destroys. Behold our God! Our God in Jesus' presence among us heals, gives hope, feeds and exhorts his disciples to care for the masses of people as he does—with pity. And with God there is always enough left over to feed the world. Do we see how the dream has become flesh in Jesus and that our way of life is to make that dream always reality in our world?

In this mountain (once Sinai, now the church in the world) God provides for all people's needs: food, drink, shelter, justice, hope, communion and peace among nations. In God's dwelling there is joy and life, forgiveness and mercy unsurpassed. This is what we have been given and what we are to share with everyone. This is life—the life of God in Jesus—this is the good news. And Jesus, once the child born in a stable in poverty now walks the earth healing, touching those in pain, the outcast and those lost to the world and others' love. God in Jesus is pity, compassion and food that fills and nourishes. We are given the Word of God and the bread that sustains us—Eucharist. And there is enough, more than enough for us, and leftovers to feed a world. What are we doing with all the leftovers, with the excess of word, bread and mercy that our God gives us daily?

Thursday

FIRST READING   Is 26:1–6
Responsorial Psalm   Ps 118:1 and 8–9, 19–21, 25–27a
GOSPEL   Mt 7:21, 24–27

Are we to be counted among the wise in God's domain? Do we build our houses on the rock of the Scriptures, the rock of the Word of God Jesus so that nothing can prevail against us? Or do we have divided bases, mixed with sand, the world's foundations of greed, self-absorption, competitiveness and violence? And so with changing weathers all that we have slips and slides and like a fool we live in a collapsing house? Only two choices: Choose—the Word of justice and truth or all the other words jostling for position—Choose and save your life!

Dreams also come from singing as well as seeing. The song reminds us to be a nation that is faithful, just, and live with a firm purpose of peace. This demands trust in the Lord. And the dream includes judgment: being humbled and brought down to the dust, or set as a strong city that protects. The judgment will be based on care of the poor and the needy in that nation. Do we hear the word of God and put it into practice? We are warned that it's not enough to cry out that God is our Lord, but we must work at making God's will the foundation of our lives.

We are called to sing, and open the gates of our dwelling place with God and let in the just, and make sure that our dwelling place with others is a place of peace and trust not only in God but in one another. Our God is with the lowly (those who do no violence) and gives to the needy what others have kept from them unjustly. Our God walks in the footsteps of the poor and this is cause for rejoicing and singing!

Jesus cries out that if we are to enter God's kingdom now and for all time than we must make sure that we are doing the will of our Father. We have heard the words for years, and pray the words, but do we practice the will of God? Are our priorities the care of the poor and the needy, the coming of justice and the making of peace, reconciliation of all peoples and doing no violence? Or are our lives built on sand?

Friday

FIRST READING   Is 29:17–24
Responsorial Psalm   Ps 27:1, 4, 13–14
GOSPEL   Mt 9:27–31

 Now we encounter two blind men following Jesus and shouting after him: "Son of David, help us!" They are acutely aware of their darkness and their need. And Jesus turns to question each of us: "Do you believe that I am able to do what you want?" They are quick to answer "Yes" and their eyes are touched and opened. Our eyes have been touched in baptism, anointed with oil, washed out with the waters of truth and joy. Are our eyes still open or have they slowly started to close, shrinking down our hearts and shutting out the light of the world? Do we believe? How do others know that we walk in the light?

God's intent is fruitfulness, beauty, abundant life, wholeness, healing and light. God is on the side of the poor and the lowly and not the side of the tyrant, the powerful or the arrogant and those whose ways are unjust and violent. We are called to reverence the Holy One and be in awe of God—in Jesus, the beloved servant-child of God. We are to be instructed and learn how to live by Jesus' example. In baptism our eyes have been touched and opened so that we can see the power of God in Jesus, the incarnation of God: human and divine. Do we cry out for the sight of God—not just to see God, but to see as God sees—ourselves and ask for pity—and others and show them pity and God's goodness?

Saturday

FIRST READING   Is 30:19–21, 23–26
Responsorial Psalm   Ps 147:1–2, 3–4, 5–6
GOSPEL   Mt 9:35—10:1, 6–8

It is Advent and Jesus is traveling the towns proclaiming hope, good news to the poor and healing. The crowds call forth waves of pity and Jesus exhorts his disciples to reach out and to pray for others, many others to join him in this work that stretches across a world and through time. The work is staggering: heal the sick, bring the dead back to life, cleanse the lepers and drive out demons—this power has been given to us as gift and our lives must be a constant gift-giving and sharing with others. Xavier did it half a world away from his home. We can go that far, but we can do it across the street and downtown, anywhere. Give!

God's words in Isaiah remind us of all that God does for his people. God is gracious to us, hearing our cries/prayers, giving us bread and water, being our Teacher, showing us the way and teaching us right from wrong. God gives seed, water and harvest and animals for toil and sustenance. But our God judges, both destroying and binding up our wounds. But we are told that we must be merciful to know the mercy of God. In Jesus everyone knows the mercy of God: healing, life, forgiveness, remembrance and goodness that is stronger than injustice. We have been gifted. Do we give as we have been given?

SECOND WEEK OF ADVENT

Monday

FIRST READING   Is 35:1–10
Responsorial Psalm   Ps 85:9 and 10, 11–12, 13–14
GOSPEL   Lk 5:17–26

✴ Amazement seizes the people. The works of God are about life, about friendship and serving one another in need, about faith in desperate times, about forgiveness and learning again to fear only God and no one else. God comes with courage, strength to stand up and transformation not only of human beings but the very ground we stand on. In the presence of our God everything matures, blooms and bursts forth with freshness and passion and grace. Does our presence in the world bring forth such peace and wholeness, such justice and grace? Make it so today!

✴ Advent—God is coming towards us. And even the earth itself, desert and steppe will respond to his presence passing by. Human beings will take heart, be strengthened and respond like earth. We are being saved, ransomed, and crowned with joy. This is God's recompense and vindication for those who wait and are faithful. Jesus' presence calls forth this freedom, this healing and wholeness. Jesus forgives and heals when he sees the paralytic's friends lowering him through the roof. Who are we bringing into the presence of Jesus? Are we living and responding to Jesus' presence among us or discussing who Jesus might be?

✴ First we see this life of God in the earth, deserts, plants, barren wastes and dead trees blossoming. Life returns in water (baptism) bringing lushness of life, food in abundance for all living things and then it seeps into humans' bones, hands, knees and hearts to bring hope and vindication. Eyes, ears and tongues are opened and loosed and human beings leap and dance in the presence of such wild life. And there is a highway for all of us to walk on now, since our God has ransomed us in the birth, death and resurrection of Jesus. We must rejoice at the coming of God in Jesus.

But there are many who do not. Jesus is moved by the Spirit of God to heal. A man's friends do everything to get him to Jesus in spite of the crowd around him (many who are cynical, and do not believe in Jesus—having their own ideas about the one who is to come should be and how he should act). But Jesus forgives the man—gives him hope/life/acceptance before God and everyone! With a word, Jesus commands the man to rise to new life and the people rejoice. But others do not. And what of us: do we rejoice in the life that God gives to others or are we annoyed that this Jesus, the child of God does not act like we want him to?

Tuesday

FIRST READING   Is 40:1–11
Responsorial Psalm   Ps 96:1–2, 3 and 10, 11–12, 13
GOSPEL   Mt 18:12–14

A parable of one hundred sheep left behind and the shepherd searching for one wandering stray—crazy! Unbelievable! Marvelous! And our God thoroughly delighted at finding the one who's lost and in dire straits. So many little ones and God doesn't want to lose a one! The bishop Nicholas took this image of God to heart and spent a lifetime rescuing the poor, giving young girls dowries for a marriage, protecting the Jews from murderous Christians, planting food, seeds, money and whatever was needed in the meager belongings of those caught in misery and sickness so that they were surprised by the goodness of God that was tucked into the folds of their garments. Look! Do a little sleuthing and searching and delight the heart of our God today!

Isaiah's visions are of a God not just of Israel, but of all nations and of the earth itself, mighty in power, vast in creation, calling every person by name. God is strength that shares its power. God is knowledge that is beyond comprehension and anyone who puts their hope in God will 'soar as with eagles' wings and will run and not grow weary, walk and not grow faint.' Are we renewing our life, our being, in this God or are we squandering our energies and attention elsewhere?

It is time to come back to God. Are we weary from doing the work of God? Do we find life burdensome because we are collecting clutter and finding ourselves tangled in the mesh of our plans and projects? It is time to take the yoke of the cross, the yoke of community, the yoke of baptismal life upon us and learn to walk Jesus' way. This way is gentle, humble, lowly, without violence, greed, grasping or fear. This yoke is the shadow of God upon us in Jesus.

Wednesday

FIRST READING	Is 40:25–31
Responsorial Psalm	Ps 103:1–2, 3–4, 8 and 10
GOSPEL	Mt 11:28–30

✺ Another of Jesus' prayers: Come to me you who are worn out from bringing the kingdom of peace to earth. Bear the yoke of community, of the cross and joy upon your shoulders and work and dance together with me. I am non-violent, meek and humble of heart and I hold you in peace, in goodness and stillness. My burden is Light! It comes shining and singing through us when we learn not to get in the way and to stand arms wide and heart open to the coming of God in Word and the poor who wait for us. Ambrose used everything he could: philosophy, politics and patience to convert and help others mature and become steadfast in faith. What can we use to ease the burden of others and be faithful together?

✺ Our God is strength, might, creating and sustaining. And God shares his strength with those who need it, an unending source of hope and power. If we rely on the Lord and put our trust in him we will run and not grow weary and even soar with eagles' wings in our lives. Yahweh graces Jesus with this strength, and he invites us to come to him when we are weary and find life hard because we have been working for God's justice, the poor and peace. We will be yoked with Jesus' cross and glory and our lives will be light. Together we will all dance. God's dreams are reality in Jesus and he wants to continue making them come true in us.

Thursday

FIRST READING   Is 41:13–20
Responsorial Psalm   Ps 145:1 and 9, 10–11, 12–13
GOSPEL   Mt 11:11–15

Isaiah's description of God grasping us by the hand, telling us not to fear and once again telling us that our redeemer is coming. We are given a vision of what we are to be—like John the Baptist, calling for judgment and what we are to be doing as the least in the kingdom of God—making sure the poor are heard, that there is water for all, that the earth and is peoples blossom and thrive so that everyone knows that the hand of the Lord does this and that God is recreating us in the person/the body of Jesus. Are we hearing? Are we heeding the prophets and Jesus' Word?

Our God grasps hold of us and tells us not to fear even though we are described as maggots and worms—not flattering. But we are given a redeemer and will be made into a thresher that is sharp and sure, ready to harvest and rejoice. It is our God who will care for the thirsty and hungry and turn every level of land into the next spacious place to dwell. Our God sees, knows what little we do and will do what is necessary. The hand of the Lord is the body of Jesus.

And Jesus praises John the prophet as the greatest in history and yet the least born into the world of water/spirit/word and bread—the kingdom of God is greater than John! There has been violence since John (beheaded) and there will be violence towards those who belong to Jesus but if we heed the words of Jesus then we will see the fulfillment of all the promises of God in his Body, the Church and those who obey him. This is what God would like for a Christmas gift.

Friday

FIRST READING   Is 48:17–19
Responsorial Psalm   Ps 1:1–2, 3, 4, 6
GOSPEL   Mt 11:16–19

We keep returning to our need for conversion: to stop doing what we are intent on and to begin to live as those intent on the coming of God in history and our lives. Are we acting more like children sitting in the marketplace complaining and whining and finding fault with everything? Do we resist the penance and asceticism of John that calls for laying bare our lives that have collected a lot of excess—and do we also resist the call of Jesus for making peace with our enemies, asking for forgiveness and reaching out to those around us that we condemn? Is there any Wisdom revealed in our words and wants? Wisdom, come and lay bare our minds and souls that we might be a friend to God who is a friend to sinners.

God is pleading and begging us to listen. If only we would heed God's Word, then God would bend to us, lead us, be our vindication and even our descendants would know the richness and goodness of God. This is the Holy One of Israel! And Jesus laments and decries his own people: acting like spoiled children, whining and complaining. We know nothing of the wisdom of repentance or the wisdom of Jesus, the Son of Man. Does Jesus look at us, disgusted and frustrated because we will not listen or obey?

Do we let God teach us and lead us where we should go? Do we hearken to God's commandments and remember that our God is the Holy One? Is our name always in the presence of God because of our goodness shared or because of our lack of response to God's Word? Who are we—in Jesus' words, we have two choices, in his time and now in our time? Are we children squatting in the street and moaning and groaning about life? Do we find something wrong with absolutely everyone—whether they come like John the Baptist or they come like Jesus, the Son of Man? Where is our wisdom—staked on the person of Jesus who comes to sinners, forgiving and preaching the Word of truth or with the world that says something different and ignores those who obey God?

Saturday

FIRST READING   Sir 48:1–4, 9–11
Responsorial Psalm   Ps 80:2ac and 3b, 15–16, 18–19
GOSPEL   Mt 17:9a, 10–13

Questions about Elijah who needs to come and set things as they have to be so that the long-awaited One can come and be recognized. But Jesus is blunt: Elijah has come and we missed him. Not only that, we treated him as we pleased—we rejected him and killed him as we have all the prophets that called for justice for the poor, peace upon the earth and hearts made pure by fasting, almsgiving and obedience to the laws of God. And Jesus knows that the same fate awaits him: the Son of Man. Jesus comes and he comes to suffer with us, to suffer for us, to suffer because of us and to suffer and transform all suffering in his own body. Suffering is a part of living. Do we ever suffer for telling the truth, for standing up for others, being the voice of the poor or standing with the Son of Man? Come stand fast.

✵ We are given a glimpse of the prophet Elijah, his fire, power, zeal, passion and disappearance in a chariot with fiery horses in the whirlwind. He is destined to reappear and turn the hearts of generations back to one another, bringing a foundation to those who wait. Blessed are those who see that time, and see him! Jesus proclaims to his disciples' that John the Baptizer is indeed Elijah returned to the people but everyone missed him again. And they will miss Jesus too, and he, the Son of Justice, the Son of Man will suffer in the tradition of all the prophets—missed and ignored. It is Advent and the Son of Man is among us. Have we missed his presence among us once again?

✵ Elijah was the fire, the wrath, the judgment of God on the kingdom of Israel, bringing punishment of famine, drought and the word of God that shut up even the heavens, denying rain to the earth. Elijah left in a flaming chariot and would come again to turn back the hearts of fathers to their children—to make peace among all. And we believe that John the Baptist is that returning Elijah, seeking to turn us all to peace and forgiveness and change of heart/life once again. Have we taken John's words to heart and have we changed? Are our eyes washed out enough to be able to see the Son of Man, who will be crucified and suffer at the hands of 'good religious and law-abiding people'? This is the child who will be born in two weeks time—who are we waiting for?

THIRD WEEK OF ADVENT

Monday

FIRST READING   Num 24:2–7, 15–17a
Responsorial Psalm   Ps 25;4–5ab, 6 and 7bc, 8–9
GOSPEL   Mt 21:23–27

Today's reading is one of blunt confrontation. The chief priests and the elders of the people are becoming more and more hostile towards Jesus. They have already decided not to listen to him. They're hearts have hardened, and they think only to protect their own beliefs and place in the community. Jesus is teaching in the temple and they provoke him wanting to know by whose authority he speaks. But Jesus has reached a point where he will not debate them, or answer their questions because there is no openness to him. And so he counters with his own question. He asks about John's baptism—whether it is of God or just human origin. And this question exposes their refusal to seriously consider any teaching.

They are more concerned with what is 'politically correct' with the people and with other factions of power. Jesus sets them up to have to face their own dishonesty and all they can answer is "we do not know." And then Jesus replies that he will not tell them where his power and authority comes from—even if it is from God, they would not accept it. This is a reading that evokes great sadness as well as anger, because it also reveals that we often react the same way. We disagree with something in the gospel--the words of Jesus but we rationalize it, or think first of how it affects factions with authority in the church or the government and we refuse to acknowledge that it is the Word of God. God is human flesh in the Incarnation—and we react against God in what we do to other human beings—they bear the brunt of our disbelief. And God then refuses to give us deeper understanding of his Word and his life, because of our refusal to obey God's Word.

Tuesday

FIRST READING   Zep 3:1–2, 9–13
Responsorial Psalm   Ps 34:2–3, 6–7, 17–18, 19 and 23
GOSPEL   Mt 21:28–32

Another story: a man had two sons (or daughters) and one says that they will obey promptly and doesn't move. The other is reluctant to obey, but does in the end. Which are we? Do we acknowledge that prostitutes, publicans are ahead of us in the kingdom of God? Do we think that we're pretty good but live without passion or grace, without obedience and without making sure that there is wine for the poor and justice and peace for all? Our God is ever-closer to us. Isn't it time to get ourselves moving and seek first God's way in our life and world? Pray to Lucy for eyes that can see: ourselves truly and God's designs for all of us.

Wednesday

FIRST READING   Is 45:6c–8, 18, 21c–25
Responsorial Psalm   Ps 85:9ab and 10, 11–12, 13–14
GOSPEL   Lk 7:18b–23

Are you the one? Go tell John what you see and hear: blind see, lame walk, lepers made clean, deaf hear, dead raised to life and the poor are given good news. That's how we know the presence of God among us. Hope runs over, life surges, forgiveness gives a new lease on life, outsiders are drawn in, and whatever is lacking is filled up and touched with grace. Tall order but every bit of peace, justice, freedom, liberation, compassion must be heralded and passed along. We walk in a dark night and yet the darkness is resplendent with the presence of the Suffering Servant who sings in our pain. John of the Cross wrote poetry with his life and sorrows and tried to reform the Carmelites and the Church—what are we doing?

Thursday

FIRST READING   Is 54:1–10
Responsorial Psalm   Ps 30:2 and 4, 5–6, 11–12a and 13b
GOSPEL   Lk 7:24–30

✹ Jesus defends a prophet: John in prison for speaking the truth to power. High compliments from the mouth of God—a prophet and one foretold in Scripture, a messenger who goes ahead to prepare the ways of God. No one is greater than John and yet, the least in the kingdom is greater than he! Wow! Everyone of us, baptized in water and the Spirit, dwelling in the Body of Christ, living on the Word and Eucharist is 'greater than he is'! We are called back in mercy and tenderness. Come home! Return! May we pray for the fire of the prophet and the truth of Jesus that our world so desperately needs this year.

Friday

FIRST READING   Is 56:1–3a, 6–8
Responsorial Psalm   Ps 67:2–3, 5, 7–8
GOSPEL   Jn 5:33–36

✹ Again Jesus praises John the Baptizer as he preaches calling him a burning and shining lamp that they were willing to watch for awhile, but now he questions them on who they think John was and who they think he is, who stands before them. Jesus couldn't be clearer—I have greater evidence than John—the works my Father entrusted to me to carry out. Jesus needs no other witness. His own presence and actions cry out even more surely than John's signal in the desert calling for repentance. The Father has sent Jesus: the Father's presence is found in Jesus' works—they are all works of life, of hope, of inclusion and truthfully gather what has been scattered by sin. Look!

FROM ADVENT INTO CHRISTMAS

WEEKDAYS OF ADVENT
From December 17 to December 24

December 17

FIRST READING   Gen 49:2, 8–10
Responsorial Psalm   Ps 72:1–2, 3–4, 7–8, 17
GOSPEL   Mt 1:1–17

Today we begin the immediate turn towards the birth of Jesus and so we go back to Jesus' origins—all the way back to Abraham. There are three sets of fourteen generations, hinting at the fullness that he bears in his person and body. And there are strangers to any Jewish genealogy included with his forebears: Tamar, Rehab, Ruth and the woman who had been Uriah's wife. It is unheard of to include women in the list, but the one to come has a human history like any others: sin, murder, unfaithfulness, craftiness and cunning, ingeniousness and passion as well as being outsiders, those who work the law and position for themselves and who bring mystery and the unexpected into his background. This is a man Jesus who is the Christ.

This is the week of rejoicing. The time approaches quickly. Now we are to assemble and listen, not just to the ancient words from more than 5000 years ago when Jacob declared to his children the promise of the Lion of Judah to come but to the words of Jesus who was born more than 2000 years ago. Jesus was born into history, a history of faith encompassing the history of the world. He was born of men and women—found in Matthew's genealogy—who broke the law to make justice happen (Tamar), of outsiders who heard the word of Yahweh and helped his people (Rahab) and of strangers who became family because of compassion to inlaws (Ruth) and even of those who conspired with murderers for position in society (the wife of Uriah) and finally of Mary, bethrothed to Joseph of the house of David. That house was once the glory of Israel, but now they are just the poor in occupied territory of the Roman empire, nobodies who still belonged to God, and are vowed to him in covenant. And the long awaited one is born into the world—and has been in the world for so long. Will he be born in us and our world this year?

December 18

FIRST READING   Jer 23:5–8
Responsorial Psalm   Ps 72:1–2, 12–13, 18–19
GOSPEL   Mt 1:18–25

Balaam was sent to curse Israel and yet when he opens his mouth the Spirit of God is what rushes forth in rapture, at the goodness and strength of God. He is eloquent in praise of what God has done for his people and their lands and what he still intends to do. And he foretells of a star that will advance from Jacob and a staff that will rise from Israel. The leaders surround Jesus, questioning what he is saying and doing, opposing him, but Jesus bests them by questioning them. Jesus is that star, recognized by the poor and the staff that will lead his own to justice and salvation. Jesus' power is wisdom and truth. Are we resistant, and in opposition to God and does God have to work through us in spite of us?

We await a child. But this child will be a man of justice, integrity and wisdom in his governance of the world. His name is 'the Lord of justice.' The history of Israel continues, out of Egypt into Israel, out of Babylon into Israel—now it lies in bondage under Rome. But they will again live in their own lands—but now this land is all the world, the kingdom of God in Jesus, born of God and humankind in Mary.

But it is Joseph, the just man who breaks a law to save the life of the woman he is engaged to because he hears the Word of God in the dream of the angel, and the words of the ancient Scritpures and the prophecies. He hopes and lives on God's word, even sleeping and dreaming God's revelation. Joseph in Matthew's gospel is the image of the one who becomes a follower of the One who is to come: the child born and named Jesus who saves his people from their sins. Joseph is the obedient one, who knows that no law can ever be used to destroy life or to harm another person. He obeys the word of God and interprets all the old into new life for all, giving his life so that others may live. And so, he becomes the man who adopts the God-child Jesus as his own son. There is so much to learn of Joseph the believer—as much as anything we could learn from his wife/friend Mary.

December 19

FIRST READING   Jdg 13:2–7, 24–25
Responsorial Psalm   Ps 71:3–4a, 5–6ab, 16–17
GOSPEL   Lk 7:18–23 / Lk 1:5–25

Now we move back further in time to the announcement of John's birth to Zechariah in the temple. This child too will be heralded by an angel for he is a prophet who will be great in the eyes of the Lord and bring joy and gladness to the people who wait on God. He will open the way for the Spirit to come—a midwife in the realm of the repentant heart! In Israel's history there is a tradition of angels' and extraordinary tidings of children that are born out of time, for God's work that belong to God and the people not their parents. Who do we belong to? What work does God hope that we will do for the people in our world?

We are drawing close to the birth of the child, with history and geography jumping around. Now we meet some of the remnant, the faithful who believed in the promises and staked their lives on them, relying on God's word in spite of the events occurring around them in history. Do we belong to God's remnant and interpret the Scriptures not from a worldly political/nationalistic way but in God's way, so that we are converted and our religion gives us God's sight? The word of the Lord comes to Manoah's wife who was barren but declares that she will bear a son, telling her to obey his commands for the 'son she will conceive and give birth to will be consecrated to God from the womb'—and he will begin the deliverance of Israel from the Philistines. The announcements follow the same pattern from the beginning. The story is told from the husband's point of view though it is the woman who gives birth. It is the same with Zechariah the priest and Elizabeth his wife. This time the word comes to the man, Zechariah in the temple. He questions how this can be and is struck dumb because he does not trust the words of God. But the words, even if not believed come true and Elizabeth conceives.

✳ God is drawing near to us and we practice seeing what is coming with marvelous stories. We hear of Manoah and his barren wife. Yet an angel appears to her and tells her of her child's birth and the child's strength and consecration to God who will deliver Israel. And Samuel is conceived and born. And the story is repeated. Zechariah, a priest and his wife are barren, but they are just, obedient, and elderly. Yet an angel appears now to Elizabeth's husband and tells him she will conceive and bear a son. But Zechariah doubts—how? And Gabriel stuns him into dumbness until the child is born. They will with the vision, silently as it starts to come true. God is seeking to be conceived in us. Do we believe?

December 20

FIRST READING   Is 7:10–14
Responsorial Psalm   Ps 24:1–2, 3–4, 5–6
GOSPEL   Lk 1:26–38

✳ And again we hear again the story of Jesus' conception and the angel sent to Nazareth to Mary, betrothed to Joseph of the house of David. This child's promise is unbelievable: he will be great, named Jesus (savior) and called Son of the Most High. God will give him the kingdom of David, and he will rule Jacob and the people forever! This is the stuff promises are made of! Mary is troubled at the words of greeting and wonders over their meaning. And with days before the birth of our God, the Word made of our flesh do the words of grace trouble us too? She says Yes to God's hope for humanity. Will we say Yes and let God use our flesh for the truth to be told in our bodies and lives?

✳ An old story: Isaiah comes to Ahaz and tells him to ask for a sign from God. But he doesn't want one—he's intent on disobeying God and seeking alliances with other nations. But he will get one anyway—a young woman conceiving a child that will be the presence of God with his people—Emmanuel. The stories repeat themselves, but with God asking permission: Gabriel comes to Myriam blessing her and asking that she bear a child on behalf of her people who will be Son of the Most High, conceived by the Spirit, and she will be overshadowed by God. Yes, she responds in obedience to the Word of God. God wants to be born in us this year. Are we saying Yes?

✷ Now it is time for the announcement/birth of Jesus to follow the pattern. First the words of the prophet intended for Ahab, the King in Israel who did not want God interfering with his reign. But Isaiah says that God is king in Israel and there will be a sign—a child will be conceived who will be Emmanuel—God with us—for the people of Israel. And a child was born of a young woman in his time. And the angel comes to Mary, as he did to Zechariah and she questions how. But she is not struck dumb. This is the beginning of the new—the new covenant and testament, the new creation, the Incarnation of God into human history and all will be changed indelibly forever.

The reading is more about who this child will be—birth announcement—rather than about Mary who will bear him into the world. He is to be named Jesus/Joshua. He will be great before God and he will be called the Son of the Most High. The Lord God is his father and David the King long dead is his father too and the kingdom belongs to him forever. And he will rule. He is born of the Father and the Spirit in Mary, and in every one of us if we obey, and accept this Word into our hearts and bodies. Nothing is impossible with God—God is to be born in us as surely as he was born in Mary. This is Christmas—not the past… but now. Are we saying: "Be it done unto me according to God's word?"

December 21

FIRST READING   Song 2:8–14 (or Zep 3:14–18a)
Responsorial Psalm   Ps 33:2–3, 11–12, 20–21
GOSPEL   Lk 1:39–45

✷ The Good News of her child to be born puts Mary in mortal danger and she flees to the hill country and shelter with Elizabeth who is also in an unusual predicament: pregnant unexpectedly in her old age. The two are kindred spirits in hope, wonder and awe knowing that their children will change not only their lives drastically but the lives of their nation and history. They recognize each other and Elizabeth's John recognizes the voice that called him into existence in the Spirit in Mary's greeting of Shalom. It is all about peace—peace come to earth in flesh and blood. Peace that is the presence of God reconciling all the earth and her children. Peace meeting the truth and blessings fall like rain upon the earth. Are we this presence of peace?

Our God is coming, the lover of the human race, coming quickly, soon, speaking to us and telling us that it is the time of spring, of life, of birth, of blooming and giving forth fragrance. Do we stand together and welcome God coming to us: "Arise, my beloved, my beautiful one, and come!" Let us hear your voice! Elizabeth hears Mary's voice and greeting of peace and the Spirit rushes upon her and her child. Do our greetings call forth the Spirit upon those who hear our voices? Do we, with Mary, trust the Word of God spoken to us and act upon it, making it come true?

God comes to us, like a lover to a beloved, one on one and he stands here in our presence, gazing at us and speaks to us to "arise and come" for it is the time of spring on the earth. Are our voices attuned to the voice and the Word of our beloved, our God who comes to us and will stay with us? Our God comes to us and we are called to rejoice for we have had our reproach removed from us and we are saved from our enemies (within and without). Our God is in our midst—Emmanuel. There is no room for fear now—in fact it is our God who will sing over us because our God has become human, one of us!

Mary goes to Jerusalem in haste (running for her life, for help from Elizabeth). She greets her, "Peace be with you!"—the Easter proclamation of the gospel. This is the Word of the Lord in Mary coming to announce his presence in the world to the one who goes before him—the voice: John in the womb of Elizabeth. God is loose in the world—now there are four who know the presence of God with us. The Spirit ricochets back and forth among the four of them. Our God comes to us in the Word—do we bring this Word to all we meet, in our need. And do we come to each other's aid, in the spirit and in the flesh? This is visitation—our God is always coming towards us. Can we see?

December 22

FIRST READING   1 S 1:24–28
Responsorial Psalm   1 S 2:1, 4–5, 6–7, 8abcd
GOSPEL   Lk 1:46–56

✺ The story breaks into a song, a psalm of praise to Yahweh the Holy One. In Mary's mouth we hear the hunger and the hopes of a people over centuries aching for the One who would come to set them free. This is Mercy that is intent on doing wonders and protecting the people. This is the work of God and of her child: to put down the mighty from their thrones and lift the lowly (as she has been lifted); to scatter the proud-hearted; to fill the hungry with good things and send the rich away empty. This is revolution— three of them: within the heart, within economics and politics. This is 'the remembrance of mercy' for those who wait on God. Do we wait on God? How's our heart today? And our economics and politics? How are the poor and downtrodden doing because of our obedience and praise of God?

✺ We keep meeting our ancestors. Hannah brings Samuel and returns him to God—as the gift was given, so she gives him back to the service of the Holy One of God. And Mary recognizes the goodness of God to her and all the poor and those faithful to God's promises. She prays Israel to hear what God has done for them since the beginning and how the promises are coming true. And her son will scatter the proud, lift the lowly, feed the hungry, depose the mighty and send off the rich and selfish, ever mindful of Mercy. The promises will come true. She is staking her life on them. Are we staking our lives and days on the promises of our God among us?

✺ Anna (Hannah) brings Samuel with her to the temple and gives him back to the God who gave him to her for this short period of time (until he was weaned, maybe 5 years old at most). He is dedicated to the Lord. This is how it is with John/Elizabeth and with Jesus/Mary. The child is not hers but belongs and is dedicated to the Lord—and so Mary sings, as once (Hannah did in gratitude and joy) of the glory of God and what God has done for her, and for her people. But she sings too of what God will continue to do for the people in this child to be born—who will scatter the proud in their arrogance, pull down the mighty warriors from their positions and raise the lowly (nonviolent), send the rich away as empty handed as their hearts and fill the poor with good things—food, justice, hope. They are all part of the remnant that clings to God's word and believes in God's promises, though they may seem to take so long to come true. Will God's promises comes through in our lives, and our hearts, and our world this year? Will we align ourselves with the Word and the will of God?

December 23

FIRST READING   Mal 3:1–4, 23–24
Responsorial Psalm   Ps 25:4–5ab, 8–9, 10 and 14
GOSPEL   Lk 1:57–66

Back to Elizabeth and Zechariah and the birth and naming of their child. His name is John as the angel commanded—it is time to obey the Word of God. And in obeying Zechariah's tongue is loosened and he begins to speak again by praising God. This child is entrusted to them, but from the beginning the hand of the Lord is with him. What is your name? What does it mean (John is beloved of God)? Is it time for you to obey the word of God? And as parents do you remember that your children have been entrusted to you but they must be about God's work in the world? God's hand is always with us now.

The prophet cries out that God is sending his messenger to prepare his way before us and suddenly the one we seek will be here. But can we bear his presence—a refiner's fire, carefully watched, until the gold is pure, God never taking his eye off of us. Are our hearts turning, our hearts becoming pure?

Elizabeth gives birth to her child and when he is named John, Zechariah's tongue is loosened and he begins to praise God. What child will this be? We are to go before the face of the Lord and prepare his way. What child of God have we become? Do we see how close the Child, the Son of Justice is to being revealed among us?

December 24

FIRST READING   2 S 7:1–5, 8b–12, 14a, 16
Responsorial Psalm   Ps 89:2–3, 4–5, 27 and 29
GOSPEL   Lk 1:67–79

David has settled in his palace and thinks of building God a palace of his own. The prophet Nathan says go ahead, but God declares that he himself will build his own dwelling place among humankind. It is God that has done everything in David's life and will give a house that will endure forever— through wars/enemies and all history. It is God who has given us everything from the beginning and given Joseph and Mary everything, including the child to be born. This is God's new house among those he has created as his own—God fulfills his promises and keeps his word. This is what he is doing! It is time to praise God, with Zechariah and Elizabeth because our God has ransomed us, visited us, remembered us and dealt mercifully with us. We should serve him devoutly and be holy in his sight. All is the work of our God who brings the Dayspring, out of the darkness so that our feet will be guided into the way of peace. Soon Peace will come to us.

It is the vigil of the birth! And we hear Zechariah's song of blessing and exuberance at what God is doing in the birth of his child John. The coming of Mercy among us is so close! This child John will grow to be a prophet strong in the Spirit who will herald a victorious Savior (no more angels, now God will use humans). We have been exhorted to be holy and righteous and serve our God fearlessly all the days of our lives. We go before the Lord now crying out that Mercy is coming like the rising sun shining on those in darkness and guiding our feet into the ways of Peace. This day guide the steps of someone into peace, into the presence of God to be born among us.

CHRISTMAS SEASON

WEEKDAYS OF THE
CHRISTMAS SEASON

December 26
Saint Stephen, First Martyr

FIRST READING   Acts 6:8–10; 7:54–59
Responsorial Psalm   Ps 31:3–4, 6 and 8, 16 and 17
GOSPEL   Mt 10:17–22

The Word dwells on earth but reaction is quick and deadly. We are thrown into the life and death of Stephen, the first to die because he is laid claim to by this Word, preaches the Word and follows this child grown to be a man into the truth and conversion. This savior Jesus will exhort his followers to be careful and on their guard because reaction to belief in him and his message of Good News will be mixed. But we are told that the Spirit will be given to us for our words in this situations of danger and death. The Spirit of our Father will speak in us. Do our words tell the truth about this child of God Jesus? Do we turn silent when we should speak the truth? Does the Spirit of our Father speak in us?

These days after the birth of the Child of God we look at what can happen if you are bound to this Child. Here, Stephen the first martyr, filled with grace and power, described in some of the same terms as Jesus his Lord, speaking of the Word, forgiving those who kill him. And Jesus' words warn us that the Word in the world does not always call forth joy. It can also call forth anger and violence against those who speak of love, of nonviolence and forgiveness. We cannot be naïve or romantic about the coming of God into our world.

The child is born to us. And the child will die with us, for us. And those who are close to him, who follow him will be born in him, and die with him. Stephen is the first to die, proclaiming who this Child truly is, Jesus the Beloved of God, prophet and crucified one risen from the dead by his Father in the power of the

Spirit. Stephen seeks to live as Jesus did, in service to his brothers and sisters and he dies as Jesus died, praying to God to forgive those who murder him. The dying and rising in Jesus the Son of God has begun.

We have been baptized into the life/death and resurrection of Jesus and we too are called to proclaim the Word of God in Jesus and if necessary to stand and speak the truth of who this child born to us is—the Son of Man, the crucified one, Son of the Father, the fullness of the Spirit. We will be given of the fullness of that Spirit when we stand as the children of God before the world. God became flesh and so now, it is our flesh that must bear God's Word to the world.

December 27
Saint John, Apostle and Evangelist

FIRST READING   1 Jn 1:1–4
Responsorial Psalm   Ps 97:1–2, 5–6, 11–12
GOSPEL   Jn 20:1a and 2–8

This is the disciple traditionally believed to be the beloved disciple. This is the preacher and lover of the Word made flesh, intimate with him, living like Jesus' shadow, closer to him than the other disciples and friends of Jesus. He saw with his own eyes and touched the Word of Life with his own hands! John was a witness, standing firm even as his word in court standing up for Jesus' truth exiled him until death away from his beloved community. So John became a writer so that those he loved would know perfect joy in the Word he passed onto them. Send a letter. Send words of joy. Shadow the Word in the Scriptures.

John proclaims in letter what he has seen and known himself intimately, and touched: that the Word became visible among us. He seeks to share this life so freely given with his children of faith, so that joy may abound. John writes from long exile, in punishment for speaking this Word of truth. John is the first of the beloved disciples, who saw and believed and lived rejoicing in the love of God given to us in Jesus; God's Word of unbounded love to all the earth.

✺ This is what we must proclaim with our lives singularly and in community, and in our words—what was proclaimed to us—life that was present to the Father from the beginning, and life that became flesh that we could touch, and see and bear witness to Jesus, the glory of the Father, in the power of the Spirit. We are to live bearing witness to our God in joy. This is John the beloved disciples' message. He is the symbol for all those baptized into the death and resurrection of Jesus, the beloved who 'see and believe', who wait upon the authority of those who do not see/believe because of their sin (Simon Peter) and who cannot see who Jesus truly is because they cling to something they want to hold onto (Mary of Magdala).

We have entered the tomb and been baptized. We have been loved and called beloved of God, with Jesus. We live to witness to Jesus' words, life and resurrection. This is our vocation, our calling and our life in community. We are all the community of the beloved disciples. We too must write love letters to the friends of God in exile not just with words but with our flesh and blood.

December 28
The Holy Innocents, Martyrs

FIRST READING   1 Jn 1:5—2:2
Responsorial Psalm   Ps 124:2–3, 4–5, 7–8
GOSPEL   Mt 2:13–18

✺ It seems that any kind of association with this child can be mortally dangerous. Just the thought of a child born to shepherd his people Israel threatens the powers that be. So the children born in geographical proximity or close in time to the birth are considered expendable if the one child can be destroyed. Murder, slaughter of the innocents, a pogrom against a group that has done nothing is set in motion when Herod realizes that the wise men will not return to give him information. Jesus' birth is marred by the cry of anguish, loss and killing. There is no comfort for so many. Jesus is the presence of God's peace in the world and peace can threaten power. We must decide if we belong to this child of resistance to evil without hard or if we subscribe to peace at the end of a sword

✹ God is light. There is no darkness in God, but there are many who still chose the dark, chose violence over light and life. John writes to his little ones, beloved of God telling them to ask for forgiveness and to remember that they live in the presence of God and Jesus who is just. And we remember the blood of the innocents, the little ones that have been butchered because they were bound to the Child. Just geographic proximity to this Child can be dangerous because the powerful of the world still hate and resist the Word made flesh among us. Who are the innocents suffering today because we sin and refuse to be the children of light?

✹ Our God is light; truth; freedom and holiness. We are born in God, dwell in God and so must walk in the light and make sure that the truth dwells in us. We are not to deceive ourselves and become liars saying that we do not sin and that there is no darkness in us. We are to keep ourselves from sin—from missing the marks of being the beloved children of God: forgiveness, love unto death, faithfulness in the face of violence and persecution, the protection of the least of our brothers and sisters, the refusal to harm others and love our enemies and to walk with Jesus, in the Spirit, in the presence of the Father.

Joseph and the child and his mother flee from Herod's viciousness/murder and slaughter as refugees. Herod when he realizes that the astrologers didn't return, takes out his rage on those who are just in the vicinity of where the child might be. This is the destruction of the innocent—those who are associated with the Child of God, all those who are victims of injustice, violence, poverty, human misery, the injustice of those in power and those who are threatened by life. We must make sure that we never find ourselves among those who do the killing and the slaughtering, in anyone's name, let alone, lying and say it is done in the name of the God of life.

December 29
Fifth Day in the Octave of Christmas

FIRST READING   1 Jn 2:3–11
Responsorial Psalm   Ps 96:1–2a, 2b–3, 5b–6
GOSPEL   Lk 2:22–35

✳ Mary and Joseph take their child to be presented to the Lord, in accordance with the law. And we meet Simeon, long faithful and enduring, living on hope that he will not die before he sees the hope of Israel. He recognizes the child, takes him in his arms and blesses God, letting go of life, for now life itself has come to resource the people. He has seen the Light and touched Peace and Glory. And he sadly tells Mary and all those who are close to the child that they will know suffering just because of their relationship to this child who will be a sign of contradiction. Mary and our swords will be pierced and laid bare by the sword of the Word of God. Have we grown sensitive to the suffering of others as we let the Word seep into our souls?

✳ Do we know Jesus? Do we keep his word/commands to us? There is only one commandment, realized in Jesus, the only light of the world—that we are to love one another. Are we in union with God, in Jesus or do we succumb to the fears of the world and continue to hate, to fear and to walk in the shadows? Jesus, first-born of Mary is brought to the temple to be given in sacrifice, dedication to God and they are met by Simeon who has long awaited the coming of the light into Israel. He rejoices that he has seen the light, but as a prophet sees that this Child will be the cause of the rise and fall of many in Israel and the world. Is this Child the cause of our rise, or our downfall?

✳ If we know Jesus than we obey the commandments. It is simple and straightforward. Do we love God—then we keep the Word of God and put it into practice all ways. This is how we abide in God. We cannot hate or harm, or cause another to fall. We must stand in love, in support and in the light and obey the only commandment—to love one another as our God has loved us in Jesus, unto death if need be.

Joseph and Mary bring the child, their first born to the temple to be dedicated and given over to the service of God. We have known this moment in our baptisms, when we are sacrificed and given over to God in the power of the Spirit with Jesus. Joseph and Mary hear the words of glory to God from Simeon who has waited so long to see the child who was to come—the

Anointed of the Lord. The child is come. And he turns to Mary, and to all who give birth to the Word in their hearts/bodies and lives and warns us that this child is a sign of opposition and will be the cause of the rise and fall of many—us included. And our hearts will be pierced with a sword—the double-edged sword of the Scriptures so that the hearts of many can be laid bare and seen for what they are. We are baptized under the sign of the cross and we stand there at the foot of the cross all our days. It is the sign of our salvation and the sign that will be opposed in the world.

December 30
Sixth Day in the Octave of Christmas

FIRST READING	1 Jn 2:12–17
Responsorial Psalm	Ps 96:7–8, 8–9, 10
GOSPEL	Lk 2:36–40

We are God's little ones, young in believing and living as God's beloved children, with/and in imitation of Jesus. His name forgives us and we are invited to know God in this Word made flesh. Has this name, this love remained strong in us? Are we intent on the will of God in the world? The prophetess Anna waited decades for the Child to come and she rejoices at the sight of him in the temple. She rejoices on behalf of all the people and the deliverance of Jerusalem that this child's very presence announces. And Jesus simply begins to grow in wisdom, age and grace before God. This is our task, our life as well.

December 31
Seventh Day in the Octave of Christmas

FIRST READING	1 Jn 2:18–21
Responsorial Psalm	Ps 96:1–2, 2–3, 5–6
GOSPEL	Jn 1:1–18

A week after the birth and we are reminded who this newborn is—the Word of God in flesh among us. This is the Truth and Loving-kindness of our God. No one has seen God, but this God-the-Only-Son makes him known, even as he is in and with the Father.

Do we receive him? Do we reject him? Is he light in our darkness, shattering the sin and despair of our lives? Are we struggling with belief and allowing ourselves to be resourced and reborn with God's glory? This week we remember so many who died violently because they believed and were known to be close to this human being who is Truth. We too must begin to die to ourselves and live in the Light, becoming light and truth in our world.

As children, we live always in the final hour, always seeking to live in love and to belong to God. We have been anointed (baptism/confirmation) and so all the knowledge that we need will be given to us to survive in the world no matter what happens. We have been given the truth—of Jesus, the Word of God made flesh among us. Our lives have been recreated and resigned with the body of Christ set as a seal upon us. Our God has come into the world as Word made flesh dwelling among us always. The light is always there in the darkness, the truth is always there among the lies. We are to testify to that light and live in it. We are to bring that light to all. But we must begin by accepting and believing in the Word and the glory of the Word—the love of an only Son for his Father in the Spirit. Our life is not in the Trinity in the world, with one another. We are to live enduring in love and with love. The only God we will ever see is Jesus' God's own enduring love made flesh. And the only God anyone will ever see is that love as it endures in us who believe. Do we live this 'love following upon love' ever more completely, every day?

BETWEEN NEW YEAR
AND EPIPHANY

FROM JANUARY 2
TO EPIPHANY

January 2 (before Epiphany)

FIRST READING   1 Jn 2:22–28
Responsorial Psalm   Ps 98:1, 2–3, 3–4
GOSPEL   Jn 1:19–28

❖ John testifies to the truth of this child grown to be a man and refuses to let the questioners dwell on who he is: he is the prophet, the forerunner, the voice in the wilderness. What is crucial is to focus on who is already in their midst: the one who stands unknown among them who they do not know. And John's words are sobering: "I am not worthy to untie the strap of his sandal." And what of us? Is this One among us? Do we know him? And will we bend before him to serve and worship him?

❖ We remain in Jesus the Christ. We have been anointed and God will continue to reveal himself to us. This knowledge must hold fast in our hearts. John the Baptizer knew who he was the voice in the desert prepariung the way, baptizing with water. And he saw the One who dwells among us, hidden even then in the world. He knew he was not worthy to untie his sandal straps, to be his servant.

Do we know who we are? The beloved children of God, the sisters and brothers of Jesus the Christ? We dwell even now in the Son and the Father by the power of the Spirit and we must be confident, living truthfully; and we must not be ashamed at his coming. Do others know who we are by the way we live?

January 3 (before Epiphany)

FIRST READING   1 Jn 2:29—3:6
Responsorial Psalm   Ps 98:1, 3–4, 5–6
GOSPEL   Jn 1:29–34

✹ Today John sees and recognizes Jesus, points him out and calls him the Lamb of God. He witnesses that this is the One the Spirit came upon, and so he will baptize with the Spirit of God. His witness is profound: "I have seen! And I declare that is the Chosen One of God." John witnesses in words as a prophet. We too are prophets, but by our baptisms we are to proclaim the presence of Jesus among us in our lives and works. Do we know this Lamb of God, who is always with those in need, those shunned and those who are the victims of the world's violence? Do we see the Lamb of God among us?

✹ We are God's children! We are to live the holiness of God, relying on the Father's love for us. We see God in Jesus now and we must be like God in Jesus and the time will come when we see God as he is and we will be like God. Amazing!
John the Baptizer calls Jesus, the Lamb of God who takes away the sin of the world! Jesus is the one who frees us from doing what is sinful, evil, unjust and violent because he baptizes us not just in water but in power and purifying fire of the Spirit of God. Now we are to testify to the presence of Jesus with our lives, living in the light of Jesus' Word.

January 4 (before Epiphany)

FIRST READING   1 Jn 3:7–10
Responsorial Psalm   Ps 98:1, 7–8, 9
GOSPEL   Jn 1:35–42

✹ John sends his disciples to follow another: Jesus. They obey and fall in behind Jesus. The first words of Jesus to them and to us are "What are you looking for?" and they do not answer, but they are invited to come and stay with him. That's all it takes. Andrew goes and gets his brother to come and follow too. It seems that if you see and know Jesus you are impelled to bring others into his company. Together we are called children to work with others to undo evil and to live uprightly in the service of love. Who do we walk with? Who have we brought to Jesus?

✤ Remember who we belong to! We are God's own children, with Jesus, born of God in our baptisms. Our actions must be holy and we must love each other, as brothers and sisters of God. To act towards others with harm, with injustice and evil is sin and declares that we belong to the devil, or those who do evil and hinder the justice of God on earth. Our way is to undo what is evil. We follow the Lamb of God, who teaches us and questions us: "What are you looking for?" and we do not often answer, but are invited to dwell with Jesus, who dwells with the Father. Once we have stayed with God in Jesus we, like Andrew must seek out our families and neighbors and bring them to Jesus to be renamed and remade into who they too were born to be.

January 5 (before Epiphany)

FIRST READING   1 Jn 3:11–21
Responsorial Psalm   Ps 100:1–2, 3, 4, 5
GOSPEL   Jn 1:43–51

✤ Once you have been caught in the web of the presence of Jesus, it is like sticky glue—more and more are drawn into the company of his followers. There is one defining characteristic that we are to be known for—no killing or harming another. We are to love, and to live without hate, even giving our lives in the service of others. But this service begins with taking care of the needs of others around us. What are we saying with our lips, and in truth, in our deeds? We are known by God. Is our God served in truth by our lives?

✤ We must make choices: between doing good or evil; between loving all others or killing them, refusing to share with we have with them , hating them. We must love in truth and in deed, remembering that God knows everything. We are either Cain or Abel, killing or doing justice.

Each person meets/sees Jesus and thinks he knows him: as the one Moses spoke about in the law and prophets, Jesus, son of Joseph of Nazareth, the Son of God (a prophet), the king of Israel. But Jesus tells us at the very beginning that we must come to know him as the Son of Man, worshipped by the angels, coming out of heaven. Who do we think Jesus is? Who must we learn to see and worship this year?

January 6 (before Epiphany)

FIRST READING   1 Jn 5:5–13
Responsorial Psalm   Ps 147:12–13, 14–15, 19–20
GOSPEL   Mk 1:7–11 (or Lk 3:23–38;
or Lk 3:31–34, 36, 38)

Jesus is making his appearance, known as the son of Joseph in a long line of believers in the covenant of God with his people. But it is John the disciple who tells us who this Jesus truly is—this man is the favor of God, God's Son who has life. There is the testimony of water, blood and the Spirit. And we have known all three in our lives: baptism, confirmation and eucharist and so have this life within us. We are called to believe: to live with all our being witnessing to the power of life and the presence of God among us. We overcome the world with life!

Jesus has overcome the world, in water, blood, and the Spirit and they are all truthful. And all three witness that life is in the Son, Jesus—life that is eternal, holy, truthful. To be in the Son in God we must believe the Word—and to believe, is to live that Word.

Mk—This is baptism. Jesus is baptized, and proclaimed by the Father to be his own beloved child, son, the chosen of God, as the Spirit descends upon him. This is our baptism, drawn into the presence of the Father, with Jesus, sharing Jesus' relationship to the Father in the power of the Spirit. We are his own beloved sons and daughters, children and chosen of God.

Lk—Jesus lives for 30 years unknown, as the son of Joseph. And we are shown his ancestry, his long line in the history of believers, in Israel, the chosen people of Yahweh.

He does not come out of nowhere, but he appears as the fulfillment of the law, of prophets' warnings and promises, of hope and the faithfulness of God. He makes his appearance, begins to make himself known. His baptism sends him to reveal himself to the world.

January 7 (before Epiphany)

FIRST READING   1 Jn 5:14–21
Responsorial Psalm   Ps 149:1–2, 3–4, 5–6, 9
GOSPEL   Jn 2:1–11

We belong to God and so we have the power within us to know the truth. We are in God in Jesus Christ by baptism and we are to keep ourselves deep in the heart of God, with Jesus. And so we can ask for what is needed, knowing that we are heard and that 'we already have what we have asked of him.' Like Mary at the wedding feast, the kingdom of the poor being fed and lack being filled we are to see what is needed and ask that others' needs be met, through our prayer, but even more through our service and obedience. Are we truly praying for the needs of others to be met and working to make sure God's word come true in us?

Monday after Epiphany
or January 7

FIRST READING   1 Jn 3:22—4:6
Responsorial Psalm   Ps 2:7bc–8, 10–12a
GOSPEL   Mt 4:12–17, 23–25

This is how it begins: Jesus responds to the violent arrest of John and moves into Capernaum, a border town. He begins to move out publically among his own people, but to those on the edge of Israel. His message "Change your ways: the kingdom of heaven is near," belongs to all peoples. Jesus is the light that has pierced the world's darkness and as he travels, the light spreads by his very presence and is enforced by his words that challenge and confront.

And his words are tied to his works: he touches people in their sicknesses, diseases and weaknesses; even in their sins. And people begin crossing borders to see him, hear him and take heart from his touch and presence among them. The world is hungry for wholeness. Do we look beyond our borders? Are we sensitive to others' pain and suffering? Do we see the kingdom near in the bodies of those all around us and in those we watch on the news? Are we the disciples of Jesus bringing light to those living in darkness and the shadow of death?

Tuesday after Epiphany
or January 8

FIRST READING   1 Jn 4:7–10
Responsorial Psalm   Ps 72:1–2, 10, 12–13
GOSPEL   Mk 6:34–44

Jesus is a shepherd who has long teaching sessions with the sheep! And then when it gets late and they are far from home, he feeds them. Or he has his own disciples model what he has been teaching. He takes their food, blesses and breaks it and has them distribute it among the crowd. The crowd learns the lesson and shares from their own small stores of food. They find that they have more than enough to feed everyone and enough leftover for twelve baskets—for all the tribes of Israel.

All those broken pieces of bread and fish, leftovers from feeding 5,000 men and 5 or 6 times that many women and children (from crowd counting) 30,000 in all. This is a new Exodus, a going out from slavery. The way out is sharing in gratitude. This is one of Jesus' primary lessons. It is Eucharist and a way of being in the world. Elizabeth Ann Seton followed in her Master's footsteps, feeding and teaching her own family and then many thousands of students through her community. Do we teach through sharing of our resources?

Wednesday after Epiphany
or January 9

FIRST READING   1 Jn 4:11–18
Responsorial Psalm   Ps 72:1–2, 10, 12–13
GOSPEL   Mk 6:45–52

Jesus sends his disciples away and goes to pray. And even as he prays he is aware of his friends in danger and he goes to them—walking on the water. "Courage! It's me; don't be afraid." And he gets into the boat with them. These words should begin our every day as we face the unknown, the unexpected and the frightening as well as epiphanies of God.

The last line describes all of us who are disciples as having 'dull minds', minds slow to see, to understand and penetrate the mysteries of Jesus' actions and words. Do we grasp the wonder of the loaves—that we can feed everyone from our resources if we share? Do we realize that to live aware of others' needs is at least as marvelous as walking on water?

Thursday after Epiphany
or January 10

FIRST READING   1 Jn 4:19—5:4
Responsorial Psalm   Ps 72:1–2, 10, 14–15, 17
GOSPEL   Lk 4:14–22

This is the work of Epiphany—showing forth in preaching the power of the Spirit of God. The words and the works are one. Jesus announces good news to the poor and his presence with them begins to make it reality. He proclaims liberty to captives and touches those outcast, drawing them in from being cast out. He proclaims sight to the blind and seeks to open their eyes and ears with words and the company he keeps. He frees the oppressed beginning with the sick, bent, broken bodies of so many, feeding them and lifting them up with the conviction that God has always cared about them from the beginning in Exodus, when He led them forth from the bondage of Egypt.

And now comes the stunning grace of a year of mercy. This year, every year is now the year of mercy—a sheer gift of God. And for all those who believe we are summoned with the power of the Spirit to live as a sanctuary for all in desperate need of God's freedom and mercy.

Friday after Epiphany
or January 11

FIRST READING   1 Jn 5:5–13
Responsorial Psalm   Ps 7147:12–13, 14–15, 19–20
GOSPEL   Lk 5:12–16

This is what setting the captives free and lifting those oppressed look like—touching lepers and those cast off, unclean, unacceptable because of their sickness, or sin or history to others in society. This is the will of God in Jesus. The will of God is welcoming, forgiving, healing and touchable. No one is beyond the reach of Jesus. And Jesus breaks all the laws that shun people, curse them or punish them for who they are or what they have done.

Leprosy was a disease that was made a curse because of peoples' fear. Who are the people we curse and condemn to a life without pity, or touch or hope because of our fear of them—public sinners, pedophiles, those who have HIV-AIDS, those who might be tainted with association with people we are afraid of and punish instead of being willing to help them return to the community? Do we stand with Jesus and say: "I do will it, be clean."

Saturday after Epiphany
or January 12

FIRST READING   1 Jn 5:14–21
Responsorial Psalm   Ps 149:1–2, 3–4, 5–6a and 9b
GOSPEL   Jn 3:22–30

Jesus and John are both baptizing in Judea. And once again John testifies that he is only a witness to the Christ. He is the friend of the bridegroom rejoicing that the time of the wedding is near. His place is to stand by, listen and rejoice in Jesus' voice loose in the world. This is John's prayer and the prayer of every disciple: "My joy is now full. It is necessary that he increase but that I decrease."

We have all been baptized. Now it is time to look at our lives and see if we testify and witness to the presence of Jesus in the world. Do we know his voice and live in joy knowing that we serve the Word? How good are we at disappearing so that the presence of God is clearly seen and heard among us?

SEASON OF LENT

Ash Wednesday

FIRST READING   Jl 2:12–18
Responsorial Psalm   Ps 51:3–4, 5–6ab, 12–13, 14 and 17
SECOND READING   2 Cor 5:20—6:2
GOSPEL   Mt 6:1–6, 16–18

The clarion call goes forth: Rend your hearts, not your garments. Fast, return to God who is gracious, compassionate. Our God relents—it's time for us to relent from evil, fast from injustice and superficial religion practiced for show or our own self-aggrandizement and the good impression of others. And the trumpet sounds the call to the whole community. We're in this together. There is to be no outward show of pious behaviors, fasting, long prayers in public, even others knowing if we give alms. This is about purity of intention and practice—we fast—the kind God wants of us in sharing our bread and justice with others, in almsgiving that protects those who receive and in prayer that rends our hearts before God, breaks our will and ego, bending us before our gracious Father who wants us to live in the freedom of the children of God—all of us, helping each other. This is the time of secrets between our God and us, in love. Father, help us to make this Lent a secret worth holding true between You who are Love and we who seek to love you back. Amen.

Assemble! Gather! It's time to come home, come back to our baptisms, to our promises to live in the freedom of the children of God. It's time that God got all our hearts and lives; not bits and pieces. And time for God to be stirred again to concern for us and take pity on us and all the earth. It is time for us to be ambassadors for Christ, so that God can appeal to the world through us. It is time for us to be reconciled to God and to be reconciled to one another. It is time to fast, to pray and give alms. It is time to relent of our evil, our self-absorption and greed, our violence and despair, and live once again with the first enthusiasm of our baptisms. It's the springtime of our souls—it's Lent.

✴ Even now, says the Lord, return with your whole heart: rend your hearts. Lent is about stopping in our ways and listening/obeying the word of the Lord who is merciful and gracious and waiting on us. And it is about doing this together as a people, a community that is mindful of its need to tap into the passion of believing and obeying once again. We are ambassadors of God—God appealing through us to the world. And what we bring always to every situation and relationship is reconciliation—that we all might walk together again with God and with each other.

This is all about hope! This time is all about making peace! This time is about living passionately, gracefully and truthfully—about getting back in touch with the intensity of our baptismal vows. Do you promise to live forever in the freedom of the children of God? Do you promise to resist evil and refuse to be mastered by any sin? Do you promise to live under no sin of power but the sign of the cross? We gather and we once again follow Jesus, picking up our cross that comes from preaching the gospel.

Thursday after Ash Wednesday

FIRST READING   Dt 20:15–20
Responsorial Psalm   Ps 1:1–2, 3, 4 and 6
GOSPEL   Lk 9:22–25

✴ Jesus summons those who would follow him, to begin to deny themselves (so that we won't deny him), to pick up our cross and come after him to death and resurrection. We are to risk losing it all, including our lives (but not likely) so that we can be saved. We are not here to make profit in this world (but to share the resources among all justly) or to damage our bodies and souls that are the children and temples of God and we are not to be ashamed before the Son of Man, the Lamb of God, the Crucified One. Who do we belong to? Who do we stand with? God, the poor, those treated unjustly, those who suffer in a world of sin and violence, evil and greed? It is time to choose who we walk with—do we walk in glory, home to the Father and belong to the kingdom of peace, without harm to others. Jesus, may we walk with you, picking up our cross, helping others with theirs and honored to belong to you alone. Amen.

✹ Life and death are set before us. Choose! We must choose so that we and all those who come after us might live. We are to love, to heed the voice of our God, and hold fast to God alone. We must choose to follow Jesus, to deny ourselves, and walk the way with Jesus rejected, put to death and risen from the dead! This is the way we save our lives and hold onto our integrity in the face of injustice, violence, and evil. Happy are we when we do not follow the wicked but give the fruit of justice and mercy in every season, planted firmly in the Word of God and the company of those who obey and delight in the law of the Lord. We do lent together.

Friday after Ash Wednesday

FIRST READING   Is 58:1–9a
Responsorial Psalm   Ps 51:3–4, 5–6ab, 18–19
GOSPEL   Mt 9:14–15

✹ We are to told to seek God daily, cry out, praying to know God's ways and practice justice. Oppression of others is not allowed if we pray or fast or do what is deemed penance. We are to fast from violence, fighting, greed, but we are to humble ourselves in breaking the yoke of injustice, bringing freedom and food to the hungry, the works of mercy (hands-on-justice) and then our God will hear and answer our call to be forgiven and to know His presence among us. Anything else is hypocritical and demeaning of God. We are to fast—from anything that makes us insensitive to the suffering of others, and to the practices of injustice. We are to bring the new wine of sharing, of forgiveness and a life without violence or harm to others. We live on new wine, wrapped in new garments of baptisms, sharing Eucharist with all our brothers and sisters. It is time to become what we speak and eat, the blessing of God on others in need. Jesus, make us beloved children of Our Father, truly your brothers and sisters.

✹ We are told to listen to our wickedness and recount our sins. We are a nation that outwardly fasts and prays but we continue with our own pursuits of war, greed, business as usual, treating laborers unjustly, striking with wicked claw. God cares not for outward show but wants justice, release from bondage of those we have been enslaved, freedom for the oppressed, and that we share our bread with the hungry, shelter the oppressed and homeless, and do corporal works of mercy. We are to do to the Body of Christ, crucified and broken among us, what we would wish to do to the Bridegroom Christ. Then we will know the dawn of God over us and the Lord will hear us. But first we must banish oppression, war, lies and accusations from our midst. It's time to face ourselves as a nation and as individuals.

We are caught off guard and told to look at and listen to our own wickedness: we quarrel and fight, strike with wicked claw; we treat workers dishonestly; we bind others unjustly; we oppressed the poor and refuse to share our bread with them or care for the homeless, the sick—we do not practice the corporal works of mercy and turn our backs on those who reach out to us in need. And then we cry out to God and expect God to immediately hear us and answer. But we are in the presence of the light, the bridegroom. If only we would do a fast for justice, from violence and terror, share what we have and forgive then our wounds would be quickly healed—this is the time of lent, when the glory of the Lord waits to be our rear guard and God seeks to draw ever closer to us. So we fast, emptying out what is evil so that God can enter it to dwell more closely with us.

Saturday after Ash Wednesday

FIRST READING   Is 58:9b–14
Responsorial Psalm   Ps 86:1–2, 3–4, 5–6
GOSPEL   Lk 5:27–32

These commands are the way to live Lent: remove the yoke of injustice, wicked words from our speech, the clenched fist, share our food, bring relief to the oppressed. Then in these days of the desert we will know the company of our God and water and light that brings strength physically renewed and our communities and church, perhaps even our nation will be made whole, healed and obedient to God. We'll have new names as a people because of what we do: Breach-mender, Restorer of ruined houses and we will know delight in God's presence. Jesus calls Matthew, a tax-collector, and all of us, no matter our jobs—all of us sinners to follow him and now the ways of greed, self-absorption and being acceptable to the world. This is the time that all of us must acknowledge our sin and stop! Lord Jesus, you are our doctor, our medicine and our wholeness—in your mercy heal us again so that we may do for others what you do for us so faithfully. Amen.

✵ Isaiah is clear about the practices of Lent: no lying, no malicious speech, bestow (gift) the hungry with your bread, and satisfy the afflicted, giving what they lack. Then we will know the presence of God as light, guidance, strength, and as what waters us deeply. We will all be rebuilt and restored. But we must truly worship and make every day—not only the Sabbath—a day that is holy. We are sinners, all of us, like Matthew the tax collector, but we are invited home. We are called to stop being self-righteous and disobedient, and turn our hearts and lives towards the Body of Christ, the children of God, and follow Jesus as we once promised at our baptism. Together we must walk Lent behind the Crucified One.

✵ Listen again to what we are to fast from and erase from our lives: oppression, false accusation, malicious speech. And instead we are to practice sharing generously our bread and our care for the afflicted. And God will respond graciously, strongly, guiding us and casting light into our lives, giving us his Word. We must begin to resist evil. We must refuse to be mastered by sin, and practice goodness and justice. Matthew is called and he stands up and follows. We are called and we are to leave behind anything that hinders us from living in Jesus' company. This is the season when we examine our lives and know that we are sinners and we need a doctor. We need a change of heart—or to bend the knees of our hearts (Irish)—and when we eat with Jesus and one another, we are called to repent once again and become the bread of life, joyfully living and drinking the cup of our salvation.

FIRST WEEK OF LENT

Monday

FIRST READING   Lev 19:1–2, 11–18
Responsorial Psalm   Ps 19:8, 9, 10, 15
GOSPEL   Mt 25:31–46

It is Lent and the readings of the Old Testament tell us where to start in our practice of obedience: Be holy like I, your God, am holy. Reach. Start with your neighbor. Don't lie, steal or deceive. No oppression, greed, injustice towards workers; no taking advantage of those in need, lacking what you have, no being a stumbling block by what we do for others. Honor the truth, treat all with the justice each deserves by right. No revenge, no nurturing grudges, no harm to others, no violence. Love your neighbor as you love yourself—why, because I, Yahweh am God and I say so. A good examination of conscience for these days for all of us publicly. And Jesus says—that was what you don't do. Now this is what you must do (rest evil, practice virtue of justice). It is right out of Isaiah—feed, clothe, give drink, heal, release the prisoner, shelter the homeless. It is not an option. This is what we will be judged on. Jesus, make us just. Make us aware of the injustice we are a part of that destroys so many others. Make us your sheep, your children. Make us holy. Amen.

We begin our recreations with the words of the Lord to Moses: "Speak to the whole community: Be holy, for I, the Lord, your God, am holy." That is what the whole law is about— imitation of God so that we reveal in our society of believers what our God looks like to others. It covers basics: no stealing, lying, swearing falsely, defrauding, robbing, withholding wages of poor, no cursing, making it more difficult for others in need fearing God and so judging justly, no slandering and do not stand idle when others' lives are at stake, no hating in your heart, and reproving carefully—in a word love your neighbor as you love your God. The corporal works of mercy in Matthew echo this code.

✹ We start from scratch: reviewing the commands of God. This version is a bit more specific than the ones we are used to—and each demands that we love our neighbor with all our heart/soul/mind/strength/resources, as we claim to love our God. It is time to look how our actions impinge on the community's struggle to believe and to obey the covenant with God. We start with what we are not to do. And then we listen to the words of Jesus and once again (we know all this stuff) continue with what we are supposed to do, especially for all those in most need. We are to practice the corporal works of mercy as a lifestyle, continuously, on our own and with each other. The Shepherd is separating out the sheep and goats—according to our behaviors, our actions and our justice (love expressed in terms of sheer human need). We are being judged. If that judgment were today—which group would each of us fall into—and which group would our community, our church find itself in? It is time to choose whether we will know the blessing of God or God's curse.

Tuesday

FIRST READING   Is 55:10–11
Responsorial Psalm   Ps 34:4–5, 6–7, 16–17, 18–19
GOSPEL   Mt 6:7–15

✹ God's word is fruitful, faithful, commanding, demanding and like the air, the rain and snow we must learn to obey and bring forth bread, seed, truth and hope from our lives as we hear God's word that is so potent for transformation and substance. Are we food for others to eat? Are we obedient to our baptismal promises and the Word of the Scriptures? Do our lives bring life, freshness and promise for the future for others? This is the practice of Jesus' prayer, our prayer to Our Father: God's will for justice, peace and no violence and word comes first. We worship God in sharing our bread, trusting in God while we give it away today; we must forgive as often and graciously as we have been and are being forgiven by our God and we must know that we are passing through a test—this world that does not honor God or make justice a norm and we must be faithful through it all and not succumb to what is evil. God is forgiveness and it is given to us but if we do not pass it on, giving life and hope to others, it returns to God, taken back from our heart and hand. Word of God, make us forgiving, giving of bread and peace this day and every day. Amen.

※ The word of God goes forth and it does not come back to God empty, but obeys what it was sent to do—always bringing life, food, seed, nourishment and hope. And so, our prayer, the words of Jesus' prayer in the Our Father must do the same. The words must become the framework of our living together doing God's will, forgiving, caring for the immediate daily needs of all, resisting evil and honoring God. Our prayer and deeds must mirror each other, beginning with forgiving as we have been forgiven. God demands this of us all.

※ We are to live on the Word as the food and substance of our Lenten practice. God's word goes forth and brings food and hope for the future and it never returns to God empty. It obeys. We must listen to the Word—in the Our Father, our basic prayer that reminds us of all the essentials of our belief. Stand before our Father, together as children (all of us), bless God, pray for and bring the kingdom to earth. Pray for our (all of us) daily bread—nobody is to go hungry for food, shelter, justice, dignity, water, health care, welcome. Forgive us, but only as we forgive others. Take us through trials and temptation daily and at the end, deliver us from evil. Back to the basics, with the added reminder again: forgive or we will never know the mercy of our Father forgiving us.

Wednesday

FIRST READING	Jon 3:1–10
Responsorial Psalm	Ps 51:3–4, 12–13, 18–19
GOSPEL	Lk 11:29–32

※ We are summoned, like the great city of Nineveh, all of us, from the greatest to the least, to turn from our evil, our collusion with injustice and to honor God, fast from violence and to know the experience of God's compassion falling upon us like soft rain and comfort. What if we only had three days time to do it? We've been given another Lent, another forty days in the desert with our community and our God and we've been given the great sign of Jesus, to follow the Crucified One who leads us to Resurrection life in our baptisms and one day in fullness. We are summoned to pick up our crosses and to follow after the Son of Man who preaches good news to the poor and expects us to be that for those who cry out for justice and life. Lord Jesus, Son of Man who stands with the poor, the broken-hearted, the victims and those outcast from our society help us, from the greatest to the least to turn from our evil and to honor you in our lives. Help us to do it now, this day and every day of our lives. Amen.

✳ Nineveh is told it will be destroyed because of the evil it has done, but the people from the leaders to the least hear the word of the prophet and stop everything to fast and pray. It is declared that everyone must turn from the evil they have done and the violence they have been a part of…and they are spared. This is our time to stop everything, and pray/fast, especially the evil and violence we do. We get no sign but the sign of Jonah, not the whale, but the call to listen to the wisdom of repentance—or the citizens of Nineveh will rise and condemn us at the judgment because we did not listen to the Word of Jesus the Lord.

✳ Jonah the prophet is sent to Nineveh (think of Los Angeles spread out) and to his great dismay they all repent. He preaches of the forgiveness of God and God's patience with us all. It is in our actions and turning from evil that repentance is known in our hearts/souls. We have 40 days too, all of us to fast, do penance, give alms and stop the evil we participate in with others, with systems, governments and corporations. From the greatest to the least we must all stop doing evil!

We must listen to the word of God, in Jesus and do what Jesus does, obeying and being attentive to the will of God, that is always life for all. There is no other sign given for we have been given the sign of Jesus crucified and risen from the dead, the sign of God's wisdom in Jesus' word and presence among the poor and those who acknowledge their sin—we need no other sign.

Thursday

FIRST READING	Es C:12, 14–16, 23–25
Responsorial Psalm	Ps 138:1–2, 2–3, 7–8
GOSPEL	Mt 7:7–12

✳ Esther fasts and prays on behalf of her people, to save them from death and extinction. And the people fast and pray with her, knowing that she will approach the king, and put her own life on the line by begging for their lives. And we are told how to pray by Jesus. To ask, to knock, to seek and it will be given and opened for us. God gives and knows what we need. We do not always ask wisely or for what is needed when we pray for what we immediately want, especially for ourselves and those close to us. We are to trust that God knows what we need—we have been taught to pray Our Father and to start with those crucial things and we are reminded that we are to pray, obey the Law and the Prophets first, remembering that we are God's people. Our Father, help us to remember all the people of the world, especially those facing death, violence at the hands of others and extinction by starvation and war and may we trust that you will continue to take care of all of us. Amen.

✳ Esther the Queen fasts and prays on behalf of her people, using her power to go before the king and beg mercy, and speak the truth on their behalf. She prays for words and courage and asks for salvation, literally from the hand of the enemies of the people. (this is the older covenant). We too are exhorted to pray, and also know what it is we ask for and that our God already knows what we need. And our prayers must have the echo of what we do to one another—treating others as we would want to be treated in all circumstances.

✳ This is the kind of fast God wants. It is a fast borne of mortal anguish on behalf of others in dire need. Esther has recourse to God, and prays. She asks the power of God for the people and asks how she can help them, using her position, her influence and even her weaknesses. Who are we fasting and praying for, so that we might be able to help, be in solidarity and communion with them this Lent?

We are to pray, humbly, asking, seeking, knocking and all will be given to us that is needed. We will be given what God wants to give us, what we truly need, whether we ae aware of that as our need or not. God is always giving us good things—beginning with our very lives, faith, relationships and time to once again worship and obey. And we are told that prayer is connected to what we do to/with one another. Treat others the way we are treated by God! Now that's something to do for Lent!

Friday

FIRST READING   Ezk 18:21–28
Responsorial Psalm   Ps 130:1–2, 3–4, 5–7a, 7bc–8
GOSPEL   Mt 5:20–26

✳ We are comforted: if we who are sinners, turn and start to observe and practice the decrees of God that are right and just, then we will live. And we are told realistically that if we don't turn then we will be charged with what we have done and the consequences of our actions will be death. And we are told that if we have done what is righteous and then turn from God and do evil, then we will be judged accordingly. God is the God of life and wants us to live, but it is we who do evil and bring death upon ourselves. We must choose. Today and everyday, in each action and word, Jesus is clear: We must be truthful and without violence in our words, our thoughts and our actions. We cannot lie, plot revenge, murder, and allow others to be killed or encourage others in violence or humiliate anyone. If we do we cannot approach God or the altar of God. We must make peace with one another before we expect to know the peace of our God. O God, you are Justice. Be justice for us and call us to account so that others may know your presence among us. Do not let us continue in our sin but turn our hearts and ways to doing justice in the world. Amen.

✳ We must look to ourselves and change. God desires us to repent and stop doing evil in our lives, so that we might live both now and forever with God. We are to, in turn, start to do virtuous deeds. These exhortations of the prophet echo our second baptismal promise: do you promise to resist evil and refuse to be mastered by any sin, evil, violence or injustice? Jesus reinforces this, saying that not only is the act evil but the intent behind it. We are not to kill, not with intention, words, slander, lies or abusive language, let alone actually murdering another. We must stop killing, be reconciled before we dare approach God in prayer.

This first week of Lent keeps returning to our relationships with others: to our own need to ask forgiveness, but our equally if not greater need to ask forgiveness from each other and to give forgiveness to others, even unbidden—as we have known it from God. We must stop our wickedness—begin with an examination of our conscience, informed by the Scripture. With others, let all of us, turn together to live in virtue.

And Jesus is as blunt as Ezekiel telling us our holiness must surpass that of scribes and Pharisees who are intent on practicing specifics of traditions rather than the spirit of the law especially as it impacts our neighbor and our poor and our enemy. Of course, murder is wrong and we must stop killing one another (under all circumstances), but we must stop letting anger control us, and rage and hate, and lies that lead to murder not only in our hearts but also in reality. We must not come to pray without asking for and giving forgiveness and releasing the grip of abuse and violence within us.

Saturday

FIRST READING	Dt 26:16-19
Responsorial Psalm	Ps 119:1–2, 4–5, 7–8
GOSPEL	Mt 5:43–48

We are exhorted like our ancestors in the desert to obey and put into practice God's commandments with all our hearts and souls and listen to his voice only. We are God's own people and we are to give him glory because he has set us apart from the nations, and consecrated us to him. We belong with Jesus to our Father and we are to obey the fulfillment of these commands: we are to love our enemies and do good and pray for those who persecute us if we are the children of God. God lets his rain fall and the sun to shine on all of us: just and unjust and we are to learn the compassion and righteous behavior of our God towards each other—towards all others. O God our Father, rain down your grace and strength upon us so that we might obey with all our hearts and souls, as your Church in the world. Make us love our enemies and remember that we belong to You alone and no nation must be obeyed if it tells us to kill. You have said we must love our enemies and that means to begin with: we cannot kill them. Make us your children and hold us fast, O Father of all. Amen.

✳ Our ancestors made a covenant with God, to hear only his voice and to obey all that he has commanded so that the other nations will see that they are sacred to the Lord. And our God in Jesus tells us that not only are we to love our own, but we are to love our enemies. This is the way our God loves all of us, the just and unjust. We must be a sign to the nations of the compassionate love our God that is revealed and expressed in our love of those we fear, hate, want to wreck revenge upon, and yet, will and act in understanding and as we would want to be treated. This is our covenant as the people of God, the Body of Christ, his Church.

✳ We dwell in a covenant with God that we have agreed to. We must hearken to God's voice so that we know that we belong to God—peculiarly his own, and we don't live like other peoples/ nations/countries. We must constantly review our lives together as his people, as communities, parishes, churches (national and universal) to see if we do indeed keep God's decrees and statutes (and not only those of our own configuring). This is the beginning of obedience and knowing God.

Jesus extends all those commands—beyond one's own family/ nation/religion; beyond all our limits and boundaries. The new litmus test or benchmark for faithfulness in Jesus' community is how we love our enemies and how we pray for those who persecute us. This is what Love demands. Our model of imitation is God our Father and how God is compassionate and merciful with those who are unjust as well as just. We must look to those who disagree with us, harm us, those we are afraid of, those condemned. And stop treating them as the rest of the world does—we must treat them as God in Jesus treats us all.

SECOND WEEK OF LENT

Monday

FIRST READING   Dn 9:4–10
Responsorial Psalm   Ps 79:8, 9, 11 and 13
GOSPEL   Lk 6:36–38

✣ Daniel's prayer must be our own, as sinners before God the Holy One, asking mercy, knowing how greatly we all need it because of our disobedience of the law and our ignoring the cries of the prophets. We have rebelled against our God and our infidelities have created a world and a nation that is scattered, without unity, hope or a way to worship with integrity. We must learn to practice the mercy of God towards others that we have known all our lives. The measure we give: in judgment, in condemning others and in forgiving others as well as in giving generously to others is the measure we will know from the hand of Our Father. O Holy One of God, make us mindful of God's mercy upon us, keeping us from death and make us respond to others with mercy, without revenge, without violence, without hate and with forgiveness. O God, be merciful to us, your children who are sinners. Amen.

✣ It is early in Lent, and like our ancestors we are in dire need of God's merciful forgiveness because we are not faithful or forgiving or obedient. We are in rebellion against our God and we ignore the commandments. All of us are in need of God's covenant. And Jesus tells us how to turn: to be compassionate and seek to understand and treat others as God as treated us. We must learn to be generous in thought and intention towards others as well as in practice and not judge harshly. What measure are we using on others these days? Careful! That is the measure God uses on us!

✤ In this season we hear from many of those who have gone before us in faith—those who were faithful, who trusted in spite of temptation, suffering and testing and spoke out on behalf of the people—as models for our own living Lent together. Daniel prays for the people who have done evil (do we?) and includes himself among them and cries out: "Justice, O Lord, is on your side." And yet, Daniel also knows God as "O lord, our God, you are compassion and forgiveness!" and he begs forgiveness for all.

Jesus exhorts us that we must be like God our Father who is compassionate—we must live with passion and mercy that is shared and given to all—even to those who do not deserve it, or think they need it and we must remember that we fall into that group first and foremost. We are to pardon, give and give without measure so that we might know the vastness of our God's compassion with us.

Tuesday

FIRST READING	Is 1:10, 16–20
Responsorial Psalm	Ps 50:8–9, 16–17, 21 and 23
GOSPEL	Mt 23:1–12

✤ We too are like the people of Sodom and Gomorrah, notorious for our evil and in need of being washed clean. Make justice your aim! Redress the wronged, hear the orphan's plea and defend the widow. The way to call forth forgiveness and become holy is to treat those most in need on the earth with the justice they have been denied by our evil doing. Jesus too is clear: we are to obey the words of Scriptures but not necessarily to imitate those who mouth them. If the leaders are dishonest/unfaithful and self-absorbed and proud they are not to be imitated. We are to follow God our Father and Jesus our Teacher and we cannot use our leaders as an excuse to continue in our wrongdoing.

✤ We do not like to think of ourselves as Sodom, or Gomorrah— a people known for their wickedness, sexual promiscuity, greed and insulting behaviors before God, but that is what and who we are—and Isaiah calls us back: cease doing evil; learn to do good. And again it is doing justice for the wronged, the orphan, the widow, the poor. If only we would obey and not continue to resist and refuse. We must choose: the sword that destroys us as our deeds come back to us or setting things right with the Lord?

Jesus uses the example of the leaders—to do what they say, but not what they do. Their words are bold and their deeds few (sadly our own leaders in our communities and church would most probably be taken to task and spoken about in the same way today). We are to take heed that our leaders bind up heavy loads and lay them on others' shoulders but don't lift a finger to help—everything that is important has to do with ritual/liturgical and social status and what is correct. Instead of following in their footsteps we are to be servants and humbly make sure that those who are burdened know our help.

Wednesday

FIRST READING   Jer 18:18–20
Responsorial Psalm   Ps 31:5–6, 14, 15–16
GOSPEL   Mt 20:17–28

✵ They plot against Jeremiah, the religious people who have no intention of listening to and obeying the Word of God in his mouth. And Jeremiah cries out both for justice and remembrance that he stood before God and spoke on their behalf—he cries out for a hearing now! And Jesus tries to tell his disciples that he will be executed, rejected, tortured and they not only ignore him, but James and John send their mother in to ask for the best seats in the kingdom to come. Jesus asks them if they can drink from his cup of suffering and know the baptism of death and resurrection. They will, but they miss entirely Jesus' invitation to share in his sufferings and death, so as to share in his glory and he reminds them to be like him (not the world) and to serve and give their lives in ransom for many. Lord, you invite us daily to take up our crosses and to follow you. You ask us to share in your sufferings, to serve one another and to give our lives as ransom, help us to share your pain, your way of the cross and your closeness to God and care for others instead of always thinking of ourselves first. Amen.

✵ Doing justice and resisting evil will not be easy and the cry for radical change is often answered with carefully calculated evil against those who speak the truth. Good often is repaid with blatant evil. Yet, the prophet, the one that is true to God's word stands before God and pleads on behalf of even those who harm him. Jesus seeks to warn his disciples that he too will suffer as did the prophets before him, even to death by rejection and crucifixion. But they are not listening and are intent on places of power and lording it over one another. They do not know their teacher as the Son of Man, servant and ransom of God for all.

✣ Jeremiah was assailed by everyone as a prophet: the citizens, the leaders and priests all sought to silence him, punish him, abuse him and demean him—trip him up. They didn't want to listen to his word, which was the Word of God—they wanted the priests and prophets that they controlled to tell them what they wanted to hear. But Jeremiah stands before God and speaks on their behalf!

Jesus takes his disciples aside and tells them what is going to happen to him—how others will plot and conspire to destroy him. He is specific, telling them in detail of his suffering and torture, rejection and physical and psychological pain. But they're not listening. James and John's mother comes in and asks for the seats of power in Jesus' kingdom—they all avoid the invitation to come and walk the way of the cross with Jesus. And Jesus tries once again to tell them of the cup of suffering/blood and that to sit at his right/or left means to die on the cross with him. Please, he begs don't be like others. Instead bend, serve and watch me and learn to give your life as ransom for many.

Thursday

FIRST READING	Jer 17:5–10
Responsorial Psalm	Ps 1:1–2, 3–4, 6
GOSPEL	Lk 16:19–31

✣ We must trust in God and be like trees planted by running water (the Word of God and the Spirit in the community that reads the Word together). We must have no fear and bear fruit no matter the weather. Our God searches us and knows our hearts and will judge us each truthfully according to our deeds. Jesus tells the story of Dives (the rich man) and Lazarus, the beggar, treated worse than the dogs at his gate. And judgment is rendered. Abraham, the father of faith takes Lazarus to his bosom and Dives is left to suffer in agony. Even then Dives treats Lazarus as a servant to ease his pain, or go tell his brothers and save them. But the chasm is fixed now—it was a gate outside a house on earth. We are warned: we must obey the law and the prophets and care for the poor, the widow and orphan, the alien and the stranger or we will not even be able to hear the Word of Jesus, crucified and risen from the dead. Jesus, help us listen and obey your word of good news to the poor and look just outside our gates now and do justice for the majority who cry out now while we can. Save us and let us see that it is the poor who call us to compassion and justice. Amen.

✹ Are we barren bushes, staking our choices on the ways of the world or are we like the tree planted by the waters of life, staying faithful and giving fruit in all seasons? Where do our tortuous human hearts set down roots? Jesus pushes us further with the story of Dives (rich man)and Lazarus (one who has been brought back from the dead), the poor man at his gate. Do we treat the poor at our gates as though they are the waters of life (where we lay up treasure in heaven) or as dead lava. It is in this life that we must connect to one another. Who's at our door, our gates, our borders, tugging at our hearts?

✹ Again we are commanded to choose: what kind of person we will be, before our God and in our works. Will we stand in a lava waste, like a barren bush in the desert or will we stand by running waters, trusting and bearing fruit no matter what the season? Our God probes our minds and tests our hearts and judges us according to our deeds and whether or not they are the ways of God.

What are the ways of God? Jesus' story of the rich man and the beggar at his gate—that was a gulf between them and the rich man never invited him in, or even gave him the leftovers of his excess to eat. And when they die, it is Lazarus (one brought back from the dead) who knows comfort and rest and Dives does not. But the gulf now is permanent—only on earth is it a gate that can open in and out. But Dives still doesn't see—he expects Lazarus to be his servant and get him water, or then to let him go to tell his brothers, 5 of them. But he has missed everything—Dives, his 5 brothers and Lazarus on earth were meant to be the Body of Christ—all seven, all the earth as one, at one table, blessed by God. Here it's still a gate—who needs to be brought in? And are we going out?

Friday

FIRST READING   Gen 37:3–4; 12–13, 17–28
Responsorial Psalm   Ps 105:16–17, 18–19, 20–21
GOSPEL   Mt 21:33-43, 45–46

Joseph is best loved of his brothers and they in jealousy and rage, plot to kill him and throw him in a well, then sell him to traders because of Ruben's pleading not to kill him. Our ancestors are just like us. We are people of intrigue, hate, jealousy, anger and murder. And Jesus reminds the people around him with the parable of the tenants who have been entrusted with a vineyard but they take the wine and then refuse to give what is due the vineyard owner. Again and again when servants are sent (prophets) to demand justice, they are seized, treated harshly and killed. Then the son is sent and they kill him. But the time of judgment will come. Jesus will be rejected. He was rejected. He is still rejected by nations and many who claim to be his followers (tenants) but justice will be done and the harvest will be reaped by those who hear the Word of God and take it to heart. Lord Jesus, let us be the ones who honor your Word, your kingdom and your will in the world and do not let us be the ones judged justly. Amen.

Israel loved Joseph best and the familiar story evolves into jealousy, hatred, attempted murder. His older brother keeps the others from killing him and he is sold into slavery for 20 pieces of silver. Jesus' story tells of a property owner and his vineyard leased out to tenants and how they, in their greed, then their jealousy take the vineyard for their own, treat the servants of the owner poorly and then drag the owner's son outside the vineyard and murder him. Same old story, but Jesus speaks of himself and his coming death that will open the vineyard to others who will care for the vines, drink the wine and obey the one who shares it with them. Who do we stand with in this world?

Joseph is best loved of all Israel's sons and this creates hatred and jealously with his brothers and they decide to kill him.

Judah intercedes for him, hoping to save him but he is dropped in a well and then sold into slavery. He is sold for 20 pieces of silver—their brother. And Jesus tells a story with many echoes of a property owner that planted a vineyard and did everything for it and then leased it out to tenants. Time for harvest and they refused to share the grapes with the owner. He sends them servants and slaves (prophets) and finally he sends his son. And with irrational thought they kill him, wanting his inheritance. Jesus questions the elders/scribes: What do you suppose the owner of the vineyard will do to those tenants when he comes? And they answer condemning themselves—and Jesus tells them that what has been rejected will be given to others—and this is marvelous to behold!

And what is our harvest like—is it rich, or do we ignore God's servants, prophets who call us to justice, to giving what is by right to God and others? Are we in collusion with those who kill, live with greed and take what is not theirs and refuse to give what is due so that all know the wine of hope/freedom and community? What would God do to us if he came today?

Saturday

FIRST READING   Mic 7:14–15, 18–20
Responsorial Psalm   Ps 103:1–2, 3–4, 9–10, 11–12
GOSPEL   Lk 15:1–3, 11–32

❋ Who is like our God who rejoices in the mercy of forgiveness? O God, show us your mercy again, trample on our wrongs and cast our sins into the depths of the sea. We cry out to God along with the prophet Micah. And Jesus eats with sinners, calling those who think they do not need to ask for forgiveness to come and listen to his Word and to sit at table with the other sinners. It is the story of two terrible sons, neither knowing the love of their Father, rejecting him outright or pretending to obey until he gets his inheritance. The younger who was brash and public about his sin comes back, not terribly repentant but is welcomed and brought in again, but the older son refuses, blind even to his own sin that dismisses his father's love and hates his brother. Both do awful wrong to the father and to one another and in witness to the town. We are all sinners. It is time to call once again on God's goodness.

Father, show us your mercy again, trample our wrongs and make us forgiving to one another, imitating your love for us. Amen.

❋ We are given a glimpse of the Shepherd to come, with staff and food, who pardons and delights in clemency, Our Father. And Jesus tells the story of the lost son to sinner and self-righteous at table, intending both of them to see God as their Father, seeking them both out, bringing them home to each other and feasting together. Both children are awful, neither knows the father, each wants something for themselves and cares not for their brother/sister. God seeks us all, with staff (word), food (eucharist) and mercy. It's always time to come home, but not just to God—to one another. We must learn to be family together, all of us on earth.

❋ Again the image of the shepherd who cares for the sheep, leading them out of bondage and into promise and pasture. Our God is so gracious, treating us with clemency, pardons us and takes us as his remnant of a people. Will we ever learn? Jesus too goes after the remnant, those who who they have sinned and seek to come home and once again know the gracious faithfulness of God. He sits at table with public sinners—who have failed the religious law who were shunned and excluded from the table/the temple by the self-righteous Pharisees/scribes. He tells the story of the lost sons, both of whom disregard their father and do not know of his great love for each/both of them.

One squanders it all and wants to come home to get something to fill his empty stomach. The other stays at home, resentful and angry, obeying his father outwardly but inwardly despising him, and hating him for giving part of his inheritance to his brother. But the Father welcomes them both back, and seeks that they will sit at the table together. It is the older self-righteous brother that is still lost and still dead. We too are part of that family, neither of us knowing God the Father and neither of us forgiving of the other—what are we going to do now that we've heard the story once again?

THIRD WEEK OF LENT

Monday

FIRST READING   2 K 5:1–15ab
Responsorial Psalm   Ps 42:2, 3; 43:3, 4
GOSPEL   Lk 4:24–30

❈ Naaman, a Syrian army commander (hated enemy of the Israelites) is cured by the prophet Elisha on the testimony of his slave girl when he obeys the word of the prophet and washes in the Jordan. He becomes a worshipper of the God of Israel. Jesus comes and preaches in his own synagogue in Nazareth and is rejected—they think they know who he is and where he comes from. Jesus reminds them of the enemy of Israel healed by the graciousness of God in Elisha the prophet when there were many lepers in Israel, warning them that if they reject him, there will be many in other lands who will come to believe in their stead. When they hear the truth of their own traditions, they seek to kill him but he leaves them and goes his way into his work among others. We see ourselves as the people of God. Have we turned and missed him altogether? Jesus, help us remember that we do not know you except in your Word and community and in how we treat our enemies. Make us who are really lepers in your sight, whole and like your children washed in baptism. Amen.

❈ Naaman the army commander, the enemy of Israel, who is a leper and he is led by his servant girl (a captive in battle) to Elisha to be healed. He must learn to obey and as he does he is healed in the waters of the Jordan. His servants help him and he becomes like a child and believes: "Now I know that there is no God in all the earth, except in Israel." An outsider who believes through the help of his enemy captive and a prophet.

Jesus preaches to his own family and neighbors in Nazareth but they refuse to take his words to heart. And Jesus, the prophet of God tells them that they are as hard-hearted as their ancestors, reminding them of Elijah and the widow of Zarephath and Elisha and the Syrian Naaman. God worked his wonders with them, as outsiders/pagans because they were so stubborn. And they are indignant and they try to kill him. But Jesus walks away from them. How long have we been close/kin/friend—or think we are with Jesus and yet do we hear and repent? Or is Jesus walking away from us?

Tuesday

FIRST READING   Dn 3:25, 34-43
Responsorial Psalm   Ps 25:4–5, 6–7, 8–9
GOSPEL   Mt 18:21–35

How many times do I have to forgive? Peter's question is one that we all ask. Seven times? No, seventy times seven—or as many times as God forgives us! The parable tells of a man forgiven a huge debt, more than he could ever repay and instead of being grateful and leaning some compassion for another, he goes out and grabs a fellow servant who owes him next to nothing in comparison with what he was just forgiven, and he demands payment and when he can't, cold-bloodedly sends him off to prison in punishment of the debt. Sounds cruel, savage, inhuman—but we do it all the time to one another, forgetting the forgiveness that is given us repeatedly by God. We are not only ungrateful and unaware of God's mercy but we do not practice it as gratitude. And so, we are told, that if we do not learn to forgive then we will know the justice of God and we will be held to account for everything we have done. Sobering. Father, forgive us—as we forgive those who are in debt to us. Amen.

Azariah stands in the fire and prays! He prays for deliverance, for all the people, that they might be received with contrite heart and humble spirit, for they have nothing left to give their God. He prays that they all will follow God with their whole heart, be saved, and so bring glory to God. The prayer sums up the life of those in covenant. And Peter asks Jesus how many times do I have to forgive my brother/sister? And he is given the sum/the core of the gospel and the following of Jesus. We must forgive everyone, everything, 70 times 7. This means: don't ask, start forgiving, but it is the way of life for one who follows Jesus and if we don't do this, then we will know the justice of God in our lives.

✳ Azariah prays for his people, in exile in Babylon and brought low because of their sins. He prays for a contrite heart and humble spirit as their sacrifice that will be acceptable. They follow with whole heart—and he prays for deliverance from the evil they have done. We, as a nation and a people, do we pray for deliverance and change, being the sacrifice that God wants? Do we even acknowledge that our sin is grave and that we do not follow God unreservedly—or much at all, only when it suits us?

And again Jesus tries to get through to Peter and to us that we must forgive all others, as often as God has forgiven us: 70 x 7…don't count, start living forgiveness. The story is told of the debtor who can't pay but is forgiven graciously. But the debtor who was just forgiven cannot forgive another who could not pay a measly sum. It is the community that is shaken and comes to the king who does justice for all. We must live mercifully or we will know the justice of God, as individuals and as a nation!

Wednesday

FIRST READING   Dt 4:1, 5–9
Responsorial Psalm   Ps 147:12–13, 15–16, 19–20
GOSPEL   Mt 5:17–19

✳ Jesus the teacher, in the tradition of Moses, comes to bring the law to completeness. It is assumed that we obey the commandments and that we dig deeper into them and obey them with all our heart and soul, and mind and resources (strength). And there is a further injunction: we are to teach them to others, in word and deed, by example and love. We must be dedicated to the law that introduces us to the wisdom of God and seeks to form us in God's image ever more truly. The kingdom of heaven is already here in the person of Jesus and we are called to imitate Jesus in his obedience to the law, and the giver of the law—God our Father who sees us all as his children, hopefully his obedient children, showing forth to others what it means to belong to God.

✲ Moses exhorts the people to observe the commands of God and thus show forth wisdom and intelligence to the nations as they in turn will be drawn to the worship of God. And they are to make sure that they are kept always before their eyes/mind and before their children's eyes in word and practice. Jesus too is concerned with the law, and fulfilling them, digging down deep into their heart/meaning and intent to transform the one who obeys them. We are great in Jesus' community if we honor the law at its deepest level, in practice with all the people of the earth.

✲ God gives his laws to his people to make them wise and intelligent. We are to obey so that others may see this wisdom and come to know our God, who is so close to us. Moses exhorts the people about the law: don't forget, be on your guard and pass them on, live them. And Jesus teaches that same law with the same passion and demand. But Jesus wants more—he wants the spirit and the heart of the law to be observed, not just outward obedience or appearances. We are not to forget what God has taught us in Jesus and we are to practice it thoroughly—as believers and as community/church, so that others may see that our God is near to us, and that God's wisdom is what sources all our actions and relationships. How are we showing forth this wisdom as a community today?

Thursday

FIRST READING   Jer 7:23–28
Responsorial Psalm   Ps 95:1–2, 6–7, 8–9
GOSPEL   Lk 11:14–23

✲ Jesus cures a man who was dumb and people cannot rejoice in that amazing deed. Instead they accuse him of being in league with Satan, who hinders people from being the children of God. Their logic is stupid—how can he cast out Satan, if he's in Satan's house? Jesus is clear: he drives out evil by the finger of God and that is a sign that the kingdom of God, of justice and peace is among us whether we want to admit to its power and presence or not. Jesus' words are sharp, demanding a choice: Whoever is not with me is against me, and whoever does not gather with me, scatters. Lord, may we choose again to be with you, to obey you and to look to you for help and direction. Teach us to rejoice in the healing and hope given to others and share in your kingdom. Amen.

✹ Walk in God's ways and God will be our God and we will belong to God. But they didn't walk in the way of God, and we haven't walked in the way of God, either or in the way of Jesus, the way of the cross, the way to the Father either. We too refuse to listen to the prophets, or to the Scriptures and sadly, in our lives and world, faithfulness has disappeared. Oh the patience of God in dealing with us. And Jesus too practices such relenting carefulness with us all. Are we faithful to Jesus' way, or do we take a piece or two and ignore the rest, and inpune evil to everyone in the world but us? Do we live under the finger of God? Can others tell, by our decisions and allegiance?

✹ Again and again comes the order, the plea: Listen to my voice, let me be your God and you will be my people. But they fail, we fail, we do not pay heed and turn our backs on God, instead of turning to face our God. When will we begin to listen to the prophets and stop being stiff-necked and doing even more evil than those who have gone before us? Are we the 'nation that does not listen to the voice of the Lord, or take correction"? Are we the people who have banished even the word faithfulness from our speech and are in need of Jesus' rebuke to cast out the evils that we practice alongside our ritual: Abortion, death penalty, war, murder, killing, nuclear weapons, disregard for the poor, hungry, the immigrant, illegal, alien, prisoner, foreigner, unemployed? Do we use violence/hate and use our relationship with God to tell ourselves, "We're good— it's 'them' who are evil?"

Jesus knows our thoughts and turns on us, telling us that anyone 'who is not with me is against me and the one who does not gather with me scatters.' What if we are those people or we are the ones who refuse to take correction and stop the evil we are doing?

Friday

FIRST READING   Hos 14:2–10
Responsorial Psalm   Ps 81:6–8, 8–9, 10–11, 14 and 17
GOSPEL   Mk 12:28–34

This is the week of the law and the call to obedience as a response to believing in Jesus' law of love. Now a teacher who admires Jesus and asks the wisdom question: Which commandment is first before all others? And Jesus answers in the tradition of Judaism—to love God and your neighbor with all your heart and soul and mind and resources. The teacher praises Jesus knowing the connection between love of God and one another and true worship or sacrifice to God. But knowing isn't enough. Jesus tells him that he is not far from the kingdom. It is a subtle invitation to believe in him, and follow him into the kingdom of peace and justice that declares to the world the presence of God among us. But it does not say that the man responded. Lord, draw us closer to your presence, intent on obeying you, not just knowing the right answers to the questions. Amen.

God is forever pleading with us to come back, come home from our defections to other countries, powers and people. God is all mercy waiting on us and wants to love us freely! We are promised freshness, blessings, fruit, understanding if only we'd walk with God...but we stumble and tread other paths. Jesus is blunt with one of the scribes. You know the law: LOVE God with everything: heart, soul, mind and strength (meaning resources) and love your neighbor the same way. The scribe praises Jesus but Jesus tells him that he's close to the kingdom, but not there yet. The law opens the latch, but you must walk the way of Jesus obeying the law in regard to all, including enemy and foe.

God is pleading again! Return and I will forgive you, heal you, love you freely! In fact God will be like dew, making us blossom, putting roots down deep, giving fruit and shade. Are we those who walk the just path and are wise, or are we sinners who stumble in the path of God? We are more than half way through lent, what are we doing? Or what are we trying to stop doing— alone and with others?

And Jesus seeks to teach a scribe, and us: to love freely, with all our heart (which is where the will is found), our soul, our mind and our strength (which means resources). And we are to love our neighbor as we say we love God—and this is the sacrifice that is worthy to give God. This is the ancient law and the scribe is close to the kingdom—only close, not in it: To be in God's presence, in the relationship of the Trinity, we must endeavor to love one another as God has loved us. How near are we to the kingdom?

Saturday

FIRST READING   Hos 6:1–6
Responsorial Psalm   Ps 51:3–4, 18–19, 20–21
GOSPEL   Lk 18:9–14

✳ Jesus tells us a parable when we are convinced of our own righteousness, demanding that we confront our souls and look at our relationship to God and how we pray. Do we tell God what we have done for him and what he should then do for us? Do we compare ourselves with others (always those who are not as good as we are—who are the problem in the world, the church and our neighborhood?) Or do we stand humbly before God, seeing some of God's goodness and power and that we exist only because of God's remembrance of us and mercy? It is Lent, time for truth-telling about ourselves and that we are not often what we claim to be, or what others to believe of us. Lord, have mercy on us. We are sinners. Save us.

✳ If we return, then on the third day he will raise us up and live in his presence. We know the reality of these words and have experienced them in our own flesh through baptism. And our God seeks to come to us like rain, the dawn—but there is judgment coming because we are not faithful; we do not endure and we do not strive to know the Lord. We forget the words of God: "it is love that I desire not sacrifice, and knowledge of God rather than holocausts."

And Jesus tells the story of the Pharisee who prays up front, about himself, telling God that he is not like others and listing all the things he's done that God is supposed to take note of and react accordingly. And the tax collector, a public sinner prays humbly, "O God be merciful to me, a sinner." He is mindful of what he has done and the gulf between him and God. The Pharisee makes a gap between himself and the sinner (and so lies to himself) and a gap opens up between him and God. Humility and truthfulness closes the gap between ourselves and God. God desires that our will would bend to his will—that is Love and the only sacrifice that we should bring before our God.

FOURTH WEEK OF LENT

Monday

FIRST READING	Is 65:17–21
Responsorial Psalm	Ps 30:2, 4, 5–6, 11–12, 13
GOSPEL	Jn 4:43–54

✳ Jesus heals the son of an official. Yet Jesus rebukes him gently (and the crowd) saying that everyone wants signs for themselves, rather than to believe in him, his words and his presence. The man pleads and the son is cured. The man believes in Jesus' word and he and his whole family become believers. How many times have we been healed, cured, cared for by God—and yet, do we believe his word to us in Jesus? Do we listen and hear his word of the Scripture and immediately go to obey—without needing proof, or some sign of Jesus' goodness and power. Do we stake our lives daily on the Word of God in Scripture and move immediately to put it into practice and make it come true in our lives. Jesus, may we believe in you and know you not for what you would do for us, but because you are Truth.

✳ God is always making something new upon the face of the earth. God is always renewing his covenant, restoring his people, bringing joy back into the hearts of those who call upon him. But there will be something unimaginable one day—we must wait and watch. Jesus is always trying to reveal that unimaginable holiness and awe to us, but even his own don't see it. He goes to Cana and Capernaum, making the rounds again and it is a royal official who approaches him, not his own people. Everyone wants signs and wonders not truthfulness, faithfulness and obedience, but still in his patience and kindness, Jesus heals the child of the one who begs from him. Jesus serves the God of life always. Do we serve that same God of boundless life, for all?

Tuesday

FIRST READING   Ezk 47:1–9, 12
Responsorial Psalm   Ps 46:2–3, 5–6, 8–9
GOSPEL   Jn 5:1–3, 5–16

✺ Jesus is in the Temple for a feast and sees so many seeking healing by a pool that was thought to be visited by an angel that stirred the waters. Jesus heals a man who has been there for thirty-eight years (almost forty—lifetime, sojourn in the desert, lent) and the man doesn't want to be healed! Jesus healed on the Sabbath and the man reports him to the temple officials, though he doesn't know Jesus' name. Jesus seeks him out (this is the Sheep Gate in Jerusalem) and warns him not to sin again—and this time the man knowingly goes and reports Jesus to the officials. Just because we have known the forgiveness of God, even been healed miraculously doesn't mean that we know Jesus at all. Jesus cannot abide disease and suffering in the world and his very presence heals. How do we repay the goodness of God to us so often? Jesus, are you saddened at what we do to one another? Do we need to hear your words again: Now you are well; don't sin again, lest something worse happens to you? Don't let something worse—that we might lose your grace within us—happen to us.

✺ This is Ezekiel's vision of the waters of the temple, rising and rising and everywhere the water flows there is lush, abundant, and copious life that is given for food and medicine. Jesus is that vision, of water and life, of medicine and food. He sees a man who has been sick for 38 years (how long have we been sick, and content to use our sickness as an excuse not to move?). He was ordered by Jesus to stand up and was healed. Yet he goes and tells the authorities that Jesus did this on the Sabbath. Jesus goes and finds him, warning him to change or something worse would happen to him. Jesus is persecuted and some of those he heals contributes to his being shunned and attacked. Are we grateful or do we contribute to others being punished for the good that has been done to us?

✸ Ezekiel is taken to the temple to see the waters rise—these are the waters of salvation, of baptism and of the temple and the church, flowing from the side of Jesus rather than the ancient building. Jesus goes to the temple and sees all the sick lying by the Sheep Pool, called Bethesda. And Good Shepherd that Jesus is, he knows that there is a man who has been sick for 38 years and asks him if he wants to be healed. The man complains and gives excuses about why he can't get into the water quick enough and Jesus commands him to "Stand up and walk". He's healed and walks.

But the man speaks with the leaders—because it was a Sabbath and he blames Jesus for curing him! He has no idea who Jesus is because Jesus had slipped away after healing him. Jesus goes and finds him (lost sheep still) in the temple and warns him to give up his sins—and yet the man goes back and informs on Jesus, causing the leaders to persecute Jesus even more. And what about us— we've been forgiven, healed, warned by Jesus—do we heed any of his words or do we use our experience with him to cause problems among others, believers and those who use religion for their own agendas?

Wednesday

FIRST READING   Is 49:8–15
Responsorial Psalm   Ps 145:8–9, 13–14, 17–18
GOSPEL   Jn 5:17–30

✸ Jesus always speaks of his beloved Father: "my Father goes on working and so do I." And he doesn't obey laws that get in the way of forgiving, healing, speaking the truth and feeding people—as the people had often done with the law regarding the Sabbath. Jesus speaks of his relationship to God-Father—that he sees and does only what he sees the Father doing. This is called the parable of the Apprentice. Do we do only what we see Jesus doing and so imitate him, in being the apprentices to God? And we are called to do great things, even greater things than Jesus! Do we? Do we imitate Jesus in his works of healing, resisting evil, speaking the truth even if others persecute us and obeying God alone? If we ignore the words of God in Jesus then we ignore God. Even the dead hear the voice of God—better than we do often. Lord, help us to hear your voice and do what is good so that we will be judged worthy of life.

✹ Isaiah speaks of wonder, of what will come if the people repent: freedom, the favor of God, light, pasture, water, pity, even the earth will make it easier for them to live with grace. All will come from afar and the earth and its people will rejoice in God who never ever forgets us. Jesus speaks lovingly of his Father, the one who does all this and more, who is at work in the world through him now. He does only what he sees God doing! Do we do only what we see Jesus doing in God? What do others see when they watch us? Are we known, like Jesus, as the ones who seek and do the will of the one who sends us out from our baptisms?

✹ Our God seeks to comfort us, to set us free, and bring us into the light, to pasture us and protect and shelter us—the Lord is all mercy and joy who never forgets us. Do we know this God who is mother to an infant and a guide, a help, a comfort to all, even for those who come from afar. Jesus seeks to tell us that "My Father is at work until now and I am at work as well." Jesus' Father is this God of Isaiah and Jesus does the Father's work and obeys his will. It is too much for many to believe—it demands not only that we change our ways of approaching God, we must also radically alter how we live with one another—to live as Jesus lived, among sinners and truthfully, calling all back to intimacy with our Father God.

And he tells us, that if we believe, we will amazingly do even greater things than he has done!!! If only we would learn to honor the Son and honor the Father, to hear Jesus' Word and heed it. But the day is coming that will be a day of judgment and Jesus' judgment is the judgment of God. Where do we stand with Jesus' God— do we seek our own will or the will of the One who sent Jesus?

Thursday

FIRST READING   Ex 32:7–14
Responsorial Psalm   Ps 106:19–20, 21–22, 23
GOSPEL   Jn 5:31–47

✹ John was a burning and shining lamp! High praise from Jesus. But Jesus' own words and works are far greater than John's ever were, because what Jesus does was entrusted to him by the Father. His works bear witness that God the Father has sent him.

These works must be accepted or rejected. Jesus is the messenger of God and if we do not believe and obey, then God's word and life is not in us, however much we profess to be believers. All the Scriptures bear witness to Jesus and yet we refuse to come to Jesus and know life. Jesus is clear—the love of God is not in us! We seek praise and acceptance from others, from power and nations, governments and money—instead of seeking the glory of God—and we will be judged by our words and deeds. We are deep into Lent, approaching the judgment of God upon us in the Cross. Lord, may we stand with you, believing and practicing your Word and not seeking to validate our lives on the words of others. May your love be in us.

✸ Moses is sent to the depraved people, no longer bound to God at all because of their faithlessness, violence and worship of other gods. But Moses pleads for them, begging God to remember all that He has done for them in the past and not letting all that go to waste because of the peoples' stubbornness. Moses cares so much for this violent people and God relents. Jesus too begs and cajoles the people to listen to him, to remember John who was the blazing light for a while and to look at the testimony of his works of healing, hope, forgiveness and search the Scriptures to know who He is. Do we have this Word abiding in us? Can we see the work of God? Jesus does not accuse us before God but pleads on our behalf. But who do we believe? And whose words do we act on?

✸ The people are depraved and turn to the worship of idols they have made out of wealth and what they have taken from Egypt, the place of bondage. But Moses pleads on their behalf yet again asking God to remember all the goodness he has lavished on his people and remember his servants of old and God relents! Jesus speaks of God, his Father, his relenting merciful God who is the Just One and all that Jesus does is God's work in the world. Jesus is sent by God the Father, more surely than Moses was sent by God to the people. And Jesus confronts the people, especially the leaders harshly for their lack of obedience and refusal to listen to him. "His voice you've never heard, his form you have not seen, neither do you have his word abiding in your hearts, because you do not believe the one he has sent. Search the Scriptures—these are Jesus' words to us as well. Who do we set our hopes on—certainly it is often not Jesus or his word? Do we plead on behalf of others, and do we listen to God in Jesus or worship our own idols?

Friday

FIRST READING   Wis 2:1, 12–22
Responsorial Psalm   Ps 34:17–18, 19–20, 21, 23
GOSPEL   Jn 7:1–2, 10, 25–30

✺ Jesus goes around Galilee but he knows that there are those who want to kill him. Even so, he goes up to the feast in Jerusalem, but in secret. He preaches and the people know that he has spoken in such a way that he is a wanted man and they are aware that he speaks freely and they do nothing publicly against him. But the people think they know him and his family and so do not believe Jesus' words. He is blunt: You do not know me or where I come from! I was sent by the One who is true and you don't know him. They want to arrest him but are afraid. Lord, we are afraid often of the truth and especially when it is directed at us and we are convicted of being lacking in belief, in knowledge and even of having a relationship with you. We are so sure of ourselves and in reality—we do not know you or the One who is true that has sent you. Teach, O Truth, and make us courageous in standing with you against anyone who would kill or lie or use religion to validate what they do.

✺ The truth incurs wrath, provokes the evil that reacts and refuses to hear. Just the presence of someone who is good, holy and speaks of God causes those who chose evil to react violently and beset the one who is a living witness against them. But the prophet and those who are just will not respond in kind. They will rely on God, in spite of torture, revilement, condemnation and a shameful death. They do not know God and they turn against the innocent. Jesus the just one is hunted for the kill by his own. He must even worship in secret. But they do not know him at all. They do not perceive in their evilness and violence that Jesus comes from God and he knows God.

The just man is a judgment on those who are wicked. And those who do evil work against the one who is holy, pure, blest and 'boasts that God is his Father." This is perversity and evil, violence and injustice directed against one who reveals goodness and God. And they know nothing of God (anyone who kills, murders, plots to destroy others). These lines reflect what happened often to the prophets, and also what happened to Jesus the beloved Son of the Father who was bold in his preaching even when they sought a way to kill him. Jesus teaches in the temple. He proclaims that he has been send by One who has the right to send. "And him you do not know, I know him because it is from him I come: he sent me." Do we know the One who sent Jesus? Do we really know Jesus, so holy and pure and true, that his very presence is a judgment on us?

Saturday

FIRST READING	Jer 11:18–20
Responsorial Psalm	Ps 7:2–3, 9–10, 11–12
GOSPEL	Jn 7:40–53

Everyone is divided over Jesus, thinking each knows how to interpret the scriptures and each looking for what they think is God's chosen one. They want to arrest him but even those who are sent to pick him up are impressed by his words—undecided but taken with the Word. Only those 'cursed people who have no knowledge of the law'—sinners and those who humbly know who they are before God can see the Truth of Jesus' words, works and person. Only Nicodemus speaks out and when he is contradicted, he returns to his silence. No prophet is to come from Galilee—fundamentalist interpretations that allows one to easily write off what is plain to see and experience. We are not allowed to use the Scriptures to avoid conversion, to seek to demean the truth or to act as we are called to—in the defense of life. They all go home. They ignore Jesus' words and intend not to be converted. We often go home too—after liturgy, after reading the scriptures and do exactly what we had intended to do. If we do not have our lives converted—then we have not heard the Word among us.

✳ Jeremiah knows that they hunt him like an animal, but he chooses to be a trusting lamb that will be slaughtered or a tree vibrant with life, cut down. The just one leans on the searcher of minds and hearts: the just Judge and trusts. The crowds are sharply divided over Jesus and who he might be, not listening to his words or watching him but using others' words to avoid listening to the Word of God in Jesus. Even some of the guards begin to hear, but the leaders insult them. Nicodemus tries weakly to stand up for him, but backs down. They each go their own way and Jesus is alone with God.

✳ Jeremiah knew what they were plotting but describes himself as a trusting lamb led to the slaughter. They are out to destroy him, cut him off from the land of the living, but Jeremiah knows the Lord, the just Judge, searcher of mind and heart who will do vengeance. Do we know the Lord as Judge and searcher of mind and heart? Do we stand with the prophets and with Jesus or do we stand with those who judge, who reject, who punish and use religion against others, and who refuse to look at ourselves and our evil and violence as insulting to God?

The people are all sharply divided over him, because of inter-pretations of theology and tradition—and Jesus speaks like no one has spoken before—yet so so few believe in him: from among the people, the Pharisees, the guards, the Sanhedrin. They don't want to listen, to be judged, to be called to account, to repent. Nicode-mus makes a feeble attempt alone to speak up for Jesus, but they put him down quickly. We must have the Word of the Lord, a com-munity to practice standing up for Jesus, and aligning ourselves with him. Do we?

FIFTH WEEK OF LENT

Monday

FIRST READING   Dn 13:1–9, 15–17, 19–30, 33-62
                                              (or Dn 13: 41c–62)
Responsorial Psalm   Ps 23:1–3a, 3b–4, 5, 6
GOSPEL   Jn 8:1–11

Jesus draws near to his death and false witnesses against him. He prays by night and teaches in the Temple by day and they bring him a woman 'caught in adultery'—only one of two that is needed for adultery. They care not for her life or person, only to trap Jesus in his own words. Either he will be just according to the law, and give them permission to kill her and loose the crowd or he will be merciful and not obey the law and give the authorities more reason to reject and kill him. But he wisely doesn't choose and makes them take responsibility for their actions—both setting him up and trying to kill someone. He turns the law on them: 'Let anyone among you who has no sin be the first to throw a stone at her'. And they are shamed and leave. Jesus forgives her and frees her. Where do we stand? Intent on using religion to validate killing: the death penalty, pre-emptive strikes, nuclear weapons, killing sanctions that only effect the poor, treaties that are unjust to the other side, giving us the benefits, claiming that we are good and the other is evil? Lord, have mercy on us and face us down in our sin.

The old story of Susanna caught in a trap by those she refused to surrender to and yet she is saved by the young prophet Daniel who tricks them with their own lies and they are meted out justice. Jesus finds himself in the same situation with the woman 'caught' in adultery (where is the man with her?) She is helpless and they intend to destroy her in their attempt to destroy Jesus. But he uses their words/deeds to trap them and to shame them into leaving and letting her live. The justice of God in Jesus is born of forgiveness, truth telling and shared suffering, for he will be caught as she was caught. But none will come to his defense; he will lean on God alone. Who do we help? Or are we in need of shaming?

✺ Ahaz will not choose to obey and wearies God. In return he is told that a sign will be given anyway. A virgin will be with child and will bear a son who shall be named him Immanuel. This is the tradition that was fulfilled in history after Ahaz and was appropriated to describe Mary and all believers who bring Immanuel into the world in our flesh and word and history. This is the day of the announcement of the Incarnation—of the coming of Emmanuel—God is with us—into the world, in the flesh of Mary, a young woman of Nazareth. The Word of the Lord comes and she is deeply disturbed and wonders what the greeting means—and what all of this Word will mean.

Mary said yes to the coming of the messiah. And Luke uses Mary as the image of all those who hear the proclamation of the Incarnation and are deeply disturbed but say Yes to baptism and to bearing the Word made flesh into their own bodies, lives and history. In the midst of Jesus' Emmanuel—God with us soon to be crucified we are called to listen to the Word of God and once again commit ourselves to believing, to obeying and to offering our bodies as sacrifice to the Lord. And say those words again: I am the handmaid of the Lord, let it be done to me as you have said."

Tuesday

FIRST READING   Num 21:4–9
Responsorial Psalm   Ps 102:2–3, 16–18, 19–21
GOSPEL   Jn 8:21–30

✺ Jesus knows—he can read all the signs—that he is going to die and that they are going to kill him. Yet it is easier for all of us to ignore our choices and complicity with evil and so they say—is he going to kill himself? And Jesus tells them that they will die in their sins—unless you believe that I am He! He is declaring himself to be the Holy One of God. And he tells them that he will be lifted up (crucified) and then they will know that he is the Son of Man, that he is the Holy One of God and that he only does what his Father tells him. He is obedient, unto death and he does only what pleases God and will never be alone, even as he dies alone. Jesus, you are the Lord of life, yet you die as one of us, with us so that we might not be bound by death and hate. Do not let us die in our sins, but come to believe that you are the Judge of Life, the Son of Man, crucified and bound to those who suffer at the hands of those who do not believe in life or cherish it. Make us your followers and save us.

☀ The people rebel against Moses when they have left Egypt and they are stricken with serpents. The cure is to look upon the seraph serpent wrapped around the pole of Moses and so look upon the evil they have done. Seeing brings healing. And Jesus declares that he is leaving and they will not see him and so will be left in their sins/evil. Seeing Jesus and seeing that he is "I AM", and that the truthful one has sent him into the world saves us, heals and makes us whole again as human beings. But we must look and see the evil, violence and injustice that we have done in the world to others, crucified and broken (the Body of Christ) and come to know God crucified and risen from the dead.

☀ The people are plagued with serpents because they again complain bitterly in the desert even though they are cared for by God. For healing they are to look upon a bronze serpent upon a pole and they recover. This is the image that Jesus will become—the Son of Man lifted up on crucifixion, nailed to a tree and yet, anyone who looks upon him in his agony and sees what hate, violence, murder, sin, injustice and evil can do will be healed, forgiven, saved and drawn into this life that Jesus shares with the Father. Jesus only tells the world the truth he has heard from his Father, the Truthful One and does only what pleases God. Do we do only what pleases God, obeying with Jesus and speaking the truth to the world? Do we stand with the Son of Man who will be crucified?

Wednesday

FIRST READING   Dn 3:14–20, 91–92, 95
Responsorial Psalm   Dn 3:52, 53, 54, 55, 56
GOSPEL   Jn 8:31–42

✳ You will know the truth and the truth will make you free. They claim to be free, through Abraham. Jesus is blunt and sharp. They sin. They are slaves and do not remain in the faith of the father's house, however, he as the son, remains. They want to kill him because of his words and so they are not children of Abraham. Jesus obeys and speaks of his father God, yet they do not obey their father in faith, Abraham. If God is our Father, then we love Jesus. And to love, is to hear, take to heart, be converted and obey, following Jesus' teachings and living by forgiveness, justice, truth-telling and defense of those in need of life. Who do we belong to?

God in Jesus' own Spirit? Or do we belong to nations and countries, groups, families and to our own designs? It is late in Lent and time for the hard truth to look us in the eye. Jesus, may we truly be yours.

✳ Shadrach, Meshach and Abednego refuse to worship the idol of Nebuchadnezzar and are condemned to death by fire. They stand fast and do not defend themselves—it is God who will defend them. They disobey the command of the king and the king sees the power of God, and praises God because of their willingness to face death. Jesus too refuses to bend to the twisted version of the law, and image of God and covenant that is presented to him. If Jesus' Word of the Scriptures finds no place in us then we are evil and the truth is that we seek to kill the Presence of God in Jesus among us. Jesus serves God alone, no religious authority, political, or economic leadership or what is fashionable to any group and so that Truth leads him to his death.

✳ The three friends refuse to obey the king and refute him saying our God can save us or choose not to, we will be faithful. The king throws them into the furnace with rage and yet they are not harmed. They walk about in the furnace, with one who looks like a son of God (a word for a prophet, one close to God) and they are freed. They disobeyed the command of power and handed over their bodies refusing to worship any idol. This is the place we stand today—do we worship idols—the gods of war, commerce, aggression, fear, terror, insecurity, money, power, who we know, our own drives?

Are we truly the disciples of Jesus, freed by the Truth? Are we slaves to sin or does Jesus' word find a place in us? Do we succumb to the powers around us or do we obey Jesus' Father and follow him, even unto death, worshipping God alone, whether we are saved physically from harm or not? Do we love Jesus?

Thursday

FIRST READING   Gen 17:3–9
Responsorial Psalm   Ps 105:4–5, 6–7, 8–9
GOSPEL   Jn 8:51–59

Jesus is trying to get across to them (us) who he is and the power of life in his words, teaching and person, but they refuse to listen, to obey or to believe in him. Jesus claims life for himself and those who obey him, forever—life beyond death and in spite of death. Jesus knows the Father—and that is life in itself, if only we know the Father, as Jesus did, then we too would have this life unbounding and life stronger than death within us. Jesus declares:

"I know him and I keep his word." And they try to kill him. Anyone who truly stands against those who resist truth and life, will be attacked, but we must seek only one recourse, our protection and one source for our lives—to be able to say with Jesus: "I want to know the Father and to keep his word." May it be so, O Lord.

God made covenant with Abraham for future generations and when they kept the covenant they were truly the children of Abraham and God was their God. Jesus claims to be the child of God and if we are true to Jesus' Word than we will not know death. We will be a covenant greater than Abraham's with God. Jesus accuses those who reject him of not being the children of Abraham and declares that he is of God, that he is I AM and they respond viciously intending to stone him to death in rage and self-righteousness. Who do we reject? What truth about other children of God do we refuse to hear and what children of God do we destroy mercilessly, self-righteously?

Abram and his descendants live in covenant with God and their part is to keep that covenant—obey God. Jesus is arguing with the people who reject him and are intent on killing him. They are misreading and not hearing anything he says—they have already decided what they are going to do. And Jesus is truthful and tells them if anyone is true to his word they shall never see death. This is Jesus' proclamation to us as we draw near to Holy Week and our own dying to evil and violence and what is not truth. Jesus is life, life forever and is God, from the beginning. In John's gospel, developed around the year 100 AD the community is declaring Jesus as God (not the emperor) knowing that they too may face death for believing in Jesus and worshipping only Jesus. They seek to kill him. Not today but the day will come when sin and evil, when violence and injustice will be the choice of people—as it still is today. Do we keep God's covenant with us in Jesus and refuse to harm anyone? Do we obey and stand with the Truth that is Jesus?

Friday

FIRST READING   Jer 20:10–13
Responsorial Psalm   Ps 18:2–3, 3–4, 5–6, 7
GOSPEL   Jn 10:31–42

✺ Again and again they try to silence and kill Jesus by stoning him to death for his words of truth that confront and convict them religiously. He stands his grounds and asks them to name which of his good deeds they are killing him for. They say they are killing him for insulting God (their God) and for being only a man, who seeks to make himself God. Jesus declares: "I am the Son of God," even according to the old traditions and they are being stubborn, resisting the power of his works that his words proclaim. He lays down the line: if I'm not doing the works of my Father, then don't believe me. But they want to kill him all the same. Do we do the works of our Father, following in the footsteps of Jesus, our Lord? Or are we found all too often among those who condemn others, not because of the good they do (conveniently just ignoring that) but because we are stung to the heart by their words?

✺ Jeremiah is trapped and all intend him harm. They will take out their vengeance on him rather than look at the truth of what he says. He calls on God and entrusts himself to God who rescues the life of the poor from the power of the wicked. Those who reject Jesus seek to stone him to death and Jesus confronts them truthfully: for which of my many good deeds that I have shown you from the Father, do you seek to kill me? He uses the words of the scripture to defend his words, and his actions. But they are murderously blind. Is there hatred, murderous intent and violence in our hearts? Do we allow anyone in our religion to do harm to others? Then the truth of Jesus words are meant to sting us to the core.

❋ The Lord is with me—the cry of Jeremiah, of Jesus and all who follow him to the cross and resurrection. Those who are punished and persecuted because of speaking the truth, the word of God cries out for the presence of God and God's vindication remembering that God has always rescued the life of the poor from the power of the wicked. Jesus befriends and calls the poor God's beloved and the power of the wicked comes after him.

They seek to stone him to death and he stands up to them—why—what good deed are you stoning me for? And they are intent to kill him for his words, for his intimacy with God, his refusal to conform to their idea of God that is narrow and self-serving of their status and interests. He tries using the Scriptures that they should know in their hearts but they are hardened against him—he tries in vain to make them realize what it means that "the Father is in me and I in him." Is Jesus still trying to make us realize that and what it means for our actions towards everyone else?

Saturday

FIRST READING   Ezk 37:21–28
Responsorial Psalm   Jer 31:10, 11–12, 13
GOSPEL   Jn 11:45–56

❋ God tells Ezekiel that he will bring the scattered peoples back, deliver them from their sins of apostasy and all their evil and violence. Instead he will make them a covenant of peace, make everlasting sanctuary among them and all the nations will know that God dwells with them. This covenant is a person who

is Peace, who brings us all back to communion with God and one another, who brings us back from the dead to everlasting life, known now in baptism/confirmation and eucharist in the Body of Christ. The raising of Lazarus is the image of all of us saved for life now and because of this power of life there are those who seek to kill Jesus. So many are turning towards this life, he must be eliminated. Do we stand with those who bring life or with those who decide that someone must die for the sake of the people. Clearcut and deadly. We must chose.

These are the promises of God to bring together his people and bring them back home, cleansing them from their evil and sin, giving them a shepherd, and a place to live in peace, and put his sanctuary among them forever. And God will make Israel holy in the sight of all the nations. This is what God has done for his people and it is what will be done for all of us in Jesus, in ways we could never have imagined.

Jesus has brought Lazarus back to life and people believe in him and there is dissension and sharp division over Jesus' person, his works and his words—and yet no matter what he does (and it is always about life) there are those who are intent on killing him, silencing him so that their collusion with Rome might continue. So it is better that Jesus dies for the people—again in a way they could never have conceived. And they plan to kill him. Where do we stand—in collusion with politics, economics, nationalistic policy, military might that uses religion when it serves their purposes, or do we stand with Jesus who is only and always life, ever more abundantly for everyone?

HOLY WEEK

Monday in Holy Week

FIRST READING   Is 42:1–7
Responsorial Psalm   Ps 27:1, 2–3, 13–14
GOSPEL   Jn 12:1–11

These are the last days of Jesus. This is the last Sabbath evening meal, prepared by Martha (who has sent her servants away to serve Jesus in gratitude for Lazarus' life). And Mary, the other sister, takes perfume worth a year's wages and anoints Jesus' feet, in homage and thankfulness. They know that now even Lazarus is in the same danger of betrayal and death as Jesus because of his closeness to him. And Judas balks at the attention and the extravagant display of passion towards Jesus. But Jesus defends her and sets her up as a model for all those who wish to do for him what their hearts cry out for—and that the poor are Jesus' gift—his own person—so that whatever we want to do for him, for God's sake, now—do for the poor. Waste at least a year's wages on them and God will take it as wasted lovingly on his own person. It is a tense night—are we for or against Jesus, the poor he befriends and those he brings back from the dead. Today is a day to choose.

This is Jesus the servant who brings justice but his ways are different than the prophets of old. He speaks softly to the poor. He will not lean on what is already trembling, nor let what is near breaking point shatter. He will not let what is flickering go out. He comes with no violence, no harm, no power that destroys. He comes with the Spirit of God, the breath of his mouth, his Word, calling us for victory and grasping us by hand for justice, for light and hope. Martha serves this prophet of life in gratitude as a servant and Mary anoints this prophet who will die violently with ointment worth a year's wages. Who do we serve and who do we generously do the works of mercy for, knowing this is the only Body of Christ we will ever have the privilege to touch and honor as we would Jesus?

✳ Again we hear that this is God's servant, the one that he upholds, his chosen and beloved son who bears his spirit and comes for justice. In Jesus we have been called for the victory of justice and it is God who grasps us by the hand to make us the children of hope, of light and freedom. God's ways are not like ours. God's way are those of power that obeys, power that serves and power that brings life and resists violence, evil, sin and injustice. This is the story of gratitude: Martha who sends her servants away and waits on Jesus and the disciples. Mary who anoints Jesus feet, as preparation for his burial, seeking to thank him for giving new life to her brother—and to all of them. This is where Jesus takes her gift and will later, at the last supper, wash the feet of all his disciples as a way of living our gratitude and obedience to God through one another. She is demeaned by others but she is defended by Jesus and we are commanded to do for the poor what she has done for the poor suffering servant of God—Jesus. We, who have known God's life in Jesus, in our baptisms, must become, like Lazarus, a reason for others to believe in Jesus.

Tuesday in Holy Week

FIRST READING   Is 49:1–6
Responsorial Psalm   Ps 71:1–2, 3–4a, 5ab–6ab, 15 and 17
GOSPEL   Jn 13:21–33, 36–38

✳ The last meal with those he loves and calls friends and the awful announcement of betrayal. The one whom Jesus loves draws near to find out and is told, the one who shares the bread dipped in the dish is the one. This was usually an act of intimacy, of closeness among friends and Jesus uses it to speak one more time to Judas, inviting him in but Judas resists. Judas shares bread with Jesus and leaves. It grows close: Jesus announces that the Son of Man will be glorified and God will be glorified in him, and very soon. Such paradox: betrayal, glorification: rejection and total acceptance. And it's not just Judas—Peter too, staunchly claims to belong to Jesus and will die for him—yet he too is warned that soon he will betray him as well. We are warned ahead of time—will we betray our Lord, our Teacher and our God? There are many ways to do it: like Judas for money, for another's agenda in collusion with government and other authorities; like Peter in cowardice and fear; like the rest of the disciples and friends of Jesus in despair and terror that his fate may be their own as well. Lord, help us to be faithful, to face the cross and to face our failures with one another and with you and your Word.

Jesus is the sharp-edged sword (Word of God), a polished arrow sent to the heart of the people, the servant through whom God shows his glory. And he is the one who will bring union and communion to all by the strength of God borne in suffering, giving all so that all may see light and know what it means to be saved—to live in God. And this Jesus sits at table with his disciples and tells them that one will betray him, one will deny him viciously three times, and all will desert him. Nevertheless he shares his life, his body and blood with them and He will lay down his life for them and leave them for his Father. The end is near. Do we see yet who Jesus is—the beloved of God, inviting us to live and die with him for the glory of God?

Jesus is the sharp-edged arrow, concealed in God's arm, the servant of God and God will show his glory through him. Jesus will obey God's word even in the face of rejection and resistance, persecution, suffering and death. This is Jesus' holiness and power that we are invited to know and share. Jesus sought to tell his disciples (and us) that one of them would betray him—they would all run in fear, but one would sell him to his enemies. But Jesus does not attack Judas, he only tells him that he knows what he is going to do—just as Jesus knows what we do in betraying him in our fear, our greed, our trying to follow both our own ways, and the ways of the world. And still we call ourselves followers of Jesus the Crucified One.

But Jesus declares that his time of glory, (God's glory) has come and that God will glorify him in his suffering and death—not because it is pain, but because he is faithful no matter what others do to him. Peter brashly proclaims that he too will lay down his life for Jesus, but Jesus tells him that he will be betrayed three times before the night is done. And who are we: Judas, Peter, the other disciples, all of whom act in fear, thinking of themselves only, and not of Jesus? This year, where are we when Jesus looks to us?

Wednesday in Holy Week

FIRST READING   Is 50:4–9
Responsorial Psalm   Ps 69:8–10, 21–22, 31, 33–34
GOSPEL   Mt 26:14–25

✳ This is often called Spy Wednesday because it remembers Judas and his betrayal of Jesus, staying among the group, sharing the last intimacies yet already intent on handing Jesus over according to prior arrangement for thirty pieces of silver. All the preparations are made to celebrate the feast of freedom and liberation while there are others seeking death and oppression once again. The other disciples are just ignoring the hostilities all around them and they have already rejected Jesus' words on his coming suffering and death. They just don't want to hear it and are intent on their own time with Jesus and what they want him to be for them. And where are we? Do we betray our God because of money, prestige, our own ideas of who and what we think God is and how God works in the world? Do we resist Jesus' call to resist evil without violence or harm to others? Do we just ignore the evil and violence all around us and concentrate on our own relationships with Jesus and what we want from God? Do we ever think that our God wants to share his cross, his rejection and suffering and death with us—calling us to share in his death so as to share in his life and resurrection? Lord, Son of Man, may we not betray you this time, but stand fast and faithful.

✳ Again we are told what we are to look like in the face of persecution, suffering and death because we have practiced justice and told the truth, offering compassion to those in need. We are told to be prophets of justice nonviolently standing and taking the pain of others into our own lives and morning after morning opening our ears to the Word of God. We must know as Jesus does that he is betrayed by one he called friend, cheaply for just 30 pieces of silver. They are all distressed at the table, but they all betray, each in their own way. How often do we betray the Lord for something small, what we want or acceptance by others? And we betray God with our friends, families, parish and nation, and yet we are feed on the bread of life.

✳ We must listen to the scriptures daily and set our faces like flint, believing that God is near and is with us. Even as we suffer we are given the word that will rouse the weary. Jesus is with us. He has known betrayal of his own. He has known the discouragement of not being understood. He has known what it is like to love and call someone his friend. They run in fear, or boast of being there when you need them. They aren't there when he is being sold into the hands of those who intend to torture him to death. It says that each of the disciples was distressed and asked: "Is it I, Lord?" And of course, the answer to that question that each of us would ask is, "Yes, it is you, who I have dipped my hand in the dish and fed. "It is not just Judas—it is each and all of us who have sat at table and shared the eucharist and known Jesus' nearness and been called his friend.

EASTER SEASON

OCTAVE OF EASTER

Monday

FIRST READING   Acts 2:14, 22–33
Responsorial Psalm   Ps 16:1–2, 5, 7–8, 9–10, 11
GOSPEL   Mt 28:8–15

✵ The women who have come to the tomb and found it empty, obey the angels' words and leave to bring the news of the Resurrection to the disciples. And in obeying the word of God they meet Jesus coming towards them on the road with the word of Resurrection: Peace! Jesus' presence is worshipped and his words change the world forever: "Go tell my brothers to set out for Galilee, there they will see me." That phrase: 'my brothers' and those two words are a world of forgiveness, mercy, new life and freedom—from sin, from betrayal, from death into hope and newness of possibility for the future. In obeying the word of God we always meet the presence of God coming towards us and we are gifted with Peace and Forgiveness. We must practice resurrection and make sure all that we meet know the extent and power of that peace and reconciliation we have been given with our God.

✵ This week we will hear the ancient sermons revealing the wonder of who Jesus truly was and is for all time. Jesus the Nazorean, prophet, healer, miracle worker, killed and raised up by God, freed from death. It was impossible for death to get a hold of the God of life, human and divine and we are God's witnesses of this grace in the world for all to see and hear. We must enter the tomb (baptism), hear the Gospel and go to share it. Then we immediately meet Jesus on the way and are given Peace, the words, forgiveness and the Presence of the Risen Lord. But still we must choose who we follow: the Prince of Peace crucified or the world that fears the life, death and truth of the resurrection of Jesus.

✹ We will hear this message again and again in these 50 days: Jesus crucified has been raised. He is God's beloved and chosen and we are witnesses to all these events. And we see how the women in Matthew's gospel run from the tomb and the angel's proclamation of Jesus' resurrection. They obey the word of God (scriptures) and Jesus approaches them with a message of "Do not be afraid. And go tell my brothers, they will see me". In an instant the message of resurrection life is the message of forgiveness and mercy unbounded. Others leave the scene of the tomb and go to learn lies, deceit, bribery and collusion of religion and nation against the Good News of God. We hear the story as those belonging to the military, the state, or those in religious circles in collusion with the state or as Jesus' disciples. And we cannot have one foot here and one foot there. We must obey if we are to see the Risen Lord.

Tuesday

FIRST READING   Acts 2:36–41
Responsorial Psalm   Ps 33:4–5, 18–19, 20, 22
GOSPEL   Jn 20:11–18

✹ Now Mary has stayed behind after Peter and the Beloved Disciple have returned to the others and she weeps, disconsolate over the loss of the body of her Master. Even though she sees angels (she does not go into the tomb which symbolizes baptism) and she even hears Jesus questioning her on why she is weeping and who she is looking for, she does not recognize him. Why? She is so bound to finding his dead body and clinging to her old life, and relationship to him that she cannot see that he is before her—and that he is much more than she ever knew him to be. He tells her that he is not hers—that he is going to ascend to his Father and her Father, to his God and her God and that she must let go of what she once had with him—for there is so much more being offered to her. Do we get lost in what was, what we had or wanted and cannot see that our God is offering us so much more in the Risen Lord and resurrection life. Time to let go of tears and what was—our lives belong to the Risen Lord and to the Father in the power of the Spirit.

✳ When we hear the story of Jesus' death and resurrection it must deeply shake us and bring us to repentance, forgiveness and the life of the Spirit. We read the accounts of the disciples (Mary) seeing the Risen Lord, and how long it takes to actually see, come to believe and change all of what we thought we knew of Jesus. Our personal relationships are tiny bits of who Jesus is and Jesus always seeks to bring us to His God and His Father, to our God and our Father, and not cling to the smallness of our grasping at God.

✳ Peter's preaching shakes the people and deeply disturbs them and they ask what they must do. All preaching must tend towards repentance, forgiveness and reconciliation that is the foundation of belief in Jesus, crucified and risen. And then the gift of the Spirit is also given to those who know they must not continue as the rest of this generation lives.

Again we hear the story of Mary of Magdala who weeps by the tomb. She is questioned by the angels: why do you weep? And she repeats her refrain that she can't find the body of her Lord. Jesus questions her asking: "Woman, why are you weeping? What are you looking for? "And still she cannot see or hear him right there with her because of her grief, but also because she has never known him as he is, only as she wanted him to be for her. One of the first lines of John's gospel is: What are you looking for? And still she does not hear and see. Once she has seen and heard, she tells the disciples what he has told her. And what of us—are our old images and what we want Jesus to be for us getting in the way of seeing and hearing the Word of God right near us?

Wednesday

FIRST READING	Acts 3:1–10
Responsorial Psalm	Ps 105:1–2, 3–4, 6–7, 8–9 34
GOSPEL	Lk 24:13–35

✳ This is the story of the two disciples running away from Jerusalem and all that has happened there and going home, in despair, having lost even their hopes for who Jesus might have been. All shattered by crucifixion and death. But Jesus walks with them and doesn't let them go that easily. He opens their minds and stirs their hearts to life with the opening of the Scriptures and all the words from Moses onwards about him and why/how he would suffer before his glory. They recognize him in the breaking of the bread, but only after he has spent hours breaking open their minds and hearts so that they can finally see and remember all that he has taught them. And they go back, to face suffering, death, fear and isolation—and the Risen Lord who now is everywhere, waiting for us and seeking to give us hope in the Word and our hearts alive again in the meaning of the Scriptures that give us faith in the breaking of the bread.

✺ It is a marvelous week hearing the vastly different accounts of the disciples seeing the Risen Lord! And hearing in the Acts of the power that comes through those who believe and carry the risen Lord within them. Peter gives what he has: belief and memory. And Cleopas and his wife are brought back to life with the Scriptures in the mouth of Jesus, bringing them understanding and hope once again. It is passed on, by word of mouth: word, story, memory, hope, life and just the telling of the story summons life back into their hearts and flesh. We must tell the story in community and stay alive in the Risen Lord.

✺ Peter grasps a cripple by the hand and raises him up in Jesus' name. The power of God begins to seep out into the world through those who witness to him. And the two disciples run away from Jerusalem, despairing at their loss. They walk with Jesus though they do not recognize him. He opens their minds to the scripture as they walk all those miles and in a moment, when he breaks bread, they see him. But it has taken all those hours on the road with him and the Word to remember/a story, Jesus' signature—the feeding of crowds, the breaking of bread. They run back to Jerusalem to tell their story of being in the presence of Jesus and of learning to see him in the breaking of the bread, after long hours of being taught to see and hear the Word of the Lord.

Thursday

FIRST READING   Acts 3:11–26
Responsorial Psalm   Ps 8:2ab and 5, 6–7, 8–9
GOSPEL   Lk 24:35–48

And the story grows! They return to the others who have stories to tell of having seen the Lord themselves, even Peter! And as they are telling theirs from the road (Cleopas and his wife) the very act of telling the story evokes the presence of the Risen Lord in their midst. They rejoice, but they're afraid it's a ghost. Jesus gently eats in their presence, shows them his wounds and opens their minds to the scriptures: the Psalms, the prophets, the Law of Moses—drawing out the depth of his place in the Word, as the Word of God made flesh and now in Resurrection with them forever. This is what we are to be witnesses to—the word of truth in the Scriptures, announcing forgiveness to all the nations and calling all to repentance—to turn towards the Crucified and Risen One as the One who is God among us.

The marvelous stories continue to be told and come true! Peter raises a lame man and tells what Jesus has done for all of us, the Author of life, murdered yet lifted up in life forever. Turn and know a season of refreshment: baptismal life and resurrection beginning now in our flesh. We must tell the story for the story shared in community summons the presence of the Risen Lord among us! In the Scriptures, Jesus, by the power of the Spirit opens our minds to memory, understanding, power. The Word made flesh among us is as sure and powerful and graceful as the bread broken among us. We must listen, tell and become the story for the world. We make the Word come true in our flesh now. This is resurrection life

Jesus is the Author of life once killed and now alive, raised by God. And what they do, they do in the power of his name, calling those who witness this goodness to repentance and to turn from evil. Peter uses the scriptures to remind them of God's words and draw them into the present reality.

The two disciples, Cleophas (and Mary of Cleophas) return and tell their story and as they tell the story, Jesus appears in their midst, with the blessing/command: Peace be with you. They are terrified, yet he calms them, eats with them and then opens their minds to the Scripture—the law, the prophets, the psalms that are fulfilled in him—especially the words of suffering, persecution, rejection and death. REMEMBER, he tells them again—all that I taught you when I was with you. We must remember so that we can preach forgiveness of sin to all the world and be his witnesses. The scriptures must be our food and drink, our lifeline and our lifeblood, to be studied and shared with others, as Jesus does here with his community.

Friday

FIRST READING   Acts 4:1–12
Responsorial Psalm   Ps 118:1–2 and 4, 22–24, 25–27
GOSPEL   Jn 21:1–14

This is Easter breakfast on the beach, with Jesus as the host, providing a warm fire (Spirit) and some bread and fish (Eucharist) calling to his still lost and unaware disciples to come and eat (Eucharist). They are out fishing as they were before they followed Jesus—they have gone back to their own lives. Jesus is on the shore, calling them children and telling them where to catch fish. The beloved disciple recognizes Jesus and cries out the Resurrection proclamation: It is the Lord. Peter puts on his clothes and jumps in the water (baptism) and they come to land. They are fed by the Risen Lord yet do not ask who he is. An awkward breakfast that is also reconciliation and forgiveness, the start of a new relationship between Jesus and themselves and each other, called now to be ministers of reconciliation and forgiveness. It's the third time they will see him, and probably the last time in the flesh.

Peter and John tell the story and imitate Jesus. With the power seeping out into the community in them and filled with the Holy Spirit, they tell the truth courageously. They are a far cry from the disheartened disciples, going back to fish and finding nothing all night. Jesus walks the beach, invites them to breakfast and feeds them. "Come children, eat your meal." Eucharist is resurrection life and baptism experienced again in community, and when we eat together we are forgiven and summoned beyond ourselves into the Body of Christ. In the bread/and fish we are made again disciples, missionaries and bringers of good news to all.

✺ Peter and John are arrested for preaching and healing and still in the fact of persecution they boldly proclaims the name of Jesus and the power of the Risen Lord to the people. The Spirit has seized hold of the disciples and they are becoming witnesses (martyrs).

This is the last story of Jesus appearing to his disciples. They fish all night and catch nothing and at the word of Jesus whom they do not recognize, they catch so many the boats are straining. They are given breakfast on the beach, forgiven, and reconciled in a meal with Jesus and nothing is said, though now they recognize him as he feeds them. He calls them, and us, children, for now they are the children of God, beloved as he is before the Father. This is Eucharist as Reconciliation and the great catch is Jesus' promise that all the world (153—all the varities of fish at the time) will be the new fishing grounds for disciples. We too are invited, whether we are faithful or not—come and eat your meal, children.

Saturday

FIRST READING   Acts 4:13–21
Responsorial Psalm   Ps 118:1, 14–15, 16–18, 19–21
GOSPEL   Mk 16:9–15

✺ Another account of the resurrection and its effects added on to the original text (1-8). This one recaps a number of other appearances: to Mary of Magdala, and to the two on the road and to the eleven while they were at table. He rebukes them for not believing one another's stories of hope, of resurrection and the promise of new life—believing in his words that were being experienced as true by others. And the disciples (and us) are commanded to go out into the whole world and bring the Good News to all creation—the good news of life over death, love over hate, forgiveness over vengeance, justice over evil, truth over lies and mercy over hate and selfishness. And we are to believe one another especially when it entails hope and the power of resurrection—attending to it wherever it happens and to whom it is given. Lord, make us attentive to resurrection and new life, hope and forgiveness wherever it is. Do not let us limit your power and goodness to our small experience of it. Amen.

✳ We jump to another gospel to hear another story, an add on to Mark's account of the empty tomb. Peter and John are running into difficulties, as Jesus did by proclaim the gospel and healing and bringing hope. They're warned. So we listen to how often Jesus appeared to his grieving followers: to Mary of Magdala, to others walking the roads, to the Eleven at table and he takes them to task for not believing one another's stories after he had been raised. We have to stand and speak, if our own don't listen to us and we must go into the whole world, even if we are persecuted, ignored and spurned. We have to if we have seen and believe in the Risen Lord.

✳ The leaders don't know what to do with Peter and John and how different they are after the resurrection of Jesus and the gift of the Spirit. They warn them sternly not to mention the name of Jesus again or to teach/preach about him. But they will obey only God and for the moment they are let go free.

This add-on ending to Mark's gospel is a summary of many of the appearances of Jesus to his disciples in shortened form: to Mary of Magdala at the tomb. They did not believe her. To the disciples on the road—And in this version of the story, they did not believe them, though it is otherwise in Luke. And a new story we don't have—that Jesus appeared to them while they were at table to chide them for not believing the proclamation of resurrection from one another—and always the experience of resurrection and the presence of the Risen Lord must lead to going into the world to preach. Do we preach?

SECOND WEEK OF EASTER

Monday

FIRST READING   Acts 4:23–31
Responsorial Psalm   Ps 2:1–3, 4–7a, 7b–9
GOSPEL   Jn 3:1–8

This feast fell in Holy Week and so is moved to Easter Week. This is the familiar prophecy of a young woman who will bear a child whose name will be Emmanuel, God is with us. And the story of Gabriel sent to the young woman Mary inviting her to obey the Word and will of God for the long promised salvation of her nation. She will give birth to a child, but the child is not hers—the child is God's, born of the power of the Spirit, born for the people and to bring hope and salvation into the world. Mary is the model for all believers and we too are invited to bring the Word of God into the world through our flesh, our words and lives. We too are called to be the handmaids of the Lord (as Moses, David, Isaiah and others were named) and we too must pray: "Let it be done to me as you have said." Let the Word of God take flesh in us, the Body of Christ and may we bring that Word into the world that waits and needs it so desperately today.

When the Spirit has been given, the disciples seem impelled to keep speaking of Jesus the Risen Lord and they don't go easy on the crowds. They speak the truth about evil, injustice, murder (death penalty) and they know some of the same reaction that Jesus knew, but they also know some of the power of Spirit that comes to them again and again. This is the lived experience of what Jesus sought to share with Nicodemus by night in his fear. This is being born again, without fear, facing the truth and standing with the risen Lord.

Peter and John once released pray to God for words, that they might be true servants of the Gospel and the entire place is filled with the Spirit and they grow in confidence. The Church, the Body of Christ grows and moves out into the world, in spite of persecution and threats.

Nicodemus comes to Jesus by night. He sits and questions he who is the Light of the World. And Jesus seeks to teach him about baptism and being born in water and the spirit, being birthed into a new life as drastically different as the one he knew in his mother's womb and the one he lives now. But this life is one of grace and Spirit, lived in community with others. Through baptism we are initiated and drawn into the Body of Christ, into the embrace of the Spirit and into the dwelling place of God the Father/the Trinity. This is our life now.

Tuesday

FIRST READING   Acts 4:32–37
Responsorial Psalm   Ps 93:1ab, 1cd–2, 5
GOSPEL   Jn 3:7b–15

We now find ourselves in the midst of Jesus' words to Nicodemus who comes by night to speak with the Light of the World. Jesus exhorts him to be born from above, born in water and the Spirit (baptism and confirmation). Jesus teaches him about the Spirit, the wind that blows where it will and we can hear its sound (Word of God). We must look to the Word of God and to the life of Jesus, especially to his death and resurrection to understand what this new life of baptism and the Spirit is like. We must look upon the Son of Man crucified and raised up to know the depth of God's love for the world and all that he has made. We must learn to listen to the Spirit in Jesus' Word, the Word of the Scripture that brings life.

The apostolic church was one mind and heart, owning all in common and sharing among all whatever is needed. They witnessed to the resurrection and no one in the Body of Christ was in need because all shared of what they had. One of those is Joseph/Barnabas—the son of encouragement who will play such a large role in the Acts with Paul. He comes and lays his property before the apostles.

Jesus continues to teach Nicodemus about the power of the Spirit of God that goes where it will and comes to rest where it will. He tells him solemnly of the Son of Man who has come down to earth and was lifted up so that all who believe might have life in him. This whole section is one of the earliest pieces of mystagogia—what was taught to the new believers after their baptism, to draw them deeper into the life of the Body of Christ through the power of the Spirit. Are we moving deeper into the mysteries of what it means to believe in and live as a follower of the Son of Man, Crucified and Risen?

Wednesday

FIRST READING   Acts 5:17–26
Responsorial Psalm   Ps 34:2–3, 4–5, 6–7, 8–9
GOSPEL   Jn 3:16–21

God so loved the world that he gave his Son so that we might have life and live like Jesus did. Jesus was born among us, lived with us, sought to teach us, convert us and turn our hearts to God alone, as he worshipped God in spirit and truth. We will know this life that Jesus knew with God if we believe and obey his words. Are we the children of darkness or the children of light? Are we the children of the truth or are we those who speak the lies of the world and confuse others' words with the truth? Do our deeds reflect the light and life of Jesus the Crucified One obedient to God or do our deeds do evil, injustice and distort the truth? We will be seen clearly for who we are and what we do. Do we live in the light of resurrection life and the shadow of the cross? Can anyone tell we are the children of God?

We hear the work of the Spirit in the early Church in Acts, alongside the words of Jesus to Nicodemus. The apostles are arrested but an angel of the Lord sets them free to preach again, boldly. They preach and are arrested again! And Jesus again and again tries to tell Nicodemus how God in love sent his Son to bring life to all the world, not condemning but bringing Good News, bring light. But the world and the children of the world (we often act more like them) prefer darkness to the light, and do evil not wanting our deeds to be exposed. We are challenged to decide again: for the light or deeds we wouldn't want exposed to the truth and light.

✴ Peter and John are arrested, but they are freed by the Spirit at night and told to preach. They obey and are arrested again the next day but the power of the Word loose in the world can't be imprisoned. If only we would preach with such zeal about this new life of baptism in Christ!

And Jesus is preaching to Nicodemus about the love that God has for the world and all its peoples. God is the God of life and in Jesus this new life is shared with all human beings. This life is light, that clarifies, that exposes, that reveals, that loves the truth. Our lives must be preaching by our deeds that are truthful, life-giving and freeing and so loving of the world and all its peoples. God's Son was given so that we could give him away again and again.

Thursday

FIRST READING   Acts 5:27–33
Responsorial Psalm   Ps 34:2, 9, 17–18, 19–20
GOSPEL   Jn 3:31–36

✴ John weaves together the images of what is above, of the The One who comes from heaven, and what he has seen and heard, and how now that he is upon earth, in the flesh of Jesus, he speaks of what he knows and bears witness, but no one accepts his testimony. No one acknowledges the truthfulness of God who refuses to receive Jesus' words as testimony about God. The mystery of God the Father in Jesus and Jesus in the Father, bound in the Spirit is found in these words: Whoever believes in the Son lives with eternal life, but he who will not believe in the Son will never know life and always faces the justice of God. Do we believe in the Son? Oh, not just in words, or creed or ritual, but in practice, in obedience to the Scriptures, in imitation of Jesus, child of God, maker of peace, reconciler, healer and one who loves, even unto death? Do we lay down our lives for one another, resisting evil without doing harm? Lord, give us life and the courage to live up to our baptismal promises this Easter season.

✴ Peter and the apostles are tried for disobeying orders. They keep speaking that Name! They continue to testify to the truth, with the Holy Spirit and the Sanhedrin wants to kill them. It is Easter time but the truth is still hard to take, hard to hear and harder still to put into our lives. Jesus speaks to Nicodemus seeking to show him the difference between those who live in the resurrection light and life, baptized and confirmed and those who do not know the God of truth and life. We must know the Father in Jesus through the Spirit and we must act according to Jesus' words, or we know nothing of God.

The pattern of what is happening to the apostles follows the one that Jesus himself experienced. When questioned about why they disobeyed and preached 'that name', they respond that they obey God and testify to the truth of Jesus' life, death and resurrection. And the Holy Spirit testifies with them. And the leaders are stung to fury and want to kill them. The Word brings revelation, exposing us to the truth/light. The Spirit bears testimony in believers to the power of God in the world.

The Father loves the Son and has given everything over to him, and the Son has given everything over to us in his Spirit! We must obey the Son and make his words come true in our deeds and ways in the world.

Friday

FIRST READING   Acts 5:34–42
Responsorial Psalm   Ps 27:1, 4, 13–14
GOSPEL   Jn 6:1–15

Jesus feeds the crowds with the bread and fish of a young boy who gives his family's food to Jesus and the leftovers fill twelve baskets. This is of course, Eucharist, but it is life in Jesus, it is core to his teaching and his knowledge of God. Communion, sharing with others what is sustenance, food, justice, life, healing, hope, possibility for the future because of the presence of the Risen One with us in Jesus, the Body of Christ—Eucharist and church, the Word of God—the Scriptures and the presence of Jesus in the poor and all that he has left with us in ritual and word. This ritual that became the mark of Jesus' presence and life is what we must do with our lives in the world after having shared it with Jesus and the community. We must live lives of sharing: bread, hope, justice, peace, freedom, forgiveness—all that Jesus has taught us to believe in, has shared with us so graciously and told us to pass on to all the world.

✹ In court again, someone speaks clearly telling them to leave the apostles alone because if they are of God, from God, then they will not be able to destroy them without fighting God himself. If not, it will die of its own accord. And they leave in joy, to teach again. They are imitating Jesus who worked ceaselessly among the crowds teaching, bringing the good news of hope, healing, touching people and feeding them from the food one young boy brought with him. They were told and now they obey: to feed the crowds, and collect the leftovers, imitating Jesus. They feed now, in word and bread of hope.

✹ Someone prevails upon the court to leave Peter and John alone and let them preach, and see what comes of it. If it is just based in human activity, it will pass, but if it's of God then they would have to fight God in destroying them. They accept this proposal but have them whipped. They rejoice to suffer for the sake of the Name.

Jesus feeds a huge crowd with the food offered by a young man, 5 barley loaves (the bread of the poor) and a few fish. It is distributed among the people and the crusts are gathered up after so that nothing goes to waste. This teaching/example of worship and life is God's way in the world—to share so that all have enough and there are leftovers to feed the whole world. Are we like the young man who gave his gift so that it could be blessed and shared as God's bread for the hungry?

Saturday

FIRST READING   Acts 6:1–7
Responsorial Psalm   Ps 33:1–2, 4–5, 18–19
GOSPEL   Jn 6:16–21

✹ Evening comes and the disciples get into the boat and head away from the shore. A storm arises and Jesus comes walking across the water to them. They are afraid, but he tells them once again: "It is Me; don't be afraid. They have eaten and they leave, back to their usual ways and places. But there were rough seas and wind—life began once again to toss them and disorient them, but Jesus is there—in the midst of the rough seas and wind…it is seems that's where we find Jesus most clearly even when our fear rises and we don't believe what is right before us. Even in the midst of need (as in the Acts, with the need for so many to be fed) the wind of the Spirit is present and new things, new ministries, new ways of dealing with life arise and are given. We are not to be afraid. Our Lord is present in all things.

✳ The community grows and with it dissension. The Jews and Greeks both have widows and the Greeks complain that their poor are not being as well taken care of as the Greeks' poor. They gather, pray in the Spirit and appoint 7 men as deacons (all Greek!) and in the name of the Church, they now care publicly for all the poor. The word continues to be preached and the community grows apace. Jesus has told them often, not to be afraid of any storms they will encounter. He is always with them, in new and creative, life-giving ways of taking care of what is at hand. Storms on the lake, in the community and our hearts—all are stilled by the Word and the Spirit in community.

✳ A new ministry—of deacons—is born in the church, out of need. The Greek widows are not being taken care of to the same degree that the Jewish widows are. The people chose 7 (all happened to be Greeks!) and bring them to be prayed over with hands imposed. And the community grows, through the preaching of the Word and the sharing of life, in care of the least. Problems that surface are the place where the Spirit seeks a new way of expressing the power of God. Just as the disciples in the boat (church) are on the lake and a storm rises—Jesus comes to them in the midst of such experiences and says: "Do not be afraid, it is I." Jesus' presence is always with us—the Church is called the sacrament of the Risen Lord. We must rely on this presence and its power for everything that develops in the church—and there is always freshness/newness of ministries in response to need—a sign of the church's vitality. What is needed in your group now?

THIRD WEEK OF EASTER

Monday

FIRST READING   Acts 6:8–15
Responsorial Psalm   Ps 119:23–24, 26–27, 29–30
GOSPEL   Jn 6:22–29

✹ Jesus fed the people and now they come looking for him again. Sadly not because they have come to believe in him, but because they were fed. Jesus exhorts them to work for lasting food that brings eternal life and that he himself, the Son of Man will give it to them. And the only work God wants us to do is to believe in the One whom God has sent. People see and yet they do not see. In Acts Stephen walks in the ways of Jesus the Lord, preaching with wisdom but they do not see and are stirred against him. Do we see? Do we see who does the work of believing in the Son of Man? Do we see those who feed the poor, and care for the widows, who speaks the truth in the face of adversity and threat? Do we see who stands with those who are treated unjustly? What food are we working for today?

✹ Stephen, one of the deacons preaches causing some to incite others to move against him (again the church is reliving what Jesus knew as he preached the truth). They stare at him his face shines with light as they falsely accuse him. His care of the widows and his preaching are two sides of one hand—he is the good news to the poor to whom he proclaims and the Spirit is strong in his words because of his care for the least.

And the people search for Jesus—and Jesus knows them. They are looking for bread, because he fed them and he tells us that we should be searching and working for the food of the Son of Man— the bread of life, of hope and justice. And we should be doing the work of God—believing in Jesus and preaching with our deeds and life, and words.

Tuesday

FIRST READING   Acts 7:51—8:1
Responsorial Psalm   Ps 31:3–4, 6 and 7b and 8a, 17 and 21ab
GOSPEL   Jn 6:30–35

Stephen preaches hard, calling the people stubborn and hard of heart and he lists the long litany of how they are just like their ancestors. They turn against him, drag him from the city and stone him to death. Like his Master, Stephen cries out in praise of the Son of Man who sits at God's right hand and forgives his murderers as he dies, handing his spirit over to Jesus who is Lord of life. Jesus' audience still wants signs, like their ancestors in the desert who were fed manna, but Jesus claims that the bread his Father gives is true bread. And Jesus bluntly says: "I am the bread of life, and whoever comes to him will never hunger or thirst. Do we want this bread, of forgiveness and justice, of peace and communion with God and with one another? Or like our ancestors are we stubborn and hard of heart?

Stephen, one of the deacons, the first martyr is stoned to death for preaching fearlessly of Jesus. He lived like Jesus, caring for the poor and preaching Good News, and he dies like Jesus, with the words of forgiveness of his enemies on his lips and entrusting his life to God the Father. Jesus too gives of his bread, his truth, his life to his community and is the Bread of life given for us/to us. When we come to this Bread of Life, as Stephen did, it transforms our life and we begin to live forever, even as death may claim us.

Stephen the preacher/deacon becomes a prophet by the power of the Spirit and tells the people and the leaders the truth about themselves: that they are always in opposition to the Spirit, just like their ancestors. And because of that, they did not listen to Jesus, the Just One and murdered him. They are stung to the heart—but they are filled with anger. Stephen has a vision of Jesus in glory and when he speaks of it, they rush at him and stone him to death. And just as Jesus did, Stephen dies, forgiving those who murder him. The blood of the martyrs begins to water the ground for the seed of the Word of God. Saul watches the killing.

✳︎Stephen lived on the Word of God, the Bread of Life. Stephen had come to Jesus in baptism and in service to the poor and he fulfills Jesus' words to the crowd who asks for God's bread always: "No one who comes to me shall ever be hungry, no one who believes in me shall thirst again." And do we live on this bread?

Wednesday

FIRST READING   1 P 5:5–14
Responsorial Psalm   Ps 89:2–3, 6–7, 16–17
GOSPEL   Mk 16:15–20

✳︎ Stephen is martyred and Saul begins to persecute the Church, going from house to house to seek out believers and jail them but even scattered those who believe and preach the word. Philip goes to Samaria to preach. Jesus tells his hearers that even though they have the Bread of Life before them, they refuse to believe. But Jesus will not turn away from the work that the Father has sent him into the world to do. He will continue, even under duress, rejection and being condemned in public. He will lose nothing of what he has been given by God the Father. Do we come to Jesus, open and ready to do the will of our Father? Do we eat and share in this bread: the word of God in the scriptures; the Eucharist shared, the work of the coming of justice and peace, forgiveness and hope?

✳︎ James sees the Risen Lord though we do not know the particulars and James is also the brother of John the Evangelist, the Beloved Disciple, cousins to Jesus. (they are also called the sons of Thunder). Philip has ties with Gentiles and asks Jesus to show them the Father at the Last Supper. It seems Jesus had to be very patient with both of them, slow to see who he is and what the consequences of his teaching will mean for their lives. The answer Philip receives: "If you have seen me, you have seen the Father!" That is enough. We too have seen Jesus, in word, in bread, in the poor, in community/Church/Body of Christ, in every human being because of Incarnation.

Thursday

FIRST READING   Acts 8:26–40
Responsorial Psalm   Ps 66:8–9, 16–17, 20
GOSPEL   Jn 6:44–51

✳ The Jews murmur against Jesus. They think they know who he is, who his family members are, which town he comes from but Jesus chides them saying that they do not know him at all. And they cannot come to him, unless drawn by the Father. But to those who come to him, he will raise them up on the last days. Jesus is speaking about his relationship to the Father and what the Father does for him, he in turn will do for all those who believe in him and honor him. He quotes that the day will come when all will be taught by God and that in his person, we can listen and learn from the Father. We must eat of this Word of truth in Jesus, his teaching, his bread and his presence so that we might live. Do we spend our days eating and becoming the Body of Christ with one another?

✳ Philip becomes a preacher/missionary and converts an Ethiopian, sitting with him and explaining the book of Isaiah to him, he connects it to Jesus crucified and risen. Along the way, (in imitation of Jesus giving understanding and revealing himself) he baptizes the man. The Spirit snatches him away and he finds himself somewhere else! It seems that if we share insight and meaning of the Scriptures with others and reveal the face of God in Jesus to others, we are taught by God and know something of the eternal life of God.

✳ The first persecution of the Church began with the death of Stephen in Jerusalem and Saul was a standby witness to his murder that persecuted the church with a vengeance. But the disciples dispersed, go and preach. Philip goes to Samaria and the Spirit's power is released so strongly that the people's response reaches a fever pitch! They listened closely to what he had to say— do we listen closely to the Word of God so that it can seep deep down inside of us? Philip meets an Ethiopian, a court official who is reading the scroll of Isaiah. Philip uses these words to preach that it is Jesus that Isaiah is speaking about. Upon hearing the Word he is baptized immediately and Philip is snatched away (shades of Elijah!) In spite of persecution, the Spirit and Word cannot be stopped.

We have both the Word and the Bread of Life—both are given so that we might do the will of the Father, in imitation of Jesus. We have looked upon the Son (on the cross) and we believe in him. We are to begin to live that resurrection life begun in baptism now—so that others can see what the Word and Bread of life means for the world.

Friday

FIRST READING   Acts 9:1–20
Responsorial Psalm   Ps 117:1, 2
GOSPEL   Jn 6:52–59

Jesus first fed the crowds, 5000 men, probably more than 25,000 in the desert and they were all satisfied, but they do not believe. Especially the leaders, keep trying to question Jesus on His words, ignoring his work and his presence, his power that comes from God the Father who sent him. His word, his life brings life and hope to all who hunger for more than survival (the poor) and all those who seek meaning and justice and life for all. Yet they refuse to accept him and what he says about his words, his teaching, that this is his body and blood—sustenance for life. His presence among them gives them life unbounded. We speak of these long passages as about Eucharist and they are, but they are first about Jesus' word, about his teaching on how to live and the Word of Scripture that is given to us for nourishment and sustenance on our journey. We become what we eat—we are the Body of Christ meant to be food for the earth. Are we this daily bread for others?

The readings from Acts and John always go together in this season. The preaching of the word of Jesus in the Scripture and the breaking of the bread of life are one and the same thing meant to be whole, unbroken that coming together in the lived life of believers. The only Body of Christ that Saul meets is the Church, the community, the sacrament of the Risen Lord and they teach him how to live: those he persecuted, Stephen, Ananias, and others. We need the word of the Scripture to teach us with others what the body and blood of Jesus, in word and eucharist means for our daily lives. We feed on God so that others might feed on us.

Saul travels to Damascus breathing murder (self-righteous religious hatred) against the Lord's disciples and on the way he is met by the light/words of the Risen Lord: Saul, Saul, why are you persecuting me? The church is the Body of Christ, suffering, crucified and risen—and this is the Lord that Saul meets. And the community though afraid of him, takes him in, feeds him, cares for him and preaches to him and he sees and is baptized. He stays and begins to preach in the synagogues of Jesus, Son of God.

Word and bread—we are given the flesh and the word of the Son of Man so that we might have life, and remain in Jesus, just as Jesus remains in the Father and Spirit. We have life because of Jesus. The Body of Christ is Eucharist and the Church—mysteries to be studied and prayed over in this season of resurrection.

Saturday

FIRST READING   Acts 9:31–42
Responsorial Psalm   Ps 116:12–13, 14–15, 16–17
GOSPEL   Jn 6:60–69

Jesus tells us that his words bring spirit and life, yet his words offend many. He asks them if they will be offended when the Son of Man ascends, on the cross and into heaven at the right hand of God as judge of the world? Jesus even loses many of his own disciples. He asked the Twelve if they will leave as well and Peter's answer is meant to be our own: "Lord, to whom shall we go? You have the words of eternal life. We now believe and know that you are the Holy One of God." But Peter doesn't know what he's saying—do we ever really know the words of our belief? Jesus tells them, reminds them that it is He who has chosen us and that one would betray him. Lord, if we are quick to say that we believe, help us to remain faithful and not to betray you before others.

The Church is at peace! Peter is making journeys preaching and healing. Tabitha or Dorcas one of the believers who makes garments dies in Joppa and Peter (like Jesus) says to her: Tabitha, stand up. And she opens her eyes and stands up. Peter brings in the widows to show that she is alive and many come to believe upon hearing the story. Jesus gives his life in his body and blood and the disciples find it hard to believe. Many drift and break away from Jesus because they cannot believe in the eucharist. And we—do we believe that the Body and Blood of Christ gives us life? It is life that is meant to be shared and given for the lives of others.

✳ The church is at peace and growing in the fear of the Lord— fearing nothing so much as to not be obedient and the consolation of the Spirit grows deeper too. And amazing things keep happening—whole villages become followers upon hearing the Word, and Peter brings Tabitha/Dorcas back to life—an echo of Jesus' raising a young girl to life. The Acts reveal the same power of the Spirit in Jesus at work in the apostles and the church—'as the Father sent me, so now I send you' is coming true. All of Jesus' words are spirit and life, yet some of them are very hard to swallow—about eating the flesh of the Son of Man and about picking up our cross and coming after the Son of Man. The Word must be preached and the invitation to follow God's holy one must be offered—are we sharing the grace that has been given to us at our baptism?

FOURTH WEEK OF EASTER

Monday

FIRST READING   Acts 11:1–18
Responsorial Psalm   Ps 42:2–3; 43:3, 4
GOSPEL   Jn 10:1–10

Jesus is the Good Shepherd who lays down his life to protect and defend the sheep from evil, harm and starvation. Anyone else who does not care for the sheep in this way, runs at danger and leaves the sheep to be attacked and scattered. The hired hand works for pay and cares nothing for the sheep. Jesus is referring to many who claim to be leaders, ministers and those who are supposed to care for the sheep—the Church. Jesus is loved by the Father because he loves the sheep and lays his life down for them. And it is amazing what Jesus is saying: that he knows us as he knows his own Father and that we will know him if we listen to his voice. Jesus' intent is to draw all together in unity, the sheep of his choosing and all those who seek him. Are we a part of Jesus' flock? Do we work at unity and communion even among ourselves let alone see to make all one in Jesus' kingdom? Do we really care for the sheep and not work for someone else or for ourselves?

The church is growing and breaking borders and boundaries for the Spirit cannot be contained in old ways, traditions, customs or to just one people. The gift of the Spirit is given as God wills. The Shepherd, the Sheepgate is Jesus—the Word of God made flesh and whoever hears his voice, and follows after him, belongs to the fold, the church. This is the Word of God who is Jesus, who comes "that all might have life and have it to the full." There is room in the fold for everyone.

Peter shares his dream with the people in Jerusalem where he was taught that what God created is clean and that he was sent to preach. When he did, those who listened were filled with the Spirit, as it had come when Jesus promised them this gift. The Gentiles too are called and blessed with repentance, life and the gifts of the Spirit. All the world is to be one in Christ. We are not to 'interfere with God". We are all the sheep of the one flock and each of us is called by name. All are invited in, to be safe, to find pasture and to have life to the full. We belong to this flock. Do we follow the voice of the Shepherd and make sure that we are not interfering with God by our exclusion of others, our customs and traditions?

Tuesday

FIRST READING   Acts 11:19–26
Responsorial Psalm   Ps 87:1–3, 4–5, 6–7
GOSPEL   Jn 10:22–30

✢ Jesus is in the temple (he is the Temple now) and is questioned on who he is, and to speak plainly. Jesus speaks plainly saying he has told them but they are not his sheep because they do not listen to his voice. And even if they had trouble with his words, they should look to his works and come to believe by seeing what he does in his Father's name. What the Father has given him is stronger than everything—the Spirit. He speaks plainly. He and the Father are one. We are invited into this oneness, this communion by the Word of the Lord, our shepherd. Do we listen? In Acts, the name Christians is given to those who follow Jesus, in Antioch after long persecutions and yet, times of mission and many coming to believe in the Word that is preached. To preach the word is to live the Word in community. Are we plain in how we preach that Jesus is Lord?

✢ The persecution of the Church, beginning with the martyrdom of Stephen gives a life force to the Church and spurs missionary activity. Barnabas and Saul (Paul) work diligently in Antioch and as the Church grows, they acquire a new name: Christians, or the followers of the Way. The word and the works of Jesus are his witnesses that lays claim to who he is truly is, the beloved child of God the Father. And Jesus' sheep continue with that word and works as witness to the presence of the Shepherd with us still.

Wednesday

FIRST READING   Acts 12:24—13:5a
Responsorial Psalm   Ps 67:2–3, 5, 6 and 8
GOSPEL   Jn 12:44–50

These words of Jesus, though spoken now in Easter are some of the last words Jesus speaks in public before the Last Supper, calling out for those who are hearing his words, but not listening to him, or obeying him to respond. He is crying out that he is the light and he is with us in the world so that we do not remain in darkness. If we hear his words, but do not keep them, then the Word convicts us. Jesus has been taught by God what to say and how to speak (the Spirit) and that God is life and all the teachings, all the commandments are about life—life for all, especially those most in need of it—life given in forgiveness and justice, in food and healing, in care and acceptance, life ever more abundant. And especially it is life in God—life that is shared by Jesus with us, in the power of the Spirit so that we might know God as Jesus knows the Father. Do we believe in the one that sent Jesus, the Father? Do we live in his light, according to his Word?

As the Church grows, the Spirit comes again inspiring the community to set aside Saul and Barnabas as those sent out to preach. The Spirit confirmed what they were already doing, but now they do it in the name of the Church. And Jesus tells his disciples that when we put our faith in Jesus, we put our faith in the one who sent him—the Father. The instruction of Jesus, of the disciples, of all those who believe is the commandment that brings life—to love without limit and to live in the light. This remains to be the mission of all in the Church.

The new ministry/mission of preaching to the Gentiles is revealed to the church while many prophets and teachers are gathered for a relief mission (care of the poor) and fast and do liturgy. The Spirit speaks and confirms what they have begun and those gathered lay hands on them and pray over them. The 2 sent forth by the Spirit go with the power of the community behind them. This is one of the ways the Word continues to spread and increase.

They go to preach Jesus, the Word, the Son of the Father so that those who see/know and believe in Jesus, know the Father who sent him. Once we have seen, we must obey and do the works of God. The Spirit is given to those who teach/preach/instruct—they do the work that Jesus did in the world—and those who preach are light, bringing light to others.

Thursday

FIRST READING   Acts 13:13–25
Responsorial Psalm   Ps 89:2–3, 21–22, 25, 27
GOSPEL   Jn 13:16–20

☀ This is what we are to look like in the world and how we are to live. We are servants who follow our Master. Jesus has just washed his disciples' feet and commanded us to do the same to one another. We are to do this not only ritually but every day of our lives. Whose feet do we wash? And then he reminds us that even though his disciples ate with him, they still betrayed him: Judas for money and power, but Peter in words publicly cursing him and the others running and hiding from any association with him. [And we will know that among the members of the Church.] But his words speak of welcome too—of those who will go before him, bringing his Word and Bread to others and that if we welcome anyone who is sent by God, then we welcome Jesus and we welcome the Father who sends Jesus. The instruction is all about openness and communion, dwelling with God and with one another in service and worship. Who are we sent to in God's name to serve? Who do we welcome in God's name?

☀ Using the history, the law, and the prophets to introduce them to Jesus, the Savior, Paul and his companions preach to the Jews who live far from Jerusalem and to all others who are interested. They had heard of John the Baptist and so Paul uses John's words, exhorting them to look for another who comes after him—to look for Jesus. And Jesus confirms this mission saying: "he who accepts anyone I send accepts me and in accepting me accepts him who sent me." We are all bound together in the Father, the Son/Word and Spirit.

Friday

FIRST READING   Acts 13:26–33
Responsorial Psalm   Ps 2:6–7, 8–9, 10–11
GOSPEL   Jn 14:1–8

✹ We are with Jesus at table before he dies. He is trying to prepare his friends for he is leaving them—violently in death but that he is going not only to die, but to be lifted up in death and resurrection and to sit at God's right hand, to prepare a place for those who will follow him in life and death. And he tells them that he will come again so that 'where I am, you also may be.' But the disciples do not know the way—they do not yet know that the way is the way of the cross, Jesus' way of speaking the truth, of being just and merciful, being the presence of God with us. He proclaims: "I am the way, the truth and the life; no one comes to the Father but through me. Have we gone through Jesus to the Father? Do we listen to his words, walk the way of the cross with him, rely on Jesus in the face of adversity and walk with others on the way, encouraging one another and reminding one another of Jesus' words? Do we stake our lives on Jesus' way?

✹ Like Peter, Paul preaches the story of Jesus, rejected, crucified and raised from the dead. And he proclaims Jesus as the fulfillment of the promises of the prophets: "You are my son; this day I have begotten you." And this is the message we take to heart: we are all the sons and daughters of God. Jesus is the way, the truth and the life and we come to the Father with Jesus' own Spirit, and we come together. Grace given to us that comes to us through others.

✹ The Good News is starkly simple (and lines and phrases are repeated again and again by Peter and John, Paul and Barnabas and everyone of us): it is the life, the dying and rising of Jesus who is God's beloved Son and his life is now our life in baptism/resurrection if we repent and believe and then do the works of God.

Jesus' words come to comfort us, to relieve us of worry, insecurity and fear. Our way in life is the way of Jesus, the way to the Father, the way of the cross, the way of resurrection life, the way of God's community that seeks to reveal in their ritual and living that Jesus is 'the way, the truth and the life' of the world. It is up to us in every generation, in each place, to preach this with the power of the Spirit, the gifts, imagination and zeal. How are we doing?

Saturday

FIRST READING   Acts 13:44–52
Responsorial Psalm   Ps 96:1, 2–3, 3–4
GOSPEL   Jn 14:7–14

Jesus continues with startling words: we do know the Father, we've seen the Father! We have seen him in Jesus. But they don't understand that Jesus is God in human flesh, Emmanuel— God with us, the presence of justice, of truth and life so clearly that to see Jesus is to see God. Philip asks him to show him the way and he is chided by Jesus—you are with me all this time and you still don't see? He says look at my works and believe, in fact if you believe that your works will be even greater than his! We need only ask the Father in Jesus' name and all that is needed will be given. We are as close to God as Jesus is, if we believe and act like Jesus does in the world. What are we doing with our lives? What are we asking for in Jesus' name? Are we praying for an end to violence and war? Are we speaking the truth to all? Are we siding with the poor, the victims of violence and evil? Are we standing with Jesus and can we say—look at my works and believe in the God of Jesus who is Father to us all?

Paul and Barnabas preach the hard word to the crowd that assembles, telling them that they are to be the light to the nations, but because they refuse the Word, they turn instead to the Gentiles, who are delighted and respond to the Word with praise. The resistance becomes planned and they are expelled from the territory. The disciples are experiencing what Jesus warned them of—rejection and refusal to believe either the words or the works of God, and yet, they rejoice because they are doing the great works of God, glorifying the Father, with Jesus. The power of the risen Jesus with us is unmistakable.

Paul and Barnabas preach first to the Jews but resistance is strong. And the Gentiles begin to come into the Church

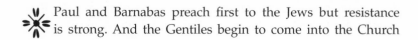

rejoicing that the Word of God is offered to them as well—no one is excluded from the invitation. With the preaching of the Gospel and the welcome of strangers and foreigners, aliens, slaves, those considered unclean comes persecution for those who preach. This is to be expected—as it was with Jesus, with the early church. Why is it not with us?

We preach the Trinity, the Father, Jesus the Word made flesh and the Spirit witness to the truth. Belief is expressed not only in words, but more clearly in deeds, in the works that we do, as Jesus did. We can ask anything of the Father in Jesus' name. Perhaps what we need to ask for is the courage to preach in deed and word so that others are drawn to the dwelling place of God—the Trinity.

FIFTH WEEK OF EASTER

Monday

FIRST READING   Acts 14:5–18
Responsorial Psalm   Ps 115:1–2, 3–4, 15–16
GOSPEL   Jn 14:21–26

Paul and Barnabas preach in Iconium and they are stoned. They flee but continue to preach wherever they go. In Lystra they once again heal a cripple, drawing him to his feet, an image of standing for belief, resurrection. And they seek to introduce the people who are in awe of them to the hidden mystery of God among them. Jesus patiently teaches his disciples that he will be with them, when they are true to his Word and that the Father will love them and they (the Trinity) will make their dwelling place with them/us. It is the power of the Spirit of God that will do these things.

Paul and Barnabas heal a cripple (the same as Peter has done). The people think they are gods and want to offer sacrifice to them. They both preach and speak of the good news of the living God now coming to the Gentiles, but oftentimes healings get in the way of hearing the Word of God.

Do we hear the Word? Jesus tells us that if we obey the commands that we have been given in the Word then we love God and the Father will love us and Jesus will reveal God to us. If we love, then we are true to God's Word. The gift of the Spirit, the Paraclete (one who stands right at our side) both teaches us and helps us to be true to the Word that has been seeded in us and reminds us of all that Jesus has taught. What is the Word of the Lord saying to the Church today and will we make it become reality in our world?

Tuesday

FIRST READING   Acts 14:19–28
Responsorial Psalm   Ps 145:10–11, 12–13ab, 21
GOSPEL   Jn 14:27–31a

✹ Jesus blesses his community before he goes out into the garden where he will be arrested and then murdered. He blesses them with Peace! "I give you my peace. Not as the world gives peace do I give it to you. Do not be troubled." This peace is strong enough to abide through injustice and evil, through violence and betrayal, even stronger than death. Jesus leaves them his peace but goes to face his death—so that all might know how much he loves the Father and does only what his Father commands him. Come let us go—it is the invitation we are given—to walk with Jesus into the world, facing down evil with the peace of God deep with us, secure in the sanctuary of Jesus' words and blessing. We are the followers of Peace incarnate. Do we bring peace by our presence, our words, our dialogue, our facing of evil, our resistance without harm, our forgiveness, all for the love of our Father? Peace—it is given. Now it is for us to give away to all the world.

✹ The persecution continues, with Paul being stoned and dragged outside the city by his friends, but he comes again to preach. They set up churches, encouraging them and telling them that they will know persecution, and then move on, allowing the Spirit build the church, after they have merely opened the door. Jesus gives the gift of Peace, his own Spirit, power and presence to abide with them, no matter their distress and trials. That Spirit remains with us still. How do we express that peace today in our church?

✹ Paul and Barnabas begin the pattern of their lives as missionaries in the name of the Church preaching the good news: they preach, they are persecuted/stoned, exiled/left for dead, pick themselves up, go elsewhere and preach. Then they retrace their steps to the new communities and encourage them, telling them what they can expect if they accept the gospel and begin to live it in their lives.

They can do this, and we are to do all that we do in the name of God because we have been given the peace of Christ. It is not anything like the peace of the world that often is no peace at all; that comes at the end of a gun, or with aggression and force. No, Jesus' peace is the peace of holiness, the peace of the Trinity, the peace of love unto death, the peace of freedom—strong enough to lay down your life in love, and forgive. It is the result of loving the Father and doing as the Father commands. It is the peace/spirit of God.

Wednesday

FIRST READING	Acts 15:1–6
Responsorial Psalm	Ps 122:1–2, 3–4, 4–5
GOSPEL	Jn 15:1–8

✹ These readings are a chance to sit at table with Jesus and listen to his last words, his testament to be cherished and acted upon in his memory, in his honor and in obedience to his commands for us. Jesus is the vine and the Father the vinedresser. We are the branches and we exist to bear fruit for the wine and the joy of the world that needs to drink of Jesus' life, death and resurrection. We remain on the vine, remain in Jesus by keeping his Word deep in our hearts and practicing it in our lives and without this Word, without the Spirit given to us, we can do nothing. We are disciples and we glorify God the Father when we bear fruit and do the work of Jesus. Are we bearing much fruit? Do we cling to the Word of the Lord and seek to make Jesus' kingdom a reality in the world? Are we truly disciples of the Vine, even in the face of suffering, hardships, exclusion and death?

✹ The issue of becoming Jewish according to the old law comes up as the preaching to the Gentiles continues. So Paul and Barnabas return to the church to tell the elders the story of their travels and the conversion, bringing joy to all. But those who were preaching Judaism as requisite were causing dissension. The church decides to convene and look into the matter. Jesus speaks of the vine and the need for pruning and cleaning to increase the yield. It is living in Jesus that the vine and the branches find their source. Apart from Jesus there is no life, nothing. Concentration on Jesus is what is primary, not on any other traditions.

✹ Controversy and dissension arise because some people want to enforce Jewish law/custom on the new believers. Paul and Barnabas begin the journey back to Jerusalem, stopping along the way to tell the churches what has happened and all that has been accomplished. And immediately in Jerusalem they are interrupted with some insisting that the new converts be circumcised according to Mosaic law. The apostles and elders convene to look into the issue. Since the beginning the Church has had to deal with people who insist on their version of life that is not found in anything that

Jesus ever did or said. But the church must look at these issues and decide with the power of the Spirit what is true to Jesus' Word.

Jesus tells his disciples that we must be pruned and all the barren branches cut away so that the fruit can grow. We live in the vine that belongs to the Father, the vinegrower and we can only bear fruit if we live in God. Apart we are withered and lifeless, without fruit. In bearing fruit we glorify God—and it is in the fruit of our works that we learn what is of God and what is simply human beings agenda.

Thursday

FIRST READING   Acts 15:7–21
Responsorial Psalm   Ps 96:1–2, 2–3, 10
GOSPEL   Jn 15:9–11

These are the most awesome words of Jesus to us. We are loved by Jesus as the Father loves Jesus and we are to remain, to stay in that love. We dwell in God if we keep the commandments, if we obey and in doing this, in obeying with Jesus, then we will also know the joy of Jesus. We are to love—everyone as Jesus has loved us, laying down our lives for one another in service, in forgiveness, in justice and care, as love demands. We are to love the poor and lift them up, giving them hope and dignity as Jesus did with all in need. This is how we remain in God. In this loving and obedience to Jesus' words there is a joy that is complete, whole and life-affirming, unlike any other joy in the world. It is the sign of God's presence among us. Are we the joyful, obedient friends of God? Are we devoted to obeying God as Jesus obeyed God? What do we know of love—only what we give to others—that is all we know of the Father.

Peter stands and announces that the Spirit has no distinction, purifying the Gentiles' hearts by means of faith, same as their own hearts. They should not have an added burden laid on them, a yoke that is unnecessary. Paul and Barnabas speak and then James, the elder of the Jerusalem church. He concurs and asks only that the Gentiles refrain from what is impure. It is decided. And Jesus is clear: there is only one commandment that all the others must serve to highlight: love one another as I have loved you and you will know the joy of God.

❋ Peter speaks first in favor of not imposing old laws on the new believers because the Spirit of God came to them without their experiencing the old law. We are saved by the favor of God, not the law. Then Paul and Barnabas recount all that has happened as they preached on mission. And James quotes the scriptures of old to speak about what God has done in Jesus and is doing now—and that they are not to hinder what God is doing by demanding circumcision but should only require those things that will not cause scandal: abstain from anything connected to idols, illicit sexual unions and the meat of strangled animals and blood. (what would those issues be today?) What are our idols—of war, commerce, selfishness, avarice, domination? The last issue is one of hygiene at the time. What would the Spirit say now?

Friday

FIRST READING   Acts 15:22–31
Responsorial Psalm   Ps 57:8–9, 10, 12
GOSPEL   Jn 15:12–17

❋ The only commandment is the one that encompasses all the others—we are to love one another as Jesus has loved us! Incredible, impossible, demanding, freeing—but we are to love all others in this way, not picking and choosing who we will love and who we will ignore or harm. The greatest love is to give life, to lay down our lives, as Jesus did for all of us. And if we do this, as he showed us—in service, in washing one another's feet, in forgiveness and mercy, in non-violent resistance to evil, in speaking the truth, in care of the outcast and the shunned, in seeking out the lost and bringing hope to all, then we will be called friends—the friends of God. We will no longer be servants, because we will know God the Father in the ways that Jesus has learned and taught us. Do we love? Do we love our enemies? Do we lay down our lives daily in service to those most in dire need? Do we make peace? Do we wash feet? Are we practicing loving as Jesus has loved us, in the Spirit given to us in baptism?

❋ The Church gathered sends out a letter declaring the decision of the Holy Spirit that is their decision as well, that they are not to lay added burdens on the new converts. It brought encouragement to the churches. Jesus' commandment demands everything: to love as God loves us, even to lay down our lives for one another, as Jesus did. Nothing else matters much in relation to this commandment and all traditions, laws and customs, rites need to be evaluated in light of the Spirit so that loving one another, all others, is what we are known for, nothing else.

A letter is sent with leaders to Antioch and the result of the meeting is announced—they tell the people that it is others who have upset them and disturbed their peace of mind by deciding to instruct people on their own. The letter brought encouragement and it supports Paul and Barnabas' work among the new Christians.

Jesus' words are so simple and direct. There is a new commandment and all must be seen in light of it: love one another as I have loved you. There is no greater love than this: to lay down one's life for one's friends. You are my friends if you do what I command you. This changes everything. All the squabbles and dissension must be seen as to whether it bears the fruit of love and unity or whether or not it destroys and makes people into slaves who do not know the Father, the Son and the Spirit intimately.

Saturday

FIRST READING   Acts 16:1–10
Responsorial Psalm   Ps 100:1–2, 3, 5
GOSPEL   Jn 15:18–21

If we begin to practice this kind of love, in imitation of Jesus, then we will know some of the rejection, the hate and the fear that this love can call forth in those who do not want to live in love. We have a choice as disciples: we can work at being loved by the world or being loved by God and often hated by the world for telling it the truth and by living the truth that lays bare injustice, sin and evil. And then we will know in some small part, the rejection that our Master knew in his life. We shouldn't be surprised if we have trouble in the world—Jesus had a lot of trouble with it! We have been warned that if we love as Jesus has loved us then we will be seen to belong to God the Father and not to the world's powers, nations and ways. Do we live passionately and strongly devoted to the Word of God, loving the people of the world as Jesus has loved us? Jesus is not just talking about loving our families and those in church or work, but loving all the world, our enemies, those different than us, those who resent us and who think of us as irrelevant, as ignorant or as trouble. Are we truly servants of the Master, the Crucified One?

✴ Paul meets Timothy and together they preach and the church grows stronger. And they travel, accepted in some places and rejected in others. The Good News of Jesus is the only thing they bring, and leave behind them. Jesus tells the disciples that we will be hated by certain groups in the world, but in this we are just like our master. We will be harried and our words disrespected, just as they were disrespectful to Jesus. But we are to make sure that rejection comes because of the gospel, and not because of our actions or scandal in the community.

✴ Paul hears of a disciple called Timothy and brings him along on his journey. They share the letter from the apostles in Jerusalem (though he has Timothy circumcised because of the people in the region). They can get into some places while they are stopped from entering others. In a dream they are called to Macedonia and so they go there. This passage reveals the shifting and shuffling of the church and individuals as very human and in a world that is filled with rejections, failures and changes yet they still try to preach the gospel. It is the same with us.

Jesus reminds us that we are in the world, but the world often hates us, rejects us and makes life hard for us, as it did for Jesus. But we belong first to God and we have been chosen by our master Jesus. What he experienced, we should not be surprised that we know too. But are we being harried and hated because of the name of Jesus?

SIXTH WEEK OF EASTER

Monday

FIRST READING   Acts 16:11–15
Responsorial Psalm   Ps 149:1–2, 3–4, 5–6 and 9
GOSPEL   Jn 15:26—16:4

✹ We draw near to Pentecost, the birth of the Church and the setting loose of the Spirit of God into the world to continue the work of Jesus. Jesus tells us that he is sending us the Spirit of Truth. Jesus' words, like the Spirit will keep us from stumbling and falling away when we begin to experience rejection, persecution, even being killed for believing in Jesus and for living out his commands. The Spirit is given for strength, for enduring grace, for imaginative and life-giving ways to resist evil and to remain faithful. The Spirit is given for the large areas that need courage, truth-telling when power needs to be confronted and the poor and the weak need to be defended. Are we praying for this gift, given to us at baptism and confirmation to take hold in us and mature us in faith and witness to love, to justice and to peace in the world?

✹ Paul and Barnabas travel on to Macedonia, a Roman colony and on the Sabbath find a place to pray outside the city, and meet Lydia who already reverenced God. She is baptized with her household and opens her house (church) for them to stay. Jesus tells his disciples that it is the Spirit of Truth, the Paraclete who comes from the Father and from him that will bear witness on his own behalf. They preach but it is the Paraclete that opens the heart of those who hear. There will be persecution and rejection, but acceptance as well.

Tuesday

FIRST READING   Acts 16:22–34
Responsorial Psalm   Ps 138:1–2ab, 2cde–3, 7c–8
GOSPEL   Jn 16:5–11

Again the disciples (Paul and Silas) are thrown into prison and flogged, but their chains drop from them and they become free. The jailer is distraught but becomes a believer, along with his household and the jailer becomes their sanctuary. Jesus' words try to comfort, yet they speak the reality of harsh times they will know, but he encourages his friends. He sends the Paraclete, the comforter to them and it is the Spirit that proves the world wrong about sin, justice and condemnation. This Spirit too is the power of truth and judgment, in the world. They will know both the sober truth and the exhilaration of faith.

In Philippi, Paul and Silas are flogged and put in maximum security. Yet that night after praying there is an earthquake the chains fall and the doors open. They can run, but they don't and the jailer asks for what will save him. He and his household come to belief and are baptized. In fact he takes them out of the jail, tends to their wounds and serves them a feast to celebrate newfound joy in the Lord. (eucharist)

Jesus continues to tell us that he is leaving and that we will grieve. But in truth, if Jesus does not leave then we will never know the Spirit, the Paraclete (alongside of us). This is the presence of the Risen Lord with us, who will prove the world wrong about sin, justice (or the way of righteousness) and condemnation (or to Judgment). We are given the Paraclete to stand firm in the world in the face of sin, evil, injustice, violence and their false judgments.

Wednesday

FIRST READING   Acts 17:15, 22—18:1
Responsorial Psalm   Ps 148:1–2, 11–12, 13, 14
GOSPEL   Jn 16:12–15

Jesus will soon ascend to the Father, leaving us with his presence, stronger than his physical body, in the person of the Spirit and he still has many things to tell us. It is the power and gift of the Spirit that gives us courage and the ability to bear the truth. It is the Spirit who teaches us all that Jesus knows—not primarily or only as individuals, but as his Body, the church and the community that is the sanctuary for those in need of the Good News. All that has been given to Jesus, is given to the Spirit, who in turn gives it to us to continue what Jesus was sent into the world to do by the Father. This Spirit is Jesus' new presence among us in the world. We dwell in the Spirit and the Spirit dwells and abides in us, holding us together in unity and diversity, maturing the Word in us and accompanying us in the world.

✴ We get to meet those who picked up the legacy and faith of the disciples. Paul preaches about the unknown god, a statue that stands in Athens and speaks of Jesus now known in word, deed and flesh. This is Jesus who will judge the world with justice, Jesus who has been raised from the dead. Only a few believe. The Word of God is fathomless. The depth is endless and there is always so much more to say. But the gift of the Spirit is given to guide us ever deeper into the truth of the scriptures. All that the Father has given to Jesus, Jesus now seeks to share with us. We are babes in knowing God.

✴ Paul preaches in Athens and uses their culture/beliefs in the Unknown God to speak about the God who creates all life and gives breath to all and about the one who is the judge of the world who has been raised from the dead. Only a few become believers, the others want to talk about these things further, and Paul goes from there to Corinth. Why do only a few believe? Perhaps where we begin to preach is important—not with creation and philosophical realities, but the Word of the Lord is what truly converts.

Jesus has more to tell us, but we can't bear it. The gift of the Spirit of Truth will guide us always and help us to believe and teach others to believe. We must make sure that we are not teaching our own words, but teaching only what the Spirit announces and what Jesus has preached when he was sent to us from the Father.

Thursday

FIRST READING   Acts 18:1–8
Responsorial Psalm   Ps 98:1, 2–3ab, 3cd–4
GOSPEL   Jn 16:16–20

✻ Jesus is trying to wean the disciples away from his physical presence. They cannot imagine life without him, or that there can be a life and a presence that is surer, stronger, more powerful and expressive, loose in the whole world that is his Presence. He is trying to stretch their minds and hearts, their belief to encompass his death and resurrection and his return to the Father, leaving us with his Presence, with his own Spirit, his own breath and life in the Father. They will weep and mourn while others rejoice but the day will come when sorrow will be turned to joy. We must learn continually to let go, no matter how good something appears to be, or an experience of God that touches us—God is always more and the Spirit stretches us beyond our limits, graces us and frees us to believe and know God more than we could ever dream. And joy will be ours.

✻ Now Paul meets Priscilla and Aquila, in Corinth (who are tentmakers) and lives with them, while he works and preaches on the Sabbath. Then Silas and Timothy join them, but he is rejected by many of the Jews, so Paul turns to the Gentiles, and the Corinthian church begins. Jesus is always trying to warn his disciples that he will leave them, but also leave them the gift of his Spirit. They will know grief but they will also know joy (as Paul does in Acts). Acts tells the story of the work of the Spirit in the churches, just as Luke's gospel tells the story of the work and life of the Spirit in Jesus. Now, it's time for us to tell the story of what the Spirit does through us in the world.

✻ Paul goes to Corinth and meets Priscilla and Aquila, who are tentmakers and they live together and work together. Timothy and Silas come and Paul preaches intently to the Jews that Jesus is the Messiah (this is the apostle to the Gentiles) and his anger is vented on them. He eventually withdraws to a house near the synagogue and then Titus' Justus and his family are baptized. And many Corinthians believe. Again we see the very humanness of the community as it lives/grows, dealing with outside decrees, the Roman government, the Jewish community and individual's shortcomings and yet the Church grows.

Jesus keeps trying to tell all of us that he will leave for a short time and then return. We will grieve and mourn but it will be turned into joy. Jesus will return with the gift of the Spirit and will return one day when the world is to be given back to God who has entrusted us with it—to make it holy. There will be mourning, but there will be joy.

Friday

FIRST READING   Acts 18:9–18
Responsorial Psalm   Ps 47:2–3, 4–5, 6–7
GOSPEL   Jn 16:20–23

✹ Jesus uses the image of a woman giving birth to a child. There is pain, suffering, hard work, stretching to let a child come into the world, to give birth to a human being. There is distress but then the joy almost knows no bounds because of what she has brought forth—new life into the world. And the disciples, and we too, will know such distress at times, such hard work, suffering, but we will know joy beyond expression because Jesus who is risen from the dead, will leave us and yet remain with us in the gift of the Spirit that he will give birth to on the cross as he dies and sends forth his Spirit. His best gift, his own presence, that is by far closer to us than any physical relationship will be given to us. It is the Spirit that will teach us how to pray the Father, in Jesus' name, for all that we need.

✹ Paul is given a vision for encouragement during persecution reminding him that God is with him and he must continue preaching. Eventually he leaves with Priscilla and Aquila and sails to Syria. Peter and Paul both image what the church is experiencing in the decades after the death of Jesus. The church is a woman in labor giving birth, grieving, struggling and filled with joy at birth. The church is being born anew wherever the gospel is preached and the joy of that no one can take from believers, even when they know suffering and rejection, even death. The joy is given and it is there always.

✳ Paul is given a dream to stay in Corinth and he will be safe and he stays for a year and a half preaching. But then the Jews want him out, he is defended by the proconsul and fighting breaks out among the Jews. When he leaves, he takes with him Priscilla and Aquila. And we are given a snippet of information that he shaves his head because of a vow (private devotion). The church is living and growing and the gospel has Jesus teaching us that life is filled with weeping/mourning and rejoicing. Life in the church, in the Spirit, in the baptized is like a woman giving birth—hard labor, pain but incredible joy at what is brought forth and the child is born.

Saturday

FIRST READING	Acts 18:23–28
Responsorial Psalm	Ps 47:2–3, 8–9, 10
GOSPEL	Jn 16:23b–28

✳ Jesus speaks in veiled language because he has not yet died and risen, yet his words are clear in the Spirit given to those as gift. The Spirit teaches us plainly about the Father. The Spirit speaks in the Scriptures, the Word of Jesus, in the community—plainly about the Father and we will be taught to pray—to pray in Jesus' name as one Body in the grace of the Spirit and all that we ask for will be given to us. The Father loves us in Jesus and in the Spirit and we must let go of Jesus—let him leave this world that limits him in his physical body—to know him and the Father and the Spirit plainly. We are so reluctant to let any knowledge or experience of God go—clinging to what we have and yet we must always let go, so that God can teach us, so that the Spirit can work in us so that we might be a part of God who is three and who is one.

✳ Now Priscilla and Aquila take Apollo home and teach him about Jesus since he has only heard about John the Baptizer. They explain the new way in great detail and Apollo begins to travel and preach, encouraging others with the Scriptures. We are told that the Father loves us and we may ask anything of the Father because we love Jesus, and Jesus is one in the Father. But what do we ask for in our prayers? Are we asking for missionaries, for martyrs, for steadfastness in persecution, for those who will encourage the church with the Scriptures, for believers to know joy as they struggle to be good news?

They arrive in Ephesus and Priscilla and Aquila hear Apollos preaching about Jesus and John's baptism in the synagogue. They bring him home and teach him more and in greater detail and depth. He goes on as a missionary and teaches Jesus as the Messiah among the Jews. The Spirit works where and as it wills, even without the church knowing of it—and when peoples/persons cross and meet each other, they need to be taken home and shared the good news in greater depth.

Jesus assures us that we can ask for anything in his name and the Father will give it to us. Our joy will be full. The Father loves us because we love Jesus and believe in him. Jesus is leaving the world to go to the Father but we can come to the Father as Jesus did. What are we asking the Father for in Jesus' name—what do the church, the world and believers need now?

SEVENTH WEEK OF EASTER

Monday

FIRST READING   Acts 19:1–8
Responsorial Psalm   Ps 68:2–3ab, 4–5acd, 6–7ab
GOSPEL   Jn 16:29–33

✣ Jesus must repeat again and again, when the disciples are quick to think they know and understand what Jesus is saying. Without the gift of the Spirit, they are on their own and cannot know the depth of what is happening, to Jesus or what will happen to them in time. Without this gift we too are glib in our belief, quick to respond without understanding and just as quick to scatter at the slightest sign of trouble. Jesus is patient, but his time is running out and he is desperately trying to make them see—he is going to die and they will all run from him, run from the cross, from giving witness to him and to acknowledging that he is their Master, their Lord and their God. He will be alone with his Father. He tells them, and us that we will have his peace in his Word, yet we're going to have trouble in the world—as did he and we will need his courage—the gift of his own Spirit. This is what we wait for—the courage of God, Jesus' own Spirit.

✣ This is the time of the Spirit that completes baptisms, deepens and confirms belief and makes us public witnesses. It is the Spirit that teaches us, guides us, encourages us and transforms our words and works, ethically and religiously into the deeds of God in Jesus.

And Jesus warns us: do you really believe? Like the disciples do we panic, scatter and run when something confronts us or we are rejected, or do we disagree among ourselves that one can't see the Spirit for all the individual agendas? They leave Jesus alone, and the church still does that sadly. It is only in Jesus, the Word of God that we find peace and it is that peace that gives us the courage to overcome our own weakness and the world.

✳ The early church had to deal with the baptism of John and those who had not yet heard of the baptism of the Spirit that he preached about, and the one who would come after him. They encountered those who had repented and changed their lives but were still waiting. They preached Jesus as the one and the Spirit came upon them, after being baptized in the name of Jesus the Lord. And what about us—have we repented? Do we listen to the word of Jesus and pray for the Spirit to come upon us so that we might preach the Word?

Jesus speaks again and again—it takes grace, the Spirit and time to understand even a small bit of what Jesus the Word made flesh is saying to us. Jesus knows that we will be scattered and we will leave Jesus alone, betraying him (though the Father is with him always). We are told to remember that we will suffer in the world but we are to have courage for Jesus' life and death and resurrection has overcome everything.

Tuesday

FIRST READING   Acts 20:17–27
Responsorial Psalm   Ps 68:10–11, 20–21
GOSPEL   Jn 17:1–11a

✳ Now Jesus prays to the Father asking for God to give him glory so that he might give glory to God. He has worked and glorified God in his words, his works, his disciples, his prayer—in everything. He has given away everything that the Father has given to him and they received it, as best as they could and so Jesus prays for them, his disciples and for all of us because we will need it. He prays that we will stay in God, that we will be kept in his Name and that we will be one as Jesus and the Father are one. We could spend years pouring over this prayer, seeking to learn what Jesus knows of God and how he loves him, glorifies him and serves him, knowing that he is rejected, misunderstood even by those who want to follow him and that he will be crucified—and glorified in dying with trust and love for God and forgiveness of those who kill him. It is close to the time of leaving us and we need Jesus' prayers. Jesus' prayers are with us always now and we know them in the gift of the Spirit.

✳ Paul is taking leave of his communities, seeking to put things in order before he goes to prison/death. And Jesus does this as his last testament in prayer to the Father, letting us listen to his words, and he prays for his friends, for all of us who come after him who keep his word. We have been entrusted with the Word and with everything the Father shared with Jesus, even his own Spirit of truth and mystery of love. We remain in the world but God is with us: Father, Son and Spirit. We must pray this prayer as our own, together.

✳ Paul speaks to the elders and tells them that he always spoke the truth to them for their own good and insisted on repentance and faith. Now he is going to Jerusalem, compelled by the Spirit, though he has been warned that there will be chains and hardships. He declares that he want to bear witness to the gospel and that he is leaving and will not see them again. He boasts of what he has done and never shrunk from announcing the good news. (Paul is not known to be a humble man).

Jesus prays to the Father for his hour to be glorified has come and he will glorify his Father. He has been faithful and done his work for the Father on earth, making his name known and giving all that he has been given by the Father to us. We have been entrusted with this message of God and know that it is the truth. We are God's and Jesus prays that we will be in the world and Jesus will be in us. What an unbelievable life we have!

Wednesday

FIRST READING   Acts 20:28–38
Responsorial Psalm   Ps 68:29–30, 33–35a, 35bc–36ab
GOSPEL   Jn 17:11b–19

✳ Jesus continues praying for us so that we will be kept in God's Name, in communion of heart and life. While he was with us in the flesh he held us together in his presence but now he is coming home to the Father and he leaves us with his words that will bring joy to us. His word is his gift to us, for protection, for courage, insight, understanding, power and truth and we are to hold fast to this Word and stay in the world and know that Jesus has prayed that we will be kept from the evil one that hinders us from living as the children of God. Jesus consecrates us in truth, in God's word and his own word to us. And we will be sent into the world, as Jesus was, consecrated in Jesus' word, and in his body given as sacrifice in death. This is the only sacrifice that God wants of us—what Jesus gave—his word, his life and his obedience in love. This is what Jesus prays that we give to God.

✢ There will be and have been times when people distort the truth of the gospel and we are told to rely on the Spirit when shepherding the Church—this is Paul's warning to the Church at Ephesus when he was preparing to leave them. He reminds them of how he has been with them and that they are to serve the needs of the poor and help the weak. And they pray and weep as he goes, knowing that they will not see him again. Jesus prays for the church, for us that we will have the protection of the Father, We are kept safe in the name of Jesus. We have been given the Word of Jesus, the Word of Scripture and Word made flesh and we do not belong to the world—as Jesus did not, but belong to the Father. Jesus prays for us so that we will be guarded and consecrated in truth, and sends us out into the world as the Father sent him. Jesus has ascended to the right hand of the Father and there intercedes for us for all time. We must rely on Jesus' prayer for all of us, for the Church.

Thursday

FIRST READING   Acts 22:30; 23:6–11
Responsorial Psalm   Ps 16:1–2a and 5, 7–8, 9–10, 11
GOSPEL   Jn 17:20–26

✢ Jesus prays for his disciples and for all those who will believe because of his disciples' preaching and lives—and so he prays for us and for all those who will believe because of our faithfulness to his Word. And he prays for oneness, for communion among us all, and oneness in the Trinity: Father, Son and Spirit. As God is one, we are to be in unity so that the world will know that in this communion Jesus loved us as the Father loved him. Jesus prays that we too will know his glory and share in it. Jesus has lived to reveal the Father to us and he will continue to reveal that love in his death, as in his life, so that this love that is between Jesus and the Father

will be in us. Jesus' prayer is staggering, is frightening in its scope
and depth and overwhelming. Jesus has prayed for us and this is
what our God hopes for us. We must listen and let God make that
prayer a reality in us, as believers and as his Body.

❈ Paul is brought before the Jewish Sanhedrin and is on trial
as a Jew/Pharisee who now believes in Jesus risen from the
dead. He slyly uses the resurrection to cause dissension between
the Pharisees and Sadducees who are split on this belief. But a
dispute breaks out and Paul needs to be rescued. At night he is told
to keep courage and to testify to the Word in Rome. And Jesus prays
for those who come after him, with the Word as their only defense,
revealing the mystery of the Trinity....Jesus would have us all in his
company, here/now and always.

❈ Paul is released from prison and he is brought before the
Sanhedrin to be tried. Paul is shrewd and says that he is a
Pharisee and that he stands before them because he believes in the
resurrection (setting the factions against each other). A riot breaks
out and he is rescued by the troops and taken back to headquarters.
Paul dreams that the Lord is at his side and he is told to have
courage. He has testified to Jesus in Jerusalem, now he will testify to
the risen Lord in Rome. Paul does have a way of enraging people—
perhaps we need to learn more from Jesus' ways and words, than
from Paul's style and weaknesses on how to preach the good news
of the crucified and risen Lord.

Jesus prays for all who believe, for all who teach/preach and he
prays that we all might be one as the Father is one in him and he is
in the Father and that all of us might be one in God, as they are in
communion. We are given to know the Father, to know the Word
made flesh, and Jesus will continue to reveal God to us in the Spirit.
Does this love and life of God dwell in us? How do we as Church
reveal this to the world today?

Friday

FIRST READING   Acts 25:13b–21
Responsorial Psalm   Ps 103:1–2, 11–12, 19–20ab
GOSPEL   Jn 21:15–19

✣ Now we skip to the days after the resurrection when Jesus has fed his disciples, his wayward friends on the beach, with Eucharist (his presence) forgiving them. But he takes Simon Peter aside and walks with him for Peter has betrayed him three times and scattered the sheep and must be brought back into the fold himself. Jesus is the Good Shepherd and teaches Peter how to be the Shepherd by questioning him on his love three times and exhorting him to care for the sheep and lambs as Jesus has tended to him in his sin. Peter is told to seek out what is lost, and bring them back as gently and faithfully as Jesus has done to him. He is told to tell the story of his sin and Jesus' forgiveness to every generation and to forgive as graciously as he has been forgiven. And he will one day, be led in the way of Jesus, to crucifixion and death as atonement for his betrayal and scattering of the sheep. This is the model of forgiveness, reconciliation, penance and atonement for all of us.

✣ Paul is brought before a Roman court in Caesarea and is kept in custody by Rome, rather than be returned to Jerusalem to stand before a Jewish court. Acts brings the story of the church from Jerusalem after the death/resurrection of Jesus to Rome, where Peter and Paul both die. Peter takes a walk with Jesus after breakfast on the beach and he confesses both his sin and his love for Jesus after betraying him. And he learns his penance and his atonement: forgiveness for all and death by crucifixion. But what is essential is "follow me."

✣ Paul's case is brought before the king, as is Roman custom and explains that it is an internal disagreement on religious issues about a certain Jesus who died, but whom Paul claims is alive. Paul asks for an imperial investigation of his case, so he is in custody until he can be sent to the emperor. Paul has gone to Jerusalem but will make sure that he ends up in Rome, using his Roman citizenship. This serves him well on occasion and at other times becomes problematic—conflicting with his citizenship in the kingdom of God.

Now we hear Peter's reconciliation with Jesus after breakfast on the beach—how the church is to deal with leaders who fail the community (and they all do at some time and cause scandal and discouragement to all). Three times he avows his love for

Jesus and three times he is reminded to care for the sheep and forget about himself. And then, after being forgiven, and reconciled, he atones—he learns how to make things at-one-ment, in the community, and restores what has been rent apart. Peter will die, by crucifixion, but when the time comes, he will know his unworthiness and he will glorify God. And he begins, as we all do, at the beginning: follow me.

Saturday

FIRST READING   Acts 28:16–20, 30–31
Responsorial Psalm   Ps 11:4, 5 and 7
GOSPEL   Jn 21:20–25

Paul is kept under house arrest for 2 years in Rome and preaches the gospel to all who are interested and come to visit. He preaches Jesus as Lord and the reign of God. Peter walks with Jesus and young John trails behind like a shadow to the presence of Jesus, and Peter wants to know about him. But there are many details none of needs to know. What is essential is to bear witness to Jesus crucified and risen. And there is so much to say, even to understand what is written in the Scriptures. How are we doing in bearing witness to the Truth of God in Jesus?

Paul lives in Rome under house arrest and continues to preach and meet with many of the Jewish community explaining that he has nothing against his own people and their customs. He stays there for two years preaching freely and teaching about the Lord.

We are coming to the end of Acts and the end of the Gospel of John, as Pentecost approaches. Now we hear the story of John who follows along behind Peter and Jesus and Peter is curious to know what will happen to John. It is a confusing piece, but what is important is that it is John who witnesses and writes down his testimony for others to take heart from and live. There is always more to learn about Jesus—so much more.

WEEKDAYS IN
ORDINARY TIME

FIRST WEEK IN ORDINARY TIME

Monday

FIRST READING

I. Heb 1:1–6

II. 1 S 1:1–8

Responsorial Psalm

I. Ps 97:1 and 2b, 6 and 7c, 9

II. Ps 116:12–13, 14–17, 18–19

GOSPEL

Mk 1:14–20

※ This is the Gospel: "The time has come; the kingdom of God is at hand. Change your ways and believe in the Good News of God." Jesus begins his work by calling two sets of brothers from their jobs as fishermen to come after him and learn the art of catching people for the kingdom of justice with peace. They are called in the tradition of prophets to convert, to confront injustice and to challenge. At this time in history, there was only one version of good news: the good news of Rome. Now there is a choice laid before them, and us—do we choose to walk in the footsteps of a national leader or the footsteps of the Son of God whose word confounds all the nations. They answer immediately and leave what they were doing. NOW—we must respond and leave something of our old ways behind. It is time to grasp a line, a piece of the net of God cast over the world.

Tuesday

FIRST READING

I. Heb 2:5–12

II. 1 S 1:9–20

Responsorial Psalm

I. Ps 8:2ab and 5, 6–7, 8–9

II. 1 S 2:1, 4–5, 6–7, 8abcd

GOSPEL

Mk 1:21–28

※ Jesus starts his preaching in synagogues (in parish churches) and immediately meets with opposition from someone who knows him and is afraid of him and his power. People were thought

to be possessed by evil spirits if they could not control their bodies and bodily functions or their words or minds. Today it would be anyone who suffered from mental illness, debilitating disease that attacks motor skills or manifested itself in fits or loss of control. Sometimes those we label as insane or unbalanced can see very clearly who someone actually is! Jesus uses his authority, his power to balance the man and to bring him back to a level of wholeness.

Jesus faces him, looks at him and commands silence. Today Jesus looks at us, faces us squarely and commands us to be silent. All of us are in need of being in the presence of Jesus and looking hard at who we are and what evil within us needs to leave and its control over us broken. Jesus, the Holy One of God empty us of our violence and imbalance!

✵ We pray today with Hannah and with Jesus. Hannah pleads for pity, as the handmaid of the Lord, promising to return the gift, if it is given, back to the Lord in gratitude. And she is mocked for her silent prayer that is torn from her. Jesus prays with the power of command, ordering silence and releasing a man from his bondage with authority. And people are in awe of him, spreading afar the story of what has happened. But Hannah obeys and those who speak of what has happened in the synagogue just talk, they do not follow Jesus. Does our prayer look more like Hannah's or those who just talk?

✵ 'Here I am and the children God has given me!" Jesus' prayer to God reveals that with Jesus we are given dominion over all things. But we have this dominion, this power of God in imitation of Jesus who has suffered death, trusted in God and proclaimed God's holiness. This Jesus begins his teaching. Are we spellbound by his words, and authority?

There is a person who has an unclean spirit who recognizes Jesus. The unclean spirit shrieks at Jesus, afraid that he will be destroyed. Jesus rebukes him sharply. "Be quiet. Come out of the man!" Jesus' work is to bring us to our senses, not to destroy us, but to still our raging minds and souls and to teach us to live with dominion, under the power of God—in our own lives and with all around us. But we must obey the Word of God to know this teaching in our bodies and lives.

Wednesday

FIRST READING   **I.** Heb 2:14–18
                                           II. 1 S 3:1–10, 19–20
Responsorial Psalm   **I.** Ps 105:1–2, 3–4, 6–7, 8–9
                         II. Ps 40:2 and 5, 7–8, 8–9, 10
GOSPEL   Mk 1:29–39

Mark's gospel moves at a furious pace in the first chapter. Baptism, the calling of four disciples, teaching in the synagogue, calling the evil spirit out of the man in the synagogue. Now he leaves the place of worship with his disciples and immediately takes the hand of Simon's mother-in-law, sick in bed with a fever and lifts her up. He grasps her by the hand for the victory of justice and raises her to life! And she, in gratitude waits on them. In the startling moment of healing we can miss the fact that she has become one of his disciples, described as waiting on them—the role of the deacon!

This is Jesus' mission: to preach, to heal, to raise up, to make disciples and to do this he prays every moment that he can steal. But it is as though he refuels and returns to his work, recharged with the Spirit he was given at Baptism. What are we doing with that Spirit shared with us? And does our prayer recharge us for the work that needs to be done now?

There is more about prayer. Samuel hears and obeys, before the Lord: "Here I am…. Speak Lord, for your servant is listening." All night he attempts to respond to the Word of God and we are told that God is with him in everything. Jesus leaves the synagogue and when he hears of Simon's mothers-in-law's illness he goes to her and raises her up. The word spreads and he spends all the rest of the day healing by touch, word, presence, yet he disappears to go and pray—to listen and wait on the Word of his Father, to resource his power that others need. We are given Samuel and Jesus as models of prayer. We must listen, get up, go and give of what we have been given to others' for their needs.

Jesus is like us in every way, merciful and faithful before God on our behalf. He was tested and suffered and because of this he is able to help us. Jesus leaves the synagogue and enters the house of Simon and Andrew and immediately (this word will be repeated often in Mark's gospel—it is a demand that we respond NOW to what is happening and being said) tell him about Simon's mother in law. Jesus immediately grasps her by the hand and raises her up—he grasps her from the grip of evil and sickness/death and raises her to life in God with him. And she immediately in bends to wait on them, to serve them and to be a disciple who follows in gratitude. Now her house becomes a church where all who need this freedom and release from bondage can come to be set free.

Thursday

FIRST READING   **I.** Heb 3:7–14
                                             II. 1 S 4:1–11
Responsorial Psalm   **I.** Ps 95:6–7, 8–9, 10–11
                          II. Ps 44:10–11, 14–15, 24–25
GOSPEL   Mk 1:40–45

This is the second story of a leper we have heard in two weeks time. Now Jesus is described as filled with pity for the plight of the man who stands before him. And he touches him but tells him, go to the authorities and be declared clean so that he might rejoin society. But the man instead begins to announce to anyone who will listen that Jesus touched him! And in so doing he makes Jesus as unclean in the society as he had been. Now Jesus can't go openly into towns, but people are so desperate that they will ignore the taboo of untouchability and go out to Jesus in the desert. Those who are obviously sinners or who cannot hide their predicaments or situations call forth pity from Jesus. And what about us—what do such desperate people call forth from us? Have we tried to touch anyone in such need?

We hear the story of the ark of the Lord, the presence of Yahweh coming into the camp of the Israelites and the awful reality of losing not only the battle, but the ark of God as well. It just seems that because God is with us does not mean that we will not suffer, or that we know or understand God among us. A leper cries out to Jesus with his prayer: "If you will to do so, you can cure me." And Jesus does will it.

His body obeys Jesus' words of cleansing but he does not obey Jesus' word and so Jesus is forced to stay out in the desert places because the uncleanliness of the leper is now his own. But those in need keep coming, breaking all the rules, traditions and ways of approaching God. Do we know God's ways among us?

Jesus has tended to everyone's needs, then goes alone to pray and is absorbed in prayer. Then he leaves prayer to preach the gospel. All seek him, even the lepers, outcasts and public sinners. The leper approaches and says: "If you so will, you can make me clean." Jesus moves in pity and touches him. This is what he has come for: to preach holiness and justice, to be merciful and to draw all to him.

Our hearts—are they hardened with sin, with habits of insensitivity and selfishness? Have we gone astray and fallen away from God? Today we stand before God, knowing that God's will in Jesus is always to make whole, to heal and to set free. But we should ask and hope for Jesus' touch and words—or we should offer those words and touch to others in need.

Friday

FIRST READING
I. Heb 4:1–5, 11
II. 1 S 8:4–7, 10:22

Responsorial Psalm
I. Ps 78:3 and 4bc, 6c–7, 8
II. Ps 89:16–17, 18–19

GOSPEL
Mk 2:1–12

Jesus is back at his new home, Capernaum, the house of Peter's mother-in-law. This is a house church where the Word is preached and the hunger for it spreads so that people bringing a man on a stretcher can't get near Jesus. But they are resourceful and ingenious. They climb on the roof, remove some tiles and lower him down. And Jesus sees their faith and comforts the man with words of forgiveness even though some teachers of the Law are horrified. They can rejoice in hope given, so Jesus puts it clearly: is it easier to forgive or to heal this man so paralyzed? And he commands him to get up and walk and he obeys and walks away! The crowd is awed and praises God.

What of us? Does our religious correctness keep us from rejoicing in the Good News of forgiveness to each and everyone? Do we think it's easier to heal physical ills in a community than it is to forgive one another? Is our faith as imaginative and hardworking as the faith of this man's friend was? Small church communities are where we must practice all this.

✴ The elders want a king and demand that Samuel ask God for a leader like other nations. Their prayer is granted and they are warned that they will not want a king and will become slaves and that one day the Lord will not answer their prayer. The people refuse to listen to Samuel's warning and they get a king to lord it over them and take them into war. They get what they ask for. And Jesus is tested by some scribes because he heals and forgives sin. They sit in their own judgments and call him a blasphemer, caring nothing for those he lifts up from their misery and pain. God answers our prayers sometimes exactly what we ask for, and sometimes with more than we could have ever imagined. But what is in our hearts—do we heed the warnings?

✴ We are invited into the rest of God, and yet by our baptisms we dwell in that presence of God, in the Trinity. But has the word that we have heard benefit us? Have we held onto this belief? And this word and belief is something we share with others. Some people bring a paralyzed man to Jesus, going up on the roof, dislodging tiles and lower him down in front of him. Jesus is moved by the man's friends and their belief, and he forgives him. This bothers some others who are more concerned with correct acknowledgement of who forgives than the wonder of wholeness that accompanies Jesus' words. He knows them, and us and asks us—What's harder?—To forgive another or to heal? Are we like the man in need of forgiveness, one of his good friends or one of those who dismisses Jesus' words?

Saturday

FIRST READING

I. Heb 4:12–16
II. 1 S 9:1–4, 17–19; 10:1

Responsorial Psalm

I. Ps 19:8, 9, 10, 15
II. Ps 21:2–3, 4–5, 6–7

GOSPEL

Mk 2:13–17

✳ Jesus alternates between preaching and healing and calling more disciples to join his company. Now it's Matthew, a minor tax-collector, a public sinner who was in collusion with the Roman empire and so despised. But Jesus is delighted to go to a party with Matthew's other sinner-friends and when he is murmured against he responds as a prophet would: first eating with them (the first announcement of forgiveness given) and then telling everyone else that he's here to call the sick to his side, the sinners and not the healthy and the righteous.

And us—who do we think we are? Not bad, trying hard, slipping here and there, but basically OK? Or do we know, as any disciple does, that we are not what we put ourselves forth to be, but are in need of a doctor, someone to teach us how to live with one another and forgive us, again and again and again?

✳ Samuel looks for the king in Israel and anoints Saul as 'commander over his heritage.' He is to govern the Lord's people and save them from the grasp of their enemies. They have been given what they asked for, instead of God as their only leader. And Jesus too, assumes his leadership, calling to him his disciples, looking for those he wants with him. He finds Levi, a tax collector and summons him to his side. Jesus is looking for sinners, not those who are self-righteous; those who know they need medicine and a doctor. Which of these are we—really?

✳ Ah, the double-edged sword that penetrates and strips, and judges thoughts and hearts. It pierces going in and rips coming out, laying all bare and exposing us to the eye of God. God is mercy and we are exhorted to come forth and take what is offered to us. This is justice and mercy, the two sides of the face/hand of God.

Jesus approaches Matthew/Levi the tax collector and summons him: "Follow me"—just as he comes to each of us. And he follows Jesus, inviting him to his house to meet his friends. But there are those who cannot rejoice in conversion and the gift of life and they complain. Jesus comes for the sick, and the sinner—for us. But are we like Matthew, or those who resist and separate ourselves from 'them' because we think we are healthy and not in need of conversion?

SECOND WEEK IN ORDINARY TIME

Monday

FIRST READING
I. Heb 5:1–10
II. 1 S 15:16–23

Responsorial Psalm
I. Ps 110:1, 2, 3, 4
II. Ps 50:8–9, 16–17, 21 and 23

GOSPEL
Mk 2:18–22

✳ Already Jesus is running into resistance from his own leaders because of his practices. He and his disciples do not fast like John's followers or the Pharisees. When questioned he tells them he is the bridegroom—in prophetic terms, the messiah! And that while his presence is with them there is no fasting. But the warning comes too: there will all too soon come a time when there will be cause for fasting when he is taken from them.

Jesus is something altogether new, like a piece of new cloth that cannot be sewn into a piece of cloth that is unraveling and torn or like new wine that will burst asunder on old skin. Jesus is shockingly new, a discontinuity in the continuity tradition—do we ever let this reality shock us into radical change? Does any area of our life burst apart because of the presence of Jesus who brings a kingdom for the poor and justice for those most in need?

✳ Saul disobeys the Lord, greedy for his own kingship rather than the honor of God. God does not want sacrifice of animals, but submission and obedience and so God rejects Saul as the ruler of Israel. This is the history of Israel, centuries before Jesus but the seeds are sown early that God does not want sacrifice of animals, or human beings, children or our enemies, or fasts. And in Jesus we discover something new: that we are guests with Jesus at the wedding feast of God, a new people in a new covenant. We are a new cloak of compassion to throw over the world. We are a new wine that will bring life to all. And this life, this Spirit is poured into us in baptism where we promise to live as Jesus did before God.

✳ Jesus offered prayers and supplications with loud cries and tears to God and God heard him because of his reverence. And he learned obedience through what he suffered—being human, limited, dying. His life/death was given for others and so he is the high priest. We are Jesus' disciples and we learn obedience in the same way. There is a time for feasting and a time for fasting; a time for reveling in the presence of the bridegroom Jesus who teaches, heals, touches and eats with us, and a time for grieving his absence, when he is taken from us. But Jesus is the new cloth, the new wine and this is the time of pouring new life into the earth and all peoples. Do we live so for others and live as the priests of God?

Tuesday

FIRST READING   **I.** Heb 6:10–20
                                        II. 1 S 16:1–13

Responsorial Psalm   **I.** Ps 111:1–2, 4–5, 9 and 10
                          II. 89:20, 21–22, 27–28

GOSPEL   Mk 2:23–28

✳ Everything that Jesus does is used to teach, to provoke and to re-examine our behavior and ideas about what is religious. As they walk along they pick grain on the Sabbath, technically an infringement of the law. But Jesus knows his scripture! And reminds them of David who did something far more shocking—he took the grain from the storehouses of the priests on the Sabbath so that his men would have something to eat! Jesus is point blank blunt—the sabbath and the law is to serve to make life more liveable for human beings and not to oppress them. His interpretations of the law are based on compassion, on need of others and on the truth that is the bedrock foundation of the law.

How do we interpret and obey the law—to honor and worship God alone, not just on the sabbath, but every day of the year? How completely do we love our neighbor—every single man, woman and child, especially those in most jeopardy and need who is our neighbor? Are we always trying to ignore the underlying reality of the law so that we don't have to do anything more than a shallow understanding of it?

✹ Samuel grieves for Saul, but is commanded to look for another among the sons of Jesse. He is looking into the heart of all his sons, and the last is David, the shepherd. He anoints him and the Spirit of God rushes upon him. God sees not as we see. Jesus walks through standing grain on the Sabbath and lets his disciples chew on the heads of grain. When he is rebuked he compares himself to David who fed his men when they were in need by going into the temple and taking the holy bread that belonged only to the priests. He continues by saying that the Sabbath and all the laws are made for human beings' life, and that we are not made for the laws. He calls himself the Son of Man who is lord of the Sabbath, and all life.

✹ 'Our God is a sure and firm anchor, and our hope is in Jesus, risen from the dead and ascended to God. Jesus is our forerunner, John the Baptist was to him. He goes before us mindful of all we do and our service to his holy people. We are to live with zeal, with passion and grace on behalf of others. Jesus teaches us that we are to live in obedience, not just to laws, but to the needs of others. There is a new rule: "the Sabbath was made for man, not man for the Sabbath. That is why the Son of Man is lord even of the Sabbath." Jesus is master of all things, and our master—we must serve the spirit and the heart of the law and be attentive to people first, not the outward manifestation of what appears to be permitted or not permitted.

Wednesday

FIRST READING   **I.** Heb 7:1–3, 15–17
       II. 1 S 17:32–33, 37, 40–51

Responsorial Psalm   Ps 110:1, 2, 3, 4
       Ps 144:1, 2, 9–10

GOSPEL   Mk 3:1–6

✹ Jesus is being watched—already many have turned against him. And Jesus knows it. It's sabbath and he cures a men with a paralyzed hand. What is the work of the sabbath? What is the honor of God? True worship of God is always to save human beings and to lift them from their suffering and oppression. He knows that when he heals, he is setting in motion those who hate him, giving them fuel for the fire that will eventually consume him. They are already out to silence him, stop him and kill him.

Jesus is both deeply sad and angry. If we are in the presence of Jesus in our gatherings for worship and church meetings is that how he would look at us and what we are doing and choosing not to do? Does our worship, our resources and our decisions for work in our church and parish reflect the needs of so many who are paralyzed, cast aside and left in their misery? Or worse do we attack those who would help them, convicting us of our lack of compassion?

The Lord has been with David and he goes to kill Goliath with his slingshot. He has protected his sheep from wolves, bandits and is protector and defender of the weak. He proclaims aloud to all that there is a God in Israel and that is not by the sword or the spear that God saves. And Goliath goes down with the one shot. Jesus too stands before his enemies who are resistant to his Word in the synagogue and commands a man with a shriveled hand to stand up in front with him He does battle with the Word of his mouth, heals the man and cries out that he is about life and saving those in pain. And like Goliath, they remain silent, closed against him

Melchizedek, king of justice and king of peace was a priest, an image of the Son of God who is priest forever. Jesus and those who are priests in his company are made so 'in virtue of a power of a life which cannot be destroyed' by any law. Jesus is priest—one who is handed over to God and his priesthood begins with both healing what is shriveled and confronting with the truth. This is the worship that God wants on the Sabbath and everyday. Jesus is watched and he confounds them with his goodness and integrity. But they grieve him with their hardness of heart, their callousness and shriveled sense of God. They plot to kill him. And what about us—if we have been healed, do we worship truly or do we grieve God still with our actions?

Thursday

FIRST READING   **I.** Heb 7:25—8:6
       II. 1 S 18:6–9; 19:1–7

Responsorial Psalm   **I.** Ps 40:7–8, 8–9, 10, 17
       II. Ps 56:2–3, 9–10, 10–11, 12–13

GOSPEL   Mk 3:7–12

※ Jesus leaves the synagogue and heads towards the lake where the crowds always gather, the unchurched, unbelievers or the lapsed and fringe folk. But they've heard and are heartened. Jesus gets into a boat and heals even as they seek to get to him. And those with evil spirits—those who are afflicted, in pain, struggling with their sin and failures, weakness and humanity—they know who he is—the Son of God. But he warns them to be quiet.

How is it that those who know evil know him and those who presume that they are religious do not know who he is or recognize his holiness? Does being self-righteous and hard of heart, of having an inflated opinion of ourselves and distancing ourselves from the human race of sinners blind us to goodness? And does that cause Jesus to walk away from us towards those who know their sin and their need for conversion?

※ David's popularity grows and so does Saul's jealousy of him. Saul's son Jonathan warns his friend David of Saul's intent to kill him, and sends him into hiding, to speak on his behalf. Jonathan pleads for David and Saul relents. David is brought back to serve the king once more. And Jesus' popularity grows apace with the stories of his healings and encounters with the scribes and Pharisees. The crowds push in on him, wanting to touch him. And some cry out that he is the Son of God—those who are deranged, with mental illness or soul sick and they are ordered to be silent. No one knows him truly and the popularity will pass and they will seek to kill him.

※ Jesus lives now to intercede for us! Jesus' new covenant is his blood/Eucharist and passion for living/dying with and for us. We know in our bodies by baptism/Eucharist that we are the Body of Christ. We know this covenant and live it with others who are the people of God in Jesus' own body. This new covenant and its freshness and power is in the person of Jesus. Crowds sought him relentlessly, to hear his words and touch him, pushing up against him. Jesus and the disciples keep a boat at hand—the new ark, the church as backup. Jesus stands between the crowds and the sea/the boat. Those who know him, know him in their sin and their disorders but he commands them not to reveal who he is. We are part of that crowd, or among the disciples.

Friday

FIRST READING   I. Heb 8:6–13
                                             II. 1 S 24:3–21
Responsorial Psalm   I. Ps 85:8 and 10, 11–12, 13–14
                                II. Ps 57:2, 3–4, 6 and 11
GOSPEL   Mk 3:13–19

As it becomes clearer what Jesus is preaching and what he is doing, he calls more people to him. He appoints twelve as apostles to preach and gives them authority to drive out demons—to name what hinders us from being the beloved children of God. He names them all, by which family they come from, nicknames, towns they hail from and lastly as one who betrayed him. Are we Jesus' apostles and disciples now? Can we name eleven or twelve of us who together follow him and seek to preach and name the truth about evil in our lives and world? How would we be described—by our family connections, the towns we were born in or live in, a nickname that reflects our personalities or behavior—or sadly would we be known as the one who betrayed Jesus. Jesus wants us all as his own and calls us to him and we go with others, not alone or separately. Are we known by the company we keep and known as his friends and companions?

Saul seeks David with a huge army of 3000 men and David and his men hid in the deep caves but it is David that finds Saul and when he has the opportunity to kill him, does not. Instead he pities Saul and leaves behind a token of his power unused. David cries out that the Lord is the one who will judge between them and take his part, and grant him justice beyond Saul's reach. And Saul relents again, praising God. And Jesus retreats to the mountains and prays, then summons twelve to follow him, sharing his power to preach the gospel and to expel demons (to release people from what bound them inhumanly and sap life from them). Who do we serve/follow? And what do we use the power of our baptisms for in our lives?

We are of the new covenant and God's laws are in our minds, written on our hearts. We are God's people and God is our God. We are forgiven and must remember that all peoples know the Lord. We must live in this new knowledge and relationship. Jesus has chosen us to be bound to him in this new testament-covenant. We hear the names of the twelve he chose, imaging those chosen from all the twelve tribes of Israel—from all the people. We know little or nothing about most of them, except their names and that they were part of his company. And we too are known perhaps only by our names, and those who are bound to us in the Body of Christ. What do we want to be remembered for: being Judas, Thomas, Peter—all betrayers or the 'sons of thunder'—not flattering, or Jesus' companions on the way?

Saturday

FIRST READING   **I.** Heb 9:2–3, 11–14
       II. 2 S 1:1–4, 11–12, 19, 23–27

Responsorial Psalm   **I.** Ps 47:2–3, 6–7, 8–9
       II. Ps 80:2–3, 5–7

GOSPEL   Mk 3:20–21

Everywhere Jesus goes he is mobbed. He has touched something in people like a raw nerve. His relatives come to 'take charge of him'—in the sense of getting him in check. They say 'he's out of his mind'—they too are afraid of him and the reaction he is stirring up publicly. But they are afraid for themselves and want to stop him and his preaching of conversion and the Good News of God to the poor and the lost sheep. It seems that Jesus has trouble with his family! Mother, cousins, aunts and uncles, in-laws? Extended families were sprawling in those days and you were associated with your blood kin and they with you, whether you agreed with them or not.

Today our families are sourced in the waters of baptism and the blood of the cross and we are bound in the Word of the Gospel and to the poor in the Body of Christ. Are we ashamed of those who publicly are associated with the poor, the sick, those who fall from grace, outcasts and those who society thinks are expendable and problematic? Do we think that prophets and those who associate with prisoners, those with AIDS/HIV, those without insurance, living on the street and of other races and religions are "out of their mind?" Are we related to Jesus really?

Saul and Jonathan are both killed and David mourns his king and his friend. He grieves in his prayer to God. His lament: "How can the warriors have fallen, the weapons of war have perished!" His prayer will have seeds in the far future where the chosen one of God, Jesus, refuses to allow his followers to harm anyone and to love one another, even their enemies. And in the gospel, the rejection of Jesus starts to deepen and spread—among the leaders, scribes, Pharisees and now into his own family who think that he is insane, and try to 'take charge of him', fearful that his words will affect their lives. What in the gospel do we reject?

We worship with and belong to God in Jesus Christ, cleansed by the Spirit of God, offered to God through, with, and in the blood of Jesus. And we dwell in God with Christ! Who is this Jesus? His family thinks he is 'out of his mind', insane, stupid, crazy, yet the crowd needs Jesus' words and presence. This Jesus is more than anyone can imagine or know: in the words of the psalm "He is the king of all the earth and rules over the nations…for in his hands are the great of the earth."

Do we know Jesus? Or are we like his family thinking he is out of his mind? Or like the crowd that just wants something from him, or the disciples who do not know what is going on? It is the Word that reveals Jesus to us—are we listening together?

THIRD WEEK IN ORDINARY TIME

Monday

FIRST READING   **I.** Heb 9:15, 24–28
        II. 2 S 5:1–7, 10

Responsorial Psalm   **I.** Ps 98:1, 2–3, 3–4, 5–6
        II. Ps 89:20, 21–22, 25–26

GOSPEL   Mk 3:22–30

Now the teachers of the Law go after him and say that he is 'possessed by Beelzebul, the chief of demons', in fact he uses this Beelzebul to cast out demons! Not very logical. And Jesus points out that if a nation is divided by civil war it falls, just as if Satan is divided in his house, he'll fall too. The word Satan means 'the hinderer'—whoever or whatever keeps human beings from being the beloved children of God. Or here, Jesus calls him the Strong One and he as much says that he has bound the Strong One by his words and presence in the world.

Who do we hinder from living and acting as the children of God? Who do we keep from living in the freedom of their baptisms? Do we find it easier to blame someone who does good and tells the truth, exposing us for what we are rather than taking to heart what all can see about us? Holy Spirit lay us bare and let us know ourselves in the light of Jesus.

David is thirty when he reigns over Israel, and will reign for 40 years. David grows more powerful because the Lord of hosts is with him. And Jesus begins to meet with resistance but rebuffs them with his examples: "No one can enter a strong man's house and despoil his property unless he has first put him under restraint. Only then can he plunder his house." And he assures those who can hear that he forgives everyone every sin except the one who curses the Spirit. He speaks to his own people who know and should recognize him from the texts and promises. What is this sin? Perhaps only God knows, but it is connected to those of us who resist and speak about Satan (the Hinderer of the children of God), calling human beings by that name and accusing them of evil. Perhaps we should be more careful of who lives in the Spirit of God and look to ourselves first.

✹ Jesus is besieged by those who resist his words and actions and they accuse him of being possessed by Beelzebul, a name for Satan (the Hinderer). But Jesus is clear about who he is and what he is doing: he is the strong man and his house is protected—no one enters who is not restrained and bound. Jesus unbinds those who have sinned and have asked for forgiveness. He holds bound those who do evil, injustice, violence, sin and restrains their power over others. Their sin was to refuse to believe in forgiveness and the presence of God among them—in the Spirit and Word of Jesus. Is that our sin too? Do we live, and seek to resist and restrain evil, be forgiving and live in the house of the strong man Jesus?

Tuesday

FIRST READING   **I.** Heb 10:1–10
                                II. 2 S 6:12b–15, 17–19
Responsorial Psalm   **I.** Ps 117:1, 2
                         I. Ps 40:2 and 4, 7–8, 10, 11
                                II. Ps 24:7, 8, 9, 10
GOSPEL   Mk 3:31–35

✹ David brought the ark of the covenant into the city, with ritual and then abandoned the rites and danced before the ark himself, then he blessed the people and fed them bread, roast meat and raisin cakes—a feast in honor of God. And Jesus is in the presence of his disciples and his mother and brothers (family) arrived but stayed outside asking for him. Jesus proclaims a new covenant not based on blood, marriage and family ties but on obedience to the will and the Word of God. The mother, brother and sisters of Jesus are those who are gathered around him under his gaze and those who obey are given intimacy beyond any familial closeness. The old ways are left with abandon and we are invited into the dance of God, bound by water, Spirit and the blood of Christ in the eucharistic feast.

What God wants of us is what Jesus gave God—his body and his obedience. Like Jesus we must answer to God and say: "I have come to do your will." We are one in the Body of Christ, offered to the Father in the Spirit (liturgy) and this is our daily offering—our life lived in obedience to the Word. We belong to and live in and are the Body of Christ. Jesus is told that his family waits for him outside—they will not come in, but send word to him to come out. But he does not. He looks around at all of us, his disciples and tells us that we are his mother, brothers and sisters and that blood ties of the new covenant are found in obedience to the will and the Word of God. This is the new family, the new offering and the new worship of God.

Wednesday

FIRST READING	**I.** Heb 10:11–18
	II. 2 S 7:4–17
Responsorial Psalm	**I.** Ps 110:1, 2, 3, 4
	II. Ps 89:4–5, 27–28, 29–30
GOSPEL	**I.** Mk 4:1–20

In these first weeks of Ordinary Time we look to our ancestors in faith and how they put the gospel into practice after the resurrection of Jesus. These men (and women) are the second generation: disciples of disciples and were often sent out two by two to preach by their very presence and way of visiting and traveling that the kingdom of justice and peace was indeed already loose in the world. They went relying on hospitality, with only the bare essentials of what they might need—no purses or bags; with no weapons or defenses—no sandals, unable even to run from danger. And everywhere they went they brought Peace as a blessing. They stayed in welcomed and remembered that they came in the name of the Lord.

If you were traveling who would you take with you? What would you consider essential? How do you (or we) practice non-violence and go without weapons or long-term financial security? Is there anything in our lives that preaches the radical presence of the kingdom of justice and peace in the world without words?

✺ Jesus is our offering and our covenant and his Word is written in our hearts and minds. We are forgiven and now live with Jesus, offering our bodies and lives back into the hands of God with Jesus. The word is sown year after year: on the path, rocky ground, in the field with thistles and finally in the field. There is a harvest: 30,60, 100 fold. The Word has been seeded in us—what kind of ground are we? Are we part of a field or are we only receiving the Word as an individual on our own and so destined probably to lose it? Does our field yield anything like 30,60 or 100 fold? (normal yield is anywhere from 3-10 fold) Who are we listening to and obeying?

Thursday

FIRST READING

I. Heb 10:19–25
II. 2 S 7:18–19, 24–29

Responsorial Psalm

I. Ps 24:1–2, 3–4, 5-6
II. Ps 132:1–2, 3–5, 11, 12, 13–14

GOSPEL

I. Mk 4:21–25

✺ Jesus begins to use images to describe what his disciples are to be in the world. Lampstands that disclose whatever is hidden, that uncovers what is not noticed. And we are warned that the measure we use for our dealings with others will be the same used by our God in measuring our value and reward. We are questioned if what we do and how we do it is for the kingdom of God or for ourselves?

Angela Merici and her companions, the Ursulines set about bringing light into the world by teaching and caring for young women and girls, giving them a place in the world, a way to develop their skills and to live with dignity and hope. Who are the people today who need this kind of lamp, this kind of protection and help to make their way in the world? Will we be remembered for making others aware of these people?

Friday

FIRST READING   **I.** Heb 10:32–39
       II. 2 S 11:1–4a, 5–10a, 13–17
Responsorial Psalm   **I.** Ps 37:3–4, 5–6, 23–24, 39–40
       II. Ps 51:3–4, 5–6a, 6bcd–7, 10–11
GOSPEL   Mk 4:26–34

Jesus paints another scene: a man scattering seed on soil and once it's sown, whether he sleeps or watches it, it sprouts and grows until ripe for the harvest. Or a mustard seed, so tiny yet it grows into a weed, a bush with branches that supports the birds of the air, giving them shelter. These are parables, stories with a twist that Jesus uses to teach his disciples what he is doing in the world and what they are to do in time. This Word that is both message and the person of Jesus is potent, far-ranging in power and effect, and it becomes something that nurtures others and protects and shelters the small of the earth—the doves, pigeons, blackbirds, the majority of birds that most would think of as a nuisance or expendable.

Thomas Aquinas, known for his wisdom and intelligence saw himself as a 'dumb ox'. He wrote theology and treatises on God but knew that nothing he could say would compare to Jesus' stories, presence and person who transformed those who were in misery to people of hope, as the children of God. What are our words and lives saying to the most desperate of the earth?

David sins, first with Bathsheba and then against her husband whom he has killed when he finds out that they will have a child together. He sins by adultery and by murder. This is the leader of the people and those with power will be held more publicly accountable than those without authority over others. And Jesus is speaking with power and authority. His very word is power that seeds, sprouts and grows, then produces a harvest. And even the tiniest bit of this Word, this presence of God on earth, the kingdom of justice and peace among his followers is potent and powerful, like a mustard seed that spreads like wildfire and takes over everything for miles around. It grows (by the Spirit's power) into a small tree, bring refuge, shelter and sanctuary for all the small birds of the earth. This is the power of God, not the power to take what you want, or kill or lie and deceive, as the leaders of the world are wont to do. Which power do we align ourselves with today?

Saturday

FIRST READING I. Heb 11:1–2, 8–19
II. 2 S 12:1–7a, 10–17
Responsorial Psalm I. Lk 1:69–70, 71–72, 73–75
II. Ps 51:12–13, 14–15, 16–17
GOSPEL Mk 4:35–41

❊ Jesus often leaves where he has been teaching, borrows a boat and goes across to the other side of the lake. A storm comes up and Jesus is asleep, oblivious to the rages of water, rain and wind. They wake him and he stands and rebukes the elements: "Quiet now! Be still!" And creation obeys him. Jesus turns to the disciples and asks: "why are you so frightened? Do you still have no faith?" They are oblivious to his presence and have no knowledge of who this man Jesus is—they are terrified that the wind and sea obey him.

Do we know this man Jesus or have we slipped into relating to him as a teacher, a man with insight or wisdom and forgotten that this is the Jesus, savior, the Word of God, stronger than any prophet of old, beloved Son of God, the wisdom of God in flesh, the power of God in a human being? What frightens us? Jesus, help us to remember your presence with us!

❊ Nathan comes to judge David using a parable that traps the king in his own justice. And the judgment is harsh, bringing the sword to David's lineage, death to the child yet to be born though God forgives his arrogance in spurning the Lord's way. David fasts and weeps but knows the justice of the God of the earlier covenant. And Jesus too, deals with power, both the power of the creation known by the Israelites and the new more incarnational power of God who calls us his friends. He stills the waves, the wind and the elements. And questions us: Why do you lack faith? Do we really believe in the power of God in Jesus? This is justice/power in the hands of God's beloved Son, tempered with human compassion, yet just and powerful still.

✳ We hear how our ancestors lived on faith, making decisions, journeying, changing and being transformed by God. And they died in faith, seeking their hopes and the fulfillment of God's promises. Even when they were tested in faith, they clung to God's word. Do we live with faith? The disciples accompany Jesus in the boat and a storm comes up—and Jesus is asleep! In fact, he is sound asleep! They panic, wake him and whine—do you not care that we are going to drown? (not much faith even in the presence of him who made the seas/winds/storms) His words resound today in our ears: Why are you so terrified? Why are you lacking in faith? We too need to be overcome by awe, be still and quiet and know that God is with us, and obey him—even learn to sleep soundly with him in the midst of storms/waves.

FOURTH WEEK IN ORDINARY TIME

Monday

FIRST READING   **I.** Heb 11:32–40
       II. 2 S 15:13–14; 30; 16:5–13
Responsorial Psalm   **I.** Ps 31:20, 21, 22, 23, 24
       II. Ps 3:2–3, 4–5, 6–7
GOSPEL   Mk 5:1–20

✺ A man who lived among the tombs, needing to be restrained, more dead than alive whose identity is legion. They recognize Jesus' power and holiness and plead not to be destroyed. Jesus demands that they come out of the man and they flee from his Word into a herd of pigs that then rush headlong over a cliff, drowning in the lake below. The man is subdued and sitting in the presence of Jesus and all who see and hear are afraid and want Jesus to leave. And the man, wanting to stay is sent home to preach the Good News done for him and show forth the glory of God.

This is Mark's gospel and the legion is Rome. Jesus' holiness and power, his presence will demand that all that makes people live in chains, more dead than alive and without hope, leave! Evil cannot stand and is overpowered by Jesus' truth and authority. The choice is to be freed or to live inhumanly. There will be reactions of fear, but those freed are sent to release others by their lives converted, and made whole by Jesus' presence in the world.

✺ David flees from his son, Absalom and weeps at the betrayal of the people but also at his own sins of murder and unfaithfulness. He is cursed, yet he does not allow his men to harm those who curse him. He is afflicted but he has done wrong. And we hear the strange story of the wild man, insane who lives in the tombs, afflicted with an illness that causes him to cut himself, throw himself into the fire and harm himself. Inside him are legion who seek to destroy him and he is helpless. Yet he recognizes Jesus' truth in his pain and Jesus names the distortions within him, calling them out and sending them into pigs that race over the cliff and into the sea below. And the man is in possession of himself again, wanting to stay with Jesus, but he is sent back home to tell others that the presence of God, God's word makes us whole, makes us human once again. This is what we are to do, tell others what God has done for us in our lives.

✳ Listen to the litany of what the prophets of old did! And then at all the sufferings, torture and rejection they lived through— and the world was not worthy of them and yet they did not obtain what they spoke of and hoped for. And yet we, who come after them—look what we have been given! Look at our world, with legions of armies, and those who suffer violence, insanity, do harm to themselves, terrify others, are condemned to live as outcasts, considered inhuman. Jesus, the Word of God made flesh, with a word commands the man to be sane, whole, in his right mind, a human being. He drives out the insanity, the violence, the injustice and terror with his Word and sends the man home to his family to tell the good news of God to everyone. This is the mercy of the Prophet Jesus. Look what God has done for us and what have we done in return? How have we relied on the Word of God to alter the world of violence and depravity? Or are we found to be among the legion in the pigs?

Tuesday

FIRST READING   **I.** Heb 12:1–4
                       II. 2 S 18:9–10, 14b, 24–25a, 30—19:3
Responsorial Psalm   **I.** Ps 22:26b–27, 28 and 30, 31–32
                              II. Ps 86:1–2, 3–4, 5–6
GOSPEL   Mk 5:21–43

✳ Long stories of healing: the twelve year old daughter of a synagogue official who comes begging for her life interrupted by the story of a woman who has suffered for twelve years both physically and by being excluded from society because of her sickness. The woman touches Jesus' cloak and Jesus takes the girl by the hand and both are healed and raised to life again. Power resides in Jesus and in everything that touches him—the power of wholeness, of life and humanness. Jesus' words to the child's father when he is told of her death are "Do not fear, just believe." That is Jesus' command to us in the face of long suffering that is endured, even in the face of those who take advantage of illness and make things worse by their insensitivity and advantage over those in need and even in the face of death itself. "Do not fear, just believe!" We are to believe in the words, the presence and the goodness of God and life in Jesus who is with us—all ways now.

✴ Absalom pursuing David is killed and David weeps over the loss of his son, to him and to life, wanting to die in his place. There was no victory, only mourning at the loss of his son. In Mark's gospel another father, Jarius is mourning the loss of his only daughter and Jesus goes to save her. He is interrupted by another daughter of Israel who has lost her savings, her place in society, herself in her disease and he heals her as she touches him. That is all that is needed to draw forth this power of God. He comes to Jarius' house and drives out all who are intent on letting death reign. He takes her by the hand and raises her up, getting her something to eat. A woman plagued for 12 years with living death and a young girl who is 12 become family with those who cried for healing and life giving touch. Do we touch with God's life?

✴ We are surrounded by a cloud of witnesses—remember them, name them, rely on them. Jesus endured the cross and they followed him—we come after with them and we are not allowed to be discouraged or abandon the struggle. We are very young in learning to resist evil. Jesus heals everyone, first a woman who for 12 years sought help and she reaches out to touch his cloak, in faith and is immediately healed by the power that goes forth from Jesus—even just his garments. She tells her story and goes to live in faith. Jesus brings the daughter of Jairus back to life, dead and alive again through the power of the Word of Jesus at 12 (when you become an adult in Jewish society). Jesus' words are for us today: Fear is useless. What is needed is trust." We must trust in the face of sickness, long illness, death, fear, insecurity, all our terrors—it is what is needed.

Wednesday

FIRST READING   **I.** Heb 12:4–7, 11–15
          II. 2 S 24:2, 9–17

Responsorial Psalm   **I.** Ps 103:1–2, 13–14, 17–18a
          II. Ps 32:1–2, 5, 6, 7

GOSPEL   Mk 6:1–6

☀ David sins again in seeking to number the people and know who is under him. David chooses a pestilence that attacks the people, but at least when he sees its effect he repents and cries out: "It is I the shepherd who have done wrong. These are my sheep, what have they done? Punish me and my kindred." David the king is slow to learn. And Jesus is the true leader/shepherd, prophet, with wisdom. But he is rejected by his own. Jesus too is distressed by their reaction to him, yet goes and teaches elsewhere. Is Jesus distressed by us and what we bring to bear on others with our sin?

☀ We are told to learn discipline and strengthen our bodies, minds, hearts and spirits to be faithful in resisting evil. We are live on the straight path (the way of holiness) and all that is halting and dislocated in our lives/actions will be healed—if we strive for peace and to carry and help one another on the way. And what Jesus experiences in his own community, family and his own country he is mocked, disparaged and disdained. He is told to do a few miracles like they've heard of in other places and they tell him he's nobody—one of them, son of Mary (a high insult for a Jew) and they know his kin and what he does for a living—a carpenter. "They found him too much for them" and Jesus found them without faith and it distressed him. And us—how do we find Jesus—do we distress him because of our lack of faith?

Thursday

FIRST READING   **I.** Heb 12:18–19, 21–24
          II. 1 K 2:1–4, 10–12

Responsorial Psalm   **I.** Ps 48:2–3, 3–4, 9, 10–11
          II. 1 Chr 29:10–11ab, 11d–12a, 12bcd

GOSPEL   Mk 6:7–13

✣ The disciples have seen Jesus heal, and now they are sent out to the villages with the authority to heal and cast out any spirit that hinders people from living as the children of God, imitating his own work. They go with nothing extraneous to their mission: no food, no money, no bag, no money for things they might need, only a staff and sandals, no extra tunic for protection. This is the way of the pilgrim, the healer, the itinerant preacher who proclaims Jesus' presence and power with word of hope, the call to repent and healing touch that strengthens and turns people away from doing evil. As believers, this is our work, our calling together—some for a lifetime, others for a time of apprenticeship and learning, others to encourage and sustain those on the road for the Lord. Those who have this authority must live more simply, more truthfully and more in the service of others. Let us pray we obey the words of our Master-healer and speaker of the Truth.

✣ There was the epiphany of the God of Sinai that was terrifying in its power and overwhelming and there is the epiphany of the God of Jesus, the first born and judge, the mediator of the new covenant that has come through the blood of the cross. This is our heritage and grace that we are to preach and share with all others. We, too are sent out two by two (who do you travel/teach with) and we are to go lightly, wear sandals and trust to those we meet to care for us. Their generosity will be triggered by their welcome of the good news of the Gospel that we bear with us. They went preaching repentance, expelling what was hindering others and anointing the sick. This too is our work as disciples, basic and necessary both for the world we live in and ourselves.

Friday

FIRST READING   **I.** Heb 13:1–8
         II. Sir 47:2–11

Responsorial Psalm   **I.** Ps 27:1, 3, 5, 8ab–9 abc
         II. Ps 18:31, 47 and 50, 51

GOSPEL   **I.** Mk 6:14–29

✣ Herod hears of Jesus' work among the people and is afraid. In the tradition of the prophets, like John whom he beheaded, Jesus' call to the people is accompanied by telling the truth about those in power. John decried Herod's killing of his brother so that he could marry her. Herod knew John was holy, liked listening to him even though he was disturbed whenever he heard him. It is Herodias, his stolen wife who has John beheaded at a dinner party, using her daughter to dance and ask for his head. Power and those who have it can be fascinated by goodness and the truth, equally disturbed by it, but if there is no conversion they will imprison it, butcher it and obscenely parade it for their pleasure. John is murdered on a whim. Jesus will be butchered legally. Truth disturbs power. It should disturb us and call us to holiness and allegiance to God, in resistance to evil in others, governments and nations. Let us pray we are faithful like John and Jesus and the prophets of God

☀ The praises of David are sung, telling both of his sins forgiven and his praises of God. And in Mark we hear the story of John the Baptizer imprisoned for telling the truth to Herod and how Philip's wife, Herodias plots to kill him because he accused them of murder and unfaithfulness. And she waits her chance and has John beheaded at a dinner party. Now Jesus arises among the people and there are echoes of the prophets of old like Elijah and John the Baptist, with the people wondering who Jesus might actually be— who are the prophets among us? Do we listen and look, and seek the Word of the Lord in those who speak out against injustice?

Saturday

FIRST READING   I. Heb 13:15–17, 20–21
II. 1 K 3:4–13
Responsorial Psalm   I. Ps 23:1–3a, 3b–4, 5, 6
II. Ps 119; 9, 10, 11, 12, 13, 14
GOSPEL   Mk 6:30–34

☀ The death of John distraught the crowds of people who had looked to him in hope and they surge around Jesus and the disciples. Jesus sends the disciples off together in a boat to rest but the people see them leaving and know where they're going and follow on foot. They are desperate, afraid and bereft without John's words. Jesus sees them and has compassion on them—they are like sheep without a shepherd. And he turns into the core of his life, accepting responsibility for all of them, herding them together, preaching them and teaching them, giving them life and hope in him. This is his way of life, the disciples' way of life and we too are called to be those who hold the people together, preach Good News and daily, life-long teach hope, a way to live in the face of murder, power run amok, injustice and violence. Let us pray that we shoulder our burden of the gospel and learn the compassion of a shepherd for so many without a sense of life's meaning and goodness.

❈ Solomon dreams, asks for a gift and is given wisdom by the Lord and a heart so wise and understanding that there has never been anyone like that up till now, and given riches and glory as well. We have been looking at the leaders of Israel in comparison to Jesus and they pale and are ghosts in reflection of the power, goodness, truth and glory of God in his beloved child among us. Yet his power and his presence draw everyone to him. Jesus takes his friends and go off in a boat to a deserted place but they are followed on foot by those desperate for him. And Jesus pities them and teaches them at great length, staying with them. Are we like our master, pitying the masses of people and being with them in their need?

❈ We are given a short list of how to live: prayer of praise, good deeds, generosity, obedience (reminding them that they will render an account) and lean on the Good Shepherd risen from the dead knowing that he wants to carry out God's will in us. Jesus has sent his disciples forth, as he sends us and we are to daily report back to him, with one another. And we are to live for others, as difficult as that might be. It was for Jesus and the disciples who sought a solitary place, a time apart and were hounded by the crowds in such desperate need. They seek the Word and presence of Jesus that they go on foot around the lake and catch them on the other side. And Jesus is the Shepherd, with pity, needing a leader, someone to tend to them and he teaches them—Jesus is the image of our leaders, ministers and who we should be.

FIFTH WEEK IN ORDINARY TIME

Monday

FIRST READING   **I.** Gen 1:1–19

                                II. 1 K 8:1–7, 9–13

Responsorial Psalm   **I.** Ps 104:1–2, 5–6, 10 and 12, 24 and 35c

                             II. Ps 132:6–7, 8–10

GOSPEL   Mk 6:53–56

Again and again we hear that no matter where Jesus is found, the sick are brought to him and people run with the news of the hope of healing, dignity, acceptance for those ill and the whole community. They beg, for his touch, to touch the fringe of his clothes and they're healed if they get that close. And this is Gennesaret where they had told him to leave before! Obviously they recognize him because the man Jesus told to stay and bring hope by his story and what Jesus had done for him, now bears unbounded fruit in his neighborhood. Now the lake that drowned the pigs, brings Jesus back and wholeness, right living (those in their right mind) now come together—the gift shared. Do we live, when we are healed and forgiven and reaccepted into God's family so that others come to recognize Jesus in our words, our lives changed and our sharing of God's goodness to us with others? This is the only gratitude God wants and that we can actually practice. Help us, O Lord of all life, help us.

Solomon dedicates the temple with the entire community, bringing the ark of the covenant that holds the law, into the presence of the sanctuary. A cloud fills the temple and God dwells with his people. Where does our God dwell now among us? Mark tells us that Jesus steps out of the boat and into the midst of the crowd that brings the sick to him. He is swamped by people in villages and towns, crossroads, the marketplace where all beg to be able to touch even the tassel of his cloak seeking wholeness and life. Where do we look for our God—among the poor, the sick, the hungry, the dispossessed, on the roadways?

✹ We go back to the very beginning covering the first 4 days: creation of light, heavens and the earth, light, moon, sun, stars, planets, dry land, and every kind of food, tree, greens. Are we in awe of what we are given? How fragile our existence is, yet how carefully made to sustain us?

Jesus is about the work of recreation, of healing, making whole and reconstituting human beings. Everyone comes to him, bringing others that need to be touched, even by the tassel of his cloak. His power is given freely to anyone who seeks it. This is the same power as that of creation, the power of God to make and keep and make ever new. Do we seek this power for others, for the earth and for ourselves?

Tuesday

FIRST READING   I. Gen 1:20—2:4a
                        II. 1 K 8:22–23, 27–30
Responsorial Psalm   I. Ps 8:4–5, 6–7, 8–9
                        II. Ps 84:3, 4, 5 and 10, 11
GOSPEL   Mk 7:1–13

✹ Jesus is engaged by the Pharisees on traditional points of practice—not the core elements of the law of Moses that sought to bind the people together in justice so that others would see the presence of The Holy One among them in their lives. Jesus condemns them (and us) "You even put aside the commandment of God to hold fast to human traditions." He uses the example of 'corban'—belonging to God, or the institutional structures of religion to excuse the commandment of caring for one's parents and family members—an insult to God's word of truth and justice. And 'we do many other things like that'. Things sadly haven't changed—what do we do that disobeys the commands of care for those in need, compassion and dignity for others and claim we ignore them because of religious ritual or spiritual practices? God, have mercy on us and convert us to obedience of the basics of being human before You.

✹ God cannot be contained in the heavens or in the temple that Solomon built. Solomon prays for protection for the temple, and that God will listen and heed the prayers of those who come to this place. He asks that God listen from his heavenly dwelling place and grant pardon. God is far and other. Jesus teaches where God is to be found and how we are to pray. We are not to get caught in mere lip service, without reverence or truth, obeying commands with empty hearts and following dogmas of human beings. God is not interested in traditions/practices that replace what is truly worship of God. God wants reverence and total sacrifice of our hearts and lives and obedience to the Word.

Now the next days of creation: waters and all that swims and all that is winged in the air; then creatures great and small and lastly us: in the image of God, male and female—the divine image (in relationship, diversity, communion). It is given to us to have dominion over—as God has dominion over all and it is all very very good. And God rests, contemplates his creation and teaches us how to live: creating, imaging, in relationship, reflecting the goodness of God, magnificent diversity, contemplation and resting with one another on earth with God.

These are the essentials and that is what Jesus is concerned with. Traditions are fine if they serve creation, life, relationships, the reflecting of the image of the divine. But they must be discarded if they do not. It is God's commandment that is crucial—not what can nullify and break the Word of the Lord.

Wednesday

FIRST READING	I. Gen 2:4–9, 15–17
	II. 1 K 10:1–10
Responsorial Psalm	I. Ps 104:1–2a, 27–28, 29bc–30
	II. Ps 37:5–6, 30–31, 39–40
GOSPEL	Mk 7:14–23

The Queen of Sheba comes to Jerusalem because of Solomon's wisdom. She is impressed by the outward wealth and prosperity, praising Yahweh for putting Solomon on the throne, giving him gifts, but she does not follow the wisdom. Jesus too, speaks wisdom and what is truly needed for purity—what is within the heart of a human being. Foods, practices and rituals do not purify or make him impure before God. What makes us impure before God is what we harbor in our minds/thoughts and in our heart. During the time of Jesus, the heart was understood to be will of a person—what we do is what makes us impure before God: violence, greed, unfaithfulness lies and deceit, arrogance and an obtuse spirit. We are what we will and do.

☀ Now another story of creation, a bit different. After the earth and the heavens, there is a stream on the earth and then comes man, given the breath of life by God breathing into him! And there is a garden for the man to cultivate (a gardener) but not to eat from the tree of the knowledge of good and evil—a warning given.

And Jesus speaks about what is good and what is evil—only what comes out of a person can be impure or evil—not what goes in. What we do is what makes us destructive of others and ourselves: what's in the deep recesses of our hearts. It is what we do that makes us impure—incapable of seeing/knowing God who is good.

Thursday

FIRST READING	**I.** Gen 2:18–25
	II. 1 K 11:4–13
Responsorial Psalm	**I.** Ps 128:1–2, 3, 4–5
	II. Ps 106:3–4, 35–36, 37 and 40
GOSPEL	Mk 7:24-30

☀ Solomon sins and turns to other gods in spite of all that God has done for him. And he is warned that the kingdom will be taken from his son, leaving him with one tribe for the sake of David the grandfather. The leaders and the people are not faithful. And Jesus is rejected by many of his own too. Yet another, a Syro-Phoenician woman comes to him begging for help. Jesus first ignores her, then speaks disparagingly against her since she is not a believer. And then it is Jesus who is stunned by her willingness to take the leftovers—what the Jews do not seem to want from him. Her child is healed and Jesus belongs to everyone now.

☀ God forms a partner for Adam out of Adam's rib, a soul-mate who is one with him in flesh and spirit. She is called 'woman'. This creation story is about the origins of marriage and how a man and a woman leave their families for one another to become one. They know no shame, and live on the earth in harmony.

Jesus meets a woman outside of Israel who is desperate on behalf of her child who is tormented (Satan, hinderer, all that keeps us from being the children of God and living in the light). The woman crouches at his feet and begs. Jesus speaks of the food for the children (of Israel) and not throwing it to the dogs. She knows and says, she will eat the food the children throw from the table to the dogs—she will take anything from him! And Jesus is amazed at her wisdom and the child is freed from what harms her. Do we care for our children, and others' children with such passion? Is our wisdom born of others' needs and begging before God?

Friday

FIRST READING   **I.** Gen 3:1–8
II. 1 K 11:29–32; 12:19

Responsorial Psalm   **I.** Ps 32:1–2, 5, 6, 7
II. Ps 81:10–11, 12–13, 14–15

GOSPEL   Mk 7:31–37

The prophets met, a cloak is torn, and Israel is divided. Ten tribes are taken from Solomon's kingdom and one is left to him, along with Jerusalem. And Israel goes into rebellion against the house of David. Israel rebels against Jesus' word and presence as we do, and Jesus goes to the other cities of Tyre, Sidon and the Decapolis. A deaf man with a speech impediment is brought to him and Jesus takes him off away from those who contribute to his illness. He touches his ears and tongue and opens them, letting him speak freely. They are amazed and seeing it, they speak to all who would hear. Jesus goes to those who will listen and be open to him when he is refused by others. Are we among the mute, the deaf and those who reject him…or has his Word found a home with us?

We read the story of the serpent that lies to Eve who eats the fruit. Eve eats because she sees it as good for food and for gaining wisdom. She shares it with Adam and they both see and know upon knowing their own self-consciousness, they also know what is good and what is evil. They hide themselves from God, knowing they have disobeyed his word.

A deaf man with a speech impediment is brought by others to Jesus. He takes him aside to heal him, putting his fingers into the man's ears and touching his tongue. He cries out and groans and the man's ears are opened and his tongue freed. And Jesus tells them not to tell anyone, but of course they do. This is a piece of a baptismal story and preparation for it: someone being brought to Jesus, who touches him, speaks on his behalf, commands him to be whole and sets him free, giving him back into the care of the community to help him speak and hear the Word. This is what we are to do for others—this is wisdom.

Saturday

FIRST READING   I. Gen 3:9–24
                           II. 1 K 12:26–32; 13:33–34

Responsorial Psalm   I. Ps 90:2, 3–4abc, 5–6, 12–13
                  II. Ps 106:6–7ab; 19–20, 21–22

GOSPEL   I. Mk 6:1–10

God comes after Adam in the garden, and he blames Eve. God goes after the serpent first—and then there are consequences for knowing good and evil: the pangs of childbirth, and the harshness of work/survival. God made garments for them to help them live and they are exiled from the garden so that they cannot eat to the tree of life. And the garden was sealed. A strange story and a strange God—but a story that seeks to explain how evil, suffering, struggle, pain and death came into the world and yet there is a God who cares for who he has created.

And Jesus is God in flesh, moved with pity for the crowd, intent on feeding them, and having anyone who is his disciple care for the needs of the masses of people—to make sure they get enough of what they need; beginning with giving away and sharing what they have for themselves. Seven loaves feed 4000 and there is enough left over—7 baskets (a number that signifies infinity—enough to feed everyone). This is our story and our God.

SIXTH WEEK IN ORDINARY TIME

Monday

FIRST READING   **I.** Gen 4:1–15, 25
     II. Jas 1:1–11
Responsorial Psalm   **I.** Ps 50:1 and 8, 16–17, 20–21
     II. Ps 119:67, 68, 71, 72, 73, 76
GOSPEL   Mk 8:11–13

The letter of James begins with a call to joy in the face of trial and testing so that we can learn enduring faithfulness and become mature. We are to ask for wisdom and faith and to live humbly, sharing all we have, not clinging to wealth which lasts for nothing. And Jesus is tested again and again by those without faith who want signs. Jesus sighs from the depths of his spirit (aggrieved) and says: "No sign will be given" and he leaves crossing the lake to the other side. Do we grieve Jesus with our want of signs and lack of faith, being immature and grabbing at what the world says makes us who we are? Lent is approaching. Time to look at our lives from Jesus' point of view.

Cain and Abel are born. One is righteous and the other resentful. Yet God speaks to Cain and warns him. But Cain kills Abel. And God will not allow anyone to kill Cain. He is marked and sent to roam earth. This is the first sin of human beings: murdering one's own family/brother. All other sins are seen in light or shadow of the result of knowing good and evil. The Pharisees (church people) argue with Jesus asking him for a sign. Jesus sighs from the depths of his being—there is sin in those who claim to be religious and in all people who kill others' bodies, and spirits and souls. And Jesus declares adamantly: No sign will be given." Do we argue with Jesus, testing him, wanting signs? Do we obey his word? Do we cause Jesus to sigh from the depths of his being?

Tuesday

FIRST READING   **I.** Gen 6:5–6; 7:1–5, 10

II. Jas 1:12–18

Responsorial Psalm   **I.** Ps 29:1a and 2, 3ac–4, 3b and 9c–10

II. Ps 94:12–13a, 14–15, 18–19

GOSPEL   Mk 8:14–21

We will be tempted, by God, but by our own passions. It is God who gifts us and wills that we be brought to birth with a word spoken in truth. Jesus finds his disciples blinded and taken in by everything around them, unable to see clearly or hear the truth. They forget to bring bread (not only to eat, but the bread of truth, the words of Jesus in their hearts). He warns them about the yeast of the Pharisees that seeps into everything, spoiling it and rotting it, but they aren't listening, looking for bread to eat for themselves.

Jesus is trying to teach them, by feeding the multitudes with what they have among them but they do not understand, caught up in their small lives, rather than the Word of God.

People are wicked and destroys life. And this offends God. God's heart is grieved. (what does God think of us today?) One man finds favor with God—Noah. He is told to build an ark and save something of each thing created and along with his family be saved while the rest of the earth is purified and recreated anew. Noah obeys, the ark is made and the waters come.

The disciples forget to bring bread except for the one loaf (they have Jesus in the boat with them!) And Jesus warns them to be on their guard—us too—against the leaven of the Pharisees and the yeast of Herod—evils that are everywhere from church/state. Do we see or hear or understand yet? Jesus feeds 5000 and there is enough left over for all of Israel, then feeds 4000 and there is enough left over for the whole world. Don't we understand that with God there is sufficiency in sharing and economics that is based on having enough? And there is evil in war, violence, theft, lies and outward maintenance of religious society that does not have true obedience that serves others.

Wednesday

FIRST READING I. Gen 8:6–13, 20–22
II. Jas 1:19–27
Responsorial Psalm I. Ps 116:12–13, 14–15, 18–19
II. Ps 15:2–3a, 3bc–4ab, 5
GOSPEL Mk 8:22–26

✹ Humbly welcome the Word that has taken root in us and act on the word. If we only listen then we deceive ourselves. The Word has to seep into every area of our life or else we do not worship. Care for the widows, the orphans and being truthful—this is what worship is. Jesus seeks to heal a blind man, taking him away from those who brought him. He puts spittle (from his mouth that speaks the truth) on his eyes and it takes time and trial to give him back his sight. He leads him away from those who blind his eyes to what is before him. And we are admonished to not go back to those who cannot see the truth.

✹ After 40 days, a raven is sent out and it returns, then a dove and it returns, and then a dove again, this time the dove brings back an olive leaf. And the waters recede. God has made peace with his people and recreated the face of the earth (literally). Noah blesses God and gives us the promise that it will not be God who dooms the earth because of our evil and it will not be God who strikes down all living beings. God will hold the earth in all seasons—that is God's promise.

Jesus is brought a blind man and he takes him aside. He puts spittle on his eyes and lays hands on him. But it takes at least twice before the man can see—conversion and living by faith takes time. Piece by piece but he is restored and can see perfectly—with the light of Christ/baptism. And he is warned not to go near the village—where people can't see. Again the story is speaking about baptism and the catechumentate, then the mystogia. Can we see perfectly? Can we see the world the way God does?

Thursday

FIRST READING   **I.** Gen 9:1–13

II. Jas 2:1–9

Responsorial Psalm   **I.** Ps 102:16–18, 19–21, 29 and 22–23

II. Ps 34:2–3, 4–5, 6–7

GOSPEL   Mk 8:27–33

James is incredibly practical. Do we treat those dressed well with respect and shun those who are poor? He reminds us that it is the poor who are chosen by God and are heirs of the kingdom. We are to love the poor as we love ourselves and show no favoritism to those who have made it in the world. Jesus is practical too and knows that his disciples don't see him clearly. The people see him as a prophet like Elijah or John the Baptizer. And who do they think he might be. They see terribly, with Peter calling him the Messiah (his version who will be king). Jesus begins to try to tell them he is the Son of Man, the crucified and rejected one who will rise. But they can't and don't want to hear and so Jesus is forced to say: "Get out of my sight, you who hinder God…you can't see by God's standards." How clearly do we see?

Again God gives Noah and his sons all the earth to enjoy, use and care for, but they are not to eat flesh or take flesh with blood in it—a decree against killing anyone, any animal. God will take into account all human life we take. A new covenant is given to Noah and to the earth and all creations. The sign is the rainbow, the arch between sky and ground—the earth will not be destroyed by God.

Jesus questions his own on who others think he is—a prophet. And then on who we think he is. The answer comes from Peter first, who says he's the Messiah, but he's ordered strictly not to say that to anyone! Jesus begins to tell them who he is: the Son of Man who will be crucified, rejected and handed over and they want no part of it—beginning with Peter who has his own ideas (like us) on who he wants Jesus to be. And Jesus rebukes us all telling us to stop hindering his way and stop judging like the world. We must learn the sight and the wisdom of God, which is the cross.

Friday

FIRST READING   **I.** Gen 11:1–9

II. Jas 2:14–24

Responsorial Psalm   **I.** Ps 33:10–11, 12–13, 14–15

II. Ps 112:1–2, 3–4, 5–6

GOSPEL   Mk 8:34—9:1

✣ We are commanded by James to put our faith into practice doing the works of justice and mercy or else our faith and our lives are dead. Jesus summons us all to the practice of faith in him by "denying our very self, picking up our cross and coming after him, to lose our lives even for his sake and so save our souls, our integrity." This is faith, not words or rituals or saying so, but walking the way of the cross, all the way to crucifixion, rejection and death itself by living and loving all with Jesus, in Jesus' way. Do we really have faith? Or is our faith and huge portions of our lives just dead?

✣ These are stories of who evil moved in the world (and still does). There was one language until they decided to work together and build a tower, make a name for themselves and be powerful. Even together as one, with one language, it is used for destruction. Evil grows and what will we do next? So the languages were confused and the people scattered and the city called Babel. We are of many languages and races, peoples and nations and we are called to come together to make one world with the gift of diversity that makes us struggle to understand one another, and so, perhaps understand God.

Jesus summons us to come after him, deny ourselves (not deny him or his words) and pick up our cross. We will lose our life, yet save everything. We belong to the Son of Man, crucified, risen from the dead, judge of the nations who will come in the glory of God the Father. Who are we—those who follow the crucified Son of Man or do we belong to those who seek to make a name for ourselves—still?

Saturday

FIRST READING   **I.** Heb 11:1–7

II. Jas 3:1–10

Responsorial Psalm   **I.** Ps 145:2–3, 4–5, 10–11

II. Ps 12:2–3, 4–5, 7–8

GOSPEL   Mk 9:2–13

Jesus takes his disciples up a mountain to pray with them. They are rejecting his words, his teaching and his call to the cross and suffering with him. He wants them to see him, to take heart and follow him in spite of their fear. He wants them to stop listening to anyone else and not to pull each other down and away from him. He prays and they see, and hear God's voice "This is my beloved, my son. Listen to him." The word listen means "to obey." They are to obey God, the Word of God in Jesus and not get caught in their own small wants, blinded by misunderstanding and weaknesses. They must look at suffering as part of the way. And so must we, if we are to be followers of Jesus.

These are people of faith: Abel, Enoch, Noah and all those who pleased God and believed in him and inherits the justice of God. Are we people of faith, offering the sacrifice that God wants: obedience to the Word of God, service to the least of our brothers and sisters? Do we obey, at least so that we might be saved from the destruction of evil?

We are invited by Jesus into the presence of God. We are allowed to pray with Jesus and to see through his body, into the light of God. We hear the voice of God, testifying to Jesus. And we are commanded: "Listen to him"—no one else. Jesus is the only reality that we must perceive the world through. And we are to follow the Son of Man even if we do not understand all that is required of us, or who Jesus is—We are to live on faith now.

SEVENTH WEEK IN ORDINARY TIME

Monday

FIRST READING   **I.** Sir 1:1–10

                                           II. Jas 3:13–18

Responsorial Psalm   **I.** Ps 93:1ab, 1cd–2, 5

                                       II. Ps 19:8, 9, 10, 15

GOSPEL   Mk 9:14–29

✹ It is time to practice all the extraordinary things that we have experienced as the Body of Christ and to be disciples for the world to see. A man comes with a boy who is so afflicted with a spirit that makes him dumb, yet his disciples cannot cure him. Just the sight of Jesus shakes the boy into convulsions. And the man asks Jesus to cure him, 'if he can'—Jesus responds that "All things are possible for one who believes." The father is desperate and cries out: "I do believe, but help the little faith that I have." Jesus commands the dumb spirit to leave him, and lifts the boy by the hand and raises him up. The disciples question Jesus and find out that only prayer—Jesus' prayer, can drive out some spirits. It is time for us now, to pray, to drive out what is evil, to believe and to ask Jesus to help what little faith we have.

✹ Wisdom is given to us from above—it's easy to recognize for it is peaceable, lenient, docile, rich in sympathy and just deeds, impartial and sincere. There is a harvest of justice sown in peace for those who cultivate peace. The disciples are having trouble without the wisdom of Jesus. They seek to heal and help and cannot make a dent in evil, illness, the trials of others. Jesus' presence commands the mute and deaf spirit of the child to leave and it obeys. And Jesus chastises us saying some things can only be driven out by prayer. Do we pray with Jesus before the Father in the power of the Spirit, in peace, rich in mercy, sincerely, doing justice. Prayer begins with words and ends in works.

✳ Wisdom is from God and it is the Lord who knows all wisdom and it is the Lord who created her and poured her forth upon all his works, upon all of us, lavishing her upon his friends. It is fear of the Lord that warms the heart, gives gladness, joy and length of days. Fear of the Lord is a gift (confirmation) that allows us to fear disobeying God and destroying his creation more than fearing anyone or anything on earth.

A man brings his child to Jesus to expel a demon from him, because the disciples can't. Jesus speaks with the father, talking with him and letting him plead on his child's behalf. And then Jesus tells him that everything is possible to someone who trusts. Jesus commands by word what torments him to leave the child. Then takes him by the hand and raises him up. Jesus says you must have wisdom to know what can only be driven out by prayer. And the man's prayer was simple: "I do believe! Help my lack of trust!" Let us pray.

Tuesday

FIRST READING   **I.** Sir 2:1–11
II. Jas 4:1–10
Responsorial Psalm   **I.** Ps 37:3–4, 18–19, 27–28, 39–40
II. Ps 55:7–8, 9, 10–11, 23
GOSPEL   Mk 9:30–37

✳ Jesus takes time as they travel to try and teach his disciples that the Son of Man will be rejected, crucified, murdered and rise again. But the disciples don't understand his words, don't want to hear him speaking like this and are afraid to ask him what he actually means. It seems the disciples (we too) don't often understand or want to know what Jesus is trying to tell us—to make us face reality in the world—to make us face the cross and our share of the burden of preaching the gospel with Jesus. They are intent on other things—like who's the greatest, and in fighting among themselves. Jesus takes a child (a word for anyone poor, without power, prestige, place in society as well as actual children who were in that category) and embraces him telling them that they must embrace the poor, the weak, the sick, the outcast, the unimportant and welcome them. Then they welcome Christ and the One who sent him. We have heard this before—this time will it sink in and become our practice?

✹ The community wars, fights among themselves, bringing conflict and divisions to everyone because of pride, jealousy and wanting to live like the world does. We are told to draw close to God and God will draw close to us! We have to learn humility, knowing who God is, and caring for others. Jesus tries to teach his disciples who have been arguing over who is the most important to be servants, to be as the least among the children of the earth, and to accompany him on the way of the cross. And they do not want to hear of it. Do we?

✹ We are warned to prepare ourselves for trials, to cling to God in times of adversity and not forsake God. Trust and hope, and fear the Lord and wait for his mercy. Hang on for the long haul! Remember that the Lord is compassionate and merciful and saves us in times of trouble. Lent begins tomorrow. It is good advice.

And Jesus too tries to warn us as disciples what is going to happen to him—he will be delivered over into the hands of men who will torture him and put him to death, yet he will rise. They did not understand and still, often we don't—that we must walk the way of the cross with Jesus so to know his glory and resurrection. We must be buried with Christ in baptism and so rise with him to a life that declares compassion and mercy through the Cross. But they aren't listening. They are fighting about who's going to be first. Jesus disarms them by setting a child in their midst—one without any power at the time, saying welcome this child, welcome the poor, the stranger—and the Son of Man who will be crucified—and you will not only welcome me, but the one who sent me—the Father.

Wednesday

FIRST READING   I. Sir 4:11–19
                         II. Jas 4:13–17
Responsorial Psalm   I. Ps 119:165, 168, 171, 172, 174, 175
                         II. Ps 49:2–3, 6–7, 8–10, 11
GOSPEL   Mk 9:38–40

✹ The disciples don't want to face what Jesus is trying to teach them and they change the subject from the necessity of embracing the poor and the unimportant and tell Jesus that they saw someone doing what they were supposed to be doing (and sometimes can't) but that this person wasn't one of them (not in the 'in' group of chosen ones). They expect Jesus to be as incensed as they are but he startles them again. Jesus says let anyone who can do good in my name, do it. "Whoever is not against us is for us." We are to assume the goodness of people until we learn otherwise! Jesus' words remind us that anyone who does good is close to him, whether they know him, follow him publicly or not. Jesus' goodness and power are not limited to those whom we think should have it or use it! Something to humble us and make us look at all people with hope and amazement.

✝ Even now, says the Lord, return with your whole heart: rend your hearts. Lent is about stopping in our ways and listening/obeying the word of the Lord who is merciful and gracious and waiting on us—and it is about doing this together as a people, a community that is mindful of its need to tap into the passion of believing and obeying once again. We are ambassadors of God—God appealing through us to the world. And what we bring always to every situation and relationship is reconciliation—that we all might walk together again with God and with each other.

This is all about hope! This time is all about making peace! This time is about living passionately, gracefully and truthfully— about getting back in touch with the intensity of our baptismal vows: do you promise to live forever in the freedom of the children of God? Do you promise to resist evil and refuse to be mastered by any sin? Do you promise to live under no sin of power but the sign of the cross? We gather and we once again follow Jesus, picking up our cross that comes from preaching the gospel.

Thursday

FIRST READING	I. Sir 5:1–8
	II. Jas 5:1–6
Responsorial Psalm	I. Ps 1:1–2, 3, 4 and 6
	II. Ps 49:14–15, 15–16, 17–18, 19–20
GOSPEL	Mk 9:41–50

✺ Jesus continues to amaze his disciples and tells them that if someone, not attached to them, treats them with kindness, even a cup of water to drink, will be rewarded because they did it for them, because they knew they bore the name of Christ. God is generous and gracious—and Jesus is trying to stretch us into the way God looks upon us all. And Jesus also warns them and us that if the way we speak, or act or when we do not act, causes one of these 'little ones'—children, the poor, the sinner, the sick and weak, the despised and cast-off, the expendable ones of the earth—to sin then we will be held accountable and treated to God's justice. We are to be careful of all others, especially those most vulnerable to scandal and seeing that we do not live up to our words and belief statements. We are to be salt—what gives flavor, healing, endurance and lasting life to all around us. We are to make sure that we are not rotting everything around us, having lost our salt—the Word and Spirit of God.

✺ These are hard sayings, in the mouth of James and Jesus. The rich are condemned for their wealth, insensitivity to others' needs, their greed, their violence and killing of the just and justice will stand testimony against them. Jesus too assails the behavior of those who lead others astray and blesses anyone who gives in his name. We are to be vigilant in our behaviors and totally dedicated to conversion of our lives in all areas. We are salted with fire….the Word of God and the Spirit of God and we must live with that Word in our hearts and at peace with one another. Hard sayings and hard practice but the core, the heart of Jesus' Word and life.

Friday

FIRST READING
I. Sir 6:5–17
II. Jas 5:9–12

Responsorial Psalm
I. Ps 119:12, 16, 18, 27, 34, 35
II. Ps 103:1–2, 3–4, 8–9, 11–12

GOSPEL
Mk 10:1–12

✺ Peter is a shepherd, an elder reminding the others that they must care for the flock. They must watch, be an example and not lord it over others—and Peter knows this, having once been the lost sheep himself, brought back with tenderness to being a follower after betraying and cursing Jesus' name in his fear.

Peter, like us, is quick to tell Jesus who he thinks he is: the Messiah, the Son of the living God! He has the words, but no understanding. The Father has shared this knowledge with him, but Peter must walk the way of the cross with Jesus before he will realize who Jesus truly is, and who he himself is called to be as part of the foundation of the new community of forgiveness and holding bound. We too stand with Peter today and are questioned: do we know who this Jesus is and who we are called to be as followers?

✳ Wherever Jesus goes, the crowds of those in need, searching and wanting follow him, and so do the leaders and teachers looking for a way to trap him. This time, the question is: is it right for a husband to divorce his wife? They know the answer—no divorce according to Moses' law, but divorce is practiced and allowed—but only for the husband to divorce his wife, not the wife to divorce her husband. Jesus is angry and says that they know the law but the law accommodated their weakness and sin because they were stubborn and hard of heart, but that doesn't change the law. Later, when the disciples want to know, Jesus equalizes both husband and wife—whoever divorces the other commits adultery, is unfaithful to the spouse. You cannot use the law on one of the two and not on the other and the law must be honored as defending faithfulness while we must admit that we fail and sin against God and one another. It all begins with the truth. All of our lives need to be looked at with truthfulness.

✳ We are called to be patient, not to grumble as we live with suffering and hardships like the prophets of old who spoke in the name of the Lord. We are to be like Jesus, like God who is compassionate and merciful, always. Jesus reminds us that he demands that we be like him, the children of the Father in our faithfulness, our relationships and in love. All of us are to be followers of Jesus' way of unbounded love, seeing the law as leading to deeper and truer commitments not as the least we are to do with one another. In marriage, in being single, widowed we are to first of all be faithful to the Word of God that has called us to life in God.

Saturday

The crowd brings their children to Jesus to have him bless them and touch them but the disciples are pushing them away—children are not important. They are trying to choose who gets Jesus' undivided attention and Jesus is annoyed at his disciples' lack of care and attention to all in that society who were considered useless, like slaves and children. Jesus rarely is angry, but he's angry at his disciples' lack of awareness of who is beloved of God. He sets the children up as a standard, appalling the disciples, telling them to watch the children and to learn to receive the kingdom like a child lives—vulnerable, open, dependent on others, needing to trust for their very survival, welcoming anyone. Jesus blesses them and lays hands on them, touching them with intimacy and acceptance and pure love. We would learn much from Jesus and instead of requiring children to go to school, allowing to know acceptance, blessing and singled out status within our churches.

There is hardship and we are to pray, and pray with others, on behalf of others, seeking to heal one another, confessing to one another and believing that our prayers will bring all of us who stray from the truth back to the Word. We are meant to be responsible for one another, saving our souls by saving each other. Jesus takes the children who come to him and sets them forth as a model for community. These poor, the anawim, those without power who need one another and Jesus are the ones who teach us how to live in the kingdom now. The children are those we despise, put off, shove away, and keep from Jesus by our blindness and evil. We must be careful not to be the cause of others straying.

EIGHTH WEEK IN ORDINARY TIME

Monday

FIRST READING   **I.** Sir 17:20–24
         II. 1 P 1:3–9

Responsorial Psalm   **I.** Ps 32:1–2, 5, 6, 7
       II. Ps 111:1–2, 5–6, 9 and 10c

GOSPEL   Mk 10:17–27

✺ Jesus is setting out on his way to the Cross in Jerusalem and is interrupted by a man who worships him and asks him the ground line question: "Good Master, what must I do to have eternal life?" But Jesus will not even let him call him 'good' for the man has his ideas and Jesus teaches him surely that only God is good, and God has other criteria than we do. Besides he knows the answer—as a Jew, obeying the law makes him holy. And he listens as Jesus recites the law—and he claims that he has obeyed them all since he was young. That in itself is amazing! Do we obey all the commandments? Jesus looks at him with love and invites him into the kingdom, into the inner circle of his disciples, invites him as close as one can get to him—and tells him there is one more thing: to sell his excess and give it to the poor, lay up treasure in heaven and come back and follow him, among his own who will be his friends. But he can't—he's too attached to all that he has and turns away. It's hard to get into the kingdom, harder still if you are wealthy and still harder to be a disciple. Are we just believers in Jesus but have no intention of being disciples, or caring for the poor? The invitation is there—how often have we saddened the heart of Jesus and refused his love?

✺ We must remember that we have been born into God, into mercy and hope and the resurrection of Jesus the Christ. We are to rejoice in that, in the face of hardship and suffering but hold fast and honor God by loving one another. Jesus is asked what constitutes eternal life, to know it now and we, like the man who asks, knows the answers. We are to obey the commandments of old. And once we have struggled to master them, there is one more thing. Sell all we have, give to the poor and come follow Jesus. There is always one more thing but nothing is impossible with our God. We are to belong to God more and more and each day give one more thing to the poor and come follow more closely. We forget so easily so often who we are.

The book of Sirach is wisdom literature, small pieces culled from around the time of Solomon and specific to Jewish schools of thought. Each piece is almost separate and can be taken at face value—and much of it isn't wisdom at all, but cultural beliefs. It should be read through the lens of Jesus' Words in the gospels and the understanding of the Spirit in community. Here is the best of this segment: how great is the mercy of the Lord!

Back to Mark's gospel, Jesus is met by a man who wants a share in everlasting life and calls Jesus 'good'. Jesus says that only God is good—our terms are relative at best. And what gives life is obedience to the law, which the man says he obeys. He is looked at with love and told there is one more thing—go sell what you have, give to the poor and then come follow Jesus. If we are to become Jesus' followers, we too must go beyond the law, towards living the poverty, the generosity and the sharing of the kingdom.

Tuesday

FIRST READING

I. Sir 35:1–12
II. 1 P 1:10–16

Responsorial Psalm

I. Ps 50:5–6, 7–8, 14 and 23
II. Ps 98:1, 2–3ab, 3cd–4

GOSPEL

Mk 10:28–31

The disciples have just watched the thirteenth disciple (perhaps) walk away and they are disturbed—how hard is it to get into the kingdom? Nothing is impossible with God is Jesus' statement—even those with wealth can let go, escape its stranglehold and share with the poor that need it. But Peter is quick to find out what's in it for him and the others and exaggerates mightily saying that they have given up everything for Jesus. (We always think we have been so generous and inflate what we have done for God) and Jesus still assures them (and us) that we will be given one hundred fold, even in persecution—mothers, sisters and brothers, houses, (community of disciples, friends of God), children, lands—missions and a place in the kingdom here welcomed by total strangers who will care for us and life everlasting—tastes of it even here and now. God is not to be outdone by any of our small gestures of giving—we haven't even begun to learn of God or learn to share with those in need.

✺ We must take to heart what was said by the prophets and pull ourselves together, and set all our hope on the gift that will be given when Christ appears. We are to be holy in every aspect of our conduct and life. We are to be holy as our God is holy! Peter, like so many of us think only of what we already have given or done, saying "I've given up everything to follow you"—oh! And yet Jesus confirms us in whatever little we have given we will know it a hundred times even in this life, along with persecution and life everlasting. We are so slow and so stingy in what we give up, what we hand over rather than staking everything on God.

✺ To obey the law, to give alms and to refrain from evil, to be generous and offer sacrifice—these are the practices of a good Jew living in covenant with the God of Justice. Jesus' words reveal what makes his followers holy, as he is holy. If we sell what we have, give to the poor and store up treasure in heaven (the Body of Christ here on earth) and follow Jesus we will know God's graciousness even now with 100 fold shared back in brothers/sisters/mothers/homes/property/children, and persecution here, and life that is everlasting in the fullness of God's kingdom. Jesus' wisdom is upside down wisdom: many who are first will be last and the last shall come first. Where do we find ourselves—first/last? What are we giving up, sharing with others?

Wednesday

FIRST READING   **I.** Sir 36:1, 4–5a, 10–17
                                       II. 1 P 1:18–25

Responsorial Psalm   **I.** Ps 79:8, 9, 11 and 13
                      II. Ps 147:12–13, 14–15, 19–20

GOSPEL   Mk 10:32–45

They continue the way of the cross, their journey and the twelve are anxious and the others are afraid and Jesus tells them again that the Son of Man will be rejected, tortured, crucified and will rise again. And then he takes Peter, James and John up the mountain to pray so that they can see who he truly is before God—greater by far than Moses (liberator of the people) and Elijah, (the disturber of the kings of Israel intent on justice for the poor)—he is the beloved Son of the Father. They are to listen only to him—not to their own fears, the murmurs around them, the rejection of others, the rising tide of hatred, only to the Word of the Lord. That is all there is when we look up—Jesus, the Word made flesh among us, who is Lord of life and Son of Man, judge of the nations, justice and mercy in human flesh. We must listen only to him.

This is a prayer to God of the universe, to put dread into the nations, so that they will know God as the Jews do, and that there is no God but God. It is a prayer for a nation, a people—a prayer of the Jews. Parts of it are still very apropos and others, in light of Jesus, in need of altering.

Jesus' prayer, life and teachings are based not on power and might but on obedience, submission to the will of God, living with no violence and forgiveness which takes us on the way of the cross. Jesus leads us to the cross and knows our fear, yet invites us to walk with him and share in his sufferings and dying, so to share in his glory and rising. Two of the disciples want power/prestige/position and ask for it, causing indignation in the group. But Jesus reminds them that in his community power is found in serving the needs of all, being the least and giving your life as ransom for many—with Jesus. We are back in Ordinary Time—time to practice all we have leaned in these last full months.

Thursday

FIRST READING   **I.** Sir 42:15–25

II. 1 P 2:2–5, 9–12

Responsorial Psalm   **I.** Ps 33:2–3, 4–5, 6–7, 8–9

II. Ps 100:2–3, 4, 5

GOSPEL   Mk 10:46–52

Now they come to Jericho and the road is crowded. A blind beggar hears that it is Jesus and desperately cries out: "Son of David, Jesus have mercy on me." And he won't be shut up, not by the crowd, or even by the disciples who are hurrying Jesus away from people and the incessant cries for help. But Jesus stops and calls him over and he throws off his cloak, runs, blind! And naked! And Jesus rather oddly asks him what he wants—he wants to be able to see again! The word 'again' is crucial. He wasn't always blind! He is given back his sight and he begins to follow Jesus up the road, on his way to Jerusalem. He immediately becomes a follower! This is what we are to do, if we have listened to all these readings this past week—we are to cry out for faith, drop what hinders us from getting nearer to Jesus, run, even blind and ask to see again—with grace and the light of the Gospel, and follow Jesus on his way of the cross. This is what Peter and the Disciples should be doing—what we should be doing. Are we?

Friday

FIRST READING   **I.** Sir 44:1, 9–13

II. 1 P 4:7–13

Responsorial Psalm   **I.** Ps 149:1–2, 3–4, 5–6 and 9

II. Ps 96:10, 11–12, 13

GOSPEL   Mk 11:11–26

Now Jesus enters Jerusalem, the place that kills the prophets and it's late so he goes to Bethany with the disciples. Next day they are on their way back in and find a fig tree with leaves, but no fruit and they are hungry—it's not the season for figs anyway. But Jesus curses the tree! The fig tree—symbol of Jerusalem, the temple, the worship of God that brings peace and justice to the land. Jesus then drives the money changers out of the temple, purifying the house of his Father, crying out that this house was meant to be a place of prayer for all nations and it's a den of thieves. They want to kill him, but don't know how to do it. And as they leave the city, the fig tree has withered and died. There is to be the new temple (the Body of Christ—people), the new ritual (prayer and forgiveness of everyone) and a new sense of God, as Father of all. In Jesus' presence and at Jesus' word, there is judgment and newness given. We must take Jesus' words and deeds to heart and turn so that our worship is pure, our forgiveness sure and our care of the Body of Christ truly worship that is the coming of peace and justice or our lives and souls are just withered trees.

✺ Jesus has entered Jerusalem and goes to the temple, but it is late and he leaves. This will be Jesus' last visit to the temple. The next day, on the way out of Bethany, Jesus observes a fig tree. It has many leaves but there are no figs. He curses it, even though it was not the time for figs. Then he enters the temple and drives the money changers and sellers out—calling it a den of thieves. After leaving, they pass by the fig tree again and it is withered to its roots. The fig tree is an ancient symbol of Israel, of peace and plenty and in this case it is Jerusalem specifically that has rejected Jesus and no longer gives life. Its religion and leaders are withered and give nothing to the people to eat. Jesus exhorts us to have faith and approach God with trust, forgive so that God the Father can forgive us. Is our life of faith bearing fruit or has it withered? Are we there when others are hungry for life?

Saturday

FIRST READING   **I.** Sir 51:12cd–20
                                       II. Jdt 17, 20b–25

Responsorial Psalm   **I.** Ps 19:8, 9, 10, 11
                                   II. Ps 63:2, 3–4, 5–6

GOSPEL   Mk 11:27–33

✺ Again, in the temple Jesus is accosted by the priests and teachers on whose authority he does these things. But Jesus is not trapped so easily. He has his own question: John came preaching repentance and baptism—was it merely human, or the work of God—answer me!

And they won't—if they answer of God, then they will be held to account for not repenting themselves and following him. And if they answer merely human, the people will turn on them, for they believe John was a prophet. They say "We don't know." And so, since they will not be honest, Jesus will not grace them with his answer. Where do we stand? Are we more interested in correct theology and power of authority or are we converted to holiness? Will Jesus grace us with answers or will he turn from us in disgust at our refusal to change?

✺ The young man sought wisdom and was instructed. Then he becomes devoted to her. What do we seek with such devotion and faithfulness? Jesus has been preaching and teaching and he is questioned on where his authority comes from. But Jesus is tired of playing word games and he knows they are not honest. So he asks them about John the Baptist and whether or not John's baptism was divine or human. And they won't answer him—afraid of the people, and then afraid that they will be confronted on their own lack of response to John. So Jesus will not answer them either. Jesus' wisdom is born of the truth and obedience to God. Do we obey Jesus, or question texts, commands and refuse to be committed wholeheartedly to following Jesus?

NINTH WEEK IN ORDINARY TIME

Monday

FIRST READING   **I.** Tb 1:3, 2:1a–8

          II. 2 P 1:2–7

Responsorial Psalm   **I.** Ps 112:1–2, 3–4, 5-6

       II. Ps 91:1–2, 14–15b, 15c–16

GOSPEL   Mk 12:1–12

✴ Now Jesus tells stories about himself in Israel's history and about how we, his disciples are to live in our nations. A man planted a vineyard (always Israel) and protected it, prepared soil, built a wine press, watch tower—did everything so that the grapes would be rich for the harvest and making of good wine. But the tenants decided that they would keep the owner's share of the fruit and they refuse to justly give what is due. Then they mock, torture and kill anyone who comes near them who has been sent by the owner. Lastly they kill the owner's son, stupidly thinking they'll get the inheritance now that there is no son to receive it from his father's hand. Jesus quotes scripture and tells them he is the son of the vineyard owner—son of Yahweh who has tended the vineyard Israel all these centuries, though his word and covenant was broken, the prophets killed and they will do the same to him—unjustly, viciously. And they want to kill him, but are afraid of the people. Jesus truth-tells them and says what a marvelous thing God is doing in him and his presence on earth. Do we see it and rejoice in it? Do we do justice or resist the will of God for justice, for wine and hope for all peoples? Are we interested in just us?

✴ Now it is time to be good news and express in our lives all the extraordinary experiences and knowledge of God that has been shared with us. Let us begin. We have everything necessary for a life of piety, devotion, virtue, self-control and discernment. Remember that we do this primarily together in community, held accountable for our growth in grace as we learn to care for one another. We are warned: just because we know of God doesn't mean that we obey God. We have inherited everything from God, but what are we doing with it?

✳ Tobit and his family lived as captives in Assyria and the book is interested in preserving the essentials of Jewish family life, values and faith as exiles. Tobit wishes to share his feast at Pentecost with the poor. But he returns with the news of a murder. Tobit brings the body home and washes and buries it—the highest corporal work of mercy for the Jewish people. He is mocked by his neighbors who know that this is his lifestyle and that he has been persecuted for it before—but Tobit is a just and faithful Jew. How faithful are we, even in times when our lives go well and we do not know persecution or exile?

Jesus tells the story of a vineyard (Israel) that was tended and when the harvest came in, the tenants kept it for themselves, murdering all who were sent by the owner, including his own son, thinking they would get the vineyard for themselves. Do we give God what is due God—as a community, his people and church? Jesus reminds the leaders of the justice of God and that God will vindicate those who are faithful and his own beloved Son.

Tuesday

FIRST READING

I. Tb 2:9–14
II. 2 P 3:12–15a, 17–18

Responsorial Psalm

I. Ps 112:1–2, 7–8, 9
II. Ps 90:2, 3–4, 10, 14 and 16

GOSPEL

Mk 12:13–17

✳ We are to live in expectation: bringing the kingdom here on earth and leaving it to God for its coming in fullness. We await the justice of God and have much to do in the interim, beginning with the making of peace, and growing in grace and knowledge of God, and again, we do this together and this is what gives glory to God. We're not to get caught in games in the world. Everything belongs to God. His image is upon us and the only God we worship and obey is Jesus' God, revealed as the Trinity.

✳ Tobit is exhausted, and sleeps. Bird droppings fall into his eyes and no matter what he does, with doctors and salves he goes blind. For four years he cannot see and his wife Anna worked for hire. He does not believe her when she brings a goat home as a bonus. His anger is loosed at her and she, in her frustration asks him bitterly—Where are your good deeds now?—your true character is showing itself. Tobit and Anna are being tried and it takes a toll on them both. [note: the readings will have little or no connection to each other for many weeks]

Factions in Judaism are set to trap Jesus. They approach him with flattery and ask him if they should pay the tax to the emperor. But Jesus will not be caught. He asks them for a coin (which they should not have in the temple) The inscription reads: Caesar est Deus and Caesar's image is on the coin. Jesus says, give to Caesar what is Caesar's and to God what is God's. But he is also aware that we are made in the image of God—each unique, and not in Caesar's image that is uniform. We are to give to God ourselves—and then what is leftover, give to the emperor/government/nation.

Wednesday

FIRST READING

I. Tb 3:1–11a, 16–17a
II. 2 Tim 1:1–3, 6–12

Responsorial Psalm

I. Ps 25:2–3, 4–5ab, 6 and 7bc, 8–9
II. Ps 123:1b–2ab, 2cdef

GOSPEL

Mk 12:18–27

✳ Again Jesus is interrogated, this time by the Sadducees who don't believe in resurrection from the dead (the Pharisees did). They insult Jesus with a ridiculous proposition of a woman who dies after being married seven times—which one will be her husband in heaven? Jesus is clear that they are wrong because they know neither the Scriptures nor the power of God and that heaven is not like here. Relationships in the kingdom are not based on marriage or blood ties, but on obedience to the God of life, the God of history and the God of those living. He's not so subtlely telling them that they are dead already! Are we wrong about a lot of things because we do not know either the Scriptures or the power of God? How stupid and misguided are we in our questions, doubts and theological issues? Do we believe in the God of life and do our lives reflect that to others?

✹ Paul exhorts Timothy to be bold and let the Spirit loose that he has been given, to express it in wisdom and testimony that is strong and loving and to be holy. We have been entrusted with the grace of the crucified and risen Jesus and we are to live in that light and power. Jesus battles the Sadducees. They mock him about eternal life, but he boldly tells them they know nothing, for life in God is nothing like life here on earth. God is the God of life, and that is meant to be ever more abundant life here and now. Hereafter follows upon our lives lived in God now.

✹ Tobit prays for mercy to the judge of the world. He asks for forgiveness for himself and his people in exile who have become a reproach to the nations. He is torn with grief and wants to die in his misery. And Sarah, the daughter of Raguel is praying as well for release for each time she tries to marry, her husband is killed on their wedding night—seven times! She is grieved in spirit and wants to kill herself. And both prayers come to God, and Raphael (the archangel) is sent to heal them both. We are all bound together whether we are aware of it or not—and all things, situations and relationships can be healed and made whole. Our recourse has always been in God.

Jesus is mocked by the Sadducees who don't believe in resurrection with an unbelievable case of a woman with 7 husbands, all brothers and no children—who would be her husband in heaven? No one is! God is the God of the living and we belong to the living God, not to any relationship on earth. Our relationships on earth are meant to express faithfully and gracefully that w are God's, now and forever. Do we know who lays claim to us?

Thursday

FIRST READING	I. Tb 6:10–11; 7:1bcde, 9–17; 8:4–9a
	II. 2 Tim 2:8–15
Responsorial Psalm	I. Ps 128:1–2, 3, 4–5
	II. Ps 25:4–5, 8–9, 10 and 14
GOSPEL	Mk 12:28–34

✹ Now a teacher of the law overheard this debate and admires Jesus for how he answered and conducted himself, but he too has a question (and wants his stand validated). What is the first commandment of all? Jesus answers with the Shema, the belief of all Israel: that God is one and we are to love God and our neighbor with all our hearts, souls, minds, and resources and all the other commandments are found in that one. Of course, Jesus' answer is correct! And the teacher adds in that this kind of love and service and obedience is more important than any ritual offering or sacrificial worship. Now it's Jesus' turn to tell the teacher he's close to the kingdom—but not there yet! But what happened after that? Did he follow Jesus, did he ask the next question—if I'm close, what do I have to do? It isn't mentioned and no one dares to take him on again in debate. Are we only close to the kingdom? Are we close in obedience and love and service, fulfilling the first commandment? What's next? Do we want to know and are we ready to spend all our life and energy obeying that commandment?

✳ If we have died with Christ (baptism) we will also live with him, and if we hold out to the end, being faithful, we will reign with him. We are to keep reminding others of this reality and stop disputing about words. We are here to preach and live the truth, not squabble about expressions. Jesus is clear as well: love God with all your heart, soul, mind, resources-strength and love your neighbor with all your heart, soul, mind, resources-strength and we'll be drawing near to the kingdom of God, here and now.

✳ Raphael travels with Tobias and they stay with Raguel to be introduced to Sarah. She is offered in marriage but with the sobering story of what has happened already. The marriage contract is drawn up and together they pray that God might have mercy on them. The story seeks to emphasize the importance of marriage within Judaism, among one's own people, and with another who shares the same hopes for Israel's return to Jerusalem.

Jesus is asked in honesty what is the first of the commandments—which every child would know: to love God and one's neighbor with all one's heart/soul/mind and strength (resources). The law applied only to those within Judaism, not to outsiders—most of the human race. The man has the insight that God wants our obedience and devotion rather than offerings, but standing near the kingdom of God in the person of Jesus—he cannot see Jesus' own power and presence as the kingdom itself—a new relationship with God and one another.

Friday

FIRST READING   **I.** Tb 11:5–17
                                                 II. 2 Tim 3:10-17
Responsorial Psalm   **I.** Ps 146:1b–2, 6c–7, 8–9a, 9bc–10
                              II. Ps 119:157, 160, 161, 165, 166, 168
GOSPEL   Mk 12:35–37

We learn how to live by watching and imitating those who obey the Word of God and part of that learning is to know that there will be suffering, hardships and even persecution if we are faithful. All that is needed is found in the Scriptures: use it for teaching, reproof, correction, training in holiness, faithfulness and wisdom. We read the Scriptures daily, food for our souls and minds, the foundation of our lives and conversions and learn more and more what it means to call Jesus: "Lord."

Raphael, the healing angel teaches Tobias how to heal his old father's eyes so that he might see again, with the fish that they caught as they began their journey. Tobit can see again and the family rejoices, blessing and praising God for his mercy. Do we bless God for being able to see, for having medicine and health care, for being able to alleviate others' pain? And do we make sure that everyone has what they need when they are ill?

Jesus is questioned maliciously by everyone who comes. Now he asks a question using the scriptures, the Word of God to illustrate what he is saying—about himself, David and the messiah. How can the messiah be both David's son and Lord? The crowd listens with delight as Jesus trumps the teachers/lawyers and scribes who have been harassing him with the intent of tripping him down. Do we read the scriptures in such a way that the Word calls us to repentance and deeper insight or do we use the Word against others?

Saturday

FIRST READING   **I.** Tb 12:1, 5–15, 20

II. 2 Tim 4:1–8

Responsorial Psalm   **I.** Tb 13:2, 6efgh, 7, 8

II. Ps 71:8–9, 14–15ab, 16–17, 22

GOSPEL   Mk 12:38–44

☀ We are to preach the Word always and be faithful. We are not to alter it so that it's easier to take or make it what others want to hear, nor take the pieces we like, or use them to back up what we want to say. It is there to transform us, convert us, make us obedient, call us to deeper love, love of enemies, neighbor, to deeds of holiness. We are not to use it on others, but let it be used on us so that we image Jesus more clearly. Jesus is clear: the widow unknown to others who gave out of her very sustenance, her survival, is the one to observe not those who are flashy and public in what it means to be a believer. We are practicing to give our lives, not for public auditions.

☀ It is time for Raphael to reveal to Tobit and Tobias that he is the one who presented their prayers to the Lord and was commissioned by God to heal him, to bring Tobias to his wife. And he teaches them how to praise God—they who enters and serve before the Glory of the Lord. He tells them: A king's secret is prudent to keep, but the works of God are to be made known with due honor. We are to do the works of God, the works of mercy and to live with honor and bless God for all things. Do we live like these men and women of Tobit's time in exile, relying on God and in due time knowing how history is being played out under God's eyes and care?

Jesus warns of religion that is not practiced but played at, in ritual, clothes, and people who parade their piety for others' benefit. The widow who gives, even out of her sustenance to survive (like Tobit and his family) are the ones who worship truly. Jesus tells us to observe this way of worship and life, not what is false and shallow and self-serving.

TENTH WEEK IN ORDINARY TIME

Monday

FIRST READING   **I.** 2 Cor 1:1–7
                                          II. 1 K 17:1–6

Responsorial Psalm   **I.** Ps 34:2–3, 4–5, 6–7, 8–9
                      II. Ps 121:1bc–2, 3–4, 5–6, 7–8

GOSPEL   Mt 5:1–12

✺ Here is the core of Jesus' teaching on who is in the kingdom of heaven already—the poor and those persecuted for justice and the gospel's sake, and who will be in the kingdom one day: those who are mourning, the gentle (non-violent), those who hunger and thirst for justice; those who practice mercy and live with pure hearts and who make peace their single-hearted love. We are blessed when we live in this way, singled out and proclaimed to be God's own people. These are practices and one builds upon the other, beginning with the practice of the virtue of poverty—living with less so that others might live, in honor of God who cares for all…then we mourn so many suffering and become non-violent, living without harm to any other, ceaselessly striving for justice for all, forgiving of all others, including our enemies who need even more than forgiveness—mercy; and seeing who God truly is and loving all for God's sake and living as Jesus did, making peace through the blood of Eucharist and our sufferings bound to His own—and often we then know persecution and rejection because we are associated with Jesus our Teacher. Where are we now? How blessed are we? Are we in the kingdom even now?

✺ As we begin our ordinary grace-filled lives expressing worship and belief publicly we are given the foundations of what we are to become and practice as communities of Jesus. First, obedience (Elijah, the story of the power of the Word in weather, lives and history). And we learn the marks of a Christed one: poverty, lowly (nonviolent), hunger and thirst for justice/holiness; merciful; single-hearted, peacemaker and at times if we do these things well, persecuted for holiness' sake. And always we are to rejoice and be prophets of the truth, the Word of God to the world (in the tradition of Elijah, Jesus and those who have gone before us in faith).

Tuesday

FIRST READING	I. 2 Cor 1:18–22
	II. 1 K 17:7–16
Responsorial Psalm	I. Ps 119:129., 130, 131, 132, 133, 135
	II. Ps 4:2–3, 4–5, 7b–8
GOSPEL	Mt 5:13–16

✹ These readings for the week to come are the Sermon on the Mount, Jesus' new law of love and the Spirit of obedience and truth. Of course we obey the ten commandments and now we dig into them and come up with layers of truth that we must seek to incorporate into our very bodies and lives. We are to be salt: what flavors, heals—cauterizes wounds, cures for eating later, brings out other tastes and highlights, replaces nutrients in our system we lose through sweat and what holds together dung for fuel. Salt was in many places coin of the land. And we are light, boundless light in the darkness like a lighthouse on the edge of a rocky coast bringing direction, protection and warning to others, a beacon of hope and warmth, and welcome. And we are to be this for the glory of God so that others can know our Father and give him praise. This isn't something we do alone—all this demands that we belong to a community and this is our practice, our discipline and our life together. Are we good salt and light?

✹ Now a widow (and not an Israelites, but an outsider) provides for Elijah and they survive together on what God provides daily for them. She listened to his word, obeyed and trusted. And Jesus proclaims that we are to be salt for the world: taste, curing of food, medicine, essential for life/survival; it was once a form of currency. And we are to be light, all of us together shining on a hill, giving direction, vision, hope, guidance, so that in all we do, God is honored and others begin to catch glimpses of our God in our lives.

✷ Now we read the letter to the Corinthians, probably the largest of the early churches, about 3 groups of 50 people each, founded by Paul, Timothy and Silvanus. They preached Jesus as the Son of God—always Yes to God. And so we pray to the Father in the power of the Spirit, with Jesus, saying Amen. We are established with Christ in God. Do we live Yes always, or do we waffle a lot?

We are the salt of the earth, humble, close to the ground. Salt is used to add flavor, to cure and preserve, to add to dung to make fire burn longer and hotter. Are we flat? We are the light of the world, a city whose inhabitants reveal the light and the truth of God in Jesus. Do our lives together as Church in our country reveal God and draw others to praise God as Father of us all?

Wednesday

FIRST READING

I. 2 Cor 3:4–11
II. 1 K 18:20–39

Responsorial Psalm

I. Ps 99:5, 6, 7, 8, 9
II. Ps 16:1b–2ab, 4, 5ab, 8, 11

GOSPEL

Mt 5:17–19

✷ Jesus is both prophet and teacher and builds on the foundation of all that has been revealed by his Father before him, fulfilling and fleshing out the laws so that they sing with spirit and depth. We must honor the law, obey it and extend it—first beyond the borders of our family and kin out towards all peoples and situations and we must then—deepen our understanding of what it calls us to do, not limiting it to 'just this' or 'only that' and the bare bones of what is the lowest common denominator. We must teach by respect of the law and what it intends to do: bind a community together that reveals in their lives the presence of God among us, that covenants us to the Holy One and witnesses to all others the goodness and justice of our God that we profess to believe in. We must learn to love the practice of obedience and call one another to it.

✹ Elijah returns and conquers the prophets of Baal and the people return to God when they see the power of Yahweh consuming everything. The prayer of Elijah is heard on behalf of the people so that they will know who is God in Israel and be converted. Jesus speaks and lives in this tradition of the prophets: speaking the truth, teaching the law, and deepening it and extending its practice to all the world. The fullness of the law is Jesus' life, words, practice and presence for all the world. We are followers of a liberator, a lawgiver, a prophet and the Truth incarnate.

✹ The Corinthian church was founded in the ministry of the Spirit and a law of life, that reveals the glory of God, stronger than even Moses' face when it showed forth God's glory to the people after seeing God face to face on the mountain. Did the Corinthians show forth that glory of God and let it come shining through them? Do we? How?

Jesus teaches the law and the fullness of the law—the law suffused with the Spirit of life, of truth and justice for all. Will we be remembered as those who broke significant commands, even small ones or will we be remembered as those who kept the law, mindful of Jesus' new command: "love one another as I have loved you" which cannot be practiced without fulfilling the older law first?

Thursday

FIRST READING	I. 2 Cor 3:15—4:1, 3–6
	II. 1 K 18:41–46
Responsorial Psalm	I. Ps 85:9ab and 10, 11–12, 13–14
	II. Ps 65:10, 11, 12–13
GOSPEL	Mt 5:20–26

✹ Jesus is trying to stretch his followers' minds in imagining other ways to act—deeper into the sense and intent of laws and their practice in creative ways to obey: who, under any and all circumstances, defying old practices always keeping in mind the image of God that is at the root of our obedience and how our God sees, knows and treats all of us. So we kill each other long before we actually pull a trigger or stab one, with our tongues, plotting, thinking about revenge and stirring up and keeping alive grievances, fantasizing ways to humiliate another. And Jesus is clear: among his own—we are not allowed to let this happen, or escalate, but stop the offender immediately: no humiliating, no shaming, no insulting, name-calling, dehumanizing others. We are not even allowed to come to liturgy without first making sure that we are at peace with others—all others. (What would this mean to a nation at war?) We must seize upon the first failure and not allow it to become public, and involve more and more people. Otherwise, one day we will know justice ourselves from God.

✺ Elijah climbs to the heights of Carmel and tells his servant to look, (seven times) for what is coming and there is a tiny cloud afar off and then he runs for the cloud. God accompanies his people in a cloud by day (Exodus). Elijah as a prophet is called to be holy and to only obey the word of God. And Jesus tells us that our holiness must surpass that of the leaders of old. The law is not just to be obeyed outwardly, though we often don't even do that. We are not to kill, and not to kill in our hearts/mind/conversations either. We are not to presume to worship without being reconciled to everyone, otherwise we stand before God already judged.

✺ A veil covered Moses' face because the people could not bear such light, and a veil covers the understanding of the revelation of God and the law. But now in Jesus' Spirit there is freedom, light and the fullness of life and we are to be transformed into the very image and glory of God. Does the splendor of the gospel showing forth the glory of Christ show in our words, our works, our relationships and way of making holy the world? Or are we blinded by other realities and values? Do we preach ourselves or are we really servants of the glory of God shining on the face of Jesus?

Are we holy? Do we even obey the bare essentials of the law—do not murder? Have we grown into any level of obedience to that command—purifying ourselves of anger, hate, greed, contempt? Do we forgive or worship without even thinking to ask forgiveness individually and as a church/nation? Be reconciled or be judged by God!

Friday

FIRST READING   **I.** 2 Cor 4:7–15
                                        II. 1 K 19:9a, 11–16

Responsorial Psalm   **I.** Ps 116:10–11, 15–16, 17–18
                    II. Ps 27:7–8a, 8b–9abc, 13–14

GOSPEL   Mt 5:27–32

Jesus tells us to look at the root, the source of what we do, whether it is the beginnings of unfaithfulness or lust or greed or harm. He uses exaggerations to get us to see what it is we begin doing: how we use our senses and reactions without thinking, just going along with whatever triggers our behaviors. We are to live aware, conscious of our birthright as God's children and to both resist easy evil as well as work at the practices of goodness. And the law is for everyone: man and woman as equals. All human beings are more than capable of evil and of change—and goodness. We are to be diligent in self-examination so that our righteousness extends far beyond anything that is superficial or shallow. Do we examine our lives, our reactions to others and our behaviors with the eye of Jesus in the Sermon on the Mount? How would Jesus describe our daily lives?

Elijah looks for God in the usual places: the wind, the fire, the earthquake, the places of power but God is not there. God comes in a whisper of wind but Elijah has difficulty seeing/ receiving God that way, because he has disobeyed. He killed the prophets of Baal, and God did not tell him to do that. No longer is he to be prophet in Israel, he must look for another because of his decision to do what he was not commanded. And Jesus gives commands to us: they are old ones: no adultery, but now they are extended to all, men as well as women and they take on depth and intensity. We are to be serious about holiness and obedience not lethargic.

Saturday

FIRST READING   **I.** 2 Cor 5:14–21
Responsorial Psalm   **I.** Ps 103:1–2, 3–4, 9–10, 11–12
GOSPEL   Mt 5:33–37

Elijah finds Elisha and calls him out. He must follow him and leave all behind and so Elisha kisses his family goodbye and gives all he has to feed the people. He obeys. Jesus is attempting to make his disciples followers with the same intensity, integrity and passion for obedience to God's word and to being holy as he is and he goes for the heart of all matters: oaths, swearing and the use of words in religion. He is interested in what is far beyond lip service, what touches in at our cores where we are who we are and where we really stand before God and one another. Nothing less than all.

ELEVENTH WEEK IN ORDINARY TIME

Monday

FIRST READING   I. 2 Cor 6:1–10

II. 1 K 21:1–16

Responsorial Psalm   I. Ps 98:1, 2b, 3ab, 3cd–4

II. Ps 5:2–3ab, 4b–6a, 6b–7

GOSPEL   Mt 5:38–42

Here are hard sayings that go against everything in our violent societies. Before it was an eye for an eye and a tooth for a tooth (and nothing past that—even this was to militage against escalation of violence). Now we are not to oppose evil with evil but learn a new way of resisting without harm, resisting and making others see what it is they are doing and that they are doing it to other human beings, not vague notions of an enemy. To be slapped and to turn and look the person in the eye and offer the other cheek is to confront the other head on. To have something taken from you and then give more is to throw the other off-balance and to reveal that you are still who you are without what was taken. To be forced into slave labor and then to do what is not asked is to demand that the other see what they are doing and have a chance to back down. Jesus lived in occupied territory with the Roman army and these were common experiences for those oppressed—these are not easy ways to act, under duress, violence and might where people despise you. This is the practice, the discipline of Jesus—do we even respect it as teaching, let alone practice it individually and with others to hold us accountable?

Ahab once again sins by taking the vineyard of a poor man Naboth. It is all that he has, but he is abetted by Jezebel who does it for him, and has Naboth stoned to death. Then Ahab goes to take the vineyard for his own. Jesus tells us in the gospels about violence, condemning it outright: no murder, no violence, no harm to another. And then goes on to say that we must learn to live offering no violent resistance, no matter what is done to us. We must learn the way of one who resists as Jesus resists, with the truth and in the Spirit, use what surprises and takes others off guard, not like those who do not believe in Jesus.

❊ Do we avoid giving offense in our ministry? We are exhorted to live with patient endurance—listen to the litany of what Paul says is to be expected if you work with the grace of God for others! There are graces abounding as well: the Holy Spirit, the power and the truth of God, and the gift of rejoicing as we share all this bounty with others. Do we really live as though we have nothing, but everything is ours!?!

Jesus wants everything from us, not just the surface response to commands. We are to live as he did: no resistance to injury—we are to live without violence, without harm to others, no matter what is done to us. What does this mean? It means to look the one who harms us in the eye, and then turn and let them see what they have done by putting oneself vulnerably before them. What others' take, give them more so that they can see what they are doing. And live with generosity. How little we have learned—sadly!

Tuesday

FIRST READING   I. 2 Cor 8:1–9
II. 1 K 21:17–29

Responsorial Psalm   I. Ps 146:2, 5–6ab, 6c–7, 8–9a
II. Ps 51:3–4, 5–6, 11 and 16

GOSPEL   Mt 5:43–48

❊ The sermon and the beatitudes all lead to these last pieces. We are to love, not just our kin and country but we are to love our enemies and pray for those who persecute us so that we act like children of our Father. Love our enemies—that means first of all—do not kill them, attack them, demonize them, blame them for everything that is wrong in our lives and economies and treat them as deserving of anything we can subject them to—all self-righteously thinking we are Christians. Our Father lets the sun and rain fall on the just and the unjust—and that includes us, not always in the just category. We are to love, not just those who love us, or who are like us, but those we are afraid of, don't know and don't want to know and those who do harm (remembering that others look upon us in the same vein). We are children of the Father, with Jesus, like Jesus and we are to be righteous and holy like our God—same exhortation as the Jews in the earlier testament, but now, more specific and demanding so that we can't just pick and choose who we'll practice on. Look around the world is waiting for this kind of love that stops evil, does no harm to the other and invites enemies to be friends of God.

✺ Elijah is sent to deal justly with Ahab over the killing of Naboth (in greed for his vineyard). And Elijah is blunt, declaring that what Ahab has done stands crying out to God and that he will be punished justly for his sin of murder and greed. His line will be cut off as he cut off Naboth's life. He repents (surprise!) and the punishment passes to his son's reign.

God does justice for the poor. God forgives but there is justice and it belongs to God. And Jesus seeks to teach us that we must love everyone, even our enemies and pray for those who persecute us, and whom we fear. God lets everyone live, the just and unjust and we are to be like God, not like everyone else. We are to learn (and it is hard) the compassion we have known from God and practice it towards all. This is the new prophet's word.

✺ The early church of Macedonia had to deal with severe poverty, severe trials and yet they knew joy and generosity—they gave themselves to God and then gave just as fully of what they had to charity (a collection for the poor of the church). Paul is seeking to touch the hearts of the Corinthians so that they will be generous— since they are rich in every respect, it seems except charity. He's not ordering them, but testing them to be generous in return for the favor that has been given to them by the poor man Jesus crucified. How gracious and generous are we—not to our own, but to those far off and those who are in desperate need? Are we more like the Macedonians or the Corinthians?

Jesus is telling his disciples that it is not enough to help your own: family, blood relations, countrymen. We are to love everyone, starting with our enemies so that we might be like our Father who is so compassionate, merciful and generous. Are we trying to be like our God and Jesus or are our spirits shriveled and stingy?

Wednesday

FIRST READING	**I.** 2 Cor 9:6–11
	II. 2 K 2:1, 6–14
Responsorial Psalm	**I.** Ps 112:1bc–2, 3–4, 9
	II. Ps 31:20, 21, 24
GOSPEL	Mt 6:1–6, 16–18

We're supposed to be good, holy and righteous but we're not supposed to be showy about it or make sure that others know this is what we're doing and what we are. We are to be secretly generous to the poor giving them dignity and learning a bit of gratitude and humility ourselves. We are to be careful of the poor, aware of them and their need, but careful not to let ourselves become the center of what we do. Even when we pray, we are to make sure it's between God and ourselves, secretly letting the Spirit teach us in the silence of being alone before God. And when we fast, we are to look good, and work at it! Again our God loves the secrets between us and him, not displays that make whatever we do cheap and mock God. Our Father would love to give to us in secret, but we have to know how to give and how to receive in such anonymous and unknown ways.

Elijah must leave, but he leaves Elisha a double portion of spirit with his mantle (of justice and truth) and the power is passed from one prophet to another. Jesus is seeking to pass on his power of justice and truth too and his teaching is forthright. We are to practice our religion for God alone, to give alms in gratitude and to pray silently and alone; to fast and not make a show of religious ritual. God who is hidden sees all and we are seen truthfully before God and will be judged on our hearts and not just by what we appear to be in public.

Do we give according to how God has given to us? This question is posed in regards to money, resources, privilege, education, food, material possessions. To believe in God our Father is to give as Jesus gave. Could we be described as those who scattered abroad and gave to the poor, his justice endures forever—and that's from the earlier testament? Do we consistently show how thankful we are to our God or do we take so much for granted?

Jesus is intent on reminding us that it is our heart that must direct our actions, in giving alms, in praying, fasting and participating in ritual. What we do for show, for others' praise and to be thought well of, (or to take off our income tax returns) is not worth much to us and does little or nothing for our well being. We are supposed to do such things, hidden with Christ in God and know then, the response of God in Christ to us.

Thursday

FIRST READING	**I.** 2 Cor 11:1–11
	II. Sir 48:1–14
Responsorial Psalm	**I.** Ps 111:1b–2, 3–4, 7–8
	II. Ps 97:1–2, 3–4, 5–6, 7
GOSPEL	Mt 6:7–15

✺ And how are we to pray—in Jesus' words. Even repeating them teaches us priorities and catapults us into a world beyond our small experience and knowledge. What are we to pray for—first, the honor of God, God's will, God's kingdom and the way it comes upon our earth in us, as in heaven; others' foods and daily needs, forgiveness of others and endurance in the face of trials; but especially forgiveness—easing of others' debts, all small things really in the face of the enormous debt our God has released us from with such mercy. Our Father, make us those who are known for forgiveness, generosity towards others and mercy—for that is the only holiness you really want from us, along with the sharing of all that you have given to us among your children, our brothers and sisters most in need. It should take us years to ever get past the first words: Our Father, our God who holds every man and woman in the world with such care and tender regard, concerned personally what happens to every one of them, and what we do to all who make up our lives….. Amen.

✺ We hear of the power of Elijah, the force of the Word of God in his mouth, his fire and passion for God that could take down kings, bring the dead back to life, anointed kings and taken aloft into the whirlwind and to come again before the Prophet that is the Word of God made flesh among us. And we hear of Elisha who carried on that word and power among the people. But we have one beyond compare, the beloved Son of the Most High God, who teaches us to call God our Father and prays with Jesus for the kingdom of peace with justice, for the will of God for all life to flourish, for bread, for forgiveness and deliverance. But it all begins and ends in forgiveness, the deep face of God in Jesus.

✹ Paul is having trouble with the Corinthians. He has been supported by the poorer church of Macedonia so he can minister to and preach to those at Corinth. And they listen to anyone who comes along—easily seduced into other forms of belief/teaching. He pleads with them, telling him of what he has tried to do for them freely (the gift of other believers) and that he loves them. But they are stubborn and slow people.

Jesus teaches us the core of what we believe by teaching us to pray as he prays to God our Father. God's kingdom may come as it is in fullness, born of hope and freedom now. Daily bread, care for all today. And so trust day to day as we share what we have with others so all have as they need. Forgiveness as gracious and often as our Father forgives us. Know that we will be tried, and pray for courage to face it and go through it and pray for faithfulness now and at the end of our lives. It is simple—intent on God's will and way and our submission. Let us pray…

Friday

FIRST READING   **I.** 2 Cor 11:18, 21–30
       II. 2 K 11:1–4, 9–18, 20
Responsorial Psalm   **I.** Ps 34:2–3, 4–5, 6–7
       II. Ps 132:11, 12, 13–14, 17, 18
GOSPEL   Mt 6:19–23

✹ More pragmatics: don't store up things here where it has a very limited shelf life! Put it where it lasts forever—where might that be? For Jesus' disciples we know that before we can come and follow him, we must take our excess and give it to the poor and lay up treasure in heaven and then come back, empty and open to Jesus' presence. Where's our hearts and treasure—in the poor where it is somehow with God! Everything in us, and our lives is of one piece. We cannot separate out our prayer from our relationships or our prayer from our economic policies or politics. Our eye must be filled with light—our hearts and consciences and souls must be drenched in the light, the Word of Jesus. We must constantly stand in that light and let it expose us, shine through us and illuminate us and our works.

It seems that the Corinthian church had a lot of folk who were making sure that others knew of their gifts and importance to the church, so Paul boasts too—of his sufferings, persecution, on and on and on—to best anyone in their church who have had it easy. He's been too busy trying to preach the gospel to have any sort of distinctions like they are claiming in their house-church. And he tells them that he is affected by their weaknesses and scandals.

And Jesus warns us not to lay up treasure here on earth—we are to give treasure to the poor and so lay it up in heaven.. Where do we put our treasure—our money, excess, resources, time, love, reputation, privilege, hope for the future? Does the light dwell in us, and shine forth in our actions, our sharing, our looking upon others?

Saturday

FIRST READING   I. 2 Cor 12:1–10
                                              II. 2 Chr 24:17–25

Responsorial Psalm   I. Ps 34:8–9, 10–11, 12–13
               II. Ps 89:4–5, 29–30, 31–32, 33–34

GOSPEL   Mt 6:24–34

We must be single-hearted and pure and not split with divided hearts—trying to juggle serving God and serving the world and our personal gain and material status in society. In reality we disdain one or the other and love one or the other but you can't have or do both. We are to depend on and trust in God for our material needs (by trusting in the Body of Christ, the community that we are publicly baptized into) that as we care for the poor, others will attend to our needs when it is necessary. We must look at the earth itself and how all creation is intricately bound together—whether it is the birds or flowers and weeds of the fields. God knows our needs. Jesus was human like us and needed to be fed, clothed, cared for, reared and protected from violence as a child and was poor, living in occupied territory. We are to set our hearts on God's justice and shared mercies of necessities for others and peace upon the earth. Where are our hearts? Where are our energies, our worries, our monies, our connections and work?

✳ Paul goes on, about the visions and dreams he has been graced with, trying to shame them with their boasting. He has known extraordinary revelations and, along with these, he has known a thorn in the flesh that he cannot control, change or get rid of. This humbles him and keeps his pride in check. It frustrates him—he has no control of it and he begs for it to be taken from him. But he is told to rely on God's grace and live with his weakness so that the power of God might be upon him. Are we content with weakness? Paul had one thorn (I suspect he had quite a few)—and we all know some of ours. Do we let God's grace work with them and on them?

Do we serve—God alone or do we dally with many other masters: money, security, power, arrogance, prestige and reputation, possessions, independence, anxiety, national security and false patriotism that betrays our home in the kingdom of God here and now?

Do we seek holiness, ask for it, ask others to help us be holy and strive with others to obey the commands of Jesus? And if we do, do we let God take care of us, sometimes or most often through others? And do we return that favor for others?

TWELFTH WEEK IN ORDINARY TIME

Monday

FIRST READING   **I.** Gen 12:1–9

II. 2 K 17:5–8, 13–15a, 18

Responsorial Psalm   **I.** Ps 33:12–13, 18–19, 20 and 22

II. Ps 60:3, 4–5, 12–13

GOSPEL   Mt 7:1–5

More pragmatics: don't judge! Don't judge others harshly unless that's the way you want God to judge you! Don't judge others with a sliding standard of conduct that demands more of some then others, unless you want God to judge you that arbitrarily or in relation to others! And if we're so good at seeing the specks of evil and wrong in others—watch out, God will be the first to point out great long planks of wood that stick out of us all over the place. If we are interested in pointing out evil and naming it and making it a spectacle, then we had best begin with ourselves—there is plenty enough there without searching out others. How clearly do we see ourselves? We are so good at finding fault with others? Can we see that what we see in others, we can only see because it resides first in us? O God, in your mercy teach us to see with your eyes, both ourselves and others.

The Lord keeps warning his people through every prophet to listen and change their ways as they live in the midst of wars, lands being conquered by Assyria, and attacks. But they are stiff-necked and do not obey. They do not believe and ignore the covenant and God 'put them away out of his sight.' This is a fearful thing but brought on by the peoples' lives. This too is the God of Jesus. We are told about judgment, which all of us do regularly...that we will receive the verdict we lay on others. We are good at seeing others' evil and shortcomings but not so good at looking at ours. Time for us to change!

✳ Back to Genesis and our beginnings as a people who
believe and belong to Yahweh/God. Abram is sent forth to
another land with the blessings of God but he moves slowly and
picks up a lot along the way: possessions, slaves. In Abram's
worships and prayers as he travels, God gives him promises as
he journeys.

Jesus tells us how to live day to day, with the people around
us: don't judge others or what we lay as verdict on them, will
be our own. As we treat others, we will be treated. We are all
one in the Lord. If we are so quick to see what is evil in others,
what about the huge injustices, sin, evil and violence we do ourselves? If we are constantly intent on seeing evil in others, can
we even begin to see the goodness of God anywhere? It is time
we looked to ourselves, in Church and in the world.

Tuesday

FIRST READING   **I.** Gen 13:2, 5–18
                          II. 2 K 19:9b–11, 14–21, 31–35a, 36
Responsorial Psalm   **I.** Ps 15:2–3a, 3bc–4ab, 5
                          II. Ps 48:2–3ab, 3cd-4, 10–11
GOSPEL   Mt 7:6, 12–14

✳ These are sayings of Jesus, collected for use as wisdom in
all sorts of situations. Don't throw your pearls to the pigs—
remember the parable of the pearl of great price—once you've
found it don't just give it to anyone. Pigs eat anything and one
thing is as good as another and it all ends up as fodder and slops
and they are violent for very arbitrary reasons and reactions. Be
careful! Not everyone is overjoyed that the kingdom of justice
for the poor and peace on earth has been found! We are to begin
way back at the beginning with the law and the prophets as
starting point—and do to others what we'd have others do to us
in every circumstance. And enter through the narrow gate—that
leads to life. Enter through Jesus' word, through baptism and
community, through obedience to Jesus' teachings and sharing
our treasure with the poor. There are few who find the road—
have we actually found the road to life? Are we on it?

✹ History impinges on Israel and the king who has not repented prays for deliverance. But Isaiah sends word to the king that God has heard his prayer for now and that there will be a remnant that lives to honor God, but it is the zeal of the Lord that does this, not the king or his army. God shields the city for the sake of those who have been faithful in the past. Jesus too is pushing his disciples to be wary of the ways of the world and to keep the treasure he shares with them from those who would not appreciate it and destroy it. The way we are offered is through a narrow gate (Jesus and the cross) but it begins with treating others as you would be treated in those circumstances. We do live in history.

✹ Abram and Lot have acquired too much for the land to be able to sustain both of their clans (early ecology and biodiversity conservation) so they split up and move apart so that they can live in harmony. The Lord promises Abram the land for himself and his descendents and Abram builds an altar to the Lord in the land, mindful of the fact that it is the Lord's and given only as gift.

We continue to listen to Jesus' sermon on very practical matters to be lived daily. We live in a world and even a church where people are disrespectful of our beliefs and practices, our call to be just and care for the poor, love our enemies and be reconciled. Therefore, we must be wise and not share the depth of our understanding with those who do not appreciate it and mock it. There is violence and we must be aware as we act towards one another that others will not always agree with us or want our care and love. But we are encouraged to go together through the narrow gate. How do we live with each other in the groups that we belong to?

Wednesday

FIRST READING   I. Gen 15:1–12, 17–18
                      II. 2 K 22:8–13; 23:1–3
Responsorial Psalm   I. Ps 105:1–2, 3–4, 6–7, 8–9
                      II. Ps 119:33, 34, 35, 36, 37, 40
GOSPEL   Mt 7:15–20

✹ Watch out—don't be stupid. Listen to what people say, especially those who claim to know the word of God as prophets. Prophets are interested in three things: the honor of God and true worship; the care of the poor and the coming of justice and for a prophet all three things are actually one and the same—God is truly worshipped by caring for the poor and taking care of the poor brings justice and justice honors God. Do those who speak care about the helpless, the vulnerable, the poor, the victims of corporate and global economics, the victims of violence, war and hate, outsiders, label people and in groups condemn them to their 'fate' as deserving what they get? Even more what do they actually do? What actions do they take in their cause—do they produce the rotten fruit of anger, violence, meanness, exclusion, killing, war, racism—they shun them and be careful. They are known by their fruit and we, too are known by ours—forgiveness, hope, comfort, healing, reconciliation, atonement, love as our God has loved us.

The high priest and the king read the contents of the book of the law that was found in the temple so that all the people might listen and obey and the covenant is renewed (again). Again and again, we begin. We must look to our lives, our relationships, our churches and communities, our ways in the world and see what fruit we are bearing for others: thorns, prickly plants, decayed trees, rotten fruit? Or grapes, figs, good fruit and sound trees: life, that nourishes and sustains and brings joy? This is Ordinary Time and we have need of lots of time to learn the ways of the Lord.

God blesses Abram but Abram is impatient for a child—he interprets God's promises of descendants in terms of a blood line. God tells him to look at the stars for they will be those who come after him in faith. Abram has many questions about what he will have and he is instructed to make a covenant with Yahweh that is ancient, terrifying and primitive—this is a theophany, a revelation of God that is personal and yet bound to a people for the future. These are our roots.

Jesus tells us that we must be known by our deeds. We are no longer known by our blood ties, families, origins, nationalities, personalities but by what we do and say and who we align ourselves with in God's kingdom. You can tell a tree by its fruit—what have we been growing and offering to others (you can't eat your own fruit, only another's)?

Thursday

FIRST READING   **I.** Gen 16:1–12, 15–16 (or Gen 16:6b–12, 15–16)

                                             II. 2 K 24:8–17

Responsorial Psalm   **I.** Ps 106:1–2, 3–4, 4–5

                                   II. Ps 79:1b–2, 3–5, 8, 9

GOSPEL   Mt 7:21–29

Just because we cry out and pray to Jesus doesn't mean we're in the kingdom or know Jesus. What everything hinges on is obedience—putting Jesus' words into practice in our communities. Even if we do miracles and healings but we don't care for the poor, hunger for justice, live non-violently, pray secretly, integrate the Word of God into every action of our lives, and our words then we really don't know God and God doesn't claim us as his own possession. If we are to be wise and build our houses, individually, but more in communities on rock it must have the solid foundation of the Scriptures and the teachings of Jesus that we are to live and model our decisions and lives on and not just empty words, pious practice and holy things. People were utterly amazed at Jesus' teaching, power and authority—they were struck by the way he taught. Jesus, strike us and stun us into seeing you and your power and may we let it into our lives to transform us.

Sarai, Abram's wife is impatient for a child too and she takes matters into her own hands. He resorts to an ancient law and offers her slave (a gift from Abram to her in Egypt) to gain a child through her relations with him. Once Hagar, a black slave woman becomes pregnant, she knows the power that she has and Sarai is enraged, and ends up blaming Abram. Abram is no better than Sarai saying 'she's in your power, do to her whatever you please.' And Sarai is so abusive to her that Hagar runs from her. Not a pretty picture of our father in faith and his wife. These people were just like us, sadly though called to be the people of God. Do we act more like them in their abusiveness and wanting to make things happen under our power than in any response in faith?

We find that Hagar is our mother in faith. She sees God and is given a promise given to Abram. She is told to return. God hears her as surely as Sarai and Abram and cares for her and her descendents.

Our mother in faith is Hagar, the woman who is considered to be the mother of Islam and we share the same father in faith.

Jesus reminds us that all are welcomed into his kingdom but only those who actually practice what we believe, beyond the words and posturing will actually know the kingdom in their lives.

Friday

FIRST READING   **II.** Gen 17:1, 9–10, 15–22
Responsorial Psalm   **II.** Ps 128:1–2, 3, 4–5
GOSPEL   Mt 8:1–4

The city of Jerusalem is destroyed, the temple burned, the kings and their families executed and the people driven into exile, except for some of the poor who stay behind. The people turned from their covenant and God was with them, but He did not save them. The religion of Jesus is about living in the world, with its sufferings, illness, wars, politics and economics, and society. And yet lives an alternative of hope: healing, drawing those excluded in, welcoming and bringing life to all in circumstances of harm, misery, hunger and lack. It is not easy but it is the will of God for life for all. This is our life daily.

Saturday

FIRST READING   **I.** Gen 18:1–15
                                                II. Lam 2:2, 10–14, 18–19
Responsorial Psalm   **I.** Lk 1:46–47, 48–49, 50, 53, 54–55
                                    II. Ps 74:1b–2, 3–5, 6–7, 20–21
GOSPEL   Mt 8:5–17

Jesus heals the servant of a Roman centurion. The man's words have become part of our liturgy, immediately before we receive Eucharist: I am not worthy to have you under my roof. Just give an order and my boy will be healed—or liturgically as we pray: Lord, I am not worthy that you should come under my roof, only say the Word and my soul shall be healed. This man has faith based on experience of obedience and power in the military and he bows to Jesus' superior authority and power beyond his experience—over sickness and death. Do we, who repeat the prayer so often, live by this kind of faith, in obedience to the power of Jesus. Whose authority do we obey? By whose authority do we decide upon our moral choices? What do we do when our government or nation's authority and power are in opposition to our church's and our God's authority. O Lord, say the Word—the Word is Jesus, the Word made flesh, our God among us—heal us, strengthen us and save us from death.

This is the lamentation prayer of the prophets who were not heeded as history swallows up the temple, Jerusalem and the people who were not faithful. They cry to God for hope, for healing and call the people to pour out their hearts and change. How strong is our faith and hope in God? A Roman centurion comes to Jesus and says, "Command my servant to be healed." As a leader he knows the power of the word and he amazes Jesus with his faith. When was the last time we amazed Jesus with our obedience to his word and expression of faith in our deeds?

The Lord appears to Abraham in the form of three strangers. They are welcomed and cared for and fed. Guests are to be treated as Yahweh's presence and Abraham recognizes that these men are somehow Yahweh's power and messengers. Sarah and the servants prepare the meal. They ask where is Sarah, telling him that they will return about the same time next year and Sarah will have borne a child. But Sarah is old and is listening at the tent flap and makes fun of what they say, laughing at such a statement. She is caught and reprimanded for her lack of belief and in her fear, lies about her disbelief. This is the woman who sought to have her own child, in her own way.

Sarah cannot believe she will bear a child in her old age. In the presence of Jesus everything becomes possible. A centurion asks Jesus to cure his servant and his faith is amazing. An outsider, a Roman speaks about obedience, having been under discipline himself, recognizing Jesus' authority and his person as the power of healing and wholeness. Jesus is delighted and announces that this man is the image of who will be a believer in his community in the future. Jesus continues his healing of the sick as part of his mission. Jesus bore our infirmities and endured all our sufferings! How deep is our faith and do we practice it, or do we just laugh things off?

THIRTEENTH WEEK IN ORDINARY TIME

Monday

FIRST READING   **I.** Gen 18:16–33

                            II. Am 2:6–10, 13–16

Responsorial Psalm   **I.** Ps 103:1b–2, 3–4, 8–9, 10–11

           II. Ps 50:16bc–17, 18–19, 20–21, 22–23

GOSPEL   Mt 8:18–22

✺ Again, the crowds are all around Jesus. Their need is public and Jesus crosses over to the other shore and a teacher of the law surprisingly comes after Jesus saying "Master, I will follow you wherever you go." Jesus is realistic with him—this discipleship isn't an easy road. Jesus tells him that even foxes have lairs and the birds have nests but the Son of Man has nowhere to lay his head. Jesus has no earthly home—his home is rooted in his Father and he belongs to all the world—to all the crowds, massive numbers of people lost and looking for safety, security, sanctuary and those who follow him will know both all the world as home and no place really that is theirs alone. And the pressing demands and needs of others take precedence over family ties—not literally (one must bury their parents) but we must be sure that we don't look for any excuse to slip away from the crying needs of so many. Is Jesus really our Master and do we follow him everywhere?

✺ The Lord and Abraham set out for Sodom and God tells him what he is planning on doing. Abraham (our father in faith) bargains with God to save the city. First he pleads for a reprieve with 50, then 45, 30,20 and ends at 10 and the Lord accepts Abraham's plea. Who do we plead for and seek to save even though their evil is crying out to God? Will we ever be known for such care for total strangers and evildoers? (or remember that we are no different than them?)

Jesus is shadowed by crowds everywhere, all the time. A scribe approaches him and wants to be his follower. Jesus tries to tell him that it won't be easy—even the foxes have lairs and the birds of the air have nests, but the Son of Man, crucified, rejected and not welcomed in the world has nowhere to lay his head. But Jesus says to us: "Follow me." Will we?

Tuesday

FIRST READING	**I.** Gen 19:15–29
	II. Am 3:1–8; 4:11–12
Responsorial Psalm	**I.** Ps 26:2–3, 9–10, 11–12
	II. Ps 5:4b–6a, 6b–7, 8
GOSPEL	Mt 8:23–27

✸ Jesus gets into a boat with his disciples and exhausted falls asleep. But a storm arises and the disciples are terrified. And Jesus just sleeps. They have not learned to be in his presence, secure and safe no matter what happens. So they wake him. Jesus chides them (and us) "Why are you so afraid, you of little faith?" Even with him they don't know him or his power. He stops the storm, orders the wind and sea to obey him. Jesus is the Lord of creation, the Lord of Life, the Lord of all history and peoples. Our God is always mightier and stronger than anything in our small lives. We must remember to relate to Jesus as God, not just personally as if we were the only peoples in the world. Who is this man? Always more than anything we could perceive, know and understand. We must grow into an awareness of the awesomeness of our Lord.

✸ God is crying out in the voice of Amos that his people refuse to listen to him no matter what he does, or what happens to them. Even though he has favored them since the beginning it makes no difference. Now "prepare to meet your God, O Israel". This is the cry of every prophet in every age, including our own. Jesus is in the boat with his disciples and he sleeps. A storm comes up and they panic, grabbing at him. They still do not know whose presence they live in/with. We must remember the power of Jesus that dwells with us always. And we have no reason to be afraid.

Wednesday

FIRST READING   **I.** Gen 21:5, 8–20 a
                       II. Am 5:14–15, 21–24
Responsorial Psalm   **I.** Ps 34:7–8, 10–11, 12–13
           II. Ps 50:7, 8–9, 10–11, 12–13, 16bc–17
GOSPEL   Mt 8:28–34

We move back and forth between ancient prophets and Jesus. Amos demands simply seek good and not evil and you will live. Let justice prevail for that is the only worship God truly wants. And Jesus expels demons—what destroys life, and hinders the children of God from living holy lives. We too are possessed by such demons: money/greed, self-absorption, nationalism, security, self-esteem, materialism, individualism, racism, the list is endless. And when Jesus frees the men possessed the people of the neighborhood want him to leave the area. Freedom is a hard and wondrous way to live, not easy but what it means to be human.

Isaac is born and at the feast celebrating the child's weaning, Sarah decides that Hagar and Ishmael must be driven out (a sentence of death to die in the desert). Abraham does it, rationally knowing that God will take care of things—which he does. Hagar cries out to God and God comes to her, speaks with her and promises her what he promised to Abraham—that she would be the mother of a great nation. God opens her eyes and lets her find water and we are told "God was with the boy as he grew up'—replacing his father who had abandoned him. Hagar is our mother in faith and the mother of Islam.

Jesus expels demons who recognize him (interestingly in the gospels many of those who truly know who Jesus is are what we would label insane, demented, addicted, mentally ill and incapable of caring for themselves.) When Jesus frees the men, he sends their energy and sickness into the pigs and the people want no part of him—they beg him to go. Do we try to get rid of people we don't understand, fear or hate?

Thursday

FIRST READING   **I.** Gen 22:1b–19

           II. Am 7:10–17

Responsorial Psalm   **I.** Ps 115:1–2, 3–4, 5–6, 8–9

           II. Ps 19:8, 9, 10, 11

GOSPEL   Mt 9:1–8

Jesus comes home and a paralyzed man is brought to him and he sees the faith of the man's friends, his community and forgives him, telling him to have courage! Not what people were expecting at all. Some of the teachers of the law are horrified and consider Jesus' words insulting to God! And Jesus knows what they're thinking and calls them on it—they cannot rejoice in the forgiveness of others, so he says to them—is it easier to forgive another's sin, or to tell him to get up and walk? They don't answer—which is easier? Jesus commands the man to stand up, pick up his stretcher and go home! And the man does! He obeys the word of God. Forgiveness frees and liberates and sets on the way to community and life in God. The crowds are awed (but it never says that any of them follow Jesus.) Do we rejoice in the forgiveness of others? Do we live so as to bring others to Jesus for help and strength to walk again into life and live in freedom as the children of God? Or are we more concerned with specifics of doctrine than the liberation of so many people in need?

The country can't endure Amos' words. Even the priests and other prophets and the king tell him to 'get lost'. And when Jesus speaks words of courage, healing and forgiveness to a paralyzed man, those around him slander him and think ill of him, never for a moment rejoicing in the hope that he brings to those who suffer and those excluded from life in the community by their disease. But Jesus heals the man anyway, proclaiming the authority of the Son of Man to forgive and make whole in body and soul. Whose words cut us to the quick and want to get lost? Perhaps the Word is closer to us than we want it to be.

God tests Abraham. He has promised him land and a nation, peopled with his descendants and now asks for Isaac, his beloved child. Abraham obeys and takes Isaac to be sacrificed. God stays his hand—teaching Abraham and all nations that God does not want our children in sacrifice (or anyone's child) and that if we trust the Lord then, in the Lord's ways and time, his promises will be fulfilled. Abraham believed. Do we? What do we refuse to give over to God in our life?

Some friends of a paralyzed man bring him to Jesus, and Jesus forgives the man because of their faith. But others are furious at Jesus for forgiving the man—accepting him as he is—at the time of Jesus it was commonly thought that you suffered illness or paralysis because of sins that you or your family had committed. Jesus heals the man, pushing those who were heartless to the man's condition (and so many others) to examine themselves on whether healing or forgiveness is harder. What do you think?

Friday

FIRST READING	I. Gen 23:1–4, 19; 24:1–8, 62–67
	II. Am 8:4–6, 9–12
Responsorial Psalm	I. Ps 106:1b–2, 3–4a, 4b–5
	II. Ps 119:2, 10, 20, 30, 40, 131
GOSPEL	Mt 9:9–13

Jesus moves on from his home town where the teachers disdained his words and even his works that recognized the faith of friends, forgive a man and gave him a future life with his family. And he calls Matthew to be one of his disciples. In joy, Matthew invites Jesus and his disciples to dinner and Jesus sits at table with these public sinners and tax collectors—all those who publicly did not live up to the demands of the law, as it was selectively enforced and practiced and who were in collusion with Rome in small ways—just ordinary people, the majority of people who did not fall into the categories of scribes, lawyers, teachers, officials of religion, priests etc.—all the people with no authority. Jesus breaks the law that admonishes people to shun such people, exclude them from companionship and not even to deign to eat with them lest you get contaminated, and like them. Jesus is sharp with people who question his company—those he breaks bread with (Eucharist) and says that God wants mercy, not empty sacrifice and ritual. Who do we welcome at our tables and share the joy of our God with?

✴ This is the heart of Amos' message: those who trample on the poor and destroy the land and live without justice, it is time to repent or else—God will visit destruction on the land and they will know famine, both of bread and water. All this because they have a famine of the Word of God. And Jesus calls Matthew, a tax collector, someone notorious for their injustice and stealing from the people. Jesus has come for sinners, for those do live unjustly and selfishly. He is a doctor of mercy, careful of sinners, but resists those who are self-righteous. When Jesus the prophet looks at us, what does he see?

✴ Sarah dies and is buried and Abraham, a resident alien in that country buys a piece of property to bury her and to rest beside her when his time comes. He asks his servant to find his son Isaac a wife from his own kindred—a dying request. The servant sets it up. Isaac meets Rebekah and they eventually marry, bringing consolation and promise.

Jesus summons a tax collector to follow him—no one is exempt from the invitation to follow Jesus, no matter what we have been working at before we hear the Word of the Lord calling out to us. Others find fault with Jesus and he tells them and us that he hasn't come for anyone who thinks they are healthy or okay. But he has come for those who know they need forgiveness, healing and mercy. Do we admit to being in such need?

Saturday

FIRST READING   I. Gen 27:1–5, 15–29
                                                   II. Am 9:11–15
Responsorial Psalm   I. Ps 135:1–2, 3–4, 5–6
                                          II. Ps 85:9–10, 11–12, 13–14
GOSPEL   Mt 9:14–17

✴ Then John's disciples come to him and ask him why do the Pharisees fast on many occasions but Jesus' disciples don't? Jesus declares that he is the bridegroom and that while he is with them, they cannot fast because of the feast of his presence, but there will come a time when the disciples will fast because Jesus will be torn from them. Jesus tells them that he is something altogether new and unparalleled—you don't patch an old garment with new cloth or else the hole gets bigger and you don't put new wine in old skins or the freshness of the wine bursts the skins and everything is lost. Jesus' newness and freshness of life that will preserve life and those who bear that life. Are we aware of the presence of Jesus and live feasting on his presence? When do we fast? Are we living fresh lives since our baptism and celebrating Resurrection?

The other side of the prophet's rage is promise of hope and so, Amos' words are now of restoration, rebuilding, being raised up and harvest of plenty, of being at home in their lands. And Jesus seeks to tell his disciples that they are not to fast while he is with them: the bridegroom, who is the image of the wedding feast of peace, abiding justice and welcome for the poor. Jesus' kingdom is a new thing, more amazing than anything the prophets of old sang of—it is new wine, life and ways of living as God desires for all: abundant life, especially for those most lacking. Do we understand? Do we live with this promise shared with the least of our brothers and sisters?

Isaac is old and can't see. He tells his firstborn Esau to go hunting for him and bring him something and in return he will give him a blessing. Rebekah, whose favorite is Jacob, plots to have him go to his aged father and pass himself off as his older brother and so get the firstborn's birthright and blessing. (Our ancestors are a fine lot—no better than what you would find in soap operas). Jacob does pull it off, though one suspects that Isaac knew the deception and it is Jacob that goes off with the blessing/promise to Isaac and Abraham before him.

Jesus is caught in the throes of teaching his disciples while the Pharisees keep questioning what he does and says—why not fast like John's disciples? They have no idea who Jesus is and that while his presence is in the world, why would anyone fast? Jesus is a new thing, unimagined and his presence/person is so strong that it will pull on the old and stretch it out of shape. We have to be made new to be able to absorb Jesus' words and life.

FOURTEENTH WEEK IN ORDINARY TIME

Monday

FIRST READING   **I.** Gen 28:10–22

                                   II. Hos 2:16, 17c–18, 21–22

Responsorial Psalm   **I.** Ps 91:1–2, 3–4, 14–15ab

                         II. Ps 145:2–3, 4–5, 6–7, 8–9

GOSPEL   Mt 9:18–26

✹ A synagogue official begs Jesus to come and lay hands on his daughter who has died and bring her to life. (The Jews believed that you were not actually dead until 3 days had passed). And Jesus stood up (he had been sitting and teaching) and follows the man with his disciples. But on the way, a woman who has suffered from bleeding for 12 years comes up behind him and touches his cloak. Jesus turns, sees her and blesses her with courage and assures her she is saved (and cured). When they arrived Jesus tells the public mourners to get out—the girl is only sleeping, not dead and they laugh him to scorn. And when they are gone, he goes in and takes the girl by the hand and she stood up. Two women, a young girl about to come of age and a woman who has been shunned and excluded for as long as the girl has lived and been loved. Both are brought back to life and into the community again. Jesus follows behind anyone who seeks life at his hand and in his words and lets those in need take as well as gives to those who ask. Do we believe—on others' behalf? How do we beg life for from our God?

✹ Hosea is the prophet of return, of being lured back into the arms of God though we are wanderers and harlots intent on our own loves, ways and wants. God's word in Hosea is sad, longing, even wistful of what was when they were close in the desert and hopes for intimacy with his people again. God longs for our faithfulness and justice so that he can give us love and mercy in return. And Jesus wants to give even more, an intimacy that frees from death, life ever more abundant, healing from our diseases and social illnesses, how we feed on death and the suffering of others. God so longs for us to be near to him.

🔅 Jacob has fled from his brother as a thief and stops to rest at a shrine. He takes a stone from the shrine to use as a pillow and he dreams of a stairway to heaven with the Lord speaking to him as he did to his ancestors. He is promised the land anew. He sets up a memorial and promises God—though it is a promise laced with 'ifs'—that the Lord will be his God when he comes back safe to his father's house. Jacob has a lot to learn—as do all of us.
Jesus is asked to heal a synagogue elder's daughter and he goes to her. But a woman who is desperate after 12 years of pain, exclusion and humiliation moves in on him and reaches for the tassel of his cloak. (this was Jesus' tallit which he would pull over his head to pray in) Jesus senses her. His power touches her. She is healed and affirmed in public and goes to life rejoicing. Jesus continues and drives out the 'official' mourners and gives the girl back her life. God is always giving us life, hope, blessing, forgiveness, another chance, even at times healing us of what we have done and the effects of our evil. Do we go rejoicing?

Tuesday

FIRST READING	I. Gen 32:23–33
	II. Hos 8:4–7, 11–13
Responsorial Psalm	I. Ps 17:1b, 2–3, 6–7ab, 8b and 15
	II. Ps 115:3–4, 5–6, 7ab–8, 9–10
GOSPEL	Mt 9:32–38

🔅 Some people bring Jesus a dumb man, possessed by a demon (a disease that paralyzed him). The demon is driven out, the man speaks and the people are dumb-founded—speechless at what they see and hear Jesus doing, but people and leaders are divided over him. Jesus is an itinerant preacher and healer bringing good news, solace and drawing people back into community and giving them a life again through his touch and acceptance. The crowds are like sheep without a shepherd and Jesus is concerned that there will be many who will do his work and lay down their life for the sheep, and reap the harvest that is sown in the Word of Good News. People have no voice—they are paralyzed by fear, loss, pain—do we give them a voice and the courage by our presence to speak once again? Are we working in our Master's fields that are ripe for the harvest?

✴ There are so many other dead idols in Israel made of silver and gold, that only reap a whirlwind of destruction. God is only aware of their injustice and how they mock him. And they do not listen or heed any of the words/laws of God that are given to save and make his people human. Jesus is about the work of making people whole, more human and bringing life—healing a mute. He preaches and his presence brings life and many are loud in his praise, but there is no mention that people change, or follow Jesus. And yet Jesus is so filled with pity, compassion that he tends to everyone and mourns the lack of others to work with him.

✴ Much later in the story, before he meets his brother whom he had wronged so many years before, Jacob takes his wives (Rachel and Leah) and his children, and takes them across where they will be safe. He has prospered and his brothers as well. But before he meets Esau he wrestles all night with an angel (or his own soul/conscience) and his name is changed to Israel. He is blessed and marked by the struggle with God and he limps for the rest of his life. His name is his people—those who contend with the Divine and with human beings but prevail—it is in itself another promise.

Jesus is brought a man who is mute and tormented (frustrated and unable to communicate or relate to others). Jesus casts out the demon (what hinders the man from being human) and yet Jesus is accused of acting in the power of a demon himself. Jesus leaves and continues to heal, his heart wracked with pity for the crowds needs, weaknesses, lacks and hopes. They are prostrate with exhaustion (think of so many countries today: Sudan, Palestine, Iraq, those hit by the tsunami, by war and other calamities). And Jesus begs us to be a laborer to go and bring in his harvest and be moved to pity by the suffering all around us.

Wednesday

FIRST READING   I. Gen 41:55–57; 42:5–7, 17–24
      II. Hos 10:1–3, 7–8, 12
Responsorial Psalm   I. Ps 33:2–3, 10–11, 18–19
      II. Ps 105:2–3, 4–5, 6–7
GOSPEL   Mt 10:1–7

Jesus calls his disciples by name and gives them authority to continue his work—to drive out what is unclean and unjust and to heal people of disease and sickness that hinders them from life as children of God. They are named but collectively called the twelve—a community of disciples, not to be seen primarily as individuals and they are given a mission to their own people first—the lost sheep—the masses and majority of people in Israel (which are the same in number and need in every nation). The message is clear—the kingdom, long awaited of the prophets that called for justice and remembrance of the poor as true worship of the God of the covenant is close at hand, near to them—near to them in his own presence and person. Do we belong to a community (at least twelve) and are we known for being good news?

Israel is lush and fertile and yet they do not give thanks to Yahweh. Instead they build edifices to other gods and their hearts are false. Sow justice, reap piety, seek the Lord so that God will rain justice down upon you instead of ruin. No one listens to Hosea. Jesus chooses the twelve to follow him more closely but one of those will betray him, and all the others will run in fear. Yet they are sent on mission to go after the lost sheep of the house of Israel. Today, do we look for the lost sheep of the church, those who have left our community because of scandals, injustice and mistreatment? Are we prophets of the new reign/power of God that is justice, forgiveness and freedom for all children of God.

Joseph sold by his brothers into slavery, has risen to the highest position under Pharaoh in Egypt. Famine strikes, but Joseph has planned ahead and there is grain. All come to him for food and his own brothers are in the long lines of those who come begging. He confines them and then tests them—letting all of them go, bringing food to their father and country but insisting that they return with their youngest brother. The brothers see this as retribution for what they did to Joseph but Joseph weeps for them in his heart. But he does not reveal himself to them. They must live with and take responsibility for what they have done—even though God has been his protector and guide all the time.

Jesus chooses 12 disciples in honor of the 12 tribes of Israel— all will be invited to become part of his new community/household of faith. They are named, with bits of detail given to some and the last described as the one who betrayed him. They are to go to sheep of the house of Israel first and to declare that God's reign is at hand. Today in your community are there 12 who are the leaders (woman included) along with bits and pieces of information about them? And there are always those who betray—often it is our own name that is found there.

Thursday

FIRST READING   **I.** Gen 44:18–21, 23–29; 45:1–5
       II. Hos 11:1–4, 8–9

Responsorial Psalm   **I.** Ps 105:16–17, 18–19, 20–21
       II. Ps 80:2ac and 3b, 15–16

GOSPEL   Mt 10:7–15

They are to do the work that Jesus does: heal, bring back from the dead, cleanse lepers and drive out evil. They have been given this power as gift and they have experienced this gift in their own lives. They are to bring peace, the teachings of Jesus. If they aren't welcomed or listened to, they are to shake the dust and leave, and leave the judgment of that place to God, as of old. They are to rely on those who are open to the Word of God and stay in that place. They are to offer a blessing of peace and wait to see if it is received or if it is returned to them. This is the community of the road; the disciples that are sent out ahead to bring hope and a taste of the justice and peace that Jesus will bring more completely. This is our vocation, no matter what our lifestyle choices are—to be good news, as the disciples of Jesus. Where do we need to go today and this year?

✳ God treats Israel so tenderly, like a child, fostering them, kissing and feeding them. Our God is tender, pitying us, overwhelmed with love for us even though he is also the Holy One among us, the God of justice and judgment. Why can we not see that? And Jesus is that love in flesh and blood, traveling everywhere and sending his disciples out to do his work: heal, bring hope, preach good news to the poor, do justice. And we are told to travel light, go without violence or protection, rely on the goodness of others, share the richness of the Word and accept what is shared with us. And when rejected, leave, but leave the judgment of others to God. It is the way of the missionary/prophet/preacher.

✳ It is Judah who approaches Joseph to beg on behalf of his aged father. He has returned without the youngest because Isaac his father couldn't bear to part with him after losing Joseph, his only other child by Rachel, his first beloved. Joseph listens and cannot bear it anymore. He cries out, has all the servants removed and reveals himself to his brothers. He forgives them and tells them that God has worked through what they have done to bring him to this place where he could help them and their people. Joseph's young dreams have become reality in Egypt through history, even of sin/violence and injustice for Joseph who has learned faithfulness and forgiveness. He sums up his life and what they did saying: "It was really for the sake of saving lives that God sent me here ahead of you." Do we believe that God works through all of history, the events of our lives and the world to save lives—if only we persevere in the fact of all that happens, remain faithful and forgive everyone all that they have done to us? Truly this is a glimpse of the reign of God to come—but extended now to the whole world, not just to those we are bound to by blood/family.?

Friday

FIRST READING   I. Gen 46:1–7, 28–30
II. Hos 14:2–10

Responsorial Psalm   I. Ps 37:3–4, 18–19, 27–28, 39–40
II. Ps 51:3–4, 8–9, 12–13, 14 and 17

GOSPEL   Mt 10:16–23

✺ Jesus gives the disciples lessons in survival in the world and uses animals that are known for certain behaviors to instill in them the need to be realistic in dealing with evil and people who are resistant to the Gospel, and hostile to it, and to them. They go as sheep among wolves, vulnerable and without violence so they must be clever like snakes! They have to know how to constantly change and be converted to the Word and know when to hide and where (community). Be on guard because you will be hauled into court for the truth telling and people will condemn them and punish them because of Jesus but they are to witness to them and to those who are not believers. Trust and hang onto the Spirit of the Father who will give the words and even when families turn against you, hang on for a dearer life, hang onto God.

✺ The people are told to return, to beg pity, to ask forgiveness and they are assured of God's mercy, love that is freely given and they will know freshness of life, blossoming times and splendor of the land and their lives. If only they would walk in justice! But they stumble instead. And Jesus sends us out like sheep among wolves telling us that we must learn to walk in the world with the Spirit that is wise, nonviolent, peaceful, clever and innocent. We are to rely on God's word, even when our own treat us harshly. We are to follow in Jesus' footsteps bringing hope and the gospel of the poor to all, until the Son of Man comes in justice/judgment. Time to be faithful.

✺ Israel (Jacob), Joseph's father goes to Beer-sheba and prays. He again has a vision and God calls out to him. He answers and God reveals himself to him, with the ancient promises given again but saying that he will return one day. So all of Israel moved to Egypt. Joseph meets his father again at long last in Goshen (where Moses will come from) and they fall into each others arms. Israel feels that he can now die, because his beloved son, first born of Rachel is alive. The promise will continue, but it is Joseph who has learned so much about his father and the God of his ancestors—Yahweh. What have we learned from our families and elders about who God is—and have we learned forgiveness no matter what?

Jesus warns us that if we preach the gospel we will have much to contend with in the world of politics, military and economic powers. We will be jailed, beaten, flogged and brought to trial (which was the experience of the church for the first 300+ years). But he gives us the Spirit to abide with us, gives us words, courage and strength to stand up for what we believe—the Father will be speaking through us. There will be violence, in families, just like there was of old with Joseph and his brothers. But if we are faithful then we will escape death—the death of the soul, the heart and the spirit. And our God, the Son of Man will one day come and there will be vindication—there will be a reckoning of justice, and yet there will also be forgiveness.

Saturday

FIRST READING
Responsorial Psalm
GOSPEL

I. Gen 49:29–32; 50:15–26
II. Is 6:1–8
I. Ps 105:1–2, 3–4, 6–7
II. Ps 93:1ab, 1cd–2, 5
Mt 10:24–33

✺ Jesus describes the community of disciples as those hounded from one town to the next, one synagogue to the next, in all of Israel—just as he has traveled all throughout Israel, seeking who is lost, and preaching to anyone who is open to his Word. And the student will be like the master—and they (we) should be glad to be like our teacher, who was maligned and rejected. But have no fear for there will be a day of reckoning and truth-telling and all will be revealed. Now, even in dark corners and hard times—preach what we have been told and cry out for justice, for the poor, for hope, for liberation and freedom as the beloved children of God. Do we live and struggle for truth in communities of discipleship and reach out beyond our small churches and parishes to bring the Word that speaks of justice and forgiveness, love of enemies and concern for the least? Are we like our Master at all?

✺ Now we meet Isaiah, the only one who wanted to be a prophet, who says: Here I am, Lord, send me! He sees the awesome power of God and he sees his own unworthiness and is purged in the fire of God. This Isaiah will be persecuted terribly, his name is the suffering servant of Yahweh. And Jesus warns us that we will be persecuted, hounded, and treated as he, our Master, was treated. But we are to proclaim the Word in the light and reveal all that has been uncovered for us and trust that God lays claim to every hair on our heads. Be afraid of nothing! Know our worth with God and let all know God owns us.

✳ Jacob charges his sons to bury him, alongside Abraham/ Sarah/Isaac and Rebekah and Leah. And when he is buried, Joseph's brothers once again worry if he will turn on them and pay them back for trying to kill him. They put words of Jacob into their mouths and ask Joseph to forgive them—as though they were their father's words. Joseph weeps and promises to provide for them and their children telling them that God works through what they have done and that he does not hold their jealousy and murderous intent against them! Joseph dies old in Egypt telling his descendants that God will lead them out of Egypt to the land that he promised their fathers before them. Joseph amazingly knew the forgiveness of God and extended it to those of his own who still did not understand that Joseph's life was bound to God and that there is nothing that cannot be redeemed and blessed by God, and evil's consequences eased.

We, as Jesus' disciples must learn that we are cared for that way and that our Father tends to us every moment. Nothing happens without God's witness and God holds our worth precious.

FIFTEENTH WEEK IN ORDINARY TIME

Monday

FIRST READING   **I.** Ex 1:8–14, 22
II. Is 1:10–17
Responsorial Psalm   **I.** Ps 124:1b–3, 4–6, 7–8
II. Ps 50:8–9, 16bc–17, 21 and 23
GOSPEL   Mt 10:34—11:1

Jesus' words startle us—do you think I've come to establish peace on the earth—no, I come with a sword. Jesus is not about the peace that reigns superficially in families, nations and groups—his life is about the sword of the Word of God that separates and divides people—into those who believe and are laid bare and those who refuse and resist change and conversion. Families will be torn apart over and divided over Jesus and his Good News. We must choose and stick to those choices in times of losing loved ones, being rejected, welcomed by strangers who take us in, and cared for by those who recognize the goodness we bring in the Gospel and when we are not spoken to by those we love most. And Jesus goes to the town of each of the disciples to preach—at home, where it's the hardest. Are we families of the Word or do we settle for an uneasy, shallow peace like the world says we should?

Hear the Word! God is appalled by the sacrifices, rites and prayers that are constant drones and festivals that only serve to cover up the blood of the innocent and the misery they inflict upon the poor. Wash yourselves clean, redress wrongs and take care of the least. It is the same always. And Jesus the prophet warns that he is here as a sign of contention, that his presence divides families, marriages and communities. We are ordered to chose where our primary allegiance lies: with others or with God in Jesus. We are to carry the cross and welcome the stranger and the poor. Are we prophets and holy people or are we wishy-washy trying to please all sorts of people in our life at the same time we claim that it is God that owns us?

✹ After several generations, a new king in Egypt knows nothing of Joseph and is afraid of the numbers of Hebrews. He enslaves them, oppresses them, puts them to hard labor to build his cities. Life is bitter for them and then he decrees the death of all the boys born to the Hebrews, to stave off their descendants rising in power by sheer force of numbers. The girls can live—for they are slaves, concubines and they can bear children, to strengthen the race of the Egyptians. Exodus begins in such misery as the stepping stone to freedom.

Jesus warns his disciples that he is not here to bring peace, contentment and harmony in families. No he is here to bring a sword—it is the double edged sword of the truth of the Word of God. And it will tear families, marriages, children and parents apart. But this is part of the cross of Christ. Our life lies not only in our families, but more specifically in the stranger, the one in need, the beggar who asks and in the welcome we give to all, especially the prophet and even the drink of cool water to the lowly. Do we live our Christian life and discipleship outside our family circle or do we use harmony in our family to avoid obeying the call to welcome the prophet, the stranger, outcast and to care for the poorest.

Tuesday

FIRST READING	**I.** Ex 2:1–15a
	II. Is 7:1–9
Responsorial Psalm	**I.** Ps 69:3, 14, 30–31, 33–34
	II. Ps 48:2–3, 3–4, 5–6, 7–8
GOSPEL	Mt 11:20–24

✹ Jesus acts as the prophet he is: denouncing the cities for their refusal to be converted even when he has done marvelous things in their midst for them to see and take heart from. He compares them to the ancient cities of sin that were cursed by the prophets. He goes after the cities where there are schools of learning and theology though they do not practice and turn to the Gospel. And Capernaum where he settled after being rejected in Nazareth he compares to Sodom, destroyed in Genesis. How would Jesus judge our cities: Manila, New York, London, Mexico City, Tokyo, Jakarta, Nairobi, Lima….how would we fare as those who have heard the Gospel yet do we repent and take God's word to heart?

✳ Unless your faith is firm, you shall not be firm. In ancient Israel, the destiny of Israel as a nation is closely tied to its adherence to the covenant. When they ignore justice and God, then they are overrun by others. Decade after decade, each generation fails and must be called back to obedience. Jesus' way is that of reproach too. Where he does the most work, healing, bringing hope, no one responds. They want the miracles not conversion, not even Jesus' presence. And there will be justice and judgment. There will be us as well, who have had the Word, the Eucharist and the Spirit

✳ A child is born, and hidden for three months, then his sister puts him in a basket and floats him down river to the Pharaoh's daughter to find and makes sure that once he is found, she provides his own mother to wet nurse the child. He is Moses—drawn from the waters. Moses grows up and sees the slavery of his own people and witnesses one of the Egyptians striking a slave. He reacts in anger and kills him and buries him in the sand. He then tries to stop two of his own people from fighting and they reject him, revealing that they know that he has killed an Egyptian. Moses flees from Egypt, it is known that he is Hebrew on the decree of the Pharaoh. And he settles in the land of Midian. This is a short rendering of the birth of the liberator and the lawgiver of Israel who will fulfill the promises of God.

Jesus preaches repentance, change, transformation of life from town to town. And some do not listen at all. Jesus reproaches them for refusing to obey his words. Today, if Jesus visited our town/city would we hear reproaches for refusing to be converted, after having given so much?

Wednesday

FIRST READING   **I.** Ex 3:1–6, 9–12

II. Is 10:5–7, 13–16

Responsorial Psalm   **I.** Ps 103:1b–2, 3–4, 6–7

II. Ps 94:5–6, 7–8, 9–10, 14–15

GOSPEL   Mt 11:25–27

And after cursing cities, Jesus turns and prays aloud to his Father, praising him for the wisdom that he gives so freely to the uneducated, the poor and those who struggle to survive among those who are learned and clever but not compassionate, just or truthful. And Jesus declares that the Father has entrusted everything to him and no one knows the Son except the Father—none of his disciples really, no one who argues with him—no one. And no one knows the Father except the Son and anyone that the Son chooses to reveal him to. Staggering words that should bring us up short. Do we know the Father? Do we know Jesus? Are we among the poor, the powerless, the unimportant of the world who learn most easily the wisdom of God? Do we let the poor teach us this incredible knowledge of God?

Now the prophet cries out the justice of God against Assyria that is intent on destroying Israel. Assyria is a saw, a rod, a staff, but it is God that wields it. It can do nothing by itself. God knows what Assyria intends, but God will bring fire not glory to them. This is the God of old, centuries before Jesus. And Jesus brings a wisdom and a knowledge of God that is of lowliness, service, the care of the most lacking and vulnerable. God is human in Jesus and Jesus sides with the bottom, with those who are always the victims: the murdered, despoiled by nations and the poor. And no one knows this God but Jesus and who he chooses to reveal him to. Do we know this God of Jesus at all?

Moses, a shepherd tending the sheep, sees a burning bush and climbs the mountain. The bush burns but is not consumed. As he approaches it, God calls out to him. God reveals himself to him, and Moses is afraid. But God tells him that he has heard the cry of the Israelites in their oppression and that it is Moses that he is sending to lead them out. Moses is told in his insecurity and fear that God will be with him and that one day all the people will worship on this mountains. God is the God of creation and life, the God of the promises to Moses' and the Israelites,' the God of freedom, of pity and human dignity. Moses is sent to set the people free.

Jesus prays to his Father and reveals that only the least, the poorest, those without power on earth, like children in his time, and now the children of God are the only ones who know God's ways. Only Jesus knows our Father, but chooses to reveal him—all that we know of God the Father is the gracious gift of the Word, the Son. Do we pray for this knowledge and wisdom?

Thursday

FIRST READING	I. Ex 3:13–20
	II. Is 26:7–9, 12, 16–19
Responsorial Psalm	I. Ps 105:1 and 5, 8–9, 24–25, 26–27
	II. 102:13–14, 15, 16ab–18, 19–21
GOSPEL	Mt 11:28–30

And Jesus continues to pray, now drawing us into his prayer, letting us see his heart and the truth of who he is—Come to me, if you work hard for the honor of the Father, the coming of justice, the preaching of the gospel, the care of the least and carry the burden of the gospel, your small share of it—come for refreshment in Jesus' word and presence. Take up Jesus yoke: the yoke of being in community together so that we can do the work of God that we cannot begin to do alone. Take up the yoke of the cross, that Jesus was tied to, the yoke that stretched his arms out so that his body was in the sign of the cross. Take up the yoke where we put our arms on each others' shoulders and learn to dance into resurrection. Here in community, in work, in suffering and death and resurrection we will learn of Jesus—learn the Jesus that the Father knows—the Jesus that is meek (non-violent) gentle, careful of others, and humble, truly bowed before God and this is the rest, the being held in God that we need.

Isaiah yearns for God in the night and for time with the earth. Its people will learn justice, and God will mete out peace to us. It is God who gives birth to us and it is a hard labor of love, that brings the dew of light and everlasting life. And this is Jesus' prayer to those who are weary and find life burdensome. Our God in Jesus refreshes us. We are given the yoke (for mission and work, the yoke of the cross and the yoke that draws us into the dance of resurrection). Our God is humble, gentle (non-violent) and if we are yoked to Jesus then our burdens are made light and we know that being bound to God is life beyond imagining.

✹ Moses asks God's name. It is "I AM" who sends me to you. This is the God of the past, the present and the future. This is the God who sends and cares about people and their dignity and life. This is the God who is personal and wants a people for himself. This is all the God of all that is. This is the God of all the nations, Egypt included even it they do not know him. Moses is to go to the elders of the Hebrews and ask for 3 days in the desert so that they may worship their God: "I AM" He is told that Egypt will resist and they will know God by power/might and force and will let the people go. This is our ancient history, the foundation of freedom and the beginning of being made into the people of God.

This God "I AM" says to us: "Come to me you who are burdened." The yoke we bear is the cross of Christ, the yoke of community that works together for the kingdom of God on earth and the yoke of joy that is given to us to refresh us and help us as we journey to fullness of life that is the freedom of the children of God.

Friday

FIRST READING   **I.** Ex 11:10—12:14

                II. Is 38:1–6, 21–22, 7–8

Responsorial Psalm   **I.** Ps 116:12–13, 15, 16, 17–18

            II. Is 38:10, 11, 12abcd, 16

GOSPEL   Mt 12:1–8

✹ Jesus is attacked for letting his disciples break the kernels of wheat to eat the grain, on the Sabbath, when they are hungry. And Jesus knows his history and scriptures, reminding the Pharisees of a time when David and his men went into the temple and ate the bread offered to God because they were hungry! And he reminds them that the priests break the law on the Sabbath but they're not guilty! And Jesus proclaims that he is greater than the Temple and that it is mercy not sacrifice that God demands from us. The Son of Man, Jesus is the Lord of the Sabbath and the law is given not for the sake of God, but for the sake of human beings. We are not to use the law to go after the innocent as they will do, in killing Jesus and condemning the innocent but the law is to be used to turn our hearts and make us more compassionate of those in need and more obedient to the heart of the law which makes us holy like our God.

Hezekiah is dying and prays fiercely. Isaiah is sent to him with words of healing—adding 15 years to his life, promising to rescue the city from Assyria, to be the shield of Israel. Even a sign is given by God's kindness. And the sign we have been given is God in human flesh in the person of Jesus who walks the earth, and worships God wholeheartedly, and reinterrupts Scriptures and history to promote life, freedom of the children of God and say again that God only wants mercy not sacrifice. This is the word and power of the Son of Man, Jesus crucified and risen from the dead. Do we hear and take Jesus' words and deeds to heart in our lives?

Egypt does not want to let the slaves go. Moses and Aaron teach the people the ritual of Passover with each family or group sharing a lamb and taking its blood to smear their doorposts with its blood. At night, they are to stand and eat the lamb with bitter herbs and unleavened bread. They will eat and leave in haste once the angel of death passes over them, striking the first born of Egypt. And finally Pharoah will let them go. This is the memorial of Passover, the central liturgy of the Jewish people, the promise of fullness of life in Jerusalem. It is the ritual and the passover experience that Jesus' own life and death and resurrection brings to reality and the experience of all people in Easter, baptism and eucharist.

Jesus lives this mystery of the Passover and the Sabbath deeply and it is for the freedom and liberation of all peoples. David took the bread from the sanctuary to feed his men and Jesus will take his life and his body to feed the hungry people. What God wants, and has ever wanted is freedom for all, mercy for all and life for all. These words of the Son of Man will be a part of what sets in motion Jesus' own Passover and our being saved from death, from sin and slavery.

Saturday

FIRST READING   **I.** Ex 12:37–42

II. Mic 2:1–5

Responsorial Psalm   **I.** Ps 136:1 and 23–24, 10–12, 13–15

II. Ps 10:1–2, 3–4, 7–8, 14

GOSPEL   Mt 12:14–21

Jesus' words and teaching infuriate the teachers of the law and they plot to kill him. But he leaves, stays on the move, continuing to preach and to heal those who come to him. The words of Isaiah the suffering servant of Yahweh are proven true about Jesus—the Spirit is upon him and he announces judgment to the nations. He is careful of the weak (the bruised reed) and those struggling to survive and live with dignity (smoldering wick) and he does not shout or argue (he speaks plainly what is just and true). Jesus' very presence is justice in the world and it will be given as gift and righteousness to all the nations. The religious leaders of his own people found him threatening and refused to listen to his Word and yet he continued to preach. There are most probably pieces of Jesus' teaching that we don't want to hear because we don't want to change—either our idea of who God is, or our behaviors and the ways we treat others—yet the Word stands to convict us.

Finally the Israelites are allowed to leave Egypt after sojourning there for 430 years. The night of vigil, is the Passover and the Lord leads them out of slavery, fear and bondage on the journey into the desert they will form them into a people, and then God will bring them to the land promised to their ancestors. Egypt is any place of bondage and the Israelites are to hold this vigil throughout every generation. It is their reason for living, their hope and their meaning in the world.

Groups within Judaism seek to destroy Jesus and yet he continues what he was born to do—preach the Word, set people free and bring justice to the nations. He does not cry out and contend but he is careful that the bruised reed is not crushed and the smoldering wick is not quenched. This is our God of life, our God of no violence, our God of compassion, our God sent to us—Beloved Son who is our hope and our Passover and our peace.

SIXTEENTH WEEK IN ORDINARY TIME

Monday

FIRST READING   **I.** Ex 14:5–18

                                         II. Mic 6:1–4, 6–8

Responsorial Psalm   **I.** Ex 15:1bc–2, 3–4, 5–6

                 II. Ps 50:5–6, 8–9, 16bc–17, 21 and 23

GOSPEL   Mt 12:38–42

℣ Now the teachers of the law want a sign from Jesus and he refers to them as an evil and unfaithful people wanting signs. But there will be a sign: the sign of Jonah, swallowed by the whale and spit forth onto land to preach again. The Son of Man will be buried in the earth for three days and will come forth again to life. The Son of Man is a judgment figure from the Book of Daniel who will come in glory to judge the nations justly and when the day comes, the people of Nineveh will condemn this generation because it did not recognize the Son of Man and repent. Have we recognized the Son of Man, the Crucified One who stands in solidarity with the poor, the victimized, those destroyed by violent systems of injustice as the one who will judge us individually and as nations? Will Nineveh rise up and condemn us?

℣ God cries out his plea against us even to the mountains. He has brought us out of bondage and set us free, accompanying us always and giving us prophets and leaders: Moses, Aaron and Miriam. And yet all God wants from us is three-fold faithfulness. We are to "do justice, love tenderly and walk humbly with our God." Jesus is being plagued by the leaders for a sign even though he obeys Micah's command publicly so that all can see and hear. He does justice for the afflicted, loves/pities crowds and walks humbly before God. And Jesus calls them to judgment—even the people of Nineveh repented at Jonah's words and he is greater by far than Jonah, than Solomon, and no sign will be given except the sign of Jonah in the whale. The sign of the cross and resurrection—that is our sign.

✺ The people leave and Pharaoh realizes what he has lost. He summons his chariots/warriors and goes after them. The people are terrified and cry out against Moses, but he pulls them all to the Red Sea and tells them not to fear, and that God will give them victory. He stretches out his arm/staff over the waters and they part so that the people can cross dry land to the other side. The Egyptians pursue them into the waters and the waters close over them. The glory of the Lord is in the life of his people. They know that he is the Lord. This is the God "I AM" that the people know in days past.

But Jesus does not operate like the God of power/might/glory and force. There will be no signs and no great displays, especially for people who do not believe. The only sign will be the sign of Jonah—Jesus buried in the tomb for 3 days before he is raised by his Father from the dead. God "I AM" will reveal the wisdom of the cross and resurrection and we have been given to know this wisdom—do we worship and bend before I AM in our lives?

Tuesday

FIRST READING   **I.** Ex 14:21—15:1
          II. Mic 7:14–15, 18–20

Responsorial Psalm   **I.** Ex 15:8–9, 10 and 12, 17
          II. Ps 85:2–4, 5–6, 7–8

GOSPEL   Mt 12:46–50

✺ This short piece of Scripture lays the foundation for church and Jesus' community. His family comes looking for him: his mother and brothers and he does not go out to them. He stays with the disciples and declares: "Whoever does the will of my Father in heaven is for me brother, sister and mother." We have never really taken these words of Jesus to heart. Intimacy and closeness in Jesus' circle is not based on blood ties, marriage or family, but it is based on belief and practice of the Word and the will of God in the community that calls God, Our Father and treats the whole human community as brother and sister. For believers, water is thicker than blood (the water of baptism) and the only blood that binds us together is the Blood of Christ, drawing us especially close to those who suffer as he did. Are we brother, sister and mother to Jesus!

✹ James: a close relative of Jesus, head of the Jerusalem church, the first of the disciples to be killed, brother of young John. He, like all of us, carried the treasure of the gospel, the presence of Jesus' Spirit within him, an earthen vessel. He was persecuted and died, but had carried the dying and rising of Christ with him from his encounter with Jesus the Risen Lord and lived, staking his life on the fullness of resurrection that would be shared with him. His mother asked for a place in glory and Jesus' asked him if he could drink of the cup that would be offered to him. He said yes, without realizing it would be his death for the sake of the Son of Man. What do we ask for and what is Jesus offering us?

✹ The sea divides with the force of a mighty wind and the people pass through. The Egyptians follow and the glance of God casts the waters back into their course. Israel is saved and the obstinacy of the Egyptians proved to be their destruction. The people sing the glory of God, in awe and praise. Are we obstinate? Are we fearful like the people? Or do we stand in the face of danger/violence/war and proclaim the power and presence of God with his people and cry out to others not to be afraid but to see how God works in all things?

The new people of God is not based on blood ties, marriage or nationality. The new community of the Word of the Lord that obeys the Father is born of Jesus' life/death and resurrection in the Spirit. We pass over/through the waters and know the awe and mystery of being born in water and Spirit. We are born to be mother, brother, sister to Jesus and each other, closer than any ancient bonding.

Wednesday

FIRST READING
I. Ex 16:1–5, 9–15
II. Jer 1:1, 4–10

Responsorial Psalm
I. Ps 78:18–19, 23–24, 25–26, 27–28
II. Ps 71:1–2, 3–4a, 5–6ab, 15 and 17

GOSPEL
Mt 13:1–9

✹ Jesus sits in a boat (on water) and tells them a story about a farmer sowing seed. The seed falls on the path, eaten by birds, on hard ground with a thin layer of soil that grabs at the seed but has no staying power in changes of weather; falls among thistles by the side of field and road and grows but choked and finally in the field. There is a harvest—different levels of growth and amount of grain: one hundred, sixty, thirty fold. If you have ears, hear! We've heard it so many times—but are we the field. The Word of God has been sown in us year after year and what is our harvest of justice, of peace, of hope and life for the poor, of truth and integrity. The Word is for the world and others that need it, for food, for survival and basic necessities for all—are we anywhere in the category of one hundred fold? Is there a harvest of justice in our world at all where 85% of the world goes to bed at night? Or has the seed fallen on hard ground?

Thursday

FIRST READING	I. Ex 19:1–2, 9–11, 16–20b
	II. Jer 2:1–3, 7–8, 12–13
Responsorial Psalm	I. Dn 3:52, 53, 54, 55, 56
	II. Ps 36:6–7, 8–9, 10–11
GOSPEL	Mt 13:10–17

The disciples are at a loss to know why Jesus keeps telling parables. A parable lets everyone hear what they need— and the point where they resist or pull back is the point where conversion begins for them. Parables are multi-layered. Every time you hear on, if you changed the last time you heard it, then you will hear something else. If you haven't changed, not only will you only hear it the same, but you will not be taken or captured by its power to transform, and reveal the truth. A parable doesn't let anyone off the hook. It's a story that carries a great weight of mystery and secrets, hiding as much as it uncovers. But if you are not open to the storyteller—to Jesus— and to the fact that you might be wrong and could use a bit of change, you can't understand it at all. Jesus is angered that people are listening to him, being healed and yet they are not choosing to follow him—the parable is Jesus' way of still teaching and touching the heart of those who are open, but at the same time, keeping the pearl of great price out of the clutches of those who do not appreciate it. We are blessed—we have all of Jesus' parables, and Jesus himself. Do we keep being changed so that the stories of Jesus come true in us and the world?

✴ The word comes to us: "I remember the devotion of your youth and how you loved me…" and yet we have discarded and ruined our relationship with God. We are a people, a nation, church, leaders that have forsaken God, the source of living waters. And Jesus speaks to us in parables because we are closed to his words and invitation. Parables force the listeners to assume that they know nothing and that all they thought was so, isn't so. You can only begin to understand a parable if you admit you know nothing and that your heart is closed, set against change and have no intention of changing. There has to be a break in one's heart and mind to hear and begin to understand. Jesus is frustrated with the closed-heartedness of those who hear him. Does he feel the same way about us after all this time?

Friday

FIRST READING	I. Ex 20:1–17
	II. Jer 3:14–17
Responsorial Psalm	I. Ps 19:8, 9, 10, 11
	II. Jer 31:10, 11–12abcd, 13
GOSPEL	Mt 13:18–23

✴ Return, rebellious children. God wants to take us back and make us know again his presence among us, so strongly that other nations will gather to honor the God of Israel and we will no longer walk in hard-hearted wickedness. The patience of God is extraordinary. And Jesus tells the tale of the sower and the seed. Potent and powerful is the seed but it can fall on hard ground, make no roots, be easily taken over by weeds and briars, or make it into a field. Ah! Even then, 100, 60, 30 fold yield. What about us—any 100 fold yield in the field of our communities, parishes. Has the seed of the Word even made it into the ground?

✴ The people arrive at Sinai and the commandments are delivered to them. We know them as the 10 commandments, the Decalogue. The first three are directed towards our worship of God alone and as a people. The fourth is directed towards family responsibilities—the bridge between God and our neighbors, the people of God (for Jews). And the last six are directed towards our fellow human beings. They are for laying the basic foundation of life together for those in covenant with Yahweh the God of the Israelites.

For us, these are already assumed and we are given the Word of the Lord. The seed that is the wisdom/knowledge of God in Jesus, the relationship given to us in baptism to the Father, with Jesus in the power of the Spirit, is seeded in us. We can receive it as hard as a path; as rocky shallow ground that eats it up and then cannot sustain any roots or with sun and rain; or we can receive it all mixed up with all the other things in our life: the desires for money, security, power, independence, reputation, etc. and it will get choked to death. Or we can be part of the field, the community and within our community we can bring forth life 100, 60 or 30 fold so that others know the fruit of our belief in God. The Word of the Lord is the new commandment and we are to obey it as the foundation of our lives together.

Saturday

FIRST READING I. Ex 24:3–8
II. Jer 7:1–11
Responsorial Psalm I. Ps 50:1b–2, 5–6, 14–15
II. Ps 84:3, 4, 5–6a and 8a, 11
GOSPEL Mt 13:24–30

❋ Again we hear of the seed sown in a field—the Word of God preached in a community. And realistically we find ourselves in a field with people who do not believe and some who claim to, but don't practice according to the word. And we're stuck together until judgment. We are to grow into wheat for the harvest: food for the hungry, justice and peace for the earth. As the parables turn, they impinge on one another. It's hard to remain faithful in a field with others—community, that is also peopled by those who resist or fight those who do believe, yet alone those on the fringes, a seed fallen here and there in clumps of thorns, on the path, stolen away. And some fields produce great harvests every year, others don't. And it is every year—the liturgical cycle where we come around to being harvested at the end of ordinary time and realize that we will be judged, separated out and our lives will be seen either as bread for the weary and hope for the discouraged, or those that contributed to the violence and evil of the world. Are we even in a community that struggles with the Word together year after year?

✳ Moses returns to the people and they promise obedience to Yahweh. They ritually accept the will of the Lord, and become his people as Moses pours blood over altar. Then he reads the book of the covenant to the people and they ritually accept all that is written there. Then he sprinkles the blood remaining blood on the people. They have shared the blood of the sacrifice—it is the people (not the holocausts/bulls, etc.) that God wants as his own, in obedience.

Jesus tells the parable of a man planting good seed in his field and his enemy plants weeds. They grow together and the question is, "Do you weed out the field?" Jesus says no, let them grow together and at harvest—when each bears fruit from their seeding and life, there will be the reckoning and separation. Are we weeds or wheat? What are we reaping from what has been seeded in us by the Word of God all these years?

SEVENTEENTH WEEK IN ORDINARY TIME

Monday

FIRST READING

Responsorial Psalm

GOSPEL

I. Ex 32:15–24, 30–34
II. Jer 13:1–11
I. Ps 106:19–20, 21–22, 23
II. Dt 32:18–19, 20, 21
Mt 13:31–35

✺ Jeremiah tries to get the attention of the people in a bizarre fashion, burying a loincloth, letting it rot in the ground and digging it up again and using it to describe Judah and Jerusalem. Hardly flattering! God wants his people to cling to him, but they tear themselves away from him. Jesus tells the parable of the mustard seed, tiniest of all that becomes a bush, a small tree that harbors and protects all the birds that no one cares about. And the story of yeast buried in dough that rises and feeds a multitude. We are to cling to God and be refuge for the lost and forgotten and feed the hungry. And we are to rejoice that we are given the wisdom hidden since creation!

✺ Moses comes down with the tablets of the law and they heard the outcry in the camp—the people worshipping the golden calf they made, drinking and dancing and committing acts of sexual degeneration that were part of pagan rituals. He breaks the tablets of the law. He destroys the calf and reduces it to powder which he makes the people drink and they get sick. Aaron is chastised for making the idol and he blames it on the people. All have sinned gravely and he goes back to the Lord to make atonement for their evil. Moses offers his life for the peoples' lives. Moses is sent back to lead the people and God will punish in his own time those who sinned.

Jesus tells the parable of the mustard seed, miniscule yet tough. Once it grows, it is unstoppable, moving into every cranny, taking over everything. And the birds love it—they come and nest and hide from those that would kill them. This is God's word and God's kingdom/community. It shelters the least and once it is loose, its freedom and power go everywhere. Yeast buried in flour—a huge amount that will feed the world in its hunger is another image of Jesus buried and risen and an image of all of us buried with Christ in God. It is hard work but the dough rises and we will all rise in Christ. Who are we protecting and feeding?

Tuesday

FIRST READING	**I.** Ex 33:7–11; 34:5b–9, 28
	II. Jer 14:17–22
Responsorial Psalm	**I.** Ps 103:6–7, 8–9, 10–11, 12–13
	II. Ps 79:8, 9, 11 and 13
GOSPEL	Mt 13:36–43

The prophet (and God) weeps over the destruction of the people. They were warned repeatedly and to no avail. Has God cast them off completely? Finally the people see what their wickedness has brought upon them. Jeremiah pleads for God's mercy once again for them. And Jesus tells his disciples inner meanings that they cannot understand because they are closed to his words. He, the Son of Man, the suffering servant is the sower and the seed is the Word of God and all too often once it is sown, there are those who are intent on destroying it, sowing dissension and injustice into the field. But there will be a judgment on all and there will be a reckoning and weeding out. We are to heed what Jesus says

Moses and the people worship at the tent where the glory of the Lord comes to rest in a cloud. The people stand at the entrance to their tents and worship while Moses speaks to God. He begs God to come along in his company. And even though the people are stiff-necked, he begs for pardon for them all and asks God to still receive them as his people. And after the peoples' worship of the idol, Moses stays with God for 40 days, fasting and praying and fashioning another set of tablets of the law. Always it is about the mercy and kindness, patience and God's love for his people as against the peoples' unfaithfulness and lack of awe or fear of God.

The disciples seek out Jesus apart from the crowds and ask him for explanations for his parables. He speaks of the Word that he preaches, the good news of God's presence and power in the kingdom of justice and peace that he brings to them and how there is much else that is sown with the gospel—hatred, jealousy, bitterness, refusal to forgive, exclusion, lack of care for the poor—weeds in abundance. They are to grow together and at the end there will be judgment and recompense, each according to their deeds. There will be those who gave up their faith, those who affected others' faith and weakened them/harmed them and there will be those who shine like the sun in the Father's kingdom. Where shall we be found—is the seed alive and growing in us?

Wednesday

FIRST READING   I. Ex 34:29–35
                                                II. Jer 15:10, 16–21
Responsorial Psalm   I. Ps 99:5, 6, 7, 9
                                          II. Ps 59:2–3, 4, 10–11, 17, 18
GOSPEL   Mt 13:44–46

Again the stories of finding, rejoicing, selling all and buying and the one that is a bit different: seeking, finding, rejoicing, selling all and buying. The treasure hidden in the field comes to the one without him looking for it (does it stumble upon it, walking through the field, or is he working in the field; it is sticking out and he happens to see it?) And the other consciously, actively spends time looking for it. There is the found (treasure) and being found (the man is found by the treasure). There is the hidden brought to light and buried again—mysteries! And always there is joy, unbounding that drives one to sell everything to have the treasure. We have the treasure! What are we doing with it? The word, the kingdom of Good News to the poor, our relationships to Our Father, with Jesus in the Spirit (for starters). Where is our joy? Why aren't we selling everything to lay claim to it, or letting it claim us for God? "Keep this treasure (light) burning in your hearts until you bring it to the judgment of the kingdom."
—baptismal ritual.

✹ Jeremiah is distraught, near despairing, wishing he had not been born, because of what he sees and what the Lord demands that he say to the people. God tells him that he is with him no matter and will deliver him from the violent. God is his strength. And the parable tells us that God is our strength, our treasure, wealth, everything. Once we find it than we must rejoice exceedingly and give everything for it. It is as though we found a pearl beyond price but we must have it—the relationship with the Father that Jesus has in the Spirit and the presence of that revealed as justice for all, in abiding peace. Do we rejoice? Have we sold anything to own the treasure and the field it is hidden in?

✹ Moses comes down with the tablets and his face is so radiant from being in the presence of God that the people are afraid and can't bear to look at him. He tells them what the Lord had spoken to him, and then he veils his face. He would remove the veil before God and put it back on whenever he would return to the people. Are our faces radiant? We who have known God in Jesus, in baptism, eucharist, the Word, the Spirit, the sacraments, one another? What does God tell us to share with others?

Jesus tells us that the kingdom is a treasure buried in a field that a man finds—buries it again! Then he rejoices and goes and sells everything to have it. Or it is a pearl of great price that once found causes great joy and everything is given to have that pearl. Do we look for God's will, God's ways, God's face in everyone with such passion and diligence? Are we willing to give up everything for this relationship with the Father that Jesus offers us? And do we live with great joy?

Thursday

FIRST READING   I. Ex 40:16–21, 34–38

         II. Jer 18:1–6

Responsorial Psalm   I. Ps 84:3, 4, 5–6a, 8a and 11

         II. Ps 146:1–2, 3–4, 5–6ab

GOSPEL   Mt 13:47–53

✹ Now the stories are found in water. A huge fishing net let down into the sea and it is dragged through the waters, collecting fish—and all sorts of stuff. Then it's sort, keep and throw away time. It's hard work, dragging anything and everyone in to the net—the circle of the kingdom so that they know it's in their world! And nets can't be dragged in alone, you need a lot of help from your friends—and it daily work—again, fish is food for the hungry. And fish, of course, is the sign of the Christians: ICTHUS, the letters for Jesus Christ, Son of God, Savior. We're called to be disciples, fisherfolk and haul it all in—from the past, everywhere, every culture, peoples, places and keep what is good and ditch the rest. It's an art to knowing what to keep and not be too quick to throw away what is useful, or beautiful and just worth having. Been fishing with your community lately? What have you caught? Or maybe more to the point: has a community ever dragged you in? If not—better look for folks who will sit down with you and comb through the Word of God.

✹ Jeremiah is sent to a potter to watch him throw a pot on the wheel. Often it turns out badly and he takes it from the wheel and begins again. This is God with his people; we are clay in his hand and God is trying to make us into something pleasing. Jesus tells stories of people, now caught in a dragnet…with all sorts of other debris as well. Time for sorting and judging, keeping and throwing away. And a good disciple is one who can go into a storeroom and take what is good and leave the rest. We are to learn how to sort, discard and take up what is essential. Justice, forgiveness, mercy, truthfulness, faithfulness.

✹ Moses builds the ark of the covenant, and puts the tablets of the law inside. And the cloud that had accompanied them through the desert comes to settle over it—the Lord fills the dwelling place. When the cloud rises, the Israelites move forward on their journey and at night the cloud was filled with fire. This is the presence of the Lord Yahweh with the people. They move together at the sign from God. It seems helpful to be a builder if you're a leader—symbols that people can see/relate to. We still have this presence of the Lord, but it is the crucified and risen One among us.

Jesus speaks of the parable of the dragnet, of God's kingdom of justice and peace being dragged through the waters and picking up everything. One day the sorting and separating will come but for now even the waters of baptism pick up everything in its wake. And it is like the head of the household that goes into the storeroom and knows to take out, as needed what is old and what is new (this is traditionally thought to be Matthew's description of himself and what he is doing in his gospel to help the new church as it separates from the Jewish nation). What is old that needs to be kept and what is new that needs to be incorporated in your Church?

Friday

FIRST READING   I. Lev 23:1, 4–11, 15–16, 27, 34b–37
II. Jer 26:1–9

Responsorial Psalm   I. Ps 81:3–4, 5–6, 10–11ab
II. Ps 69:5, 8–10, 14

GOSPEL   Mt 13:54–58

The Lord teaches Moses and Moses in turn teaches the people how to order their time partially according to the seasons, but more so according to the remembrance of what they have known in their experience with God—the Passover and the Sabbath rest. These feasts are times to gather, to offer sacrifice, to stand before the Lord, to be thankful and to become more a people that belongs to God alone. They put work and survival in perspective, teaching the people that it is more important to live aware of God than just to live. Do we remember to stop, gather and share with each other in the presence of God?

Jesus seeks to teach in his own place and the people reject him, thinking they know who he is and where he has come from—he is 'altogether too much for them'. And Jesus says aloud that no prophet is accepted in his own place. In Matthew's gospel, Jesus is The prophet of God, the new Moses, lawgiver and liberator of the people, the new Passover into life—not in a place but in relationships everywhere. And it is too much for them to accept. What do we refuse to accept about Jesus, the Word of God that we find in the Scriptures?

Jeremiah preaches the harsh word of judgment and the coming destruction if the people do not change. And the priests, prophets and people resist, grab hold of him and are intent on killing him. The Word is spoken and it provokes a response: for life or for death. It's our choice too. Jesus preaches in his hometown and most reject him out of hand—they know him, who does he think he is? And Jesus responds saying that he is a prophet and will know no honor in his own place. Do we listen to Jesus as a prophet, like Jeremiah, Amos, Hosea, Isaiah, seeking to turn us back to the intensity of belief and practice, to convert us or do we think we know him and do nothing?

Saturday

FIRST READING   **I.** Lev 25:1, 8–17
                       II. Jer 26:11–16, 24

Responsorial Psalm   **I.** Ps 67:2–3, 5, 7–8
                 II. Ps 69:15–16, 30–31, 33–34

GOSPEL   Mt 14:1–12

John the Baptist has been executed—beheaded at a dinner party to please his brothers' wife who he had taken as his own, after murdering his brother. Herod had long wanted to kill John but was afraid of the people who saw John as a prophet. When his wife and his step-daughter trick him into killing John he is displeased but he kills him nonetheless. The voice in the wilderness crying out for conversion, for hope and justice, for repentance is stilled forever but his voice and soul echo in the world. There is no way to silence the Word of God. Then Herod hears of Jesus' teaching and works and in fear, believes it is John returning to haunt him and terrify him. John's body is claimed by his disciples and after they bury him, they bring the news to Jesus. How did Jesus react? Grief, anger, sorrow, such stupidity of evil and violence! The one who went before his face is gone—now he sets his face towards Jerusalem of the prophets. Do we listen to our prophets today?

The leaders demand Jeremiah's death for his words against the nation/people and Jeremiah repeats the words of God, saying that he is in God's hands, and they must repent. But if they kill him, they will bring his innocent blood on their hands. The people side with Jeremiah, but not the leaders and Jeremiah finds protection. And Jesus has to cope with Herod who has killed John the Baptist, who thinks that Jesus is John come back to haunt him. When John is killed, his followers come and tell Jesus. Jesus now lives in the shadow of death, knowing that he too walks in the way of the prophets.

✷ Moses is taught to celebrate the Day of Atonement, which begins with a trumpet blast to summon the people. The fiftieth year is the year of the Lord and liberty is proclaimed to all the inhabitants (not only Jews). It is the jubilee year. There is to be no work, no sowing, harvesting of the earth and its trees or vines. The land is redistributed to the people so the people are urged to be honest in their dealings, in the buying and selling of their crops in every year so at the jubilee year each family can repurchase what they have lost or sold at a fair price. This is the year that people must depend on God's bounty and share with one another. It allows the land and the trees to rest (good ecology) and visibly reminds the people that we are all inter-related—all that God the Creator has made and sustains, as he sustains us.

Herod has John the Baptist killed. He had him imprisoned because he personally decried Herod's behavior as a Jew/King by killing his brother and marrying his wife Herodias. She hated him and sought an opportunity to have him killed—it comes at her birthday party when her daughter dances for him and he promises her anything. Her mother tells her to ask for John's head on a platter. And so the one who went before the Lord to prepare his way, the voice crying out in the wilderness who sought to bring out those in darkness, dies in chains in a dark prison and is beheaded as a reward for pleasing a king. John's fate is the fate of every prophet, as it will be Jesus' own. Evil resists the gospel of God in service to its own message of power, arrogance and violence.

EIGHTEENTH WEEK IN ORDINARY TIME

Monday

FIRST READING   **I.** Num 11:4b–15
       II. Jer 28:1–17

Responsorial Psalm   **I.** Ps 81:12–13, 14–15, 16–17
       II. Ps 119:29, 43, 79, 80, 95, 102

GOSPEL   Mt 14:13–21

The disciples are sent off in the boat, and Jesus goes off to pray. But the boat is rocked by waves and wind against it. Terrified by the storm first, then they are terrified by Jesus coming to them on the water. But his words: "Courage! Don't be afraid. It's me!" causes Peter to climb out and come towards Jesus. Initially elated, the waves rise and Peter gives in to his fear and cries out "Lord, save me!" And he is grasped by the hand and chided—for his doubt, even as he could still see Jesus right in front of him. This is the story of most Christians' lives: rocked by circumstances and events, terrified of God's presence, encouraged by the words of God and then we initially rush forward to be overcome again in doubt, letting our fears control us. When will we learn to lean on and lean into the presence of our God in word and strength?

Hananiah the prophet preaches what the king and people want to hear, takes the wooden yoke Jeremiah wears as symbol of what will happen to the people and breaks it. But Jeremiah cries out that now the yoke is forged of iron and that the false prophet raised false hopes in the people and he will die within the year. We forget often that Jesus lives in the shadow of Herod and Rome, and that most of what he says and does is in response to death. Now John the Baptist is dead and the people are scattered and fearful so Jesus feeds them with words of hope and bread together, knowing he too will know the fate of the prophets before him.

Tuesday

FIRST READING   **I.** Num 12:1–13

II. Jer 30:1–2, 12–15, 18–22

Responsorial Psalm   **I.** Ps 51:3–4, 5–6ab, 6cd–7, 12–13

II. Ps 102:16–18, 19–21, 29 and 22–23

GOSPEL   Mt 14:22–36

Israel is wounded and there is no one to attend to their sores or plead their cause, but the Lord wants to restore them so that they will live and rejoice and sing once again. God wants still to be their God alone. Jesus has fed the people and goes off to the mountain to pray while his disciples get into the boat and head out on the lake. A storm comes up and they panic. Jesus knows of their fear and comes to them walking on water and Peter braves the storm to come to Jesus. But it only takes a moment and he's sinking because he stopped looking to Jesus. Jesus saves him and pulls him out. And continues saving people—bringing them hope, life, courage, healing. If only they could touch his cloak!

Miriam and Aaron speak against Moses. They are jealous of how God treats Moses and want a share in his power. The three are summoned and God defends his treatment of Moses. Miriam becomes a leper when God departs (it seems that it is she who instigates the complaint) and Aaron begs Moses. Moses prays for her healing. The power of God is God's choice and there is nothing anyone can do but accept it. Our ancestors quarreled and fought, were petty and narrow-minded, and did all the same things that we do. You would think that we would learn, but every generation, every family and every person must learn for themselves. The stories are told to help us see what is happening among us.

We are to rely on Jesus, the presence of God with us, in each of us, he is closer than he was with Moses or any of the ancients. We are not to be afraid, but to draw ever closer to Jesus in every situation, especially when we are in trouble, and distraught. Do we really believe that Jesus is the Son of the Most High God?

Wednesday

FIRST READING   **I.** Num 13:1–2, 25—14:1, 26a–29a, 34–35
      II. Jer 31:1–7

Responsorial Psalm   **I.** Ps 106:6–7ab, 13–14, 21–22, 23
      II. Jer 31:10, 11–12, 13

GOSPEL   Mt 15:21–28

❉ Jesus leaves his own place and go out to the cities. He is being rejected by his own: both leaders and people and his own disciples are having trouble with what's happening. A Canaanite woman (the original dwellers in the land) cries out to him, shadowing him to help her daughter. And Jesus ignores her. The disciples want him to shut her up. They are in foreign territory among gentiles and the last thing they want is a scene. But the woman is relentless and no matter what Jesus says or does, she responds and comes back at him—and he is delighted and amazed. She gets what she needs—her daughter's healing and Jesus gets what he needs—recognition that he belongs to the whole world, not just Israel. It is the turning point of Matthew's gospel—Jesus turns towards the world.

❉ God has loved us with an age-old love and is always restoring us, bringing us back to serve him and be a light to other nations. This time it is a remnant that is delivered. It is the same in ordinary time with us, year after year, needing to hear the cries and stories of the prophets of old and the prophet/God Jesus. Usually it is outsiders who believe when we take Jesus for granted or ignore him, or reject something he teaches. A Canaanite woman pleads on behalf of her child and amazes Jesus in her need—she take anything he gives, leftovers, what is thrown to the dogs, what others who claim to believe in God don't want. Who do we plead for? Do we look for leftovers, anything from the hand of God?

❉ They are approaching Canaan and it is time to send out scouts to reconnoiter the land before they enter—since it is already occupied. It is as Moses described—a land flowing with milk and honey. But the report disheartens the people—and it doesn't help that some of the men exaggerate what it will be like to enter the land while so many others are already living there. The people wail and the Lord God hears them. Because of their constant grumbling and lack of faith they will stay in the desert 40 years for the 40 days they did not believe even after having seen the Promised Land. They will have to learn to be a people that does not oppose God. Long have we been opposing God in Jesus and wailing and discouraging each other when our God in Jesus heals anyone with faith. And it is often outsiders who believe more deeply than we do.

Thursday

FIRST READING   **I.** Num 20:1–13
                                     II. Jer 31:31–34
Responsorial Psalm   **I.** Ps 95:1–2, 6–7, 8–9
                                     II. Ps 51:12–13, 14–15, 18–19
GOSPEL   Mt 16:13–23

☀ The question comes again—and again! Who do people say I am—and who do you think I am? And they all think that he is a prophet! A prophet is dedicated to the true worship of God, care for the poor, work for justice and no violence allowed among the people. And Peter answers theologically—unlike him. He answers for the community of Matthew (the gospel written after the destruction of the temple, with Christians struggling outside of the Jewish community for an identity of their own, since they have been rejected and exiled from their tradition and society for refusing to defend the temple against the Romans). Peter and the church of Matthew is told that nothing will prevail against them: not the Romans and the Jews who are persecuting them, not their own infighting and not even the gates of death. The church will survive and forgiveness and justice will be loosed in the world. We are given courage to stand and endure faithfully.

☀ The Israelites camp and Miriam dies and is buried. They rebel against Moses for their thirst and having to live in the desert (Miriam was their water-diviner as they traveled). Moses takes his staff and in the presence of the disbelieving people strikes the rock—but he strikes it twice (he was told only once) and the water gushes forth for the people. And at the waters of Meribah; Moses knows that he will never enter the Promised Land because in his anger at the people he reacted and did not show forth the glory of God. Between Moses and God, God knew what was in Moses' heart. The place is known as the site of contention between the people and God and Moses' great loss.

Jesus is intent on asking us who we believe Jesus to be: a prophet, the messiah (according to our personal wants or nationalistic hopes), the Son of the Living God—all partially true. But do we know him as he knows himself to be before God, as the Son of Man who will be rejected and crucified and be raised? And are we following him or judging by our own standards and wants?

Friday

FIRST READING	I. Dt 4:32–40
	II. Na 2:1, 3; 3:1–3, 6–7
Responsorial Psalm	I. Ps 77:12–13, 14–15, 16 and 21
	II. Dt 32:35–36, 39, 41
GOSPEL	Mt 16:24–28

This portion of the scripture follows Peter's betrayal and rejection of Jesus' call to the cross and what will happen to him in Jerusalem. Jesus turns his back on Peter and the disciples and call the crowd—everyone who would follow him to 'deny yourself' so that we will not deny him publicly, and then "take up the cross and follow him." It's a call to wholehearted acceptance of suffering and even death if necessary in defense of the good news to the poor and the person of the crucified Lord. It is about life and death, here and forever. Have we ever truly decided, committed and singleheartedly turned into the way of the Cross, the way of Jesus the Lord to the Father, relying on the Spirit? Today would be a good day.

Nahum the prophet cries out rejoicing and deliverance of Judah and the destruction and woe for the city of Nineveh that will be destroyed. Always the choice is the same: do we chose life, obedience, justice for the poor, the true worship of God or do we choose greed, injustice, violence and the mockery of empty prayers/ritual? Jesus is clear; if we are to follow him then we must deny ourselves, pick up our cross and come after him to death and resurrection. There will be judgment, repayment, life and death. We're supposed to chose life now, over and over again, daily, as we sign ourselves.

Saturday

FIRST READING   I. Dt 6:4–13

                                               II. Hab 1:12—2:4

Responsorial Psalm   II. Ps 9:8–9, 10–11, 12–13

                                    I. Ps 18:2–3a, 3bc–4, 47 and 51

GOSPEL   Mt 17:14–20

The prophet Habakkuk cries out to God to see those who do wickedness and how they appear to flourish and rise, doing violence to the people of God. But God responds saying: "Write down the vision. Its time will come, wait for it. Those who do violence have no integrity but the just will live." This is the truth of the Word of God. Jesus is approached by a man begging for the life of his child who is demented and always trying to harm himself. Jesus heals the child, when his disciples cannot. They (and me) lack trust to face evil in the world. We are weak in faith and need to be converted as surely as the young child needs to be delivered from what harms him. Every generation must change.

Moses seeks to instill a passion and awe for God into the people so that they can pass it on to the next generation. The law is their hold on God and God's hold on them. He warns them that when they come to the land and settle in it they will forget; they will turn aside and take for granted all that they have been given. But they are to tell the story of God's power, of bringing them out of bondage and slavery, and never forget that they were slaves once and it was God who set them free, and they are to serve him alone. Jesus heals a man's child that is demented and a danger to himself. The disciples cannot heal him and Jesus calls his own followers an unbelieving and perverse lot! The child is cured by a reprimand from Jesus, and Jesus reprimands us saying that we have so little trust. Even a mustard seed's worth could move a mountain. Do we trust, not in ourselves, but in God in Jesus, not just as individuals but as a community of disciples? Or are we in need of a reprimand from our Lord?

NINETEENTH WEEK IN ORDINARY TIME

Monday

FIRST READING   **I.** Dt 10:12–22
                         II. Ezk 1:2–5, 24–28c

Responsorial Psalm   **I.** Ps 147:12–13, 14–15, 19–20
                         II. Ps 148:1–2, 11–12, 13, 14

GOSPEL   Mt 17:22–27

Once again Jesus tries to tell the disciples what awaits him in Jerusalem: rejection, delivered unto death, being killed and raised again. They are deeply grieved. They cannot abide it, not even the thought of it. And they go back to Capernaum, home for them and Jesus asks Simon (his name when he doesn't follow Jesus first) about "who pays taxes or tributes to the kings of the earth: their sons or the other people? It is a strange question—aimed at Peter's lack of belief in Jesus as the Son of the Father, Lord of heaven and earth. He is told: "the sons are tax-free'. Peter, and we hardly understand what he is saying. He is told to go get the money and pay it because they aren't ready yet to declare that they belong to Jesus, to God alone. They are divided at heart and so their practice is half-hearted as well. Are we followers of the God Father of Jesus, even unto the cross and resurrection or are we still 'this people easily offended' and without understanding who pay the taxes and serve two gods: and so serve neither well.

Ezekiel sees four figures of incredible power, and a throne and someone like a man. He describes it as "the vision of the likeness of the glory of the Lord." Jesus is the human image of God and the face of the Son of Man, rejected, crucified and maimed is also this vision of the likeness of the glory of the Lord. The disciples are overwhelmed with grief and reject the vision Jesus presents them. And the collectors of the temple tax (in collusion with Rome) ask Peter if Jesus pays the tax. He says yes. And Jesus tries to teach Peter (and us) that it is not necessary to pay the tax, only do it so as not to 'disedify' people. In Matthew the tax is paid. Who are we afraid of 'disedifying'? A nation or God?

☀ The requirements of the Lord never change: fear the Lord, obey, love and serve the Lord and know that the Lord is God, creator, keeper of all things. Bend before God and do justice, befriend the alien because we once were aliens/slaves in Egypt. Hold fast. But we hold fast not only to the limited understanding of Yahweh God of the exodus but we hold fast to his beloved Son, Jesus the Lord. We stay near the one who is rejected, crucified and risen. We are in this world, having to cope with politics, economics, nationalism and intrigue but we must remember that we are not citizens of these places, we are foreigners in every nation on earth, because we are the people of God first and foremost. Do we believe this? And if we do, then how are we to deal with nations and peoples that continue to crucify the children of God worldwide?

Tuesday

FIRST READING   **I.** Dt 31:1–8
                                             II. Ezk 2:8—3:4
Responsorial Psalm   **I.** Dt 32:3–4ab, 7, 8, 9 and 12
                    II. Ps 119:14, 24, 72, 103, 111, 131
GOSPEL   Mt 18:1–5, 10, 12–14

☀ The disciples are clueless asking about who is the greatest in the kingdom of God. Jesus' example of the child would have shocked them: a child was in the same category of those without any power like: slaves, servants, the poor, the sick, outsiders, gentiles—the lowly of the earth, the meek and those who do no violence to others. These are children, like Jesus himself. We are not to despise any of these children: the massive numbers of the poor, the weak and those thought inconsequential by society. Jesus, the Father, even the angels are more concerned about one lost sheep, the least of our brothers and sisters than any of the ones who think they are not lost, even if they are the ninety-nine. Jesus has come for the lost, the sinners, the sick, the poor and those who have never known life. They are his beloved lost ones and with him they come first. And with us: who comes first?

✳ Moses prepares the people for his dying telling them that the Lord will cross over the Jordan before them. He appoints Joshua as their leader, exhorting him to be steadfast (with this people, that is a necessity). They march into the land, facing all the peoples that actually live there. This is the God of the older covenant who conquers peoples and transfers land. Our God in Jesus is never violent and never allows his people to be violent or harm another, not even an enemy. We are exhorted to live with courage and live without power—like the children of Jesus' time. We are to welcome all but especially those with no place in society. We are to seek after the lost and the straying and to work at community and unity making sure that all the people of no account in this world, count first in our hearts and households. This is our God, our Father God.

Wednesday

FIRST READING

I. Dt 34:1–12
II. Ezk 9:1–7, 10:18–22

Responsorial Psalm

I. Ps 66:1–3a, 5 and 8, 16–17
II.B Ps 113:1–2, 3–4, 5–6

GOSPEL

Mt 18:15–20

✳ This is a judgment scene, Ezekiel's vision of an angel marking with an X those who mourn and weep over the evil that is done, starting in the temple, and then out into the city. And the glory of the Lord leaves the temple. And Jesus brings a new form of judgment upon us. It begins with forgiveness so graciously given to us. And we must give that to others. We must try individually, with 2 or 3, with elders, with small groups and the larger church and then even, treat those who have sinned the way Jesus has treated the Gentiles and tax collectors—with more kindness and mercy. And we are to pray first and always for forgiveness for others and unity among ourselves.

Thursday

FIRST READING

I. Jos 3:7–10a, 11, 13–17
II. Ezk 12:1–12

Responsorial Psalm

I. Ps 114:1–2, 3–4, 5–6
II. Ps 78:56–57, 58–59, 61–62

GOSPEL

Mt 18:21—19:1

❁ Peter is at it again: how many times do I have to forgive? Has he been listening to anything that Jesus says? So Jesus is clear—don't count! Just start forgiving. Any number with seven in it is infinite in the Jewish numerology, fullness of life—all creation and time. So forgiving is never-ending, a lifestyle, a way of breathing and being a Christian, a follower of Jesus. And the parable is clear—each of us is forgiven massively for our sins against God and so we must forgive in turn the things that others do to us. Otherwise the mercy we have known from God will be turned to justice, since we have not learned from our God's dealings with us to be merciful to one another. How good are we at forgiving—or consistent—everyone, all the time, for everything? As good as we are at expecting God and others to forgive us? Clare prayed for others, forgetting herself, do we pray for others' forgiveness?

❁ Ezekiel's words are ever present reality. The prophet lives in the midst of a rebellious house. They are blind, deaf and stupid. Does it ever change? Do we think for a minute that this is not describing us as individuals, church, parishes, nations? Jesus' parable seems harsh. We are to forgive everyone always, as a lifestyle because we have been forgiven by God that many times, or more, for everything. And if we don't we will know justice from God. What we have received we must give or God will treat us as we treat others. Do we ever learn?

❁ The book of Joshua begins, the transition from the desert to being a people in the land. He summons the people to listen to the word of God and to remind them that the living God is in their midst as they enter the land. They go, carrying the ark of the Lord before them and the people cross the Jordan on land land—a mini passage through the Red Sea. And the whole nation arrives at the end of their long journey from bondage to freedom. It has been a long and arduous time learning to be free.

Jesus teaches us that freedom is rooted in forgiveness—not counting how many times but as a lifestyle practiced in every regard towards everyone, always. God forgives us everything—what we could never repay (the debt in the Our Father that we ask forgiveness for) and in exchange we must forgive others what they owe to us (the debt in the Our Father that we are required to forgive others who are in debt to us). This is a ground line requirement for Jesus' followers, the people of God and God will treat us as sincerely forgiving as we have forgiven one another. Sobering and demanding, but freeing.

Friday

FIRST READING   **I.** Jos 24:1–13
              II. Ezk 16:1–15, 60, 63 (or Ezk 16:59–63)
Responsorial Psalm   **I.** Ps 136:1–3, 16–18, 21–22 and 24
                II. Is 12:2–3, 4bcd, 5–6
GOSPEL   Mt 19:3–12

❋ Jesus is set up again with a question on marriage—can a man divorce his wife for any reason? (They knew he could according to the law, though not according to the scriptures— and that a woman could not divorce her husband for any reason. The law was not applied equally). Jesus reiterates the Word of God from of old and is blunt in telling them the only reason Moses changed the law back then was because their hearts were stubborn. But Jesus is interested in faithfulness for everyone; love unto death; love as service of life; love between equals; love as he has loved us. So he condemns them. But tells his disciples, all of us that each of us is called to faithfulness whether we are single, unmarried, married, separated or divorced. All we are is for the kingdom. Like those of old with stubborn hearts we have a long long way to go to learn faithfulness and forgiveness among us all.

❋ Jerusalem is not born of God, a cast-off, orphan yet God has spread the corner of his cloak over the people and entered into covenant with them, giving them everything as lovers do. But Jerusalem cares nothing for God, only for itself but God will once again remember them and love them and pardon them. We hear this message practically every day for months. Do we realize it's about us, as a people, church, nation? Jesus deals with it in the covenant of marriage and that both men and women are called to be faithful, imaging God's own faithfulness. No matter who we are or our status, we belong first to God alone.

✸ Joshua summons the entire people and retells the story of their promises, of deliverance and God's choice of them as his people. They must remember their past and especially keep in mind what God does for them always, no matter how they have been towards God. They have been given a land that belonged to others, land and crops that they did not till and produce that they had no hand in planting or harvesting. They deserve none of this; it is all the bounty of their God.

Jesus teaches about the hardness of peoples' hearts and that Moses changed the law of marriage—so that men could divorce their wives—but just because it was changed does not mean it was the original intention of God. Men and women were meant to live as one. Men are not to divorce their wives and women are not to divorce their husbands—this is the prophetic teaching of Jesus/God. We must begin here and face unfaithfulness and failure and make excuses, change the law and harden our hearts because we have sinned.

Saturday

FIRST READING
                                                I. Jos 24:14–29

Responsorial Psalm

I. Ps 16:1–2 and 5, 7–8, 11
II. Ps 51:12–13, 14–15, 18–19
Mt 19:13–15

✸ In light of this call to faithfulness, parents are bringing their children to Jesus for him to bless them. He lays his hands on them in prayer and the disciples who don't listen or hear very well are indignant, pushing them away and telling them to keep their children to themselves. And now it is Jesus' turn to be indignant— those we don't think deserve to have time apart with Jesus, closeness and intimacy: children, the poor, servants, slaves, the sick and the weak—all those who don't count in society—they are the ones he wants to touch, to bless and be with, unlike us. This is Jesus' way, not the way of the world or our way. Who do we think does not deserve to get near Jesus? Who do we hinder from the kingdom in our self-righteousness? Is Jesus indignant at us more often than not?

The line for the First Reading: I. Ezk 18:1–10, 13b, 30–32 appears as second option.

✺ God judges each of us according to our ways, telling us to cast off our crimes and make a new spirit and a new heart in us. God does not want us to die—to know the consequences of our evil on us and those we love, or to die without God's nearness. Return and live! And Jesus wants us to live fully now. He wants us to live as the beloved children of God. He wants to bless us and lay hands on us and pray with us and give us the kingdom of justice and peace now. Does the kingdom belong to us? Or are we like the disciples in need of a scolding?

✺ Decide today who you will serve! Get rid of your other idols if you decide that you will serve God alone. And the people vow to obey God, knowing that God is holy and will not forgive if they do evil and worship other gods. They raise a stone to witness their covenant renewed once again with God, recording in the book of the law what is expected of the people. Joshua has ushered them into the land and set them each to their own heritage/portion and he dies. The transition from slavery to freedom is completed—now their life in the land of Israel begins.

Jesus blesses the children that are brought to him and rebukes his disciples for trying to hinder them from coming to him. We must be as children—with no power, no arrogance, no place in society, having to obey everyone, treated primarily as slaves, servants (at the time of Jesus). Children stand for those who are weak, need help from others, cannot make it on their own and are treated as cheap available labor. Not just children but all those under the age of 15. We must do religiously—this is our law from the Lord—what they are caught in by age, circumstance and others' power. Are we the children of God?

TWENTIETH WEEK IN ORDINARY TIME

Monday

FIRST READING

I. Jdg 2:11–19

II. Ezk 24:15–23

Responsorial Psalm

I. Ps 106:34–35, 36–37, 39–40, 43 and 44

II. Dt 32:18–19, 20, 21

GOSPEL

Mt 19:16–22

Ezekiel is told not to mourn the death of his wife, the 'delight of his eyes'. This is what will happen to the sanctuary of the Lord and when it happens the people are not to mourn its loss aloud either—because they will rot on account of their sins and groan to one another. The Word of the Lord sounds desperate and is consumed with grief beyond express on us. A man comes to ask Jesus what he has to do for eternal life. He is told the commandments and he says he does those already. Can we answer that? Then he is commanded to sell his possessions (he is a rich man) and give to the poor and then come and follow Jesus, but he will not. He is bound to what he has, rather than to Jesus. He goes away sad. Do we? And do we sadden the heart of God in our refusal to follow?

The book of Judges tries to organize the loose federation of tribes into a people in the land, calling them to the law and holding them together in the face of many peoples in the land, with many other gods. And the people begin quickly to take on the practices of the peoples they dwell with and worship the idols. They would be taken over by the peoples they dwelled alongside and always lost and were oppressed. The pattern began early: forgetting their covenant, worshiping other gods, given judges to pull them back to faithfulness and obedience and straying off again, to be conquered by still another group. It is the history of Israel, but in reality it is the history of our church as well—with the leaders becoming those who stray along with the people and the need for prophets to arise. Our law is based on the 10 commands of Moses but we must move on from there—towards care of the poor, singlehearted devotion to the kingdom of God coming to earth in peace and justice and following Jesus with all our hearts/souls/minds and resources. Do we go away from Jesus' invitation to closeness because we are possessed by what we own.

Tuesday

FIRST READING   **I.** Jdg 6:11–24a
                                              II. Ezk 28:1–10

Responsorial Psalm   **I.** Ps 85:9, 11–12, 13–14
                II. Dt 32:26–27, 27–28, 30, 35cd–36ab

GOSPEL   Mt 19:23–30

Jesus seeks to teach his disciples the hard realities of the kingdom: how hard it is for the rich to enter the kingdom. Hard as a camel, stripped down, pulled through the eye of a needle. Impossible!—nothing is impossible with God. Grace and the Spirit can call even the rich, the middle class, and the poor alike to give what is their excess, and even what they need to those who need it more—the poor of the earth. He encourages them to live beyond the present, unto the end of time when there will be judgment. If they share in his way of the cross then they will share in his glory and even in this life they will know the graciousness of God in community, in shared hope, courage, dwelling places, friends who are the friends of God, the presence of support and life everlasting. How little we believe in the goodness of our God and what he hopes for us—even now, even here!

The people have been conquered and an angel is sent to Gideon to rouse the people. The pattern is here as well—Gideon comes from the meanest house in Manasseh and he is the most insignificant of his family. This is whom God chooses. Gideon does sacrifice and realizes that he has been speaking to the messenger of God (angels and God are almost interchangeable in the earlier testament—they are the word of God given to a person who needs to do something for the people of God). He is told to be without fear.

We are to live without fear, without greed and hoarding. We are to live with graciousness to the poor, sharing what we have to others, so that we have our treasure in heaven. Nothing is impossible with God: Incarnation, Resurrection, the Body of Christ—nothing is impossible with God—the rich giving up their clutching of their riches to give to the poor and becoming the followers of the Crucified one. Nothing is impossible with God. What impossible thing do we should do and become today?

Wednesday

FIRST READING	I. Jdg 9:6–15
	II. Ezk 34:1–11
Responsorial Psalm	I. Ps 21:2–3, 4–5, 6–7
	II. Ps 23:1–3, 3b–4, 5–6
GOSPEL	Mt 20:1–16

One of Jesus' strongest parables: the vineyard owner (the Father) who goes out to hire workers for his vineyard (to pick the harvest to make wine!). The first group has a contract in justice for a daily wage: the usual and they know they will work, and eat and have dignity that day. Then four more times he comes out and chooses more, until at the end, with just an hour to go, he sends still more out. But at the end of the day everyone gets paid the same!!! What's going on here? And those who worked hardest and longest are made to wait on those who worked the least! And those from the beginning are angry and won't deal with the foreman (Jesus) and go back to the owner—claiming injustice. But God's justice is just this: that all are given hope, salvation, life for the day (what we pray for in the Our Father) and that all deserve, from the richest to the poorest, to the healthy to the sick, all are human beings, all are the beloved children of God. We should be grateful to know (if we start early) that we know and have the honor of working for the wine of the kingdom and have pity for those who come late and have missed so much. Who are we? Do we like, or love this God of the least, the last, who puts us all on the same footing? Or are we angry, wanting God to treat us differently than 'them'?

Ezekiel rails against the shepherds of Israel who pasture themselves at the expense of the sheep, letting them die, be scattered and lost. And God will come among those shepherds and take the sheep from them and care for them himself. Jesus' parable mirrors the state of Israel, its leaders and people, using the image of a vineyard instead of a sheepfold. All the workers will be paid the same, justice and what they need. While those who came early think they deserve more, but the owner made a just deal with them. Now he chooses to give mercy to others. God will take care of all of us, but the poor, the sick and those in need first. We should be honored to be in the vineyard and able to serve God.

Thursday

FIRST READING
I. Jdg 11:29–39a
II. Ezk 36:23–28

Responsorial Psalm
I. Ps 40:5, 7–8a, 8b–9, 10
II. Ps 51:12–13, 14–15, 18–19

GOSPEL
Mt 22:1–14

Another parable, about a wedding for a king's son. The guests are invited and none of them want to come—excuses are sent. The guests ignore the second call to come: they go off to their fields, business, livelihoods and then insult and kill the messengers. Then the king sends his troops to destroy them—his judgment on their actions. And the invitation goes out still again—to the people of the road, the wayfarers, the poor and the folks who live on the edge, on the fringes of society and all are drawn in—the good and the evil alike! Some wedding feast! As the king goes around, some are found without garments—they were given garments as part of the invitation as custom—where are they? What have they done with them? And out they go. We have all been invited and we have our excuses and we do our killing and insulting. All of us, good and evil have been invited into the Good News and we have been given garments. There will be the judgment and the feast—will we still have the garment of our baptisms? Or will we find ourselves outside, disappointing our God—again?

The spirit of the Lord comes upon Jephthah and he vows to save the people from the Ammonites. And if he does triumphs he will give God "whoever comes out of the doors of my house to meet me when I return in triumph." And he shall offer him up as a holocaust. Was he expecting a servant? What he does is against the law of Yahweh. From the time of Abraham there has been no human sacrifice in Israel so what Jephthah does is against everything in the tradition—it is his choice and his sin. It is a despicable story that is to instill horror. This is primitive society and primitive religion and they have much to learn of God's true nature and a long way to go in developing what it means to obey God and imitate God and give God what it is that God desires. And he never desires the life of anyone ever. Jesus himself was killed, equally horribly and it was excused as necessary by leaders and people alike—but we belong to the God of the banquet who welcomes all and there are no enemies...

Friday

FIRST READING
I. Ru 1:1, 3–6, 14–16, 22
II. Ezk 37:1–14

Responsorial Psalm
I. Ps 146:5–6ab, 6c–7, 8–9a, 9bc–10
II. Ps 107:2–3, 4–5, 6–7, 8–9

GOSPEL
Mt 22:34–40

Jesus has been arguing with the Saducees who were insulting (they did not believe in resurrection) and the Pharisees come to him. One lawyer asks him the theological question that many discourses began with: Which is the most important law? And everyone knows what the answer is! Jesus answers with the Shema, the groundline prayer and statement of belief for the Jewish people: Love God with everything you have and then he adds on how that law is expressed: love your neighbor, love human beings with all the heart, soul, mind, strength (resources) that you proclaim belongs to God. All other words, scriptures, law, theology rest on these. It is still the foundation of everything Jesus teaches but he has added something unbelievable—his way of loving. And so now we are to love God and everyone, including our enemies who come to test us as he has loved us and loved his beloved Father God. Everything comes down to this. How do we love?

Ezekiel has his famous vision of bones that hear the word of the Lord and they start coming together and coming back to life in the desert! Bones, then sinews, then flesh and finally spirit. This is Israel who has been dead but will be brought back to life and they will have the spirit of God placed in them. God vows this! And Jesus tells us clearly what this Spirit is and what life is: to love God and everyone with all that we are and have been given, with all our life's force. Are we alive in God? How alive? Or is there a great deal in us that is still dead and in need of the Spirit?

Saturday

FIRST READING	**I.** Ru 2:1–3, 8–11; 4:13–17
	II. Ezk 43:1–7ab
Responsorial Psalm	**I.** Ps 128:1b–2, 3, 4, 5
	II. Ps 85:9–10, 11–12, 13–14
GOSPEL	Mt 23:1–12

✳ Now it is Jesus' turn to speak his mind about those who have sought to test him and to make him look stupid or ungodly. We are told to obey the teachers of the law in what they say when they teach, quoting Scripture, but not to obey them or follow them in what they do. They are hypocrites, and worse, they lay heavy burdens on others and do not lift a finger to help them. They are cold-hearted, demanding and unlike Jesus' Father. They are self-righteous, demanding attention and public respect while inwardly shallow and filled with pride. We are not to be like that—we are to be servants of all, humble and lowly before all, knowing our God sees into our hearts. Are we good models? What are we teaching by our behaviors, decisions and lifestyles? Why are we religious, devotional? Are we truly servants?

✳ The glory of the Lord returns to the temple and Ezekiel lies prone before the power as it enters. And the words he hears are ones of homecoming. "This is where I will set the soles of my feet; here I will dwell among the Israelites forever." And it is Jesus who has set the soles of his feet upon the earth, dwelling with us, and calling us to observe the law that has been given, but not to imitate the actions of those who lead, yet disobey the laws they teach. Jesus, the Word (scriptures) is our teacher and we are called to serve, as he served us.

The book of Ruth is about an outsider, named Ruth married to an Israelite and has become a widow. She casts her lot with her mother-in-law, Naomi and returns with her to Israel. Naomi seeks to have Ruth meet one of her kinsmen to marry and settle—they are two widows, a precarious position in the land. She meets Boaz in the field and he instructs her to stay with his women servants and follow field to field to glean. And he soon marries her. She is praised in familiar terms of blessing with a twist that is crucial to note: "He will be your comfort and the support of your old age, for his mother is the daughter-in-law who loves you. She is worth more than seven sons!" Amazing blessing and she is the great-great (many greats) grandmother of Jesus.

An outsider in Israel obeys the law and goes beyond the law to care for her mother-in-law. And in Israel Jesus is chiding the people to listen to their leaders but not to do what they do. They are hypocrites who lay burdens on others (usually widows and the poor) and who lord it over others and know no humility. Ruth is an alternative model to imitate.

TWENTY-FIRST WEEK IN ORDINARY TIME

Monday

FIRST READING   **I.** 1 Thes 1:1–5, 8b–10

                            II. 2 Thes 1:1–5, 11–12

Responsorial Psalm   **I.** Ps 149:1b–2, 3–4, 5–6a and 9b

                            II. Ps 96:1–2, 2–3, 4–5

GOSPEL   Mt 23:13–22

✴ We begin a letter from Paul, Silvanus, and Timothy with the grace and peace and blessings of God called down upon us. The leaders give thanks for us who believe and whose love grows even as we endure persecution and trial. The leaders pray for us that we might be worthy of our call and glorify God with Jesus. And Jesus looks at the leaders of his time and declares that they shut the door of God's presence in the faces of the people. Jesus as a prophet calls down woe and judgment upon leaders who uses their place of authority among the people, liturgically and ritually for their own gain and who do not enter the kingdom, and keep others out. What kind of leaders are we? What kind of leaders do we have? What should we be praying for?

✴ Paul begins his letter with prayers for what they are doing and growing in their belief and practice of the faith—the power of the Spirit is strong in them and word is spreading of their conviction and service. The churches are in communication with each other as they grow and develop, learning from one another, and praying for one another. This is the corrective of what Jesus is pointing out with those leaders of religion who are frauds and shut the door to the kingdom of God in the faces of those seeking to enter. He calls them blind guides, fools—laying stress and importance on things of no value or worth. They care more for the gold and the gift of sacrifice than they do the temple and the altar. Their priorities are twisted and destructive of others' search for truth. What of us—are we laboring to have others know the kingdom's justice and forgiveness or are we shutting doors in peoples' faces because of our pettiness and blind priorities?

Tuesday

FIRST READING   **I.** 1 Thes 2:1–8
                                             II. 2 Thes 2:1–3a, 14–17

Responsorial Psalm   **I.** Ps 139:1–3, 4–6
                                      II. Ps 96:10, 11–12, 13

GOSPEL   Mt 23:23–26

Jesus attacks those who have sought so insistently to contradict him and interrupt him as he preaches the good news to the poor, and seeks to heal the sick and those condemned by the lawyers and leaders of the Jewish community. And he is devastating in his condemnation of them. They forget (conveniently) the foundations of law—that binds and holds the community together, especially giving the poor and the weakest shelter, dignity and life—justice, mercy and faith. Instead of practicing these core-heart issues, they are interested in taxes, tithes, their own status, use and misuse of power. There is no mercy or justice in them. They are heartless, blind, self-absorbed and swallowing camels, keeping the mosquitoes out to torment others. We are horrified when we hear Jesus like this—angry. But does he have equally good reason to be angry at us—the good people of the parish?

Paul and his companions preach at Thessalonika after being rejected at Philippi. He tells them that they have been treated gently like any nursing mother would treat her child, caring for her little ones. They came to share God's good news and would share their own lives with them, they have become so dear to them. Look at the contrast with the way Jesus accuses the leaders who not only neglect the weightier matters of the law, (justice, mercy and good faith) but nitpick details while allowing huge evils to happen. Jesus is furious with them because of their impurity that is more vicious and vacuous than any law they enforce like the one which describes how a cup or a dish becomes unclean. They are filled with loot and lust—this is the anger of God at leaders who destroy the community. What would Jesus say today to our leaders, to us and how we treat those we bring the gospel to?

Wednesday

FIRST READING	**I.** 1 Thes 2:9–13
	II. 2 Thes 3:6–10, 16–18
Responsorial Psalm	**I.** Ps 139:7–8, 910, 11–12ab
	II. Ps 128:1–2, 4–5
GOSPEL	Mt 23:27–32

✴ Paul and the others make themselves the models that are to be imitated, working day and night on their behalf, not even depending on them for food. Those who can work are supposed to work and peace is to be the mark of their gatherings. Jesus is about the hard work of telling those among the people who have authority that they are whitewashed tombs, rotting, with holy exteriors, frauds and hypocrites and liars. They would have joined in with their ancestors in shedding prophets' blood. And they will be a part of shedding Jesus' blood. And who are we—frauds, rotting inside and very devoted on the outside? What would Jesus have to say to us?

Thursday

FIRST READING	**I.** 1 Thes 3:7-13
	II. 1 Cor 1:1–9
Responsorial Psalm	**I.** Ps 90:3–5a, 12–13, 14 and 17
	II. Ps 145:2–3, 4–5, 6–7
GOSPEL	Mt 24:42–51

✴ We are warned: Stay awake for we don't know when our Lord is coming. When will the kingdom come? When will judgment come for the earth? When will it come for our nation? When will it come for us individually? When will our God come in glory? It will be unexpected—like a thief breaking into our houses! That's unnerving. Each of us has been put in charge of something in God's kingdom. Are we watchful, obedient and good servants or are we fighting with one another, forgetful of the master's will and hopes for his kingdom on earth among us? Will be we caught unawares; dismissed and cast out with all the others who didn't claim to be servants but served the gods and powerful of the world? It's growing late in ordinary time and we are must examine whether we are actually living as the servant of the Jesus the Risen Lord who has great expectations of our continuing his work on earth.

Paul rejoices that the witness he bore to the Corinthians has been rewarded richly in their speech, knowledge and confirmation of belief. He prays for continued growth and strength and blamelessness, more grace and peace among them so that they will be holy. Could this be a description of us? Jesus is warning his own to 'Stay awake' because we can't know when the day of the Son of Man will come, when judgment will come upon the earth. We are to be like servants of the master who is away, who are faithful, not like those who take over, take the master's house for our own, beat one another and get caught. We will be judged and punished if we act like those he has been criticizing and calling to task. If the Son of Man came today what would we be doing?

Paul expresses his gratitude to the Thessalonians for all that they have done for him and his fellow preachers and missionaries. Their standing firm in the Lord gives them heart. They are prayed for fervently night and day that they might see them face to face and that God the Father will light the way to them. It is a prayer that we can say often for all the groups in our churches, in our nation and worldwide that we cling to the same hope and become holy—all of us.

We are to be prepared always, as servants awaiting the master's return. The Son of Man has entrusted us with his household and to dispense food to those in need: the bread of life, reconciliation, justice, peace, mercy. How we treat one another will be the basis of Jesus, the Son of Man's judgment upon us. Are we faithful, and good servants so that no one in the household lacks or wants for anything?

Friday

FIRST READING	**I.** 1 Thes 4:1–8
	II. 1 Cor 1:17–25
Responsorial Psalm	**I.** Ps 97:1 and 2b, 5–6, 10, 11–12
	II. Ps 33:1–2, 4–5, 10–11
GOSPEL	Mt 25:1–13

✳ The parable of the ten bridesmaids who go out to wait for the bridegroom to come to the bride's house with their oil lamps. It was the custom for the bridegroom to party with his friends and then come sometime in the night to collect his bride and take her to his own house with her bridesmaids lighting the way. Five have oil for their lamps and five don't—ridiculous. If you had that honor, not to know that it could be a long wait, or a short one revealed you as insensitive, not really concerned about the wedding at all. When the moment comes they run off to try at the last minute to get oil—while the procession would have proceeded without them. They come to the locked door and aren't allowed in—they missed their chance! The words are harsh: "Truly, I do not know you." How much oil do we have in our lamps: the oil of gladness, the oil of chrism from our baptisms and confirmations; the oil of prayer and almsgiving, of the scriptures and the work with others for justice—which brings the bridegroom and bride together? Does our God truly know us or are we stupid, foolish, unthinking and not really concerned about the feast of justice for all and peace on earth?

✳ The gospel is preached with focus on the cross, though it appears to be complete absurdity to those who do not believe. This is wisdom for God, to save us through obedience even unto death on the cross and the crucified is the only wisdom we must study and imitate. It seems often in this year B, that it is one long continuous call to conversion, a long Lent. But it is the core of baptism and the gospel. Now we get to decide if we're wise or foolish. Do we have oil (Scripture/Spirit) in our lamps or are the empty? Does God know us or are we going to be left outside the door?

✳ We must always make great progress, in instruction and in practice so that we may grow in holiness. We are to be careful in all that we say and do, and how we treat one another in the grace of the Spirit. This is the Word of the Lord calling us back always to imitation of Jesus and obedience to the Word of the gospel.

Jesus tells us the story of the 10 bridesmaids awaiting the coming of the groom, some with flasks and oil in their lamps and others with none. Flasks of oil—the anointing and gift of the Spirit given to us in baptism/confirmation for the life of the people at the wedding feast of the Lord. Have we used our oil or do we keep our lamps lit and our minds and lives attentive to the Spirit of God. Are we so wrapped up in ourselves that we are forgetful of what has been given to us and our place in the community awaiting God's coming to us?

Saturday

FIRST READING
      I. 1 Thes 4:9–11
      II. 1 Cor 1:26–31

Responsorial Psalm
      I. Ps 98:1, 7–8, 9
      II. Ps 33:12–13, 18–19, 20–21

GOSPEL
      Mt 25:14–30

Another parable about the master who goes away leaving his servants in charge, leaving silver with the servants in differing amounts. One gets five, another two, another just one. Two are very entrepreneurial and double what they were given in trust; the other doesn't do that sort of risky business and buries it so that it will be there when the master returns.

And return he does and what to do how things have fared. The first two reap the master's goodwill and are given more power. The last describes the master terribly: he's unscrupulous taking and making profit on what he doesn't work for, dishonest at best, violent at his worst. And the one talent (a huge sum of money) is taken from him and given to the one who is most adept at making money for the master. Is this our God: Is this the Father of Jesus? And then the dictum is given: for to all those who have, more will be given, and they will have an abundance; but from those who are unproductive, even what they have will be taken from them. This is the way of economics, nations and the world, not of our God. In this world those who do not play the games of the world are useless, but at judgment (the next parable of the sheep and goats) they will be in the kingdom they served from the beginning-God's care for the poor and justice and peace.

We are called; and most of who were called weren't wise or influential, but lowborn and despised in the world. But we have life in Jesus, who is our wisdom, justice, sanctification and redemption and we are only to boast in the Lord. Does that look anything like us? Jesus tells the story of the talents, a huge amount of money given to servants while the master went on a journey. He returns to hold them accountable for what they've done with what they were entrusted with—sounds like the world—and it is, not how God judges, but the way the world does. Are we more intent on making it in the world's judgment or in the eyes of God?

We are to love one another—and it is God who teaches us how, in Jesus, in the word of the Lord, in community. "Make it a point of honor to remain at peace—to work at making the community more whole and holy, and to take care of everyone as an example to those who are not believers. No one is to want for anything. This is how we are to live as Jesus' company.

We are told the parable of the man who goes on a journey and gives away a great deal of money to be disbursed according to the abilities of each, 10,000, 5,000 and a 1000. He is away a long time and when he returns, there is an accounting. Those who invested wisely get more power and management and the one who just keeps the 1000 tells the master he is a hard man and reaps what he doesn't sow (obviously this is not Jesus' Father, but the way the world works). And the servant is thrown out—this is not about making it in the church/parish but whether or not we actually belong to God as his servants caring for others or whether we still belong firmly to the world and are making it among the corporations and nations—where are we rooted really?

TWENTY-SECOND WEEK IN ORDINARY TIME

Monday

FIRST READING   I. 1 Thes 4:13–18
II. 1 Cor 2:1–5

Responsorial Psalm   I. Ps 96:1and 3, 4–5, 11–12, 13
II. Ps 119:97, 98, 99, 100, 101, 102

GOSPEL   Lk 4:16–30

✺ We are reminded of the core-heart of our belief and practice—Jesus Christ Crucified and that we do live 'in fear and trembling', reliant on the word and Body of Jesus, the power of God in the Incarnation. This is all we have: the Word of God made flesh in Jesus and what we, with Jesus are baptized for: to bring good news to the poor. And, with Jesus, we will most likely be rejected by family, neighbors and fellow believers. If we live in that power of God, the Spirit, as prophets then we will share to some degree the rage of those who are sure that their god is god, yet have not met God the Father of Jesus Christ's Spirit.

✺ We are reminded of our belief about death and resurrection. We live in hope and die in hope. We live resurrection life from the moment of our baptisms, practicing it in our lives and in death we are entrusted to the Lord of Life. The church thinks that Jesus will come back soon and they speak of it as if they know what is going to happen, using language that is familiar to literature about the end times. We are to console one another but not with the end of the world/time but with the life that is ours now in ever greater depth and power. We leave the world's end to God's hands. We are to be concerned with now—today. We are to do the five things that are God's work in the world, and make God's words in Isaiah and in Jesus come true in our lives and worlds. Today this Scripture passage comes true, when we hear it, believe it, obey it and stake our lives on it. This is life and we are called to make this life available for all. Do we ever preach well enough with our lives that we are rejected even?

Tuesday

FIRST READING I. 1 Thes 5:1–6, 9–11
II. 1 Cor 2:10b–16

Responsorial Psalm I. Ps 27:1, 4, 13–14
II. Ps 145:8–9, 10–11, 12–13ab, 13cd–14

GOSPEL Lk 4:31–37

Jesus begins preaching publicly in the synagogues and is confronted by a man who is possessed by an evil spirit—the traditional way of describing someone who was often not in control of their bodily functions (spasms, epilepsy, mental illness, etc. and in the same sense we'd talk about people addicted to drugs, alcohol, etc.) It seems those who are most damaged as human beings see clearly who Jesus is and he has power over all their ills and lacks. He commands with his word that the man be whole, so that the man can live without harm to himself or others. This is the work of Jesus: to peach the good news to the poor, to heal and restore people to their dignity and life as children of God, to teach with authority and to have power over everything in heaven and on earth. It begins in the synagogue and will spread out into the world. We have been restored to our dignity as children in our baptisms; now we are to share that holiness with others outside of our churches.

The Spirit teaches us the depths of God! The only way we learn the mind of Jesus is through the power of the Spirit, found in the Word, the Scriptures. Jesus' words are filled with authority that comes from within him, not given to him from outside by others. There are those who know that Jesus is the Holy One of God, but they see only destruction in Jesus' presence. Do we know Jesus as the vibrant, commanding power of God to transform destruction into life? Do we live by Jesus' authority and Word?

The day of the Lord will come, but probably not in our lifetime. It has been over 2000 years since Jesus ascension and as a church in the eye of God's creation we are very very young. We are to live in this world as God's children and not be running around after the peace and security of the nations. We are one in God—those of us who live and those of us who have died believing in Jesus and struggling to allow Jesus to transform us and release us from whatever holds us in the grip of evil—we are forgiven and freed, and graced in the presence of Jesus in Word, sacrament, community and the Spirit. Do we know this Jesus now?

Wednesday

FIRST READING   **I.** Col 1:1–8
      II. 1 Cor 3:1–9

Responsorial Psalm   **I.** Ps 52:10, 11
      II. Ps 33:12–13, 14–15, 20–21

GOSPEL   Lk 4:38–44

Jesus leaves the synagogue and goes to Simon's house and cures Simon's mother-in-law. She rises and waits on them (in gratitude surely). The imagery is that of raising up, of baptism into new life and ministry. She has been drawn into the circle of disciples—waiting at table on Jesus and the others. And the word spreads and so many come for healing. So many of us are still in need of healing, of wholeness, of release from debilitating sin, self-absorption and the effects that our actions and others have on all of us. Jesus lays hands on each of them (as in confirmation) and those who 'know' him because of their illness and sin are told to be silent. These are not acts of faith, but fear and distance from Jesus. And then Jesus retreats to a deserted place to pray, to be alone with his Father. And then they find him and he is off again to the towns, synagogues and houses to do his work on earth. This will be the pattern of his life. It should be ours: to preach the good news to the poor, to comfort, heal, bind the sick, to speak the truth to those who suffer from doing evil, or are the victims of sin and to pray, seeking strength from our God—but to always come back to those who are lost and in need. This is what we are sent to do as well.

The Word of the Scripture is our food and we've been eating it since baptism. But are we still acting like ordinary people, with divisions and claims to who is more important than the others? Are we still acting like irresponsible children rather than working with God for the growth of the human community? Jesus leaves the synagogue and immediately goes to work: healing, freeing, bringing hope and solace, to Peter's mother-in-law, and then to everyone who hears the good news. We too are sent with Jesus to proclaim the goodness and power of God in Jesus. Is this what we are known for, after praying?

✳ Paul begins each of his pastoral letters with a hymn to the Father, Son and Spirit—the Trinity. This is prayer that was developing along with the practice of the teachings of the apostles (which was the teaching of Jesus that is eventually written down in the four gospels). They are letters, with details of people and who brings news of the communities to Paul as he travels. They must always be seen in light of the Word—as effects brought forth in the lives of those who sought to obey Jesus' words.

Jesus leaves the public place of prayer and goes to his disciples' house and is told of Peter's mother-in-law's illness. He goes to her immediately, grasping her and pulling her up to life. And she responds by waiting on them (deacon description). Where do we go after public prayer? Do we immediately go as church to visit those who are sick, dying and in need in our homes and communities? What he did for her, he will do for everyone, when it is requested and sometimes without being asked. Jesus came for healing and holiness, for justice and reconciliation, for peace with God and among us all.

Thursday

FIRST READING   **I.** Col 1:9–14
                                 II. 1 Cor 3:18–23
Responsorial Psalm   **I.** Ps 98:2–3ab, 3cd–4, 5–6
                            II. Ps 24:1ab–2, 3cd–4, 5–6
GOSPEL   Lk 5:1–11

✳ We return to the beginning of Luke's gospel and Jesus' call to his first disciples while they are washing out their nets. The call comes in the midst of their work, their livelihood, with their families and friends. Jesus borrows Simon's boat and preaches from there. Then he commands him to put out into deep water (most fisherman didn't know how to swim and they trawled along the shore, only about 100 yards out). In spite of his protestations, they catch so many fish that they need help to haul it in and Simon falls on his knees as he sees that he is in the presence of a holy man, calling him Lord. It is the beginning of his apprenticeship and learning who this man Jesus truly is. He is told not to be afraid, and he'll need to hear that over and over again, but he's caught and the adventure begins. We've been caught awhile, do we know who's presence we are in?

✳ Have we learned the wisdom of God or are we still useless when it comes to what God would like to do with us? Do we boast that we belong to Christ and Christ belongs to God, remembering that this is the Crucified One? We have been summoned to put out into the deep, to trust in the power of God, leave everything we have spent so much energy on for ourselves and follow Jesus. God in Jesus has been seeking to catch us for the work of God. Have we been caught or have we managed to wiggle out of Jesus' net?

✳ We are meeting the churches of Paul as he travels. We see his pastoral concerns with each of them, and how they are developing and staying faithful to the teaching they have been given. There are prayers for knowledge and wisdom (gifts of the Spirit) and that we will live a life worthy of our baptisms (calling). Jesus preaches this Word and life and then gets into Peter's boat and commands them to set out into the deep—they obey and catch so many fish they almost sink the boats. Peter gets a sense of who this man Jesus might be and asks mercy and forgiveness. We must always go back to this—that we are meant to go out into the deep with our God, ask mercy, be not afraid, leave all and follow Jesus into the depths of God. Time for taking a risk?

Friday

FIRST READING	**I.** Col 1:15–20
	II. 1 Cor 4:1–5
Responsorial Psalm	**I.** Ps 100:1–2, 3, 4, 5
	II. Ps 37:3–4, 5–6, 27–28, 39–40
GOSPEL	Lk 5:33–39

✳ Jesus is put on the spot: why don't your disciples fast like other teachers? And Jesus declares that his presence on earth is a wedding feast (echoes of Isaiah and the coming of the one who would bring feasting to the poor and justice to the nations). But he is also realistic and tells them the day will come when they will fast from his presence because of the evil people do. And in two short parables: the torn cloth and patches, and the new wine in old skins he tries to impress on them the newness and radical difference his presence brings to the world, to everything realities and celebrations of life. So many will prefer the old and spurn the new. He is the new thing that God is doing in the world: incarnation—our God made flesh among us. Do we rejoice and make sure that others know the bridegroom is in our midst?

✳ Christ is the image of the invisible God—we could pray with that forever. Christ is in all things, the holiness and power of God in a human person. Jesus' main work and mission was to reconcile us to one another in God the Father. He has made peace among us and with us by obedience to God's Word and his cross—the symbol of our being made one with God. Our God dwells with us in Jesus— in Word, Bread, the poor, the Spirit—and so there is a time to fast and a time to rejoice in God's nearness. Are we new garments and new wine—shelter and food, life for the world? We need to examine ourselves on the quality and the depth of our relationship to Christ the image of the invisible Holy One.

Saturday

FIRST READING	I. Col 1:21–23
	II. 1 Cor 4:6b–15
Responsorial Psalm	I. Ps 54:3–4, 6 and 8
	II. Ps 145:17–18, 19–20, 21
GOSPEL	Lk 6:1–5

✳ It's Sabbath and Jesus and the disciples are out walking through a corn field and they run their hands along the heads of grain and crush them, chewing on them. It is thoughtless in their hunger and they are condemned for an infraction of the law. Jesus chides the Pharisees trying to get them to see things with some sort of proportion—reminding them that David and his soldiers in their hunger raided and ate the temple bread! His take on the core of the Sabbath: the Son of Man is Lord of the Sabbath. And so his life, suffering and death will change the emphasis on what constitutes keeping holy the Sabbath and breaking its spirit. And making sure hungers are filled always is in the spirit of the law. God is pleased with feasting and sharing of food. It is and has been true worship that reveals liberation and freedom among the people of God.

※ We are not to take sides and divide the community. Our leaders are to stand behind the community, following at the end, falling in behind Jesus, bearing their crosses and trials, encouraging those they have taught the Gospel to, to live as fools for Christ. Are we known as Christ's or do we belong to one faction or other, forgetting the Word of God among us? Like the Pharisees at the time of Jesus are we nitpicking about inconsequential issues while ignoring hunger, true justice and worship of God? We are called to remember that our Lord is Jesus, the Son of Man, master who is crucified for standing for the Truth.

TWENTY-THIRD WEEK IN ORDINARY TIME

Monday

FIRST READING   **I.** Col 1:24—2:3

                                              II. 1 Cor 5:1–8

Responsorial Psalm   **I.** Ps 62:6–7, 9

                                   II. Ps 5:5–6, 7, 12

GOSPEL   Lk 6:6–11

✳ Sabbath again and Jesus is intent on preaching by example what is the true worship of God. It is not ritual alone, but it is healing that is broken and sick, filling up what is lacking and make human and whole again. He sees a man with a paralyzed right hand and calls the man out (discipleship) and commands him to raise his hand. He obeys. And Jesus examines them: is it lawful to do good or to do harm, to save life or destroy it? And, it seems, not to do anything because of a law is to do harm and destroy life! He heals the man by his word, but they the teachers and leaders are furious and already they begin to figure out how to get rid of him. He's dangerous, preaching wholeness, inclusion of the sick, the weak, the lost, those without power, previously shunned religiously. He reveals their own shallowness and insensitivity, by acting with such compassion. Who do we look more like today?

✳ Do we take pride in our lives, our weaknesses and failures to live up to the Gospel and stand before one another as though we were not called to live in the Body of Christ? What kind of yeast has each of us become: leavening the dough or seeping through it and making it all rotten, inedible? Are we in need of sincerity and truth directed at us by the suffering Christ? God knows our thoughts too and will do good in spite of us, even in our presence. How do we deal with the Jesus that speaks the truth of our own evil to us?

✻ Paul speaks not only of his sufferings for the gospel but also his joy because he fills up what is lacking in the sufferings of Christ, on behalf of the church. The mystery of Christ that is preached is the mystery of the cross and resurrection. Our life in Christ, bearing our cross and dying and living in the Lord together. We are struggling for and with one another, strengthening one another and we are to be united in love. We are to remember that we live in mystery with Christ in God!

Jesus heals a man with a withered hand on the Sabbath and the hearts and minds of those who are withered with insensitivity, self-righteousness and judgmentalism are indignant. Jesus is about life, giving life, preserving life for all and most for those whose lives are on the brink, on the edge. This protection of life, this healing and care of all people from the womb to the tomb provokes a frenzy of rage. And they intent at going after Jesus. Do we share Jesus' dedication to the truth and his care of other human beings?

Tuesday

FIRST READING   I. Col 2:6–15
               II. 1 Cor 6:1–11

Responsorial Psalm   I. Ps 145:1–2, 8–9, 10–11
         II. Ps 149:1–2, 3–4, 5–6a and 9b

GOSPEL   Lk 6:12–19

✻ After Jesus has healed or had a run in with those who reject his words, he goes off to pray, spending the whole night with his God. And when he rises from his prayer, he calls those who he will ask to share his work, his words, his care for the sick, the lost and the excluded with—this first twelve disciples. We know their names and in many cases, not much more than that—as is fitting, because we are to disappear into our Lord, our master and God, as Jesus did, doing only what he sees his Father asking and willing, in his prayer. Only the one who betrays is singled out. Are we in a list of disciples? Who do we publicly follow and belong to? And how will we each be remembered? Will we disappear into our God or be remembered for our sin and treachery in our community?

✹ The saints going to court against one another! This is scandalous behavior for those reconciled to God in Christ called to reconcile one another. What kind of people have we become, that the Church acts just like everyone else both in doing evil to each other and then acting as though we were not forgiven and reconciled to God in Christ. We have all been called to be the men and women who are heal, and draw others to Christ by our lives and presence. Have we instead become traitors and tormentors of others struggling to believe?

✹ We must continue to live in Christ Jesus the Lord and in the Spirit in which we received him. We are to continually learn, be taught and to share in gratitude the grace of Christ with others. Our lives are to mirror Jesus' own life. We are his followers and we are to pray, before making any important decision daily. We are to live with others and hold each other accountable to God. We are to do the work of healing (medicine and health care for all) and we are to touch all with the power of God. This is our calling, our vocations and our life in baptism/confirmation and eucharist. Do we go back to our baptisms and back to the Word and our communities to be held accountable for growing in the mystery of dying and being born in God?

Wednesday

FIRST READING   **I.** Col 3:1–11
                                  II. 1 Cor 7:25–31
Responsorial Psalm   **I.** Ps 145:2–3, 10–11, 12–13ab
                        II. Ps 45:11–12, 14–15, 16–17
GOSPEL   Lk 6:20–26

✹ Jesus begins the most densely packed sermon in Luke's gospel: on the plain by raising his eyes to his disciples, which means he is kneeling on the ground before them, as servant. And he gives the four blessings and the four woes that bind others to him: blessings for the poor, those hungry and weeping and for those rejected, hated and insulted and treated poorly, as he was treated. And woes for the wealthy, the secure and full, those oblivious to others' needs and happy in their insensitivity and those who are deemed successful and blessed in this world. There are only two choices at distant spectrums. Where do we stand? Or how close to our suffering servant master do we find ourselves because of what we do and who we share our lives with? Jesus kneels before us and invites us down to where he kneels, humbly upon the ground.

※ This is Paul's opinion, not Jesus', for Paul is expecting the end of time to come quickly and so he does not consider marriage to be important, as well as children and the long faithfulness of being an alternative of hope in the face of the ways of the world. Instead he sees immediacy of the present, intent on preaching as primary. The world isn't passing away—we are to transform the world and we do this by the beatitudes. All of us are called to live blessed lives, poor, hungry for justice, weeping over injustice and evil and its consequences and joyful always as we preach the Good News to the poor to those who do not want to hear of it and reject us. What is the heart of Jesus' life with God is to be ours as well: living with and like the Son of Man, beloved child and crucified because of being truthful.

※ Paul's letters are all written in the plural and we have a tendency to read them as if they come to us personally, rather than as a community of believers being called to live together and be accountable to each other. We are in Christ's company—those we break the bread of life and the word of truth with daily—and we are hidden with Christ in God. We are to daily live our baptismal promises and pragmatically root out evil, sin, injustice, and violence in our lives and we are to make sure that we do not hinder others in living their baptismal vows. We are one in God, all of us—every nationality, language, culture, gender, economic group, even religious persuasion and we are to be ever formed anew in the image of the one who created us all.

Our program of practice and being formed anew: to become poor, to hunger and thirst for justice and holiness (they are the same word), to be compassionate with those who are suffering and stand with them and to rejoice if we are honored to be persecuted for the sake of the gospel and the Son of Man. And we are to be careful not to be found among the rich and insensitive, those who are full and do not share, those who live without care of the pain of others and those who court prophets who tell you what you want to hear. Are we as Church among the blessed or have we become like those who think 'you can have it all'?

Thursday

FIRST READING **I.** Col 3:12–17
Responsorial Psalm **I.** Ps 150:1b–2, 3–4, 5–6
GOSPEL Lk 6:27–38

✣ We are God's holy, chosen ones; God's beloved. We are to clothe ourselves in the garments of our baptism into Jesus and the Spirit. We are to live and act, speak and pray as Jesus. This is a blueprint for building up the life of a believer. The basics to be practiced by everyone. We make peace the reality of our lives with each other, in the Body of Christ and in the world.

Jesus' words are like sword to our hearts and souls: love your enemies, do good to those who hate you, bless and pray for those who harm you. We are to live with the peace of God, without harm, violence or provocation of others. We are to respond with life-giving imagination, creativity and a chance at conversion in every situation. We are to lend and give generously even if we think that nothing may come back to us. We are to be holy and compassionate and forgiving, living like God in relation to everyone. What kind of measure will we be getting back today this year?

Friday

FIRST READING **I.** 1 Tim 1:1–2, 12–14
Responsorial Psalm **I.** Ps 16:1–2a and 5, 7–8, 11
GOSPEL Lk 6:39–42

✣ We return to the last section of Jesus' sermon on the plain—where the most difficult commands are found: we've just been told love your enemies, don't judge or condemn and forgive. The example: a blind person leading another blind person, both falling into the ditch. Who are we like: the blind or our master Jesus? Do we pay attention to Jesus' words and actions or are we busy looking for the speck in others' eyes, disregarding the huge planks in our own? Do we have a highly inflated opinion of ourselves and 'lord' it over others, rather than remember how our Lord relates so patiently with us? We had best get clear about one thing: the measure we deal with others is the measure God uses with us.

Saturday

FIRST READING	**I.** 1 Tim 1:15–17
	II. 1 Cor 10:14–22
Responsorial Psalm	**I.** Ps 113:1b–2, 3–4, 5 and 6–7
	II. Ps 116:12–13, 17–18
GOSPEL	**I.** Lk 6:43–49

The sayings of Jesus continue: what fruit do we bear (and trees usually bear every year as do grain and cereal crops)? What do others gather from our behaviors, choices, relationships and associations? Figs or thorns? Do we listen to Jesus' words and then act accordingly or do we listen to the words and go our own way, along with others, building our foundations on sand instead of stone. Do we listen? The word listen means to obey? Who do we obey? Daniel Berrigan once said that he spent his whole adult life looking for someone to obey? Are we heading for a disaster? Or are we building on the solid foundation of the Word of God, justice, care of the poor, love of enemies and being peacemakers and the children of God?

We feed upon the bread/body and the cup/blood of Christ that makes us all one in his own Spirit. And we are not to anger the Spirit of God, given to us in baptism, confirmation and eucharist by our actions and those of our communities. Are we sound or rotten trees? Do we draw goodness from our lives, fruit for others to feed and feast upon? What fills our hearts? Do we glibly call Jesus "Lord" yet do not obey? Are we shallow believers, without foundation, substance and practice? This is a good examination of conscience using Jesus' own words.

TWENTY-FOURTH WEEK IN ORDINARY TIME

Monday

FIRST READING   **I.** 1 Tim 2:1–8

II. 1 Cor 11:17–26, 33

Responsorial Psalm   **I.** Ps 28:2, 7, 8–9

II. Ps 40:7–8a, 8b–9, 10, 17

GOSPEL   Lk 7:1–10

✸ Jesus turns from preaching and goes to Capernaum (home for him on the road). A man in the Roman military hears of Jesus and sends the Jewish elders to him. Though he was a Roman in occupied territory he obviously had good relations with the community, even building their synagogue for them. His words are stunning: Sir, do not trouble yourself for I am not worthy to welcome you under my roof." Just give the order and it will be done. Jesus is stunned. Faith can be found anywhere (even among enemies of the people) and he praises him and responds to his request. These are our words before receiving Eucharist. We use them for ourselves (not on behalf of another in need). Do we wait with this kind of attention for Jesus' order? Has Jesus ever had good reason to be stunned by the depth and expression of our faith in him?

✸ Factions in the community: it started early and it distorts even the Eucharist. Those who are rich eat their own gift before those who are poor, coming with their gifts can even arrive (servants coming late after their masters). In liturgy they embarrass those who are like the poor man, Jesus. They are eating and drinking not to the life of the Lord, but to their own judgment and death. Jesus heals us all, those with power on earth and wealth and those with none. And sadly, it seems there is often more faith in outsiders than among believers. Wouldn't it be great to astonished God today? What could we do?

✺ We are to pray for those in authority so that we can live our lives undisturbed, but we must remember that God is one and that God wants all people to come to the truth. We must also give our lives as ransom for the many and speak the truth to all, including or especially those in authority. We are live truthfully, without anger. What does this admonition call us to in our day?

Jesus heals the servant of a centurion. He was part of the occupying force, but respectful of the people and their customs/religion. The servant dies but still he asks, for he knows what it is like to live under authority and he recognizes Jesus' power as stronger than Rome's—stronger than death. And Jesus praises his faith. By whose authority do we live and do we keep the authority of our nation/state in perspective—that it is nothing in comparison to the authority of God and must be challenged/disobeyed when it stands in opposition to God's authority?

Tuesday

FIRST READING   I. 1 Tim 3:1–13
                                                    II. 1 Cor 12:12–14, 27–31
Responsorial Psalm   I. Ps 101:1–2, 2–3, 5, 6
                                                    II. Ps 100:1–2, 3, 4, 5
GOSPEL   Lk 7:11–17

✺ Jesus continues on his journey halting at the gates of the town of Naim as a funeral procession exists, with a widow mourning her only son. Two people leave the town, one to be buried and the other, as widow with no support to become a beggar, destitute and alone, dead to her society. And Jesus abruptly tells her "Don't cry!" wow…and he touches the stretcher and tells her son "Awake, I tell you." Older translations are clearer: I say to you Arise! And he does. And he gives him back to her (shades of Elijah giving the widow back her child). God has visited his people—Jesus has brought two people back from the dead and refuses to let society and especially his own people condemn anyone to a life that is walking death. Don't cry! Do something, like Jesus and begin to raise up the hopes of the widow, the orphan, the poor, the sick, those without insurance and health care, the refugee and immigrant, the outsider and outcast, so that everyone knows that God is visiting his people again, in us.

✻ We have all been baptized into the Spirit of Jesus to honor our God, our Father. We are citizens of God, part of the Body of Christ. Those with the most authority or power are those who serve the most members of the Body and we are to be servants, first and foremost. Jesus, the servant of God looks first for those most in need: a widow whose only son has died. In fact, with no one to care for her, she would have died too. And Jesus raises the son and brings them both back to life in the community. Do we live to bring and share life with others? Are we the prophets of life not just in word, but our action?

✻ Do you want to be a bishop? You have to be married only once! Irreproachable, a good teacher, not addicted to drink, a man of peace and you cannot love money—among other qualities. A bishop must manage his own household, because he will be managing the household of God. And deacons must follow in these same patterns—and all should be put on probation first! And the women who serve in these ministries must be trustworthy—the requirements are the same for all. We seem to have forgotten and have lost much of the wisdom of the early Church in regard to bishops/deacons for both men and women. Who in your church would make worthy ministers?

Jesus heals a widow's only son and in the tradition of Elijah the prophet gives him back to her. We do not often see Jesus so clearly as the prophet of God—his Word bringing us back to life. Do we listen and come back to life?

Wednesday

FIRST READING	**I.** 1 Tim 3:14–15
	II. 1 Cor 12:31—13:13
Responsorial Psalm	**I.** Ps 111:1–2, 3–4, 5–6
	II. Ps 33:2–3, 4–5, 12, 22
GOSPEL	Lk 7:31–35

✻ Reach for the higher gifts! Love, unending, enduring with grace, no violence, no thought of self, no reward, rejoicing in others' gain, forgiving, not taking offense, delighting in the Truth of God, ready to excuse, hope, and serve. Are we adults or still just children when it comes to love? What are we, the men and women of this generation like? Are we selfish, petty, stupid, irreverent of those who cry justice and without harm obey the commands to love and serve the least among us? Do we have any Wisdom at all?

☀ Who do we worship, follow and put our faith in—the one born in the flesh, vindicated in the Spirit, worshipped by all of heaven, preached to the nations and now in glory and believed in throughout the world? Jesus questions the people of his day (and ours) on what we are like—peevish children squatting in public and calling out to their playmates, whinning and complaining. Not a pretty picture. They neither responded to John the Baptist's call to repentance or to the Son of Man's call to sinners in mercy. They found something wrong with both of them, and did nothing. And what about us—have we listened to John's call to change so that we can see who is coming? Have we listened to Jesus' summons to the cross and reconciliation among us?

Thursday

FIRST READING   I. 1 Tim 4:12–16
Responsorial Psalm   I. Ps 111:7–8, 9, 10
GOSPEL   Lk 7:36–50

☀ Timothy is young but mature in his faith. He must be devoted to reading the scriptures, to preaching and teaching, and he is to be absorbed in his service so that others can see and take heart from his example (as well as his words). This is how Timothy is saved and many of those around him. This is how we are saved—and this is what opens us to the awareness of others who are seeking faith and salvation.

Jesus is invited to a Pharisee's house for dinner but treated shabbily, not as a guest. Yet a woman arrives who in public attends to Jesus, with honor and personal service. The man is scandalized because he knows who the woman is (how?) yet Jesus knows what he is thinking—how he has judged her harshly. His story makes it clear—everyone is in debt to God and some owe a little and some owe a lot. But all are forgiven. And who loves God more?—the one whose debt was great. She is sent home with praise, respect and thanks and made the model of how he must learn to love, in gratitude. Do we need to learn this too?

Friday

FIRST READING

I. 1 Tim 6:2–12
II. 1 Cor 15:12–20

Responsorial Psalm

I. Ps 49:6–7, 8–10, 17–18, 19–20
IC Ps 17:1, 6–7, 8 and 15

GOSPEL

Lk 8:1–3

✺ Here we are introduced to other disciples, who accompanied him from the beginning in Galilee as he preached and gave away the good news of the kingdom of God, journeying through towns and countryside, on the way to Jerusalem: women, some not named, others clearly singled out as disciples in their own right: Mary called Magdalene healed of her afflictions, Joanna wife of Chuza, Herod's steward, Suzanna and others who provided for them (the twelve). All told, there are another twelve named in the gospels, women (not counting Mary his mother). This is their company—those who they break bread with, share life and wealth and the struggle to bring the kingdom with. Do we have twelve—each of women and men that form our company as we make our way to the cross and resurrection today?

✺ We stake our lives and our dying on the resurrection of Jesus and we are committed publicly to being witnesses to this truth in the face of the world's choices based on so much death. In baptism we died with Christ and rose with Christ and live with Christ in God. Our lives are seeped in resurrection if we live in God. And we belong to the company of resurrection, those called by Jesus to be known together as followers: twelve named men and in this reading, three named women disciples: Mary of Magdala, Joanna, Suzanna. But there are others who made choices based on the truth of the resurrection. Who do we provide for out of our own resources, and are we among those who follow, named or anonymous?

Saturday

FIRST READING   **I.** 1 Tim 6:13–16
                                II. 1 Cor 15:35–37, 42–49

Responsorial Psalm   **I.** Ps 100:1–2, 3, 4, 5
                               II. Ps 56:10–12, 13–14

GOSPEL   Lk 8:4–15

A crowd gathers and Jesus tells stories and parables. First we hear the sower and his marvelous seed and it is lavishly thrown everywhich way. Onto footpaths where birds carry it off; on thin shallow soil where it spouts quickly and just as quickly shrivels; on the patches where the weeds reign and finally in the field. The farmers would have been nodding knowingly, but then comes the jolt. And it produced: some 100 times as much! What? Thirty-fold return, sixty, ninety, one hundred-fold return. Impossible. The usual yield in a really good year—maybe 6-8%. Anything past that and you could expand your fields, pay off your debts, hire someone to do the planting and harvesting for you, keep the best seed, put in irrigation ditches, build a new house. Anything over 20-30 and you were the only provider in that area! Some seed! So—has any seed fallen in our fields? Has Jesus' word taken over our lives, monies, decisions, neighborhoods, morality, politics, economics or is it clear to everyone that it's fallen somewhere else?

Do we ask stupid questions too? Our bodies have been sown in the Body of Christ, buried with Christ in God and we already have been raised in glory with Christ. The rest of our life since baptism is practice of resurrection that will come one day in fullness for all, and for the earth. Our lives, the ground we dwell in has been sown with the Word of God and that Word is powerful beyond imaging. But what is our ground like: our bodies, our lives and souls? We've heard the Word, but what has it done in us? And this is not just about our individual lives, but our communities that yields yearly harvests of justice and peace for others. What have our hearts reaped on behalf of other hungry hearts?

Jesus faced Pontius Pilate and spoke truthfully. We too must stand our ground before the nations/powers of the world and keep God's command over and above any command of the state. Our only ruler and lord is Jesus the crucified and God the Father/Spirit who dwells in inapproachable light—yet we dwell within them by our baptisms. We are to live so as to honor them alone. How deep is our devotion to God? How do we live in the reign of our God, the reign of justice, peace, forgiveness, unity and communion with all?

Jesus tells the story of the seed/sower and the ground. There is the footpath, shallow soil, and edges of the field choked with weeds. If the Word falls in any of these places it can barely get going and then dies/chokes or is blown away. If it falls in the field (community) then it can be harvested—100 fold! Amazing havest. Do we understand? Every year we hear the Word—every year God waits for the grain/justice/food, the meal/Eucharist we share and our excess that belongs to the poor of the world. What does God get from us this year?

TWENTY-FIFTH WEEK IN ORDINARY TIME

Monday

FIRST READING   **I.** Ezra 1:1–6

                                        II. Pro 3:27–34

Responsorial Psalm   **I.** Ps 126:1b–2ab, 2cd–3, 4–5, 6

                                   II. Ps 15:2–3, 3–4, 5

GOSPEL   Lk 8:16–18

Jesus notes that no one lights a lamp and covers it up. No, it's put on a stand so that the light can penetrate and spread throughout the entire space it is in. It can be everything from a lighthouse to a candle in a cave or prison cell. It must expand to fill the emptiness of the darkness around it. This is what we are to be in the world, as Jesus was in his time and place. All will be revealed, even if now, much lies covered. We are to listen to the Word with care and obey, and produce. And our judgment depends on it. Our lives are not our own. From the moment of our baptisms we were told: you live now, no longer for yourself alone, but now you live hidden with Christ in God." Are we lamps burning bright, wicks steady in oil, lighthouses, even just oil lamps or long-lasting bulbs? Do we cut through the darkness and shadows of evil and lies to reveal the light of Christ?

A few bits of folk wisdom couched in proverbs: never refuse a kindness to someone begging for it and do it now! Do no harm to another. Do no violence. Be humble and truthful. Basics for being decent human beings, no matter your religious beliefs. Jesus exhorts us, his community in a short parable: be a light welcoming people into the kingdom. Make clear what is secret and reveal the wisdom that has been given to us in baptism's Spirit and the Word of Jesus. Be aware and don't lose the light that has been entrusted to us! These are foundational ways of being in the world.

✸ Ezra tells the history of the people who come back from exile
and strangely enough it is a foreign king Cyrus of Persia
who allows the Jews to return, to go back and rebuild the temple
to their God and to once again dwell in their land. The exiles go
back and bring all they have acquired and made in the land where
many of them flourished. It is amazing that Cyrus was inspired
by God—there is only one God—and God inspires all men and
women in the world towards goodness, unity and life with dignity
and freedom.

Each person is called to be a light, not hidden but displayed, so
that it can be used by anyone who needs it. We are to be the light of
Christ in the world—and that light, that truth exposes everything
and what each person does with the inspiration that God gives to
him/her. And there will be a reckoning when all know what each
has done with their knowledge and gifts from the Lord. How much
has been given to us who have known Jesus the Word of God made
flesh? How many have we shared/given back to others?

Tuesday

FIRST READING   I. Ezra 6:7–8, 12b, 14–20
                                 II. Pro 21:1–6, 10–13

Responsorial Psalm   I. Ps 122:1–2, 3–4ab, 4cd–5
                            II. Ps 119:1, 27, 30, 34, 35, 44

GOSPEL   Lk 8:19–21

✸ Jesus' family arrives: his mother and relatives but they can't
get near him because of the crowd. Someone alerts them to
their predicament and surprisingly he doesn't care. They are not
his family. They were his family of origin, but he is now about his
Father's business of preaching the Word of good news to the poor
and bringing the kingdom among those in desperate need of hope,
of life and forgiveness, justice, mercy and peace. He is clear on who
is family to him; what constitutes intimacy and closeness in the
family of baptism and grace: "My mother and brothers and sisters
are those who hear the word of God and do it." That's the blood
tie, the water ties of baptism and the blood connections of eucharist
and shared suffering. If we want to be Jesus' mother, brother or
sister, then we must listen to his Word, obey and make it come true
in our lives.

✦ God weighs our hearts and is interested in our practice of justice and truthfulness. We are watched always by the Just One and it is known when we ignore the cry of the poor. As we have heard and responded, so our God will respond to us. This is justice. And Jesus is clear with his disciples that if we wish to know intimacy and closeness with him and God our Father than we must hear the word of God and put it into practice. This is justice in Jesus' family. We are bound by Word, not by family ties, blood or marriage. How close are we to Jesus and to the Father, really?

✦ King Darius lets the people work on the temple and be repaid from the royal revenue! The people work, encouraged by the Word of God through the prophets with them: Haggai and Zechariah. They finished a portion of the temple (nothing like the earlier one's majesty) and celebrated the dedication by keeping the feast of the Passover for the first time back in Jerusalem since it was destroyed. They have come back and God has used foreigners who had conquered them and many other peoples to allow them this privilege, and to help them, though they did not believe in the God of Israel.

Who are the true brothers and sisters, mothers of Jesus? Not anyone bound by blood or marriage but those who hear the Word of God in Jesus, or are inspired by God and obey it—beyond any line of blood, marriage, religion, nation, economic bracket, personal connection. We are all called to be the family of God. We must remember and pray for and work with all peoples as the children of the one Father, kin to Jesus in the Spirit.

Wednesday

FIRST READING	**I.** Ezra 9:5–9
	II. Pro 30:5–9
Responsorial Psalm	**I.** Tb 13:2, 3–4a, 4befghn, 7–8
	II. Ps 119:29, 72, 89, 101, 104, 163
GOSPEL	Lk 9:1–6

✦ The Word of God, in the prophets and in Israel, are the shield of those who take refuge in God. And those who know the word know what is essential: enough bread to eat, to live truthfully and honor God. This is the wisdom of those who do not know Jesus, the Word and bread of God in community. Jesus' words are pointed: go lightly with only what you need now, live on the kindness and generosity of others, and leave without saying anything to those who reject you. And go the Way of Jesus preaching and living the good news to the poor in the world, healing and setting the world right. God is with us in Jesus

✹ Ezra prays to God afraid to raise his face because of the peoples' injustice and sin, even after they have been punished, exiled, put in captivity. They have been given mercy and the remnant was allowed to return. They have been given relief in their servitude but they are still slaves in their own land and it is being restored—yet the people, priests, leaders, all continue to do what is wicked.

Jesus' mission sends forth his followers with the power and authority to heal and to overcome demons (evil and all that hinders individuals and groups from living truly human lives—addictions, bad habits, vices, etc.). They must travel in the power of the Spirit like/with Jesus—no walking staff (used to protect), no traveling bag, bread and money! They are to be a community that relies on the hospitality of those who are waiting to hear the good news, as a sign of the radical change in society for those who believe in God's kingdom where all are family in God. How can we do this today?

Thursday

FIRST READING   **I.** Hg 1:1–8
                                                       II. Eccl 1:2–11
Responsorial Psalm   **I.** Ps 149:1–2, 3–4, 5–6, 9
                                 II. Ps 90:3–4, 5–6, 12–13, 14 and 17bc
GOSPEL   Lk 9:7–9

✹ Herod the Jewish king who killed John the Baptist now hears of his cousin, Jesus and is distressed and disturbed (as was his father when he heard of the birth of this child from strangers to his kingdom). Who is this man? Is he what his worst fears and superstitions scream: John back from the dead? Is he a prophet like Elijah of old (called the disturber of Israel and every king who saw him coming knew that he was in trouble with Yahweh)?

Is he one of the ancient ones, teachers, lawgivers, prophets come back to life?—of course come back to haunt him. Herod lived in fear and guilt having murdered and schemed and stolen from the people, living in opulence while his people lived in misery, living in collusion with the occupying force, accommodating his religious practices to suit his own ends. And he's anxious to see him. Anxious—not hopeful, not in expectation of justice and fulfillment of the peoples' long wait, not about to be converted. Anxious. How do we feel about this Jesus?

☀ Folk wisdom that sounds like Zen sayings: woe, everything passes away; all things are wearisome, back to circling around. Nothing new on earth, nothing remembered. A bit bleak. But such a description of life, describes the one who says these things and their belief or lack of it, not life itself. And it is echoed in the words of Herod who sees Jesus as just John the Baptizer returning. Yet is anxious to see Jesus. What if Jesus and his words are life and hope and something new upon the earth? Do we live lives that are a new thing for the world to be amazed at? And do we live resurrection life now surprising people as Jesus did?

☀ Haggai, one of the prophets of the return—the people have come back and built their own dwellings first—leaving the temple in ruins. They have picked up their old lives where they left off—planting, harvesting, making wine, making a living, but they have been without spirit and soul or heart. They must begin to build the house of the Lord for God's glory.

We know that our God no longer dwells in houses/temples/ even churches but the glory of God dwells in Jesus the Word made flesh and in the Body of Christ of which we are all members. This person Jesus, the prophet in his time is God made manifest in human flesh. Even Herod (the corrupt leaders of nations/who use religion as they use everything else for their own ends) is curious about Jesus but does not understand what Jesus is doing. How can he? He does not wait for God's word to come true. He cares not for the worship of the true God. Do we at heart care for God's will upon the earth?

Friday

FIRST READING   **I.** Hg 2:1–9
                                           II. Ecc 3:1–11

Responsorial Psalm   **I.** Ps 43:1, 2, 3, 4
                            II. Ps 144:1b and 2abc, 3–4

GOSPEL   Lk 9:18–22

Jesus is praying not far from his disciples and asks them what Herod has been thinking about: who is he? What do others think? What do they think? The answers are surprisingly the same—prophet, one of the ancient ones, John the Baptist returned, like Elijah. Peter blurts out: the Messiah of God, meaning the anointed one, the prophet who would come to fulfill the hopes of the people for justice. But it's a problematic title, one that Jesus never uses and won't let others use either because for many it meant a king, an earthly ruler who would overthrow the Romans, rebuild Jerusalem and make Israel a nation to be reckoned with in the world. That's why he says—don't, for God's sake tell anyone that. Instead he calls himself the Son of Man who will be rejected, suffer greatly, be crucified and rise again. It is the beginning of the call to the cross, the way he has walked since incarnation, as have all those who were prophets and truthtellers before him. Who do we think Jesus is? Do we remember that he disturbed everyone, was a prophet of God, the Word made flesh, God in our midst? Crucified and scorned?

The people barely remember what the house of the Lord/ temple looked like, because their exile had been so long. But they are to take heart and have courage for God will be with them in their work. God remains with them as their God, and they are his people still. The day will come when God will dwell with them once again and the future glory of the Lord will be greater than the former—and his dwelling place will know the gift of peace.

This dwelling place where the glory of God is greater than any former dwelling place is the body/the person of Jesus. He is thought to be a prophet like of old, or like John the Baptist. And Peter calls him the Messiah of God—the hope of those who have gone before them waiting on the promise of God. But Jesus tells them that he is the Son of Man, the judge of the nations, the glory of God hidden/

revealed in the Crucified one—and he is peace, God's peace upon the world. Do we know our God in Jesus like this?

Saturday

FIRST READING	I. Zec 2:5–9, 14-15a
	II. Eccl 11:9—12:8
Responsorial Psalm	I. Jer 31:10, 11–12ab, 13
	II. Ps 90:3–4, 5–6, 12–13, 14 and 17
GOSPEL	Lk 9:43b–45

Jesus preaches, heals, speaks truthfully, releases people from bondage and gives them hope and many are amazed (but not many follow in his footsteps). So he reminds his disciples again: I am the Son of Man (from Daniel, one who will come in glory to judge the nations with justice, but one who has suffered terribly at the hands of people). The disciples don't understand—they don't want to—they don't even want to hear this kind of talk—it's not what they expected when they decided to come after him. It says 'something prevented them from grasping what he meant and they were afraid to ask him about it.' That something is rejection, their ideas of what they want him to be for them and what following him could mean: power, prestige, a place in his kingdom. Their fear and disappointment, their own and others' demands and expectations are what took over. It is the beginning of their rejection of their own master. And us—do our fears and others' words and ways make us avoid and ignore the core of the gospel—the call to the cross and suffering and death, as prelude to resurrection?

God will bring us to judgment. Sobering reality to hear. We are to remember our Creator, and look to the world that has been made along with us to teach us wisdom and the reality of life bound to death. God gives all breath in life and takes it from all as well. This Creator is the Son of Man, who will give his life so that everything might live forever and be renewed and blessed again and again. Do we understand this yet? Are we still reacting in fear to the words of invitation to come and follow the Son of Man, whose power is steeped in creation and life, but not in the power of men and women? Lord, help us see the meaning of you, Son of Man.

TWENTY-SIXTH WEEK IN ORDINARY TIME

Monday

FIRST READING   I. Zec 8:1–8
Responsorial Psalm   I. Ps 102:16–18, 19–21, 29 and 22–23
GOSPEL   Lk 9:46–50

✳ The disciples just don't get it. They ignore what they don't want to hear and act like everything is going according to their plans. Who's the greatest is the subject under discussion. Jesus knows about their petty arguing and brings forth a child and puts him or her by his side! "Whoever welcomes this little child in my name welcomes me; and whoever welcomes me, welcomes the one who sent me." Listen (and obey) the least among you is the greatest, the servant is the one who goes before the others—to the cross and on the way. They are to forget about power and seek to serve, to follow and to disappear and to forget about others who aren't in their group—leave them be and let God work in them as He wishes to. Who's the greatest? Remember the child is the one without status, power, influence, place in society, has to obey everyone bigger or stronger, has no rights and was considered nothing more than a slave or person servant at everyone's beck and call. How are we doing as children of God, welcoming others in God's name?

✳ God speaks of returning to Jerusalem and the people he loves and wants them to be his faithful city, like the mountain of God where the law was given and the covenant was proclaimed and accepted. A remnant of the people will be brought home, for nothing is impossible for God. The people will be rescued and they will be brought back from all the places of exile. God will take them back closely to himself again.

Jesus seeks to draw all people but especially those who claim to be his own. He takes a little child into their midst and says: "Welcome this child and you welcome me and the One who sent me. The least among you is the greatest." The child in Jesus' time had no power, they were seen as slaves, with no rights. Some were loved and many were not—they were like outsiders, outcasts, the ill, all who had disobeyed the law (not until they became adults at 12 did they figure into the community). Jesus tells us that all these are the ones we are to welcome—to place in our midst as honored and blest. Do we?

Tuesday

FIRST READING

I. Zec 8:20–23
II. Job 3:1–3, 11–17, 20–23

Responsorial Psalm

I. Ps 87:1b–3, 4–5, 6–7
II. Ps 88:2–3, 4–5, 6, 7–8

GOSPEL

Lk 9:51–56

✳ Jesus is following the plan of the prophets—heading towards Jerusalem, but makes a side trip—to the Samaritans, the hated enemies of the Jewish people. He sends ahead some messengers so that they have a place to stay but the people there won't receive him because he was on his way to Jerusalem (a point of doctrine and belief). James and John want to call down fire on them, destroying them, indignant, but Jesus' reaction is drastically different, even opposed to that suggestion. He rebukes his own for this violence and hatred and reaction and they go on their way—the way of the cross, of forgiveness, mercy, nonviolent response to rejection, set on what is important. Have we learned anything from Jesus about rejection, or are we as violent and stupid in our responses to the gospel and the presence of goodness as his cousins?

✳ Job suffers and curses the day he was born, wanting to die, grieving and bitter of heart. He cries out to God, who appears to have given light to him, yet he does not see his way and God seems to hem in on every side. Jesus too faced pain, suffering, hardship, grieved at others and the evil that was done to him, yet he does not pray bitterly like Job. In the face of rejection, from the Samaritans he rebukes his disciples for calling down harm upon them, and simply goes off to others who will hopefully listen to him. How do we deal with rejection or the prospect of death because of being truthful—like Job or like Jesus?

Wednesday

FIRST READING   **I.** Ne 2:1–8
II. Job 9:1–12, 14–16

Responsorial Psalm   **I.** Ps 137:1–2, 3, 4–5, 6
II. Ps 88:10bc–11, 12–13, 14–15

GOSPEL   Lk 9:57–62

They continue on the way to Jerusalem and a man comes and says to Jesus that he'll follow him anywhere he goes. Jesus must look at him rather ruefully and realistically responds to him saying that the foxes and birds have places to rest, but the Son of Man has nowhere to lay his head. He will be utterly rejected and even be buried in a borrowed tomb. Others have other things more pressing and then they'll come: funerals, goodbyes to family, work, relationships—all sorts of things can get in the way, become a 'good' excuse to avoid following Jesus more closely. Jesus' words examine us: "whoever has put their hand to the plow and looks back is not fit for the kingdom of God!" How fit are we for God's work and reign in the world? Are we wafflers at best, good at excuses and fast with our words? And yet, Jesus still hopes that there will be some who come with him to Jerusalem.

Job knows that he cannot be in the right against God. It is God who is wise and who has made creation, and that God's strength and power is about life, sustaining the earth, sky, seasons, stars and human beings. And man is judged by this awesome entity, and Job wonders seriously if God even hears his voice. Jesus is that awesomeness of God yet human like us, among us, calling us to singlehearted devotion, letting go of everything and trusting that God will care for us. Do we act like Job, or look back even though we've said yes to following God? Are we like Francis, the poor man passionately in love with the Son of Man who has nowhere to lay his head—and looks to us to be his friends?

Nehemiah is a servant, attends the king and his sadness is revealed. He tells the king of the city of his ancestors lying in ruins and he asks if he can return to rebuild it, and then he would return as the servant of the king. He is given leave (surprisingly) and he also receives letters for safe-conduct, for wood. The favoring hand of God is upon him! Again it is unbelievers, those outside the land/people/covenant of Israel who enable prophets and people to once again worship God in their own place. Do we appreciate others not of our faith, nation, covenants who are wise, gracious and generous towards those who dwell in their nation and yet seek to serve another God?

We claim to be followers of Jesus, the Son of Man who had no place to lay his head, no home/no shelter, no family. But those who said they would follow him and his Father, do no other work but the work of God. They obey God's will, bringing hope and true worship of God to all, along with the good news that what we do to one another, our God takes as done in honor to God himself, for our God is one of us, Jesus, the prophet, whose very word is flesh.

Thursday

FIRST READING   **I.** Ne 8:1–4, 5–6, 7b–12
                                     II. Job 19:21–27

Responsorial Psalm   **I.** Ps 19:8, 9, 10, 11
                            II. Ps 27:7–8a, 8b–9abc, 13–14

GOSPEL   Lk 10:1–12

Job cries pity from his friends, wanting his words forged in stone so that others will know what he suffered, yet he declares that God is his Avenger, the Last and that he will one day set him close to him, take his side and let his eyes gaze on him, who is his rock forever. Jesus goes to his friends, sending them out to bring others into his community, seeking others with the reality of Peace, sharing what is given them, offering the kingdom in return—the presence of God among us in Word, Body and community. We are told again that the kingdom is near—are we aware of how close our God is, and how close judgment is upon us too?

Ezra reads the scroll of the law and all the people stand and listen attentively! This is the liturgy of the word with the book held high for all to see. The people are blessed and they prostrate themselves before the Lord. The law is interpreted and when the long reading is finished the people are told to rejoice for the day is holy unto the Lord. And when they feast, all are included and fed.

The disciples are sent out to preach the Word of hope, the good news of God to the people, in pairs. They are to preach not only with words, but with the way they dress, travel, where they stay, and the peace that they bring forth with them. They are not to 'shop around' for a better place to stay but stay where they have been welcomed—where the people have listened to and responded to the Word of the Lord. If the Word is refused then they are to leave. The Word must be preached and people must have the chance to take it to heart or to ignore it. Do we honor the Word as these people do?

Friday

FIRST READING   **I.** Bar 1:15–22
                                 II. Job 38:1, 12–21, 40:3–5
Responsorial Psalm   **I.** Ps 79:1–2, 3–5, 8, 9
                                 II. Ps 139:1–3, 7–8, 9–10, 13–14ab
GOSPEL   Lk 10:13–16

Jesus cries out in judgment of the cities that rejected him even though they had seen him work miracles, heal, preach, teach and comfort with the good news to the poor. They were given so much and they would have nothing of it. He judges them, worse than Tyre and Sidon (pagan cities that did not claim to believe in Yahweh) as did these townspeople. And then he speaks of Capernaum, the place he made his home after Nazareth rejected him—even they will be thrown down as though dead. And he speaks truthfully not just about those who rejected him and his words, but all those who will reject the Gospel, the words of hope to the poor, of justice for all and reconciliation, forgiveness and the making of peace in a world torn and destroyed by hate and violence. All peoples, cities, nations, governments, individuals will be judged on whether or not we obeyed the Word of God. What will happen to our towns, cities, countries, churches and parishes, our families and friends, to us—we have seen and been given so much? Have we returned any of that favor to God by sharing it with others, by giving life, hope, justice and peace to others?

✳ God answers Job from the center of the tempest, and basically declares that he is God, the maker and creator, the keeper and sustainer of all that is: time, seasons, the earth, the abyss of waters, the expanse of sky, even life and death for all on earth; the light and the darkness. What does Job know of anything, let alone of wisdom? And he learns to be silent. And Jesus echoes God's words: cities, groups, churches, parishes have seen so much of miracles, you would think we would repent, but we do not really listen—and so we do not obey. Are we among those who listen or reject the Word of God?

✳ Baruch begins with the message of every prophet: Justice is with the Lord our God and we have not been just or obedient to the Word of God but have disregarded the voice of God. Instead each and all serve other gods/idols and our hearts are wicked and we do evil in the sight of the Lord. Does this refrain touch our hearts today? Are we any different than our ancestors?

Jesus too, as a prophet judges that it will go ill with whole cities where he preached and worked miracles and yet no one repented or converted or obeyed the voice of God in Jesus' own Word made flesh. Have we heard and obeyed or rejected the Word of the gospels and so rejected God?

Saturday

FIRST READING	**I.** Bar 4:5–12, 27–29
Responsorial Psalm	**I.** Ps 69:33, 35, 36–37
GOSPEL	Lk 10:17–24

✳ It seems there are seventy-two disciples and they come back in joy! Jesus reminds them that he has shared his own power and authority over evil, his own strength and grace with them and that nothing can really harm them, (though that doesn't mean that they do not know rejection, suffering and persecution as he did—the cross). And Jesus prays aloud for the small of the earth, those without learning and influence who are taught wisdom by God: these are the poor, the sick, dying, rejected and without rights, spurned by the earth and struggling to just survive, hoping for life and desperate for God. This is the mystery of the Trinity—that only Jesus knows the Father and it is he who reveals him to those he chooses to—and that only the Father knows Jesus. Yes, we are blessed, like the disciples and those who knew Jesus because he has revealed the Father to us—in the Word of Scriptures that reveals his presence as surely and powerfully as does the Eucharist, in the poor and those who struggle to be a voice for God in the world. We've seen and heard!

The prophet cries out to the people that they find themselves in such dire straits, as slaves because of their disobedience to the Lord. God let their enemies take them and yet God is like a widow mourning her lost children, who always remembers them and only waits for them to call out for him. He waits to give them joy and save them—if only they would cry out to God! Do we seek God in all times—the hard ones and the good ones—knowing that God is with us always, and what we do either causes God to grieve over us or rejoice?

The disciples return from their mission and they are exuberant at what they have been able to accomplish in the name of the Lord. They get carried away with what they have done but Jesus reminds them that what is important is that they must be the least of God's children so that they might learn the wisdom of God the Father and the Son—we must be like the child of God, Jesus before his Father, our Father. And Jesus seeks to reveal his beloved Father to us. Are we listening or too wrapped up in our own works?

TWENTY-SEVENTH WEEK IN ORDINARY TIME

Monday

FIRST READING   **I.** Jon 1:1—2:1–2, 11

                                        II. Gal 1:6–12

Responsorial Psalm   **I.** Jon 2:3, 4, 5, 8

                 II. Ps 111:1b–2, 7–8, 9 and 10

GOSPEL   Lk 10:25–37

Jesus is always being questioned: "Master, what shall I do to receive eternal life?" And the teacher of the law already knows the answer! Love God and love your neighbor with all your heart, soul, mind and resources. But he's intent on trapping Jesus—who is my neighbor. Narrow it down to the least I have to do for the smallest group of people. And he is told the story of the Good Samaritan. For a Jew, there is no such thing as a 'good' Samaritan. He is the enemy, the apostate, irredeemable. And Jesus uses the 'enemy' to reveal the goodness of God, telling the teacher that his neighbor is everyone, extending even to those he would rather die, than take help from himself. And the man is furious, for when he must answer who was compassionate, he refuses to even say 'the good samaritan', but 'the one'.... he is told to imitate his enemy's goodness and compassion and he will have life now! Our enemies—do we see their compassion and goodness that reveals God to us and imitate their goodness, rather than excluding them and so many others from even being our 'neighbor'?

Paul is dismayed at how quickly his baptized turn away from the Scriptures and try out a new version, ignoring what the servant of God taught them. The Scriptures are the revelation of God in Jesus Christ, not to be treated as we would any other teaching. It is to be taken to heart, obeyed and put ourselves in the position of being transformed by it. This is Jesus' parable of the Good Samaritan—no such thing, (like saying a Good Terrorist today). It seeks to tell us that those we reject as human beings can teach us truly about God! If our interpretation of Scripture does not make us compassionate and filled with pity for our enemies, then it is not the Word of God, and brings us no life here or ever.

☀ This is the story of Jonah, a prophet that is sent to preach against Nineveh (like Los Angeles, London, Delhi, Bejing, Singapore—places not known for their religious devotion, and certainly not to the God of Israel). And Jonah is reluctant—he boards ship and runs from God. A great storm arises and he knows he has put them all in danger because he has not heeded the Word of God. They find him out and throw him overboard hoping that they will save their own lives. And a large fish swallows Jonah for three days and three nights and then the fish spews him out on the shore. It's a grand story—how do we run away from calling others to repentance, reluctant to do so ourselves? Do we spend most of our time trying to run away from our responsibilities in and to the world?

A lawyer asks Jesus what he's supposed to do. Jesus questions him on the law, "Do this and live." But the lawyer is running away from the reality of loving his neighbor and wants to know just who that might be. In Israel, one's neighbor was considered to be only their fellow Jews. But Jesus makes it clear that it begins far outside ones kin and nation, with one's enemy and the ones that we despise and fear—the Samaritan, the Muslim, the terrorist—the one we will not name as "Good." We must learn to love our neighbor—everyone, as they love. And then, as now, we all have much to learn.

Tuesday

FIRST READING   **I.** Jon 3:1–10
                                             II. Gal 1:13–24

Responsorial Psalm   **I.** Ps 130:1b–2, 3–4ab, 7–8
               II. Ps 139:1b–3, 13–14ab, 14c–15

GOSPEL   Lk 10:38–42

☀ Jesus is on his way to Jerusalem and stops in to stay with his friends; Martha, Mary and Lazarus (though he is not mentioned). Martha waits on him and the other disciples and Mary sits listening to him. This short piece is the ending of the story that has come before—the lawyer who wishes to justify his behavior and the good samaritan and Martha who wishes to justify her behavior and make Mary act like her. She too is rebuked by Jesus—no, Mary has chosen the better part. She has chosen to 'get into the ditch and care for the one beaten and left for dead on the road to Jerusalem'. Jesus is on his way to be crucified and Mary stays near him—that's the better part—to stand and live close to those who are beaten by others, who are crucified and left for dead. All else must serve that, and those who stand close by the cross. And we—do we seek to justify what we do in the church, rather than look to those who work for justice and care for the suffering and dying, stand with those condemned, crucified and put to death, remembering what is the heart of our religion? Francis learned that and bore the marks of the crucified in his own body.

✣ Paul gives his confession how he turned from violence as a persecutor, zealous in the tradition of his ancestors to the Gospel and a life of revelation as an apostle. He turned from destruction to the glory of God in the life of the Lord. Jesus is the presence of life and the Word of God present among us. We are challenged to listen and to obey and sit at the feet of the one who will be in the ditch and left for dead (Good Samaritan parable) and to remember that only one thing is most crucial: being attentive to those crucified, suffering and innocently abused. That's the better part: no violence, just mercy towards those who hurt.

✣ Again Jonah is told to go to Nineveh and this time he does. He walks for days crying out for them to repent, and they do! From the greatest to the least they begin to do penance and ask God's forgiveness. And God sees their repentance and so he does not harm them. What is we all repented from the evil that we do—leaving the homeless on the streets, not providing people with health care and nutrition, constructing bombs, nuclear weapons, land mines to murder people and disrespect for others? We are called to repent—not just a person here or there—but all of us in every church and synagogue and mosque and temple.

Martha welcomes Jesus to her home and prepares to feed him, while her sister listens to Jesus' word. She, like the lawyer in the previous story, wants Jesus to justify her actions and make her sister do the same. But like the lawyer, Martha and all of us must learn the better part is to accompany those who have been the victims of violence and to care for those who are broken and murdered because they have spoken the truth—as the good Samaritan did to his enemy and as Jesus will do for all of us.

Wednesday

FIRST READING

I. Jon 4:1–11

II. Gal 2:1–2, 7–14

Responsorial Psalm

I. Ps 86:3–4, 5–6, 9–10

II. Ps 117:1bc, 2

GOSPEL

Lk 11:1–4

These four lines reveal the foundation of Jesus' person, strength, mission, relationship to his Father and how we are to be formed in his image. Jesus prays and when he is finished (when he has become the words and desire and hope of his prayer, submitting and handing himself over to his Father) he teaches us how to pray. These are the crucial things: OUR Father...we pray in community to our Father, and Jesus' Father, for his will, his kingdom of justice and peace to come (what Jesus came into the world for). Give us what we need just for today so that we all share and live in communion together, aware of others' need. Forgive us, but only as we forgive one another and stay with us, through it all, even through the last test: death. Is this the way we pray? Does it impact our lives? Does God come first and everyone else with us or does our prayer rattle on with "I, me and I want?" We pray with Jesus to the Father in the power of the Spirit.... Our Father....it is as much our discipline of life, as it is the words of our mouth and hearts.

Paul preaches to pagans (those not Jews) and Paul and Barnabas together with the other leaders of the Church go to preach the good news and care for the poor. They agree in the Spirit but when they start doing what was decided upon, James, the other Jews and even Barnabas renege and go back to their old traditions.

They do not respect the Word of Jesus. Jesus teaches his disciples a new way of praying: to Our Father (no distinctions among the human race), the seeking of God's will and justice with peace for all, food and justice for all daily, forgiveness and strength as we are tested. This is the gospel of the Lord! Have we drifted away from Jesus' priorities to practice what others say we should be doing—but these practices have nothing to do with making us children of Our Father?

✹ Jonah is distressed that the people repented! He wanted to see the wrath of God come upon them! He is miserable and wants to die. He pities himself and goes out into the desert to wait and see—and God provides a plant for him—shade. But then the plant dies and Jonah groans and wants to die. Jonah is more concerned over the plant that shaded him than the whole people of Nineveh. God is concerned about all the peoples of the world and all that he has created.

Jesus is often found having gone off to pray—for the world and all the peoples. He came to bring God's message of forgiveness, love, justice and peace. He also teaches us to pray as he prayed. We are to be concerned with what God is concerned about and we are to care for everyone as God does. We are not to single ourselves out, but see ourselves as part of God's children, all in need of food, forgiveness and strength for our lives. Is this how we pray?

Thursday

FIRST READING
      I. Mal 3:13–20ab
      II. Gal 3:1–5

Responsorial Psalm
      I. Ps 1:1–2, 3, 4 and 6
      II. Lk 1:69–70, 71–72, 73–75

GOSPEL
      Lk 11:5–13

✹ There is more on prayer. A friend comes to us in the middle of the night, in need of bread for visitors to his own house and knocks and knocks. Eventually we get up, give him what we have because he is a friend in need and he passes it on in hospitality (one of the most important demands of Jewish society). Our God is like that—gives us what we need to pass onto others. And he gives better and truer than we do—who gives to our children and those we love what they need. But it is what is needed, not what is simply wanted! And what is most needed is the Spirit. We must ask for the Spirit of God for others and for otherselves for that is the deepest gift that will transform all our lives and world.

✹ Are you mad/stupid? The Galatians have slipped back into thinking, the law saves them rather than the Spirit of Jesus in their baptisms and in the Word of God. Do we slip easily into thinking that it's because of what we do that God answers us, cares for us, forgives us, listens to us and gives us what we need? What do we ask for—does it have anything to do with God's will, what others need right now, or the gift of the Spirit that inspires, teaches, corrects and makes us like Jesus, friends and beloved of God? Will we ever learn?

✹ Again the prophet repeats the reasoning of those who have turned from God because they do not find it productive, or it does not let them profit off of others' needs. They are proud and call themselves blessed. But God listens and there is a record of everyone whether they feared the Lord or not; whether they mocked him, or were compassionate and just towards others; whether they were wicked in their dealings or not; whether they served God or they refused to. And the day will come when the sun of justice comes with its healing rays for those who were just or burning like an oven for those who were not. How will we face that sun?

Jesus speaks of prayer and of what we ask of God our Father and how we ask—whether we will respond to people in need in the middle of the night, if only to be able to get back to bed. Then how is it with our Father who knows all our needs. Even parents who are not so gracious take care of their children and give them what they need—how much more so with our Father who takes care of all, whether they ask or not. And if we really want to receive from God, then we are to pray for the gift of the Spirit—the first and best gift of God.

Friday

FIRST READING   **I.** Jl 1:13–15; 2:1–2
II. Gal 3:7–14

Responsorial Psalm   **I.** Ps 9:2–3, 6 and 16, 8–9
II. Ps 111:1b–2, 3–4, 5–6

GOSPEL   Lk 11:15–26

Jesus drives out demons—all that hinders human beings from being and acting as the true children of God that they were created to be—in compassion, strength and the power of God. And others refuse to look at the good Jesus does, ridiculing him and claiming that he does it as one who serves Satan (the Hinderer) rather than God. Jesus is the Holy One of God and his power has come among us on earth and this power and presence of God is stronger than any other force or kingdom. God's justice, peace, attentiveness to the poor and the lost, and mercy unbounded in forgiveness shatters all the evil of the world. But we must accept and take to heart the Holy One of God or else we will be in a worse condition than we were before we encountered Jesus. We have been baptized into the Body of Christ. Have our households, souls and lives been broken into by the kingdom of God or do we live with divided hearts serving other gods of violence, greed, selfishness and lies, while claiming that we belong to Jesus?

Do we rely on faith, like those who have gone before us, or do we keep relying on the law, observing the letter, as proscribed? Or are we learning to rely on Christ who has saved us from the law, remember that crucifixion—obedience unto death, on behalf of others' needs is what has saved us in Jesus? This is the blessing of Jesus—the gift of the Spirit that takes us beyond the law, and deep into its heart. Do we let Jesus cast out what hinders us from obedience (the meaning of the word Satan—hinderer) and do we stand with Jesus, gathering others with him? Are we worse off than before our baptisms because we do evil claiming to belong to Jesus? These are hard questions that must be asked.

Joel attacks the priests and ministers of the community and tells them to fast and then to cry out to the people, gathering them all into the house of the Lord. And they are to warn the people that the day of the Lord, the day of judgment, is coming and it will be a day, like nothing that has ever been seen before. There will be a day of judgment, sometimes in this life and we believe at the end of life and the end of time. Are we ready for that day today?

Jesus is accused of serving the devil—of serving and doing evil by evil's power. But what Jesus does is only good—healing, curing, forgiving, including, giving people food, hope and the good news. Jesus warns them that there will be a day of judgment for them and we must be careful that we have not become evil ourselves, while thinking that we are just fine, that all is well because we believe in God. Are we mindful of others' goodness or are we always looking for evil such that we often put it there where it was absent before?

Saturday

FIRST READING	**I.** Jl 4:12–21
	II. Gal 3:22–29
Responsorial Psalm	**I.** Ps 97:1–2, 5–6, 11–12
	II. Ps 105:2–3, 4–5, 6–7
GOSPEL	Lk 11:27–28

Jesus is speaking and others are listening to his words. A woman breaks out in praise of Jesus' mother, ancestry and blood ties of family (you are Jewish through your mother). And Jesus rebukes the woman directing the blessing elsewhere— away from Jewish and family, or blood tie connections to what constitutes true discipleship and being a beloved child of God in his family of water and the Spirit. "Blessed are those who hear the word of God and keep it as well." This is what draws us into intimacy and closeness with Jesus—nothing else. Jesus is out to shatter the dependency of people on kinship and family and marriage ties—stretching and expanding peoples' hearts so that they are steeped in the Word of God, in obedience to God's family that includes all the children of the world. (note: Mary is holy, not because she gave birth to Jesus physically and is his mother, but because she too learned to 'hear the word of God and to keep it as well.') This is what will make us holy and bless us, in this life and world and forever.

✺ Sin is a reality: injustice, violence, evil, selfishness. The law condemned us, judged us in everything we did, but we live in Jesus the Christ of God and are justified by believing in Jesus— by living in Jesus' word. We are all one in communion, forgiven, forgiving and free. So we rejoice in that—but are we really living in that freedom as the children of God. We want to cry out blessings on the woman who gave birth to Jesus, but he is intent on proclaiming " More blessed still are those who hear the Word of God and keep it!" God is concerned with our hearing the Word and keeping it more than any devotion or praise. This is what we are being judged on now, as believers in the Word of God in Jesus.

✺ There will be judgment. All the nations will be involved and God will be known as the only God. There will be restoration for Jerusalem—for those who have been faithful and those who have done evil, and have enslaved and destroyed others, they will know the violence of their own choice coming to visit them. The Lord is the Lord of justice and one day all will be set right and will be revealed. We hear the book of Joel at the beginning of Lent. As the year comes to an end we are called to look and to see if this year has been the Year of the Lord.

While Jesus is speaking the Word of God, the truth, a woman cries out in blessing for the woman who came him birth and nursed him as a child, but Jesus refuses to allow that blessing to stand. He says, "No, rather blessed is the one who hears the word of God and keeps it." This is more important than any relationship of human kinship, marriage, family and parents. We are given birth in the Word of God and we must make sure that this Word grows within us.

TWENTY-EIGHTH WEEK IN ORDINARY TIME

Monday

FIRST READING   **I.** Rom 1:1–7

              II. Gal 4:22–24, 26–27, 31—5:1

Responsorial Psalm   **I.** Ps 98:1bcde, 2–3ab, 3cd–4

          II. Ps 113:1b–2, 3–4, 5a and 6–7

GOSPEL   Lk 11:29–32

✳ Jesus is blunt: people of this time are evil people asking for a sign and nothing will be given them. Jonah in the whale was a sign and now the Son of Man will be a sign—calling first for repentance and then buried and spewn forth into life again—from a whale and from a tomb. The call is once again for repentance, conversion of heart and life. Nineveh was 'sin city' and repented. Others from outside the covenant recognized the wisdom of Soloman (and so Yahweh, Israel's God) and now there is someone far greater than Jonah and no repentance, only questions, rationalizations and rejection. We have known the Son of Man, crucified and risen from the dead, sitting at God's right hand and do we repent of our selfish, greedy and violent ways—or will many cities and lands rise up to judge and condemn us in this age?

✳ We are the children of God, free in baptism and we are meant to remain free by standing firm and refusing to submit to any yoke of slavery. The yoke we bear is that of the cross of Christ, together working for justice and peace for all. This is the only sign that is given to us: the sign of the Son of Man, rejected, crucified and risen. This strangely enough is the wisdom of God and all other wisdom fades into oblivion in the face of God in Jesus. Have we repented at the preaching of the Gospel? Or will we be known as another wicked generation and be condemned?

✳ Paul begins his letter to the church at Rome, giving his credentials that he is preaching the gospel of the Son of God, who is holiness itself, raised from the dead, Jesus the Lord. He is both servant and apostle sent to spread the name to everyone. He writes to those in Rome called to grace and holiness and blesses them with the peace and grace of God the Father. This is a variation of the beginning of all Paul's letters. Pastorally this is the core of what Paul's work consists in—preaching, reminding and praying that those called to believe will indeed become holy like God.

The crowds press Jesus and he calls this an evil age that wants signs instead of repentance. But there will be no sign—only of Jonah, three days/nights in the tomb and then resurrection. Others come looking for wisdom to Israel, but Jesus' wisdom is far greater than anything in Solomon's time, or ever. Nineveh repented at Jonah's preaching, but have we repented after having heard the Word of the Lord—Or are we part of this evil age?

Tuesday

FIRST READING	**I.** Rom 1:16–25
	II. Gal 5:1–6
Responsorial Psalm	**I.** Ps 19:2–3, 4–5
	II. Ps 119:41, 43, 44, 45, 47, 48
GOSPEL	Lk 11:37–41

✳ Jesus preaches hard truth and is invited in for a meal. Immediately he is thought badly of because he does not adhere to practicing the outside rituals of washing hands in an elaborate show of cleanliness. But Jesus knows them well and condemns them for being full of greed and evil but publicly going through the formalities of being pure. Jesus speaks always of his God, Father who makes both the outside and the inside of all creation and knows everyone inwardly no matter what we're doing outwardly. Jesus is clear that the outward show of giving alms doesn't immediately clear one of all sin, especially sin that is right at the heart of our lives, thoughts and behaviors. Ordinary time is for looking into our hearts and lives, changing and seeking to live with integrity and whole-hearted obedience to the core of our religion. And we follow the Truth. It must be what scours us purely within so that our actions reflect our hearts.

✴ Stand firm, stay free, stay with the grace of Jesus, shared with us in the power of the Spirit. What matters is the expression of our faith in actions that bring love to others: food, clothing/shelter, medicine, support, release from burdens, oppression. What we do for the Body of Christ—this is living our faith. Jesus too is intent on teaching us that it is not the law, or details or traditions that make us faithful, but our intent and practice. We are to touch those in need, give alms and treat people with respect, just as our God treats us.

✴ The gospel reveals the justice of God and God's truth—revealing who is evil and perverse and who is just. God is clear to us now and so our actions and our lives reveal whether or not we remain in God, or if we have degenerated into people that are not human in our behavior. Do we treasure the glory of God that has been shared with us in baptism? Do we take it for granted? Or have we laid it aside by the way we do evil in our hearts, with others and against others?

Jesus is invited to a Pharisee's house to dine. But Jesus does not perform the customary ablutions before eating. The Pharisee notices and Jesus knows that his heart judges him harshly. The Pharisee is concerned with outward appearances while inwardly his heart (and ours) are disgustingly filled with viciousness and evil. God knows—God who has made both inside and outside. But if we wish to be made clean, we can give alms. Perhaps we need to look to ourselves, and the groups we belong to and see what alms we must give in order to be made clean before our God.

Wednesday

FIRST READING	I. Rom 2:1–11
	II. Gal 5:18–25
Responsorial Psalm	I. Ps 62:2–3, 6–7, 9
	II. Ps 1:1–2, 3, 4 and 6
GOSPEL	I. Lk 11:42–46

✴ Jesus curses the Pharisees and as a prophet of old is very specific about the evil that they do—obeying tax laws that they benefit from immediately as part of the temple structure but refusing to practice justice and love of God. They are cursed again for making a show of their religiousness in public so that others are impressed with them but another curse calls them tombstones of the dead that one day will be ignored and stepped on by people. They will one day be forgotten and no better than rotting flesh in dirt—which in reality they are already. These are not words to endear Jesus to anyone. Do we need to hear them or do we think that he is talking about other people? Are we the ones known for the practice of justice for those who need it most and for making sure that it is God who is revered instead of us?

✴ We are all judged before God and should be careful of judging others because usually we are doing the same things we call them to account for. Are we hard and impenitent in our hearts? If the judgment of God was upon us today would we know God's honor for the good we have done, or would we be revealed for what we have done that is evil?

Jesus takes up his refrain: "Woe to you Pharisees who pay tithes on little things—(herbs) and neglect justice and the love of God." These are what is essential to religion. Do we practice our religion so that others see and are impressed by our piety? And yet what are our hearts really like? Jesus insulted them—the lawyers and anyone in a position of authority in liturgy and teaching. Jesus is furious telling them that they lay burdens on others and do nothing to lighten their lives. What is Jesus saying to us today in our churches, communities?

Thursday

FIRST READING

     I. Rom 3:21–30
     II. Eph 1:1–10

Responsorial Psalm

     I. Ps 130:1–2, 3–4, 5–6
     II. Ps 98:1, 2–3ab, 3cd–4, 5–6

GOSPEL

     Lk 11:47–54

✴ Jesus continues extending his curses not just to the Pharisees, but to the teachers of the law who make life unbearable for so many people, interpreting the law so that heavy requirements and burdens fall upon so many and then they do not lift a finger to help them. There is no compassion, no spirit and no concern in them. They are cursed again for building memorials to those of their ancestors (in unfaithfulness) killed and they agree with those who went before them—'they got rid of the prophets for them, not they can build!' And then he turns on everyone—calling them to account for the murders of so many who spoke the truth on behalf of those in need of justice and life. And the curse is upon those who had knowledge of the law and prophets, the keys of the kingdom but never entered it. The result of Jesus' words are endless questions, traps, harassment. And what of us—do we kill the prophets, silence the truth, make life unbearable for so many and do not raise a finger to help anyone? Is our God cursing us today?

✺ Always the blessing of the Father, Son and Spirit—the Trinity— upon all believers. We were chosen to dwell within our God and to be holy like Jesus, beloved sons and daughters of the Father. We are forgiven, graced and freed so that we might share in the plan of wisdom that brings everything together in Christ. What a calling we have been given!

Jesus is appalled at what some of the leaders of his own people do in the name of religion: the bad example, being stumbling blocks to those seeking God and even to slaughtering the prophets who speak the truth. And they in turn, attack Jesus, seeking a way to catch him in his own words. Do we remember who we are and what God asks of us, and how what we do affects others around us?

✺ Luke has stayed with Paul while others have left him and he asks Timothy to come and join them and bring Mark along too—they were friends in the work of the Lord. Poor Paul complains about others and his case in court. He says that everyone abandoned him, and yet Luke remained with him. Luke was an evangelist, a preacher and missionary, a leader in the early church, a companion to those in ministry and a good friend it seems.

Luke's gospel speaks of a community that goes out in twos to preach and to bring in the harvest that the Lord has created in others' hearts. They are people dedicated to being a radical presence of the kingdom of God—where all are taken care of and everyone relies on the hospitality of one another. This is the image of our God who is hospitable to us in Jesus and the Spirit. The message is that of peace—the peace of the Risen Lord, the peace of forgiveness and new life, the peace of the reign of God—justice, mercy and initiation into the life of God in Jesus. Luke left the Word of the Lord as his best gift to the early church and to believers for all time.

Friday

FIRST READING   **I.** Rom 4:1–8
           II. Eph 1:11–14

Responsorial Psalm   **I.** Ps 32:1b–2, 5, 11
      II. Ps 33:1–2, 4–5, 12–13

GOSPEL   Lk 12:1–7

The crowds around Jesus swell in size and Jesus addresses his disciples publicly—warning them to beware of the yeast of the Pharisees. They are plotting to destroy him and one day all will be known and everyone will be seen and revealed for what they were—as will we in our times. And he warns them about fear—not to fear those whose power who can kill your body, but those who are intent on murdering your soul and separating you from God. Jesus uses the birds—sparrows by the millions—and not one ever forgotten by God. This is our God who will care for us much more than sparrows. We are not to fear anyone on earth. We are only to fear betraying our belief, our God, our friends in Christ. Who do we fear? Who on earth controls our words, our choices and our commitments? Are we mindful that our God holds us dear?

We are God's own, chosen to reveal God's glory, and to live in hope with Christ. This is the message of truth we have been given and stamped with the seal of the Spirit. Do our lives reveal the glory of God? And this is what the crowds are hungering for: the truth and integrity of the Word of Jesus, who warns them against hypocrisy. We must be fearless and speak truly and do not fear what others might do to us, and remember that our God counts every hair on our head and we are worth so much to God—with Jesus.

✺ Abraham was a believer and he was credited to him as justice. He knew that it was God who called him, sustained him and gifted him with all that he had, including his sons and that is justice—recognizing rightly who is God. David knows this too—human beings are forgiven and our God does not let us incur guilt for our deeds—This is our God!

Jesus is trying to warn his disciples (and us) about anyone who acts like some of the Pharisees—they are hypocrites. What is shown in their lives belies what is in their hearts. But one day all will be revealed and be seen for what it is. We are to be careful that in protecting our lives, we do not lose our integrity and our souls. We are to be careful of those who could destroy our souls, even more than those who could kill us. God keeps each of us, everyone of us close, and dear. This is why we are to fear nothing! Except perhaps we should fear forgetting or betraying God just because we want to live or have longer lives.

Saturday

FIRST READING	**I.** Rom 4:13, 16–18
	II. Eph 1:15–23
Responsorial Psalm	**I.** Ps 105:6–7, 8–9, 42–43
	II. Ps 8:2–3, 4–5, 6–7
GOSPEL	Lk 12:8–12

✺ Jesus is blunt: if we stand witness to Jesus, then the Son of Man will stand up for us and if we do not, then the Son of Man will stand against us. Pardon will be given even for those who deny the Crucified One when they repent but for those who slander (declare untruthfully that the Spirit is one of death, evil and injustice) the Spirit of Holiness—there is nothing but condemnation. The Spirit is Truth and if we stand with Jesus then the Spirit is given to us to speak when it is needed for defense in public. Jesus is trying to impress upon his disciples, and all of us, that the truth must be spoken and defended at all costs and that there will be persecution. But at the same time the Son of Man, crucified and risen will be standing with us, sharing his Spirit with us and we are not to let fear control us. We are to throw in our lot with the prophet Jesus who belongs to God. Do we stand publicly with the Crucified One or do we let others slander God's name attributing what they do in evil to being done in God's name?

✹ Paul constantly remembers to pray for the Ephesians, and to be thankful for their faithfulness. He prays wisdom upon them, constant growth in understanding, and the fullness of revelation. They must know Christ who is above every authority, power and sovereignty upon earth and they are to submit to Jesus, the Body of Christ and the Spirit that fills all of creation. Jesus too exhorts his followers to be faithful to the Son of Man, the Crucified, suffering and risen one of God. He warns us that we might share in his own persecution and sufferings, but that the Spirit will teach us everything we need for that moment. What do we pray for, for one another and the Church?

✹ Hoping against hope, Abraham believed—on behalf of all his descendents and so he is father to many nations. Do we hope against hope in the face of what happens in our lives and do we hope and live in that hope on behalf of others, even the nations all around us? More than half of the world has never even heard of Jesus except in the person of those who brought slavery, nuclear weapons, consumerism and individualism to their countries. Is our hope and so our faith shriveled and selfishly kept to ourselves, and so dying?

Jesus tells us that if we acknowledge the Son of Man, the Crucified and Risen One, in the presence of the world then we will be acknowledged by Jesus before God! But do we speak against the Son of Man in word or deed and sin against the Spirit of God? Have we ever had to stand up for what we believe? Or have we ignored the issues that must be faced and resisted: care for the poor, justice for all, equality for all, no war, no destruction of the earth and other human beings of greed? This too is to sin against the Spirit—to avoid having to stand up for what we believe, or only picking one issue that is an acceptable one. With this we do not know the Spirit, only our own words.

TWENTY-NINTH WEEK IN ORDINARY TIME

Monday

FIRST READING   **I.** Rom 4:20–25

      II. Eph 2:1–10

Responsorial Psalm   **I.** Lk 1:69–70, 71–72, 73–75

      II. Ps 100:1–2, 3, 4ab, 4c–5

GOSPEL   Lk 12:13–21

Someone in the crowd tries to get Jesus to publicly side with him against someone in his family on an issue of money and inheritance. But Jesus will not because the demand reveals the underlying violence and greed of all our hearts. He begins by warning everyone about greed and that it is not what gives life. He tells the story of the man who has a good harvest, gloats, plans to tear down his barns, build bigger ones, store up and live without responsibility or cares the rest of this days. First those who listened would have been horrified because the harvest came from God and first fruits belonged to God—10%, then it was expected that more was to be given to the community and especially to the poor and then you could keep the excess. But Jesus goes to the heart of the matter—the man is going to die, the way he has lived—with his greedy heart thinking only of more and how to live insensitive both to God and others' connection to him. Fools! Anyone who lives thinking of themselves first will lose it all. Do we amass fortunes, life, possibilities for others and for hope, serving God or are our hearts shallow and grasping? Are we fools too?

We once were dead, doing evil, living unjustly, selfishly, living under the anger of God. But we were/are loved mercifully and we've been brought back to life (resurrection-baptism) and we have a place with Jesus. Always there is the gift offered and we are being made into God's work of art! Jesus in the gospel deals with the details of inheritance, family disputes, greed, selfishness and demands that cause divisions. And Jesus tries to show us the larger reality that we live in and are called to remember. Where do we put our treasures? We are God's treasures—what are we doing with our lives now?

✴ Are we faithful? Do we believe in Jesus risen from the dead and stake our life on that reality. Are we no longer far from God but have been drawn near to God in Jesus? Do our actions reveal our faith or contradict our words of being belivers? Jesus is asked to intervene in a family dispute over inheritance and make the other give him what he thinks is his (this we do all the time—wanting God to move on our account, against others in our family, work, nation, church even). But Jesus won't be caught in such a useless endeavor that belies the larger issues. He tells the story of a man who will soon die and all he can think of is what he is going to do with all his money since he is doing so well. Are we fools, making plans without thought of God and what is demanded of us, here and now, let alone as a final accounting?

Tuesday

FIRST READING	I. Rom 5:12, 15b, 17–19, 20b–21
	II. Eph 2:12–22
Responsorial Psalm	I. Ps 40:7–8, 8–9, 10, 17
	II. Ps 85:9ab–10, 11–12, 13–14
GOSPEL	Lk 12:35–38

✴ We were so far from God, now we are brought so close in Jesus' life/death/resurrection and we share in that in our baptisms/eucharist. Jesus is our peace with God and one another; we are all one in the Body of Christ, reconciled, so close in God: we are saints, being built into a sanctuary together where God lives. Do we realize we are to be light burning, waiting, as servants intent on obedience and answering our Master's needs? If we are true to our baptisms, then Jesus will wait upon us! If only God finds us 'at the ready' today and everyday!

✴ God is the gracious gift of life—on a human level, and on every other level. Do we live in that gift that has been given to us in Jesus where it abounds for all? Do we live with overflowing justice and obedience, in imitation of Jesus who has brought us salvation in living justly so that we may know how to please God and bring life to the world? As the Christian year winds down, Jesus warns us to live with our lamps burning ready and belts around our waists ready to go at the word of God. Are we ready to open to God our hearts and lives, our relationships and communities? Would God find us wide-awake and so, would serve us? God would serve us! We must pray for one another that together we will live lives of justice and obedience to the Word so that all of us will be ready whatever time God would come—either in our deaths, or in judgment at the end of time.

Wednesday

FIRST READING	I. Rom 6:12–18
	II. Eph 3:2–12
Responsorial Psalm	I. Ps 124:1–3, 4–6, 7–8
	II. Is 12:2–3, 4bcd, 5–6
GOSPEL	Lk 12:39–48

✳ Again Jesus tries to warn us: pay attention to your life, to what is going on around you and how all this is perceived in God's eye. We are to live 'at the ready', on our marks, waiting and living passionately because we don't know when the Son of Man, the crucified and risen one will suddenly be among us again. We are to be wise and faithful stewards of the earth, of all that has been given to us—acting with justice, integrity, serving those in need and making sure that the master's accounts and resources are used for those they were meant for—the poor. Is our God going to find us attending to the words of justice, mercy and care in his kingdom or find us wrapped up in our own pursuits and material pleasures. We have been given so much—do we remember whom it belongs to and that all is given in trust to us? Are we sharing the gifts of God with those we are meant to serve? God has trusted us—have we honored that trust?

✳ The mystery of Christ is limitless, yet revealed in the Gospel and by the Spirit, to prophets, apostles and numberless people. We are servants of the Gospel: to proclaim and to explain, to delve into the mystery once hidden but is now the wisdom that can be known endlessly in Jesus. Are we awake, on our guard, waiting for the Son of Man, the mystery of God's presence with us, to burst in upon us? We've been given a share in the household, as servants and so much has been given to us. What are we doing with this gift shared among us? What does our God expect of us today, in economics, politics, among the poor, sharing with the world as truth?

☀ We have been offered to God and so we must live in holiness and make sure that we do not do evil. We are to do justice and live by grace. We do not live under the law but we live in the Spirit of the law, far surpassing what is superficially expected in obedience to the law. We are the slaves of God—willing slaves of justice, freed from doing evil so that we can do the works of God.

God is always coming and we must live with the realization that God always comes when we least expect him and in ways we would not think of. We must be on our guard. The Son of Man, crucified and risen is watching whether we are farsighted and faithful servants, intent on doing our master's will here in the world today. We have been put in charge of God's kingdom on earth, to care for the least of his children and to be the heralds of forgiveness and peace. These are our master's wishes. We have been given so much. Do we do anything near what is required of us, let alone what we should be doing in response to the Spirit in gratitude?

Thursday

FIRST READING   **I.** Rom 6:19–23
                                 II. Eph 3:14–21
Responsorial Psalm   **I.** Ps 1:1–2, 3, 4 and 6
                    II. Ps 33:1–2, 4–5, 11–12, 18–19
GOSPEL   Lk 12:49–53

☀ Jesus has come to bring fire: the fire of the gifts of the Spirit, of judgment and of purification and transformation but there will be baptism first—of blood and water in the cross. Jesus has come with demands, expectations of us. He has come to drive the wedge of truth into every relationship of family, marriage, friendship, social status. Do we side with the Son of Man, crucified or with others? Ground line. There is to be no peace on earth that is not based on belief in and following of the Son of Man, crucified and risen from the dead. All else is false peace. There is only the Peace of Christ, Pax Christi, the peace that holds all together in justice, truth and forgiveness—the peace that often provokes violence, persecution and death for those who share Jesus' own anguish until the kingdom comes. Do we settle for an uneasy false peace or the Peace of Christ, seeking to avoid suffering and so betray the Spirit given to us as gift of God

✴ Paul's prayer is for the power of the Spirit of God to make strong our inner souls that our outward lives may reflect the depth of love that has been given to us. And the prayer is of praise for Jesus the Christ of God and that we may be his glory in every generation. Jesus has come to bring fire (the Spirit) upon the earth, blazing, transforming in a baptism of fire. God desires us in Jesus to be holy and to be truthful, even if it divides family, marriages, societies. Jesus knows distress until we are made holy as God is holy. Are we made of fire and truth, reflecting the love given to us? Or are we more concerned with keeping everything the way it is in our families and communities, adding to Jesus' distress?

✴ We have all sinned with our bodies, sexually and in relation to others in regard to justice and forgiveness. But now we are the servants of justice so that we may be made holy. We have known what death/sin/evil/injustice and violence does in our lives and in others. Now we are to know what holiness, grace, the Spirit and love—that is the life of God—and what it does in our lives and others. This is the gift of Jesus the Christ in our lives at baptism that we carry around in our bodies.

Jesus intends to light a fire on earth—it is the baptism of light and the Spirit. Jesus has not come to make everything 'nice' but to stir up what has been lying dormant and dead—to call each of us to commit ourselves to passionately obey God. This will cause dissent and division in our families, churches and the world. This is a baptism of fire that can bring anguish because it is rejected by many and accepted by a few. Have we accepted this baptism of fire?

Friday

FIRST READING   **I.** Rom 7:18–25a

                                                  II. Eph 4:1–6

Responsorial Psalm   **I.** Ps 119:66, 68, 76, 77, 93, 94

                                       II. Ps 24:1–2, 3–4ab, 5–6

GOSPEL   Lk 12:54–59

The collected sayings of Jesus continue with words about how to read the signs of the times, beginning with the weather patterns. Everyone knows that clouds portend showers coming from the west and a south wind harbors heat. If anyone can catch those portents how come we are so stupid as to miss the signs of deeper and more powerful things happening around us? What criteria do we use to decide what is fit? Do we try to settle things 'on the way', on the way following Jesus to the cross or do we wait until the last moment, the moment of judgment and condemnation? Will we ever see what is demanded of our lives now: forgiveness, the truth, justice and obedience to God's Word in Jesus or will we have forfeited so much that at the end we will have nothing to fall back on? Justice will be served and all will know it. Are we a part of it now or are we part of the injustice, collusion with evil and selfishness of the world? Are we as shallow as the people around Jesus were?

Paul pleads for his community to live up to their baptisms, to live in service, selflessly and with no violence and patience, preserving the Peace of Christ that binds them together. This is the Body of Christ, one Spirit before God the Father—we dwell in God! This is the bedrock of our lives/faith. And are we, like so many Jesus speaks harshly to, more concerned with watching the weather and not judging what is right? We are told to settle with one another, forgive and not cause scandal and be imprisoned for what we do that is not of God. There will be justice for all, including we who have been baptized into the Peace of Christ.

Paul often does what he doesn't want to do, and doesn't do what he wants to do. He does not accept the grace and power of God to be conformed to the life of God within him instead, he reverts back to his old ways. He is wretched and asks who can free him from this wretched body under the power of death? Often Paul sounds like he has forgotten the incarnation and that our bodies are holy and it is not a question of being freed from our bodies, but remembering that God dwells in them. We are the temple and the dwelling place that God lives in the world. We are at home in God, the Trinity, by baptism and we must not let our feelings and old beliefs pull us into looking at what God has made in a negative way.

We must read the signs of the times—religiously through the eyes of God. We can read the weather signs and interpret the portents of heaven and earth but we are not so astute at reading what is just and good. We had better learn how to be just and forgiving with one another or the courts of the world will do their form of justice on us and we will pay. How do we live with one another as Christians? Do we resort to courts of law and betray the power of God in Jesus in us by baptism?

Saturday

FIRST READING	I. Rom 8:1–11
	II. Eph 4:7–16
Responsorial Psalm	I. Ps 24:1b–2, 3–4ab, 5–6
	II. Ps 122:1–2, 3–4, 4–5
GOSPEL	Lk 13:1–9

Jesus grows more and more passionate about calling people to see and repent. He reminds the people of those who they think were evil and so were caught without time to repent, cut down while they were offering sacrifices and caught in a disaster that claimed so many at once. Who are sinners?—it was thought that God allows the good a chance to turn before they would die. Jesus tries to make them aware that they must change and give forth the fruit of justice and peace. A fig tree in a vineyard, with no fruit. Year after year—nothing. It only sucked the nutrients and water out of the vineyard. It took nearly seven years for fruit—first years were too bitter, hard. The first good figs belonged to God…but there's nothing here. It needs help—drastic measures—manure—enough alkaline to either kill it or jump start it and strong chopping and hoeing around its root structure—produce or else! And what about us? How long have we been in the kingdom (vineyard of God) and are we just sucking up everything around us but producing nothing? Do we need a good dose of manure dumped on us and our roots wrenched so that we will finally produce justice and peace? Or will we, in the end, be cut down because we gave nothing to anyone?

We live in the power and the law of the Spirit of Jesus and in the freedom of the children of God. Do we live according to that Spirit in all things? The Spirit needs flesh to work in the world, to work in our flesh. We must make sure that all we do tends towards life and peace. If we revert back to being controlled by our desires and the world's selfishness than we cannot please God. But we have the Spirit of God and so we live with justice. The Spirit that raised Jesus from the dead is the Spirit that has been given to us and we are to know that resurrection in our bodies even now. Do we practice resurrection?

Jesus warns those who listen to him that we all must repent and change. What happens to people—how they die, or are killed—doesn't necessarily mean that they are being punished. We are all guilty of evil and injustice but we are all given the command to bear fruit that is holiness and goodness. It is late in the year—maybe a month left before we offer this year 2007 to God—is there fruit that God would want or are we sadly lacking and without anything to give God for this year? There is still time—repent!

THIRTIETH WEEK IN ORDINARY TIME

Monday

FIRST READING   **I.** Rom 8:12–17

                                      II. Eph 4:32—5:8

Responsorial Psalm   **I.** Ps 68:2 and 4, 6–7, 20–21

                             II. Ps 1:1–2, 3, 4 and 6

GOSPEL   Lk 13:10–17

❋ Jesus is in a synagogue on a Sabbath, teaching and sees a woman bent double for seventeen years (she would have been in the back of the gathering). He cries out freedom for her and leaves the front, cutting through the crowd—everyone would have parted like the Red Sea so the women wouldn't have touched him. He lays hands on her and raises her up! And she stands and praises God loudly. And bedlam ensues. The synagogue leader tries to get order back, by quoting the law, and telling people not to bring people to be healed (no one brought her or had anything to do with her for seventeen years)...and Jesus becomes prophet as well as preacher. He declares them all hypocrites, intent on outwardly worshiping and obeying laws, but bending them for their own convenience when it suits their livelihood (taking their animals to water) but not caring at all about human beings bent under economic, social and accepted evil (Satan means anything or anyone who hinders one from living as a child of God). She is the only daughter of Abraham, true believer and worshipper about them! Do we ever really worship God?

❋ Be friends! Forgive, imitate God and be a sacrifice on behalf of others as God has been for us in Jesus. Our lives are to be pure, singlehearted, faithful in relationships, our sexuality, so that everything we do is suffused with light! Be what we proclaim we are: the children God loves. A woman unnoticed by all is healed by Jesus' word (on a Sabbath—it is truly worship of the God of freedom and holiness). But others are incensed, breaking the law to help someone! Jesus is furious: we break laws for our own convenience but not to set others free and relieve distress. We do not worship God this way. She is a faithful and true daughter of Abraham, faithful in suffering/isolation—which side of the sanctuary do we find ourselves in today?

✵ We must live in the Spirit of God as the sons and daughters of God. We are the adopted children of God in Jesus, with Jesus as our brother. We call God 'Abba', Father, and have the same relationship to God as Jesus. This is the gift of the kingdom of God, the good news that Jesus brings to earth in his body. We must live in our bodies as Jesus lives in his—to the glory of God—for we are heirs with Jesus, in suffering and in glory.

A woman who for 18 years has been bent over is seen by God. He goes to her, touches her and raises her up and she blesses God. The synagogue and those in attendance are horrified. In setting her free from her bondage, Jesus has broken the Sabbath laws and their customs. They cannot rejoice with her or with Jesus. Then Jesus tells them Sabbath worship consists in this—setting others free and not in following empty laws that make us feel like we are righteous. This is what our God looks for in us.

Tuesday

FIRST READING	**I.** Rom 8:18–25
	II. Eph 5:21–33
Responsorial Psalm	**IA** Ps 126:1–2, 2–3, 4–5, 6
	II. Ps 128:1–2, 3, 4–5
GOSPEL	Lk 13:18–21

✵ Jesus has just healed this bent woman and he goes on with his sermon. He gives two images of his presence in the world, his kingdom on earth. A man who plants a mustard seed in a vineyard—creating havoc in those orderly rows—growing into a bush, and small tree where the birds of the air come for shelter (and they eat the grapes too!). And a woman who buries yeast in masses of flour—mixed with the right amount of water, sweetness and heat and works strenuously to make the mess rise and become bread for the earth. He has just showed them what it looks like—the bent woman, like the masses of people in need of liberation, now free and brought to shelter in the tree (the cross) and all those who will be feed on Word, bread of Eucharist and justice's compassion because of baptism, the Spirit and the struggle to bring the Good News to the poor in reality. Do we dwell in the kingdom of God? Are we hard at work making bread for the masses of people and raising those in despair and brokenness to life?

Bend in obedience. In marriage bend to one another, loving and faithful, making one another holy—love one another as Jesus has loved us. The mystery of marriage is that of equality and freedom with one another, as we are in the Trinity. Jesus seeks to share the mystery of the kingdom of God—the relationship we are all given in God upon the earth, the same that Jesus has with the Father, in the Spirit's power. What was seeded in us in our baptisms is to grow and grow, thrive, spread like a weed, giving shelter and protection to the least. And the Word/Spirit is buried in us so that we might be bread, and leaven for the world, offering something unbelievably fresh and true.

We suffer, but we must see our lives in the light of forever, in God's eye and God's vision of glory and hope for us. We are here to reveal the good of God to all the world and to live in freedom, sharing that life with others. All the earth and all that God has made groans in hope, in expectation for what is still to come in grace and wholeness for everything. And we who have this Spirit knows that we wait for the fullness of redemption that has been seeded and begun in us in baptism. We wait with patient endurance. We live fully knowing that the Spirit of God is redeeming everything in us and in the world.

The kingdom of God—Jesus' power and presence in the world— is like a mustard seed, so tiny as to be unnoticed. But once it is planted it can take over an entire field, just as it is meant to take over our lives and the lives of all around us. It grows to be a sheltering presence for others. And it is hidden like yeast that is kneaded into bread that can feed a world so that all can rise to life now and for eternity.

Wednesday

FIRST READING   **I.** Rom 8:26–30
                                 II. Eph 6:1–9
Responsorial Psalm   **I.** Ps 13:4–5, 6
                      II. Ps 145:10–11, 12–13ab, 13cd–14
GOSPEL   Lk 13:22–30

☀ Jesus leaves the synagogue and continues on his way (towards the cross) and someone wants to know if only a few are going to be saved. Jesus warns them to enter by the narrow door—the way of the cross, the way of the good news to the poor, laying up treasure in heaven and following him. It will be harder any other way. We can walk with Jesus and yet not follow in his footsteps, but keep our distance and not allow our hearts to belong to him in obedience. Many will be left outside, but by their own choice—Jesus keeps preaching to all who have ears to ear and open hearts until the very end. Do we hear and obey? So many have heard from the east and west—so many have responded but oftentimes those who are closest and consider themselves already 'in' and saved are nowhere near the kingdom or Jesus in their actions and priorities. And what about us—do we walk the way with Jesus or are we hesitant to follow?

☀ The Spirit is there for us in our weaknesses and prays in us, teaching us how to pray and praying with and for us. The Spirit teaches us with words, with groans, and senses and hopes that cannot be worded or imaged. But our hearts are searched and the Spirit prays for what we need, each and as God's people. All things in the world work together. As horrible and violent as they may be, all things are redeemable because of Jesus, the beloved Son's obedience and dying and rising. We are called to live and die and rise with Jesus, in our baptisms, in the pattern of our lives and one day, forever.

Jesus tells us that we must come in together, and through the narrow door—of the Word of God, the kingdom of the least and the poor and living in imitation of Jesus. Just because we have been baptized or have shared eucharist does not mean that we are saved, or even on the road—the way of the cross, the way of justice and peace, the way of the children of God to the Father in the Spirit with Jesus. There will be others we never dreamed of who are in the kingdom of God, while we thought it was all ours. We need to be careful for God knows the others who will be first and perhaps we will end up last, if we are in at all.

Thursday

FIRST READING   **I.** Rom 8:31b–39
                                          II. Eph 6:10–20
Responsorial Psalm   **I.** Ps 109:21–22, 26–27, 30–31
                                     II. 144:1b, 2, 9–10
GOSPEL   **I.** Lk 13:31–35

In an unusual move, some Pharisees (Jesus' own group) come to him with a warning about Herod who is intent on killing him. They tell him to go his way and leave this place. Jesus is clear—go tell that 'fox', insulting but truthful that he is about his own work, the work of his Father and the kingdom and no one will threaten him or cause him to stop what he must do. He will do what he has come to do. But he knows what Herod is capable of and will do and he will move on—because he also knows the prophets are killed in Jerusalem. Jesus' way leads to Jerusalem. Jesus is a prophet: one who speaks the truth, cares only for the honor of God, the care of the poor and the work of justice and because of that he will meet his death in Jerusalem—and Herod will collude with the Romans in his murder. Do we tell the truth? Do we honor the prophets, warn them and listen to them? Do we continue to do what is necessary and walk the way of cross in our lives if necessary? Do we at least pray for those who do know the cross because of their words and works?

Friday

FIRST READING   **I.** Rom 9:1–5
Responsorial Psalm   **I.** Ps 147:12–13, 14–15, 19–20
GOSPEL   **I.** Lk 14:1–6

A new letter to the church at Philippi begins with a blessing and calls down God's grace and peace upon them, with gratitude to God for the community's faithful adherence to the gospel. And further, Paul prays that God will bring his work to completion right up to the end, and that they will learn love and goodness, practicing their new life ever more in the praise of God. Jesus, on the Sabbath, holy to the Lord, asks self-righteous believers if it's against the law to heal on the Sabbath, but they are silent. Jesus heals the man and then tries to teach them compassion as worship of God, but they still do not speak. What is God trying to teach us today?

Saturday

FIRST READING	I. Rom 11:1–2, 11–12, 25–29
	II. Phil 1:18b–26
Responsorial Psalm	I. Ps 94:12–13, 14–15, 17–18
	II. Ps 42:2, 3, 5
GOSPEL	Lk 14:1, 7–11

✳ Jesus tells a parable when he sees guests at a party jockeying for the seats of honor. He reminds them that the host may have others in mind for the seats of privilege, close to him. And if they have moved into them without this relationship of intimacy, then they will be humiliated when they have to move out and down to whatever is left over when everyone else is seated. Instead Jesus says, go to the lowest and maybe you will be moved up higher. It isn't a false sense of humility—so that you will be moved up, but a call to recognize who each of really is—just a servant in the kingdom. And it will be up to God who judges and sees with the heart where we truly deserve to sit—how close to our God we actually are. For us, we are to be servants, bend before others and not take to ourselves what is not given. Most of us don't do this well—or even often! Who do we think we really are? Do we really live as the beloved servant-children of our God?

✳ Paul is struggling with whether it is better to live or to die since he is facing that reality all too closely himself. His dilemma is solved by relying on the necessity of preaching Christ in living, and among the living and leave his dying in the hands of God. And Jesus struggles with those he is at dinner with who are resistant to what he does on the Sabbath. He tells a parable of guests invited to a dinner and their seats at table. Which seat do we take when we come in, and why do we chose our seats. Are we humbly aware of our relationship to God, or do we think we are closer than we actually are—and that there are many who would be seated nearer to the host? What draws us closer to God is compassion, not religious devotion or legalism.

Most of the early members of the church were Jews. Jesus was a Jew but many in Israel did not come to believe that Jesus was the awaited Messiah because he was more than that, more than what was awaited—he is God, for those who believe that he is the fullness of the promises, the law, and the hopes of all the years of waiting in Israel. Now God in Jesus belongs to every tribe and nation. But Israel is beloved of God always. They were his first people, his dearest treasure and God's gifts are irrevocable. We must be careful not to let Paul and others' words influence negatively how we feel and relate to the people of Israel. And we must make sure that we live in such a way that our lives reveal the presence of God in Jesus crucified and risen now in the world. We must live humbly, truthfully and with respect for all.

THIRTY-FIRST WEEK IN ORDINARY TIME

Monday

FIRST READING   **I.** Rom 11:29–36
                                      II. Phil 2:1–4

Responsorial Psalm   **I.** Ps 69:30–31, 33–34, 36–37
                                     II. Ps 131:1, 2, 3

GOSPEL   Lk 14:12–14

✤ Jesus addresses the man who had invited him to eat with him and tells him that his guest list needs some revamping. He is supposed to invite the poor, the hungry, the weak and the sick, not his family and friends, the wealthy and influential who can reciprocate later and invite him back—an enclosed group. He will be repaid by them, not by God. Jesus is talking about the wedding feast, the kingdom where the poor and the weak and those most in need are taken care of first, but this is supposed to be reflected in all our decisions and meals, work, use of money and resources. Who we choose to eat with (at eucharist, at the table of the Lord, at our own tables and in our own homes) will speak for us, either for good or for condemnation at the resurrection of the dead and our own time for judgment. We live and have been called to walk in the company of those who follow and love Jesus. Company means those we break bread with—and who we lavish our resources and income on—are we truly among the company of Jesus or would he be ill at ease among us and who we dwell with and hang around with? Are we the upright and the just? Who is welcome at our table?

✤ An urgent heartbroken plea from Paul, "Be united, if all that has been given means anything to you." There can be no competition, no pride or arrogance, instead there must be an attitude of attending to the other's needs. It is a faint echo of Jesus' exhortation to think first of the poor, the hungry, the outcast, the sick, the blind, lame, crippled—those who cannot pay us back. We are to do this, not just among ourselves (that's practice!) but we are to be those who are attentive to the least, the forgotten and the excluded of our society. What would Jesus say to us, today, if we were hosting him?

※ God's gift and call are irrevocable, whether they are to Israel or to each/all of us called to baptism and conversion in Christ. We have known the mercy of God—how do we respond daily to God's goodness. Our God is vast, beyond description and yet we know God in Jesus. And Jesus is a strange God. He exhorts us to care for the poor, the least, the outsider and sick, the many who cannot survive in the world and to treat them with dignity, graciousness as though we were inviting God to our tables—because we are. By the incarnation what we do to one another, our God takes as done to himself. Are we delighted to be able to do for others what we would want to do for our God? Do we rejoice that this is the wisdom and knowledge, the mercy of God among us?

Tuesday

FIRST READING   I. Rom 12:5–16ab
                                        II. Phil 2:5–11
Responsorial Psalm   I. Ps 131:1bcde, 2, 3
                           II. Ps 22:26b–27, 28–30ab, 30e, 31–32
GOSPEL   Lk 14:15–24

※ This is the hymn of Jesus, the humble servant, crucified and obedient as a human being before God, the Father of us all. And because of his emptying out of himself on behalf of all of us, God has lifted him, on the cross and in glory before the entire universe. This is the One that we follow and seek to imitate daily in our bodies. Jesus invites us into his life with the Father, and yet so many of us have excuses, our own agendas and plans and we basically say to the invitation: later…later…not now. We've been invited so often. What are we missing that the beggars and the street folks know and experience from God?

✻ We are all gifted by God, to serve and nurture the Body of Christ, our communities and the world. We must be sure that our faith grows in the giving of our gifts and that we are loving, just and sincere in our service and relationships. Do we rejoice and bring others cause to rejoice? Do we help each other stand firm and bless our persecutors and have compassion on all? A short examination of conscience—what will we have to present to the Lord when this year is handed over? Happy are we who eat bread in the kingdom of God here on earth, among the poor and those welcomed so graciously by our God into his feast. We who eat the bread of thanksgiving—Eucharist—must also be sure to share our bread/justice/money/resources with all. And we must be careful that we do not refuse the invitation of God because we are engrossed in work, profit, our personal lives and what we think is more important right now. Are we going to even taste a morsel of what God would like to feed us?

Wednesday

FIRST READING   I. Rom 13:8–10
                                          II. Phil 2:12–18

Responsorial Psalm   I. Ps 112:1b–2, 4–5, 9
                               II. Ps 27:1, 4, 13–14

GOSPEL   Lk 14:25–33

✻ It is God who forms us and matures us in faith and practice. Paul just reminds us that we are to do all without complaining or arguing so that we shine like stars in a dull world. He is facing death rejoicing, do we face life day to day with the deep joy of being the children of God? Jesus too, is drawing near to Jerusalem and he tells us that if we follow him we must leave all we love behind, if we are to pick up our crosses and walk with him. This is a long endeavor that will take all the energy, devotion and planning of our lives. Have we counted the cost? Or have we handed over all that we have to the service and work of the kingdom, being willing to accept the cross if it is offered to us?

✻ Do we think of ourselves as being in debt to one another in love? How deeply and faithfully do we love? And do we love all our neighbors, from our enemies and strangers to our friends and loved ones? Do we need to look at what needs to be undone and corrected? Jesus is clear about the depth and breadth of what commitment to following him means in regards to our families, our work and our own personal lives. Do we pick up the cross—what is laid on us because we live our lives in public, devoted to Jesus' justice, the care of the poor and the proclamation of the truth of God's Word? Are we serious about our baptismal promises—at least as serious about them as we are when we start a new job, or a business, or building a house, or an addition to what we have? Are we as astute in our dealings with one another and making peace among all, and with God, as we are when it comes to our finances and future? Is our future wrapped in God?

Thursday

FIRST READING	**I.** Rom 14:7–12
	II. Phil 3:3–8a
Responsorial Psalm	**I.** Ps 27:1bcde, 4, 13–14
	II. Ps 105:2–3, 4–5, 6–7
GOSPEL	Lk 15:1–10

Jesus tells two stories, out of three in a row about a lost sheep, one out of a hundred and the shepherd leaving the one hundred to their own protection and going after the lost and wandering one. And another about a woman losing a coin off her dowry belt and searching high and low for it and calling a party with her neighbors to celebrate finding it (and keeping the belt from continuing to unravel). This is the way the angels rejoice and God delights in finding one who is brought home. The story is told at a party with sinners who have come back, while those who don't want to eat with 'them' overhear the story. Who are we? Self-righteous and indignant, not wanting to be reminded that we have all been lost and the invitation to eat at the table of Eucharist goes out to all, but in accepting forgiveness we must forgive one another—all of us and eat together. Jesus, forgive us our spitefulness, our arrogance and inflated images of ourselves. Draw us all into your company of sinners lost and found. Amen.

✺ We are the servants of the Lord and we are responsible in everything to the Lord. Are we mindful that we belong totally to God? How often do we ignore our own duties to God and are quick to see and point out others' shortcomings and failures, disregarding our own glaring lacks? Do we bend before our God: our hearts as well as our knees, our bank accounts, and our tongues to the truth? Are we ready for an accounting before God and all the world?

Are we sinners who are the friends of Jesus or are we self-righteous? Surely we are friends of God, and we know that 'they' are not friends of God—because we will not even think of speaking or eating with 'them'. If that's the way we feel about anyone or any group, they are the ones whom Jesus will go looking after and he will leave us with all the rest of the 99 who couldn't care less about that one. Are we really dead and lost but are not aware of it?

Friday

FIRST READING
I. Rom 15:14–21
II. Phil 3:17—4:1

Responsorial Psalm
I. Ps 98:1, 2–3ab, 3cd–4
II. Ps 122:1–2, 3–4, 4–5

GOSPEL
Lk 16:1–8

✺ We are drawing near to the end of liturgical time, to judgment and reflections upon the end of all things, all history and the stories call us to attend to our own histories and turn, once again into the heart and Word of God. Now it is a rich man who has a steward who has to render an account of his service, because he is going to be terminated. He's in a quandry on what to do, so he tries to undo some of the cheating he has done in his master's service. He calls in those who owe debts and cuts them, half here, a quarter here, a bit there. The master hears and is pleased because he was so astute in providing a position for himself when he is out of his master's service. Are we so astute? Do we need to undo some of what we've done but forgiving others' debts? Do we need to be as careful and astute about what God has entrusted to us as this wily steward. Lord, have mercy on us and help us learn to use all our resources to serve the needs of others and live in your kingdom now and forever. Amen.

✳ Be united and study others who live in community, under the cross of Christ. We live under the power of God in Jesus that will continue to transform us utterly, so that we resemble more and more his risen Body. In fact, this power is loose and is about the work of transforming the whole universe. We have been given a share in this life and like the steward in the parable we will be asked to give an accounting. The steward is stealing from the master, and slyly gives back some of it to the creditors so that the master looks good and he still has some of his stolen money and he makes friends with others so they will take him in. If only we were as shrewd in taking care of the work of the kingdom, as we are at taking care of ourselves!

Saturday

FIRST READING

Responsorial Psalm

GOSPEL

I. Rom 16:3–9, 16, 22–27
II. Phil 4:10–19
I. Ps 145:2–3, 4–5, 10–11
II. Ps 112:1b–2, 5–6, 8a and 9
Lk 16:9–15

✳ The exhortation on yesterday's parable continues. It is blunt and brutal—use filthy money to make friends for yourselves, so that when it fails, these people may welcome you into the eternal homes. Are we using our resources in little things (money) to care for the needs of others or are we doing all so that our own nests are covered? Are we trustworthy with what has been given to us? Are we trustworthy with the true wealth of the kingdom: justice, forgiveness, the peace of Christ, the Word and Bread of God shared with us? Are we trying to serve two masters—which one do we really hold in contempt? Are we intent on making sure others think highly of us? O God, you know the hearts of each and all of us. Look hard at us and let us see ourselves in your eyes for what we truly are and turn us back to you. Help us to radically do an accounting of our lives, and forgive the debts others owe us now. Amen.

✳ Paul is touched by the Philippians concern for him, especially in the midst of his hardships. He is even more moved by the fact that they alone seem to have remembered him in his need. In turn he prays for them, that God will fill their needs as lavishly as God does in Jesus, for all of us. The gift was of money, for necessities, for survival and making life a bit easier. And Jesus tells us to use money to make friends. That might sound self-serving, but it is what we have done for those most in need, the friends of God and that this will save us and get us into heaven. What master do we really serve in this world?

✻ Prisca and Aquila (wife and husband) are leaders in the church at Rome who serve and have risked their lives for Paul and many others. Paul greets the workers, the members of the Body of Christ in Rome, old Christians and new ones, those who are at liberty still to preach and those in prison. And the letter contains personal greetings from the one who pens it. And always it begins with praise of God who has given us Jesus, the Word made flesh who reveals the Father in the Spirit so that we might become ever more human and holy.

And Jesus tells us to make friends—either in the world, or in the Body of Christ—so that we may rely on one another and come to one another when we are in need. What master do we actually serve— God or the world we are making for ourselves, for our families and for our friends? Does our small world and its members serve God and God's kingdom of justice for all where there are no poor among us because we are trustworthy and obedient to God's Word? It is high time we put our lives in order for this year of the Lord.

THIRTY-SECOND WEEK IN ORDINARY TIME

Monday

FIRST READING   **I.** Wis 1:1–7

II. Tit 1:1–9

Responsorial Psalm   **I.** Ps 139:1–3, 4–6, 7–8, 9–10

II. Ps 24:1b–2, 3–4ab, 5–6

GOSPEL   Lk 17:1–6

✳ Jesus is realistic: scandals come in the world and the church because people fail and others will fall because of them. But woe to those who brings about the fall of others because of their words and deeds, or inactions. But, still we must forgive—and forgive, ceaselessly, without fail, walking a thin line between condemning what has been done yet leaving the judgment of the person to God. And they pray for an increase in faith. How deep and great is our faith—like that of a mustard seed (nearly the smallest seed of all)? If so we could uproot trees and replant them in the sea! Lord, increase our faith! Help us to forgive and forgive! Make us realistic, both seeing the truth of failure and sin, yet not being drawn into it or despairing because of others' actions. Water that seed within us, O God. Amen.

✳ A new letter from Paul and Titus, born in faith and they are setting up the structure of the church, with elders who will exhibit the traits and practice of belief that can be imitated. Faith is primarily taught in the power of the Spirit by example, found in the lives of those who express what they believe daily for all to see. The foundational mark and practice of a Christian is forgiveness, not counting how often or on what account, but as a way of life that must become the sincere response to everyone, always. Forgiveness, with its depth and breadth, is the mark of faith. How faithful are we?

This is wisdom—love justice and seek the Lord. Are we those who have learned wisdom and are apprentices to the Spirit of truth and gentleness (meekness and nonviolence) or do we do evil, speak untruthfully and destructively and so, are in need of God's rebuke? Jesus warns us that there will be scandals—in the world and among those who believe. We had better be on our guard that it is not we who give that scandal and cause others to stumble and fall. We must make sure that we are forgiving, that we correct with kindness and that we are not the reason that others sin. If only our faith were as small as a mustard seed, we could change the situations in the world that are so unjust, destructive of human life and cause so many to live in misery and without hope. Let us pray for faith—a faith that is wise and does justice for those most in need.

Tuesday

FIRST READING

I. Wis 2:23—3:9
II. Tit 2:1–8, 11–14

Responsorial Psalm

I. Ps 34:2–3, 16–17, 18–19
II. Ps 37:3–4, 18, 23, 27 and 29

GOSPEL

Lk 17:7–10

Here is a stark parable. A servant is called in from the work of the fields plowing or tending sheep (missions in the church that we are all called to practice daily) and the master doesn't say— here, sit down, rest, eat! No, the servant is told to prepare dinner, put on your apron and wait on me and you can eat after me. (this speaks of the table of Eucharist and the servants as well as work in the world as servants who put others first). Then, is the servant thanked—NO! We are reminded: "When you have done all that you have been told to do, you must say: "We are no more than servants; we have only done our duty.' These words are truthful, declaring who we really are before God—servants. We are beloved servants it is true, but graciously called to wait on God, obey the Word of God and do the work we were sent into the world to do by our baptisms. We are to serve others and eat last. How are we doing? Lord, make us servants. Make us humble. Make us mindful of how you have been servant to us everyday of our lives and that the only way to thank you is to be servants of one another, especially those we have been commanded to remember first. Amen.

Each group of people, according to their age, vocation and position in the community must be careful that their lives reveal the extent of their belief. Grace is always present and available to everyone as we live in hope for the fullness of blessings. We are not just individual believers, but the people that belongs wholeheartedly to God. And Jesus reminds us that we are a servant people. Servants are expected to obey, to wait on their master, to serve meals and to do the work of the master's domain. Is God grateful for our work? Are we grateful to be servants in God's house? Are we even doing what is just our duty?

We were born to live forever! And those who die are in the hands of God, knowing peace and the judgment of God because they were faithful and strove to be holy for God's sake—that was their sacrifice. One day they will be as stars and know God forever. This is our hope and we live this hope through obedience and fulfillment of our baptismal promises now, this day, this year of the Lord, before we die. Do we examine our lives and see if our deeds tell the truth of our words—that we are the servants of the Lord? Are we willing and grateful servants, working for the kingdom of God, planting the seed of the Word and harvesting bread for all and making sure that the communities/nations of the world are gathered as one? Or are we even more useless than the servants in the gospel who 'do all that they have been commanded to do' and still have far to go in being of use to God?

Wednesday

FIRST READING	I. Wis 6:1–11
	II. Tit 3:1–7
Responsorial Psalm	I. Ps 82:3–4, 6–7
	II. Ps 23:1b–3a, 3bc–4, 5, 6
GOSPEL	Lk 17:11–19

We are to be especially respectful in public, among others who are not believers, knowing that we are being watched. We are to be obedient to officials in the government, but only in areas that do not contradict what Jesus has revealed in his word and life. The Holy Spirit has been given to us so that we might be righteous on behalf of others. Jesus is met by ten lepers, one of whom is a

Samaritan and he heals all of them. Only one returns, the outsider, in gratitude, worshipping Jesus. Look at everything that God has done for us in Jesus. Are we the one who returns to worship? Or are we like the other nine who took the immensity of life that was given and do not return to give praise to God?

✺ The Word of God warns the leaders of the world that they will be judged, not just as individuals but for all the effects of their actions/decisions in the world. And God's judgment will be swift and terrible on those whose choices disobeyed the laws of God, and disregarded the care of the people and the lives of all. Those who were great in the world will know the judgment of God as surely and more clearly as those who had no power. If those in power are wise, they will seek the Word of the Lord. We need to pray for and speak this wisdom to our leaders, in the church and in our nations. Jesus heals ten lepers, all of them—all of us in our churches/communities. He commands that we do what is necessary according to the law so that we can live in society and contribute to it. But only one gives thanks, only one acknowledges Jesus' power and goodness and blesses God. And this person was not even a believer. Does God look at all of us—the other nine and say, "Where are you?"

Thursday

FIRST READING   **I.** Wis 7:22b—8:1

II. Phlm 7-20

Responsorial Psalm   **I.** Ps 119:89, 90, 91, 130, 135, 175

II. Ps 146:7, 8–9, 9–10

GOSPEL   Lk 17:20–25

✺ Where is the kingdom of heaven? What does it look like? Jesus is being questioned and the Pharisees are pushing him to be specific. But he refuses, answering in a one-line parable: the kingdom of God is among you—and of course, he's referring to himself, his presence in their midst which they are blind to recognize. And to his disciples he warns them, that they too want to see his glory, but not to get caught in that trap but remember that he has warned them that the Son of Man will be rejected and suffer many things first before they see his glory. Are we discouraged at such words? It is time to face the long road ahead relying on the Word of God among us and his presence hidden in the poor and all of history.

✺ Philemon owned a runaway slave—Onesimus—and Paul has taken him in, baptizing him up as a believer and child of God. Now Onesimus is returning and Paul writes that he must accept him as he would Paul! Now he is no longer a slave, but a blood-brother in Jesus, dear to Paul, and hopefully will be dear to Philemon too. He is to put new heart into Paul by welcoming Onesimus. This certainly takes the heart out of any practice of slavery! Jesus proclaims to those who do not believe in him that the kingdom is among them—in his presence, his body. But there is much to come and Jesus will be rejected and suffer before he comes as the Son of Man in glory. How we treat one another, slave or free, how we treat Jesus, the Body of Christ here among us, is the measure of our faith.

✺ Do we pray for wisdom? Do we seek others who are wise— who act as God acts—to teach us and to share their company? Are we one of those people who in this generation are the friend of God? Can our communities be described in this way? Obviously all things are not governed well—in our churches and families, our work places/corporations and nations—so we are in desperate need of wisdom. Do we long for wisdom? And do we long for the coming of the Son of Man—crucified and risen—who comes in judgment of every human being and nation—and judges justly, on the side of those who never knew justice or the care of those who often claimed to believe in God? We are told that we must suffer and be rejected by this present age if we are faithful to God. Are we faithful? Can God rely on us?

Friday

FIRST READING	**I.** Wis 13:1–9
	II. 2 Jn 4–9
Responsorial Psalm	**I.** Ps 19:2–3, 4–5ab
	II. Ps 119:1, 2, 10, 11, 17, 18
GOSPEL	Lk 17:26–37

✴ Jesus speaks much more clearly, pushing his disciples to recognize the seriousness of what he is saying, comparing the days ahead to those of Noah as he made the ark as those around him mocked him and the flood came. And again, Sodom is presented with its ruin of fire. The Son of Man will come in judgment and we must not be paralyzed with fear. Instead we must give our life now and everyday and make faithfulness to the Word our practice. But we do not know the time, any of us. What we know, is that we must be converted and be baptized and then continue in that way of the cross all our days. Like Martin who left the military to be baptized and then became a hermit, a monk, a bishop and someone who tirelessly defended heretics and suffered for protecting them, we must change again and again, radically as we come to see people in need of our love and service.

✴ John writes to a woman friend of the commandment of love, pleading for understanding of its meaning and practice, and that all who read the letter to watch themselves and not be deceived by others. The Word, the teaching, is somehow the presence of the Father and the Son within them, by the power of the Spirit. Watch! Jesus cries out—we don't know when the Son of Man will come in judgment and justice upon the earth, for all of us. It is not important to know the precise time: what is essential is that we live faithfully everyday, so that day will be welcomed, not feared. Is the Word and the Father and Spirit within us? Are we keeping watch and loving one another?

✴ Are we wise or foolish? What do we know of the awesomeness of God or God's creation and thoughts? Creation is often called the first book of wisdom and revelation of God. How are we treating this revelation and using its resources: air, water, land, trees, plants, and all its riches shared with us? Do we keep reading what the universe says of God to us? And what does our God in Jesus say to us? God will come to judge the nations and each human being. If that judgment was this year, soon to come, would we be able to rejoice that it was time for our lives to be rendered before God and to give God back this world that has been entrusted to us for our living, our use and our sharing with those who come after us? Or would we be begging for another chance, another year, another lifetime, to make amends and heal the earth and one another? These are the questions of this year's endtimes, and always it is a gift of God's patience offered again to us.

Saturday

FIRST READING	**I.** Wis 18:14–16; 19:6–9
	II. 3 Jn 5–8
Responsorial Psalm	**I.** Ps 105:2–3, 36–37, 42–43
	II. Ps 112:1–2, 3–4, 5–6
GOSPEL	Lk 18:1–8

✷ Here is a parable on praying and not losing heart. A widow and an unjust judge. She rails against him and he is slow to give her justice. We think of ourselves as the widow and we make God into an unjust judge. What if God is the widow and has spent all of history and all our lives trying to get our attention and give God what is due to him: worship and our lives? We must pray because God is God and we belong to God. We must cry out and be faithful no matter what is happening in history. God will be faithful! God may you find faith on earth today. Amen.

✷ John commends the Christian community for the love they show to the brothers and sisters, and especially to strangers. The community is encouraged to give its support for anybody who works for the kingdom. And Jesus teaches us to pray with full confidence, with persistence, constantly nudging for God's attention. And if a dishonest judge can give in to a widow's pestering, how much more will God heed the pleas of his own children? But the question remains: when the Son of Man comes, will he find faith on earth?

✷ God's Word has bounded down from the heavens in the stillness of night and this Word is a sharp sword that brings death and new life, either decreeing freedom and life and awe before God, or death for those who stand against God's will. This is what happened at the Red Sea and, we believe, this has happened in the Word become flesh among us still in Jesus the Lord. We are to pray and reflect upon the Word of the Lord, and let it transform us and call us to account in our own lives. God is the widow, intent on making us do justice, care for the poor and acknowledge God's will in the world. It has been so since the beginning. But if the Son of Man, the widow who pleads on behalf of her rights and the rights of all those in the world without justice were to come now—would our God find us faithful or would he find us with the unjust judges of the world, only occasionally doing justice because we are afraid of widows, orphans and the Word of God?

THIRTY-THIRD WEEK IN ORDINARY TIME

Monday

FIRST READING   **I.** 1 Mac 1:10–15, 41–43, 54–57, 62–63

II. Rev 1:1–4; 2:1–5

Responsorial Psalm   **I.** Ps 119:53, 61, 134, 150, 155, 158

II. Ps 1:1–2, 3, 4 and 6

GOSPEL   Lk 18:35–43

※ A blind beggar cries out: "Jesus, Son of David, have mercy on me!" He is silenced by the crowd and even by the disciples but Jesus has the man brought to him. "What do you want me to do for you?" Obvious but he says: "Lord, that I may see!" And he sees by faith and he follows Jesus. Jesus is on the outskirts of Jericho and is close to Jerusalem and his death. This blind man sees and becomes a follower, unlike his followers who do not see what they are walking into, or about to face: Jesus rejected and crucified. Jesus, have mercy on us and give us the courage and hope we need to walk through evil and follow you wherever you lead us.

※ An angel reveals to John, who writes down for all the word of Jesus Christ. Blessed are we if we read and take the words to heart. Always in everything, there is the grace and peace. We are commended for being tested and holding true, but we are also devastatingly charged with loving less than when we first believed! The beggar cries out to Jesus over and over again: have pity on me. And in spite of the disciples trying to keep him quiet, Jesus calls to him and he gets up and runs to him. It is time for us to cry out for pity, and come when we are called. Sight for the journey will be given and we will follow Jesus to the end.

※ There arises an evil king and many of the people of Israel become ashamed of who they are and their heritage of the covenant, and they begin to practice the customs of the Greeks.

Then the king demands that they abandon their ways and their religion. The law is destroyed, the altars profaned and those who remained obedient were killed and many die. This is the short story of a long time of horror. We barely know what persecution means—are we faithful or are we seduced by whatever new way or fad comes along?

Jesus heals a blind man on the side of the road. Having heard it is Jesus, the blind man cries out but the crowd and even the disciples make it difficult for him to attract Jesus' attention. He asks for sight and is given it and he follows Jesus up the road—the road to Jerusalem and the cross. Do we cry out for sight from Jesus or are we part of the crowd that hinders others from coming to God? Sight is seeing by faith, seeing through the Spirit, the wisdom of God. We are all in sore need of this sight.

Tuesday

FIRST READING
I. 2 Mac 6:18–31
II. Rev 3:1–6, 14–22

Responsorial Psalm
I. Ps 3:2–3, 4–5, 6–8
II. Ps 15:2–3, 3–4ab, 5

GOSPEL
Lk 19:1–10

✳ A follower is added to the company of Jesus—Zaccheus the tax collector who climbs a tree to try and catch sight of Jesus. For his trouble, Jesus invites himself to his house for dinner! And in gratitude, even when others grumble against him he radically changes his life. He gives one-half of his goods to the poor and does justice, returning four-fold anything that he might have cheated in another. Amazing! And Jesus rejoices over a lost sheep found. This was thought to be the criteria for baptism in Luke's community: what if we turned our lives around with one-half to the poor and four-fold restitution for those we have treated unjustly? Is it even thinkable? Lord, may we respond generously to your invitation to sit and eat with you and dine and dwell with you in your kingdom

✳ The letters to the churches continue: are we dead or alive? Time to wake up, repent and go back to the intensity of our first devotion and practice. What do our baptismal garments look like?

Are we lukewarm and will God spit us out? God wants to reprove us, refine us in fire, heal us and share his life with us. And Jesus invites everyone to sit with him in glory, even the most unlikely and despised, sinners and those who profess belief but publicly live in collusion with evil. Everyone is in need of repentance and radical change of behavior: to do justice, care for the poor and welcome Jesus into our lives. Do we bring delight to the Son of Man, or are we still murmuring against one another?

✳ Individuals endure horrific tortures in refusing to break the laws of their religion (as insignificant as they may appear to be to us). Even the elderly and those who have access to power are called to obey or to die. The old man knows that his choice and his dying will impact many. So he proclaims this so as to give courage to those younger than him. What example do we give to those who are younger than us—in our lifestyles, in what we chose to refuse to do or be a part of and in standing against our nation when it is necessary in regards to moral issues of life and death? Anyone can at any moment decide to follow Jesus—like Zacchaeus a nortorious tax collector who was wealthy (probably by cheating his own people and taking more from them than was required). Yet Jesus invites himself to his house. We must be careful that those we speak ill of and despise may be more intimate with Jesus than we ever have been. We need to examine ourselves.

Wednesday

FIRST READING I. 2 Mac7:1, 20–31
II. Rev 4:1–11

Responsorial Psalm I. Ps 17:1bcd, 5–6, 8b and 15
II. Ps 150:1–2, 3–4, 5–6

GOSPEL Lk 19:11–28

✳ A parable of pounds (money again) and a king despised by his subjects puts ten of his servants in charge and goes off. Some of them make a profit for him, doubling his investments. Two are mentioned and one is hauled in and everything taken from him. The king is vicious, interested only in profit and vengeance, killing anyone who has resisted him. What happened to the other seven servants who weren't mentioned? Would Jesus talk about God his beloved Father in these terms? Or is this Herod and historically the way he treated his servants, rewarding them with power over his provinces and killing his enemies ruthlessly. And when the story is told, Jesus goes ahead of them into Jerusalem to die. How do we live and who do we serve? Margaret though a queen knew violence and murder among her family and Gertrude sought to use her learning to speak to her own contemporaries in a language they were familiar with. They knew who they served. Do we walk with Jesus into Jerusalem and refused to be caught in the corruption and greed of the world?

What is the future like? Through the eyes of God there will be glory, judgment, the praise and acknowledgement of God, in all of heaven and on earth. True worship: bending before the One who has made all and that it is by God's will that we continue to exist. This is Jesus' last parable, seeking to warn his disciples that he will be killed, they will be scattered and some of them will be martyred because they will follow him one day. We are all servants living in this world and must choose which leader to follow. After the telling Jesus goes on ahead, up to Jerusalem. It is getting closer to the end of Jesus' life.

To the servants who did their Master's will, Jesus describes them as faithful. Why is this word important to us today? It is important because unfaithfulness has pervaded our society. Faithfulness, on the contrary, demands courage, sacrifice and risk-taking. Only the convinced can take this risk as we see in the faithful servant of today's gospel. The wicked servant betrayed the Master's trust and toasted it with insults. The reward for faithfulness is more trust and the Master's approval; the punishment for unfaithfulness which Jesus described as wickedness is a loss of the Master's favours and damnation. It really pays to be faithful.

Thursday

FIRST READING   I. 1 Mac 2:15–29
                                                  II. Rev 5:1–10

Responsorial Psalm   I. Ps 50:1b–2, 5–6, 14–15
                  II. Ps 149:1b–2, 3–4, 5–6a and 9

GOSPEL   Lk 19:41–44

✺ Jesus weeps over the city of Jerusalem, the city of prophets and the temple. "If only you'd known the ways of peace!" Jesus is speaking of himself, the Peace of God reconciling and freeing everyone in his body and the gospel that he has brought to the people and yet it has been rejected and he will be tortured and crucified for speaking such bold truth and hope. And he weeps over the destruction of the city that did not welcome his coming. He visited them and they turned aside. Such sorrow Jesus carries. He came among the poor and sought to give them life. Do we, like Elizabeth of Hungary care for the poor of the kingdom and weep with Jesus over the state of affairs in our world?

✺ Only Jesus, the Lion of Judah, the Lamb of God, the Crucified and Risen One is worthy to open the scroll and read it. This is Jesus, God and human, savior of all people, who serves God alone and so will rule the universe. This is our God that we are to look to as the year ends, in the midst of turmoil and war, and as our own lives will one day come to an end. Jesus looks over the city he loves, the people of his nation and weeps for it will all come to ruin. The temple, the city, the people will be taken down by Rome, and they will not recognize him as their hope. Do we recognize what we are offered in Jesus?

✺ Mattathias and his sons, as leaders in the community are urged to disobey so that the people will follow and so that they will be friends of the king, given bribes and eventually become richer. He refuses and then he kills someone who breaks the covenant and he also kills the messenger of the king. This is political/religious war/revolt / not faithfulness. It may be zeal but it is misplaced. They flee into the desert with others in order to live. This is the earlier covenant, ancient history with primitive responses to equally harsh and brutal powers. But it is not anything like Jesus' response to such violence (the Romans occupying Israel throughout his lifetime). Jesus, the prophet and the obedient servant of God, weeps over the city of Jerusalem who slaughters the prophets—(much like the twisted zeal of those who think that killing their enemies makes them acceptable to God). The result will be destruction and more killing. Those who belong to God in Jesus must weep and mourn but not harm anyone else no matter what happens in history.

Friday

FIRST READING   **I.** 1 Mac 4:36–37, 52–59

II. Rev 10:8–11

Responsorial Psalm   **I.** 1 Chr 29:10bcd, 11abc,

11d–12a, 12bcd

II. Ps 119:14, 24, 72, 103, 111, 131

GOSPEL   Lk 19:45–48

So close to his own torture and death, Jesus enters and drives the merchants out, crying out that "My house shall be a house of prayer; but you have turned it into a den of robbers." These people cheated the poor when they came to offer sacrifice and made money off the worship of God, stealing even from the Holy One. Jesus speaks the truth in public and his enemies gather wanting to kill him but can't find the right moment because of the people who are "hanging on his words." He will hang on a cross for those words. These past days all the saints we remember were known for their care of the poor and the sick. Rose Duchesne founded schools for Native and African Americans. Does our work in the church reflect true prayer that precedes the work of justice and mercy for others?

John must eat the scroll, bitter in his mouth and then turning sweet as honey. He does, swallows it and it turns sour, and he must continue to speak what he sees to all nations and countries, the powers of the world.

Jesus The Prophet, the Word of God in flesh and blood, drives out of the temple those who would have worship and religion serve their economics and politics. Then he teaches there daily. The people are hungry for his Word and the leaders seek a way to destroy him. The confrontation between powers in Jesus' life and history are converging.

In every generation, we must chose who to follow, to obey and what we are willing to stake our life on. We must choose.

Judas Maccabees, the leader of the revolt at the time of the liberation of the sanctuary, brings the army and the people to rededicate the building to the worship of Yahweh. And the people rejoice for eight days. This Feasts of the Lights (a candle for each day), still celebrated around in Judaism at this time—the reclamation of the Temple. Jesus too reclaims the temple (a house of prayer) for the worship and praise of God. He ejects the traders, using force, but harming no one, a prophetic and symbolic gesture meant to highlight the necessity of severing the ties between economics/politics and religion. The worship of God does not serve anything but God alone. And today, there are many still—within church and without—who seek to destroy anyone who speaks as clearly as did Jesus on this issue. Let us examine ourselves to see whether the way we practice our religion serves the dominant culture, government, and economic system more than it calls us to transformation and conversion to Jesus' good news to the poor.

Saturday

FIRST READING	**I.** 1 Mac 6:1–13
	II. Rev 11:4–12
Responsorial Psalm	**I.** Ps 9:2–3, 4 and 6, 16 and 19
	II. Ps 144:1, 2, 9–10
GOSPEL	Lk 20:27–40

The Sadducees are trying to trap Jesus and make him look stupid, proposing to him an impossible situation—they do not believe in resurrection. But Jesus will not be caught in their games. There will not be the same relations after death and resurrection as there were on earth. We will be the sons and daughters of God, born of life everlasting and forever free. We are born into this life in our baptisms and no matter our vocation we are to live professing the power of life over death and practicing resurrection, dying and rising with Christ until the day we die. Lord, may we practice resurrection and bring hope to others today.

There are visions of prophets murdered, wars, victors gloating and others in misery, and death rampant and vicious. There will be times of witnessing to the truth and paying for it with our lives, but we are not to do war on earth. It is in God's hands to breathe life back into us and judge justly in the face of enemies. Whatever the afterlife is, however judgment will take place it is in

God's hands. And Jesus is mocked by the Sadducees who do not believe in resurrection with an absurd case. But he refuses to be mocked and tells them they know nothing about life, or about the God of the living or of the life to come. Do we hear and take to heart Jesus' words of life?

The king hears of the revolt of the Israelites and their reclamation of the Temple, destroying the idol he had enshrined. He saw himself as benign in his rule of others, and as beloved by the people. But now he realizes the evil he has done and he sees himself dying as an alien. Sickness, loss, the ruin of our plans, when we are intent on our own designs, often bring pangs of conscience—a bit late, but necessary.

When faced with the reality of death there are those who do not believe in an afterlife, in a judgment and a reckoning of justice for all. The Sadducees (a sect within Judaism at the time of Jesus) were of this confession. And so they approached Jesus to mock him with an absurd case, in the process, they mock the law of marriage as well. And Jesus uses their own scriptures to show them their ignorance and their evil intent, reminding them that God is the God of the living, of their ancestors, of history, and of all time. Do we remember who God is truly and act accordingly?

THIRTY-FOURTH WEEK IN ORDINARY TIME

Monday

FIRST READING   **I.** Dn 1:1–6, 8–20

       II. Rev 14:1–3, 4b–5

Responsorial Psalm   **I.** Dn 3:52, 53, 54, 55, 56

       II. Ps 24:1bc–2, 3–4ab, 5–6

GOSPEL   Lk 21:1–4

Only days left in this year, Anno Dominum, 2006. At the end of history there will be a throng of believers, marked with the name of the Lamb and the Father on their foreheads who will sing the glory of God and follow the Lamb, as they did on the earth. They are those who speak the truth and do not abide in evil. On earth, Jesus proclaims what they might look like here: the widow who gives all she has to live on. She who was poverty-stricken anonymously gives God everything. She is just like Jesus. And we, are we giving God everything, imitating Jesus who serves us, yet is the King of Glory?

Daniel resists the king's command, his food, his lifestyle and his domination. He offers a test so that he and his companions can prove that they will not only survive but thrive on their obedience to their God who is God alone. They become known for their knowledge and wisdom and prudence (knowing when to be public and when to lie low in the face of evil and persecution). We have much to learn from these young men who know how to be faithful to their covenant with God and the people yet know how to survive in a climate of slavery, oppression and being conquered.

And Jesus tells us to observe the woman who gives a mite—it is all that she lives on. She is a true believer and worshipper of God. Even though she has been beggared by poverty, by the taxes of Rome and by her own religious leader, she still gives to God. Jesus points out that he is in collusion with her! And he wants us to be sure that we do not put others in the position she finds herself in. And yet we are to imitate her in giving all that we have to live on—like Jesus who gives even his life so that we might have life.

Tuesday

FIRST READING

I. Dn 2: 31–45
II. Rev 14:14–19

Responsorial Psalm

I. Dn 3:57, 58, 59, 60, 61
II. Ps 96:10, 11–12, 13

GOSPEL

Lk 21:5–11

☀ People are praising the temple and its artwork and Jesus sees its coming destruction. His disciples are fearful and Jesus tries to warn them of the coming destruction of Jerusalem by the Romans and times of nations raging against one another and the destruction of the earth through war, floods, famines and earthquakes. Jesus was describing the last one hundred years before him and the following one hundred years after his death, and every era on earth because of evil, injustice and sin. This is the world and his disciples must be realistic about how the world works. Today we remember Cecilia, a young woman caught in that horror, tortured and yet faithful. Our world is no different. Do we stand look at the world through the eyes of Jesus and know we must try to make holy the world in obedience to God's Word, yet suffering and evil are ever-present along with grace abounding?

☀ The vision is of harvesting: wheat, grapes and then it is subjected to God's anger. The anger of God is righteous, doing justice, making right what is wrong, revealing what was, is and should never have been on earth. There will be judgment and justice for all. And Jesus overhears some speaking of the glory of the temple in Jerusalem and sadly tries to tell them that it will be no more—utterly destroyed. And immediately everyone wants to know when/how/where. But that is not given for us to know. There will be wars, dissension, natural disasters and signs in the heavens, but we are not to be afraid, because even when these things happen—the end is not so near. How do we live today—that is what is of issue here?

✳ Daniel reports on the king's dream and is truthful in telling the king that another will replace him, and that the kingdom will be divided into alliances made by marriage and that all will shatter and fall. But there will be a kingdom without end, set up by God. It will be stronger than all kingdoms on earth. Daniel, the slave becomes Daniel the prophet of God, speaking the truth to the mightiest power in his lifetime/history.

And Jesus too speaks as a prophet while he watches his disciples contemplate and admire the buildings of the temple (the restoration that has just recently been completed). But, as with all buildings, all kingdoms, all institutions, dynasties and leaders it will one day be utterly destroyed and gone. And they want to know when. But Jesus wants them to be truly religious, not bound to their externals, but internally bound to the community, to obedience and trust in the face of history. Our history is being described—this is not only about Jerusalem and the temple, but also about the United States, Europe, Asia, every country and rulers, even the Vatican and all buildings. Do we live with the heart of our religion and not its superficialities?

Wednesday

FIRST READING   **I.** Dn 5:1–6, 13–14, 16–17, 23–28
     II. Rev 15:1–4
Responsorial Psalm   **I.** Dn: 3:62, 63, 64, 65, 66, 67
     II. Ps 98:1, 2–3, 7–8, 9
GOSPEL   Lk 21:12–19

✳ Jesus tries to tell us that we will be caught, persecuted, delivered up to torture, imprisoned and called to witness to the truth of Jesus. But it is not a time to worry, for the Spirit will be given to us in words and wisdom that no one will be able to contradict. But we will be betrayed and some killed. Yet, paradoxically even if they kill us, we will not be ultimately harmed. Faithfulness will save us. We have been reading Daniel for days and the stories of the young men, and Daniel who refused to worship any God but Yahweh, their sufferings and their vindication. There will be vindication. We must hang on for a dearer and truer life, as our Master did on the cross. We draw near the end of the year and ask ourselves how we want to live our lives now and until the hour of our deaths. Jesus be near to us.

✻ In the midst of anger and judgment there is glory and acknowledgment of both the power of God, and his goodness and those who stood by and were faithful in the midst of all the horror. They sing the song of Moses/Exodus and freedom now in fullness. God is the King of all nations and worthy of all human beings honor. Jesus tells us we will know persecution, being hounded to death, torture, and yet we are to bear witness, as he has to the truth, and his Spirit will be with us as our defense and support. God, this God of power and might, of servanthood and humility is with us.

✻ The king uses the treasures of the temple at his party and a hand appears writing on the wall. Daniel is summoned to interpret because it is thought that the Spirit of God is within him. He doesn't want the king's gifts and informs him that he has rebelled against God, profaning the vessels but worshipping idols while ignoring the God who holds his life in his hands. He ruthlessly reveals the destruction of his kingdom and boldly speaks in the name of God in public.

Daniel faces what Jesus warns us will happen if we speak the truth to the powers of the world: nations, governments and even religious leaders who have ignored the God who holds all life in his hands. But he also tells us that the Spirit of God will be with us and will give us the words, the wisdom and the courage to stand our ground in public and say what needs to be said. Even families will turn against one another (and churches) but patient endurance save us. Who do we serve with our words?

Thursday

FIRST READING **I.** Dn 6:12–28
II. Rev 18:1–2, 21–23, 19:1–3, 9a

Responsorial Psalm **I.** Dn 3:68, 69, 70, 71, 72, 73, 74
II. Ps 100:1b–2, 3, 4, 5

GOSPEL Lk 21:20–28

✻ This is the description of the destruction of Jerusalem, but it could be any landmark, any country as it falls from power, any nation brought to ruin by another nation and then made slaves to those who conquer. And it is harder for women, children and those about to give birth. And it is about the end of time, the end of all history and all world power, at the end of the world when the Son of Man comes to judge the nations with justice. There will be justice and glory will touch the earth. This woe ends with wonder: "stand erect and lift up your heads, for your deliverance is drawing near!" The martyrs, the prophets, those who worked for justice, those who befriended the poor and were the friends of God—fullness will be given. No matter what transpires in the world today we are to stand in the freedom of the children of God, practice resurrection and know our God is near, always drawing nearer to us.

Daniel is caught praying and is cast into the lions' den, though the king is partial to him. In the morning he goes to see if Daniel's God has saved him and Daniel is alive. The king in his brutality casts the men who accused him, their wives and children into the den to be torn apart and eaten and declares that the God of Daniel is to be reverenced and served. He has caught a sense of the power of God, but certainly nothing of his forgiveness and mercy and enduring faithfulness to his people.

Jesus warns that the destruction of the city and temple will come (he could read the signs of the times in the hostilities between Rome's iron hand and those who would revolt. There will be distress in the land and no one will be spared. Luke's gospel is written more than 25 years after the actual destruction that has severed the believers in Jesus from the Jewish community and put them at peril to both Rome and the Jewish factions. But Jesus speaks not just of persecutions to come, but of the end times when all will know who is God—the God of Jesus the crucified Son of Man who holds both justice and mercy in his hand. This is our God.

Friday

FIRST READING

Responsorial Psalm

GOSPEL

I. Dn 7:2–14
II. Rev 20:1–4, 11—21:2
I. Dn 3:75, 76, 77, 78, 79, 80, 81
II. Ps 84:3, 4, 5–6 and 8
Lk 21:29–33

A story of a fig tree to help us know when our deliverance is close at hand. We are to watch the ways of history and what happens (and they happen in every generation) and know that there will be summer, new life, hope and the coming of the kingdom of God in more and more fullness, spreading through the world like the season of summer coming upon us. God's word will prevail. God's presence will renew the face of the earth. God's peace will abide in us and we will know God's nearness. In the face of evil in the world we must stand fast, with heads lifted high to catch the Son of Justice on our faces. The year is ending with both judgment and promise, the reality of death and the declaration that life will prevail. Lord Jesus you died and brought a life unbounded to us—may we cling to you and one another in faith all the days of our lives.

The visions are elaborate, detailed, and symbolic: evil will be destroyed. The dead will be raised, judged before life; the old earth will pass away; there will be second deaths of judgment and there will be a new heaven and a new earth. What will they be like? We only know that holiness will prevail and it will be born of God. Is it close? Jesus says to look at the fig tree, every tree—watch the signs. Is God near? God is always near and every year there is judgment and newness of life. One day there will be ultimate justice and redemption. But for this year, do we belong to God?

Saturday

FIRST READING	**I.** Dn 7:15–27
	II. Rev 22:1–7
Responsorial Psalm	**I.** Dn 3:82, 83, 84, 85, 86, 87
	II. Ps 95:1–2, 3–5, 6–7
GOSPEL	Lk 21:34–36

This is the last day of the liturgical year 2005. We stand turning from the past into the Advent of our God who comes again into our weary and war-torn world. We stand judged and knowing we are in desperate need of another year, another chance at believing in and living the Gospel. There will be an end to everything on the earth, even the earth itself. And there will be an end to our lives and our endeavors, nations and agendas. We must examine everything in the light of the coming of the Son of Man to judge history, judge all who ruled with power and each of us. We stand before the Son of Man coming in a cloud with power and great glory and cry out for justice in the world and mercy upon us all and bless our God who is holy: Father, Son and Spirit. Glory be to God forever and ever. Amen.

On this last day of the year we are shown the river of life rising from the throne of the Lamb and flowing into the earth, bringing healing, grace, power, light, food; and we will see God face to face. There will be no night and the light will come from within God and us: all that God writes will come true and God will be with us again. Jesus' words cry out: "Watch!" The day will come. Stay awake and pray for strength so that no matter what happens we can stand before the Son of Man with confidence. One day we will all stand before the Son of Man, but for today we can give this year and all we are/have back to God, knowing that tomorrow and every day, another year is gift of life/light and the presence of God among us.

This is the last day of the liturgical year. Daniel is given visions that fill him with anguish and fear for his people who sought to be faithful and were persecuted until the Ancient One arrived and judgment was pronounced in favor of those who remained holy. He tells of the vision of his time and the vision whenever those who belong to God remain holy. They are given over to God and not to history and a reckoning happens. And his vision speaks of the last judgment and the time when all the earth will be held in the scales of justice and there will be the last break with the powers that ruled this world—often in opposition to God's justice and merciful forgiveness and life. Jesus warns us, "Do not get caught up in the day to day cares of living in the world. "We live, but we live in God's time too and we must pray to stay attentive to God's day and God's presence." The Son of Man will come in glory; he comes in the poor and the crucified daily. The Son of Man is always coming. Are we ready to stand secure before the Son of Man?

PROPER of SAINTS

SOLEMNITIES, FEASTS, MEMORIALS

The difference between the three basic categories resides in their importance, which in turn reflected in the presence or absence of different liturgical elements. Solemnities are the highest degree and are usually reserved forthe most important mysteries of faith. These include Easter, Pentecost and the Immaculate Conception; the principal titles of Our Lord, such as King and Sacred Heart; and celebrations that honor some saints of particular importance in salvation history, such as Sts. Peter and Paul, and St. John the Baptist on his day of birth.

Solemnities have the same basic elements as a Sunday: three readings, prayer of the faithful, the Creed and the Gloria which is recited even when the solemnity occurs during Advent of Lent. It also has proper prayer formulas exclusive to the day: entrance antiphon, opening prayer, prayer over the gifts, Communion antiphon, and prayer after Communion. In most cases it also has a particular preface.

Some solemnities are also holy days of obligation, but these vary from country to country. A solemnity is celebrated if it falls on a Sunday of ordinary time or Christmastide. But it is usually transferred to the following Monday if it falls on a Sunday of Advent, Lent or Easter, or during Holy Week or the Easter octave.

A feast honors a mystery or title of the Lord, of Our Lady, or of saints of particular importance (such as the apostles and Evangelists) and some of historical importance such as the deacon St. Lawrence.

The feast usually has some proper prayers but has only two readings plus the Gloria. Feasts of the Lord, such as the Transfiguration and the Exaltation of the Holy Cross, unlike other feasts, are celebrated when they fall on a Sunday. On such occasions they have three readings, the Gloria and the Creed.

A memorial is usually of saints but may also celebrate some aspect of the Lord or of Mary. Examples include the optional memorial of the Holy Name of Jesus or the obligatory memorial of the Immaculate Heart of Mary.

From the point of view of the liturgical elements there is no difference between the optional and obligatory memorial. The memorial has at least a proper opening prayer and may have proper readings suitable for the saint being celebrated. The readings of the day may be used, and the lectionary recommends against an excessive use of specific readings for the saints so as not to interrupt too much the continous cycle of daily readings.

On the other hand, the specific readings should always be used for certain saints, above all those specifically mentioned in the readings themselves, such as Martha, Mary Magdalene and Barnabas.

During Lent and Advent from December 17 to December 24 memorials may be celebrated only as commemorations. That is, only the opening prayer of the saint is used and all the rest comes from the day. November 2, All Souls' Day, is something of a special class that, without being a solemnity, still has precedence over a Sunday. It is also important to note that the same celebration may have a different classification in various geographical areas, as some celebrations and saints are venerated more in one place than in another. For example, St. Benedict, an obligatory memorial in the universal calendar, is a feast in Europe since hs is one of its patrons. But he rates a solemnity in the diocese and abbey of Montecassino where he is buried.

Finally, the decision on whether a solemnity such as the Body and Blood of the Lord is a holy day of obligation falls primarily upon the bishops' conference, which deides based on the pastoral reality of each country. Some have maintained the traditional Thursday celebration and kept it as a holy day; others might have maintained the day but without the obligation. Many have preferred to transfer the celebration to the following Sunday so as to ensure its celebration with the greatest number of faithful.

The Vatican, for example, continues the traditional Thursday celebration and thus the Holy Father's procession with the Blessed Sacrament is held on that day. The Diocese of Rome, however, along with the rest of Italy, celebrates it on the following Sunday.

JANUARY

CONVERSION OF PAUL, apostle

FIRST READING   Acts 22:3–16 (or Acts 9:1–222)
Responsorial Psalm   Ps 117:1, 2
GOSPEL   Mk 16:15–18

✳ With the resurrection of Jesus, all disciples are sent out into
the whole world to preach the good news of forgiveness,
baptize, learn new languages and to continue the work that Jesus
began in the world. Paul, the apostle who was knocked from his
horse, blinded by the presence of the Risen Lord learned that in
persecuting the Christians, he was, in fact, persecuting Jesus. Paul
was converted and he turned from his violent and murderous ways
of attacking Christians and learned to walk in the way of the Gospel,
and then to preach to the nations of the earth.

We don't often think that we are persecuting Christians or that
we are sent to preach the gospel to the world, but we are sent by
our baptisms and confirmations to stand up for what we believe
in a world that is sorely tried by persecutions, killings and making
others suffer for their religious beliefs. In this day, we are called
to look to ourselves and see who we are harming and know that
we are, in fact, harming Jesus the crucified one among us in our
Islamic, Jewish, Hindu, Buddhist and other believers who are our
brothers and sisters.

✳ Paul meets the presence/person of Jesus in those whom he
persecutes and threatens when they proclaim the good news
and follow Jesus, the Son of Man. He hears and is blinded and then
given sight by one who believes in Jesus and Barnabas vouches for
him and helps him to grow in the faith in the community. Paul
learns what this new Way is that is the way of Jesus, the way of

CONVERSION OF PAUL ✦ JANUARY 25   **441**

the cross, of loving one's enemies and loving as God has loved us, the good news of life for all ever more deeply and he learns to be a preacher, a missionary and one who brings this gospel of the way to others. But this is the vocation of all baptized as Christians and we are told that we are to 'make holy the world' and live the resurrection now in our lives (Vatican Council documents). Do we live by the name of Jesus, saving those who hunger, thirst, for food, justice and life?

Acts 22—Paul's history before encountering Jesus on the road to Damascus was persecuting and arresting Christians—this is the only Jesus, the Body of Christ that Paul ever met and knew—the Crucified in the community of believers. And in the light of the Word of God he is missioned and told to be baptized and forgiven. It is the story of each of our own conversions, over and over again in our lives.

Acts 9 In this version of the story, Saul must obey and go into the city and learn from those he has persecuted what he must do to be forgiven, saved and converted. Others in the community are sent to Saul to help him change and learn the ways of Jesus. It is fraught with violence/fear and insecurity for the church must seek out and help those who have harmed them. And Saul's conversion took a lot longer than the change of his name to Paul.

Conversion to the Gospel, to the good news of Jesus Christ who heals and saves, forgives and accompanies his community the Church throughout all history is what we are called to preach and to be ever-more converted to daily, both as individual believers and as the company of Jesus' disciples. None of us goes home alone, we go in Jesus' company and we are to be light, blinding searing light for the entire world.

TIMOTHY and TITUS, bishops

FIRST READING	2 Tim 1...1–9 (or Tit 1:1–5
Responsorial Psalm	Ps 96:1–2, 2–3, 7–8, 10
GOSPEL	Lk 10:1–9

Jesus describes how his followers who share his power with others must live. They are to go forth two by two and live as workers bringing in the harvest that is given by God (which they did not necessarily sow). They are to live with courage, but as lambs among wolves, nonviolently, protectively, keeping the flock together, without scandals and without reliance on a purse (money) or more than what they need for the moment. They are to bring peace, and share what is given to them, not looking for a better deal with others. They are to heal (bring medicine and health care, hope, dignity and a sense of life for the future and preach God's kingdom of justice and peace so near to us.) These are the roles and ways of bishops along the Way of the Lord.

2 Tim—Timothy is addressed with prayers and saluations in the Body of Christ and the Trinity, and as a member of his family of believers: his grandmother Lois and his mother Eunice. They seed him with the fire of the spirit and his faith was brought to flame in the laying on of hands by Paul in the presence of the community—and that spirit is ours too.

Tit—Titus is addressed as a son in the faith, in the Lord Jesus, by Paul, prayed for and with and encouraged to share the faith and knowledge that he has been given by growing in it and passing it onto others. Always the grace and peace of Christ is with him/all of them.

Lk—The harvest is waiting in every generation for those with strength, generosity and gratitude to bring it in. Jesus sends 72 out, two by two (the usual way to do any form of ministry, evangelization, preaching, teaching outside of the community and to go before the Word and the community—as Timothy and Titus did (as Lois and Eunice did) as all of us are called to do. We are to bring the Peace of Christ, healing and hope, and the words of the Gospel. That is essential. That is our calling, our sending and our hope.

FEBRUARY

February 11

OUR LADY OF LOURDES

FIRST READING   Is 66:10–14c
Responsorial Psalm   Ps Jdt 13:18, 19
GOSPEL   Jn 2:1–11

❉ Isaiah comes to bring joy and comfort to the city of Jerusalem, bringing peace to her at long last, overflowing and rushing towards her in a great river. And they are told that they will "be nursed and carried in her arms and fondled upon her lap." This is the description of the wedding feast of Isaiah, the coming of the kingdom of God in fullness for the poor and those who hunger for food and justice and life that is the symbol of the wedding feast of Cana. With the presence of Jesus in the world there is abundance of wine, of mercy and rejoicing. We are reminded to share that abundance among those who need it most.

February 22

CHAIR OF PETER, apostle

FIRST READING   Is 66:10–14c
Responsorial Psalm   Ps Jdt 13:18, 19
GOSPEL   Jn 2:1–11

❉ Peter has learned as an elder in the faith through witness to the sufferings of Jesus and others, facing his own martyrdom to be a shepherd, guarding it willingly, generously and serving them all as Jesus, the Good Shepherd taught him by his own forgiveness when he betrayed his Master publicly, scattering the sheep. Jesus questions the disciples on who he truly is—and Peter answers prophet and more, the Son of the living God. Jesus tells him he is blessed because he was given that knowledge by the Father. And he is given another gift: the power to forgive on earth, as Jesus did, as well as hold bound those who do evil, as Jesus also did. The Church and its leaders, like Peter, have known the Good Shepherd's forgiveness of their public betrayals and failures and in turn they go out looking for the lost sheep, bringing them back with forgiveness. It is only the witness and experience of suffering that makes this power of God shared with humans a source of hope and a gift among peoples. Father, teach your Church how to forgive, how to seek out those lost and how to speak the truth to power that is unjust and evil. Make your Church and its leaders servants and martyrs, even if we are slow-learners, like Peter. Amen.

The leader/teacher of Jesus' church is to be on elder and a witness to the sufferings of Christ, hoping to share the glory too. It is not being old, but being steeped in suffering and caring for others as a shepherd does his/her sheep, generously and leading by example that makes for one who keeps the Church in imitation of Jesus the Good Shepherd who lays down his life for the sheep. Nothing can stand against the Church but those who lead and those who follow must be subject to the Father of all standing in the world, but also against it when it must do so to be true to the crucified Christ.

Peter is a shepherd, an elder reminding the others that they must care for the flock. They must watch, be an example and not lord it over others—and Peter knows this, having once been the lost sheep himself, brought back with tenderness to being a follower after betraying and cursing Jesus' name in his fear.

Peter, like us, is quick to tell Jesus who he thinks he is: the Messiah, the Son of the living God! He has the words, but no understanding. The Father has shared this knowledge with him, but Peter must walk the way of the cross with Jesus before he will realize who Jesus truly is, and who he himself is called to be as part of the foundation of the new community of forgiveness and holding bound. We too stand with Peter today and are questioned: do we know who this Jesus is and who we are called to be as followers?

APRIL

April 25

MARK, evangelist

FIRST READING   1 P 5:5b–14
Responsorial Psalm   Ps 89:2–3, 6–7, 16–17
GOSPEL   Mk 16:15–20

✹ Today is the feast of Mark, the scribe of the Spirit, the writer of the first gospel. Mark obeyed the command of Jesus after the resurrection to "go out into the whole world and proclaim the Good News to all creation." Mark wrote words, and traveled with Paul and Barnabas on missionary journeys calling people to conversion and forgiveness, believing that Jesus remained with them in Word, in Bread, in community and in the work that was given to him to share in with Jesus. We, like Mark, are called to share in Jesus' suffering and to know his glory too and it is the Spirit of God who strengthened and confirmed and established Mark. And we have been given this same command and same Spirit. We who know the truth and marvel at his gospel are called to be Good News in our way, in our time, in obedience. Peace to us all—the Peace that Mark served and we are to be in the world.

✹ Mark, the disciple and companion, spiritual son of Peter and the one who was inspired to write the Gospel of Mark. Mark's gospel ends with the proclamation to go forth into the whole world and preach relying on the Lord being with them in word/deed and saving power. Peter is in jail facing death by crucifixion and sending greetings of faith, of hope and love to the community. Mark's words (written around 63 AD) would come after Peter's death but they have been spoken daily before they were written down for us. Mark was a young follower, running from the garden in fear, but standing in the tomb, unafraid and preaching the resurrection. We too must learn to do the same.

446   MARK, EVANGELIST ✦ APRIL 25

꤫ Mark's symbol is the lion—and his gospel enables us, the
꤫ followers of Jesus to stand firm and resist the devil that
seeks to hinder us from being the beloved children of God. The
life of baptism/confirmation/eucharist is one of resistance, of
undergoing suffering for the sake of the Gospel. Peter sees Mark
as his son, in the Lord and Mark will write his gospel with Peter
as the image of the believer who fails, betrays and is afraid and
yet because of the resurrection will stand firm and become solid
in faith. Mark's gospel is the first one we have and it calls us to
'deny ourselves, pick up our cross and come after Jesus', learning
to be faithful and free in the Word and presence of the Risen Lord.
Some say that it is Mark who was in the tomb, proclaiming the
Gospel, because once in the garden that night Jesus was arrested,
he too ran in fear.

MAY

May 1

JOSEPH THE WORKER, foster father of Jesus

FIRST READING   Gen 1:26—2:3 (or Col 3:14–15, , 17, 23–24
Responsorial Psalm   Ps 90;2–3, 3–4, 12–13, 14 and 16
GOSPEL   Mk 16:15–20

꤫ The telling of creation reminds us that each of us is made in
꤫ the divine image: man and woman together reveal the glory
of God. And all that God has made has been entrusted to us. We
are given dominion but it is the dominion of an interdependent
world. And part of the dominion is to rest, to contemplate the
goodness of God in imitation of the One who gives us life and
sustains us. It is the image of those who work, who create, who
bring life and nurture it.

Christ's peace is what is to reign in our hearts as the Body of
Christ. We are to work/live with thanks, with peace for the glory
of God the Father, in the name of Jesus. We are to work with our
whole being and do the work of God in the world, transforming

and making all holy. We are the slaves of the Lord, sent to free the world, revealing its goodness.

Joseph was a father, a husband and a worker, a carpenter, a man made holy by his work and his relationships in the place he lived—Nazareth. And he taught Jesus his trade, working with him building, felling trees, making crosses for the Romans out of rough hewn trunks. He protected his family, sheltered them, cared for them and sought to live with dignity and freedom and instilled those virtues and hopes in his son, Jesus. We are made holy in the places we live, dwell, study, work and seek to make hospitable and welcoming.

We are made in the image of God who did the work of creation, making all things so good. And we were given dominion over all the earth and its creatures. Dominion, meaning "lord," but we are to lord it over the earth, the way God lords over us, his creation, caring for it, protecting it and nurturing it, safe-keeping it and passing it along so that all enjoy its richness, and see in it the glory of the Maker. Jesus is the son of Joseph the carpenter, who worked to keep Jesus alive, protecting him and Mary from violence, breaking the law to save their lives and provide for them. Today we honor Joseph who adopted Jesus, the son of God as his own beloved son, and taught him how to be a man, a human being and a Jew, how to walk the earth with us. That was his work and ours too.

May 3

PHILIP and JAMES, apostles

FIRST READING	1 Cor 15:1–8
Responsorial Psalm	Ps 19:2–3, 4–5
GOSPEL	Jn 14:6–14

James is the first of the Apostles to be martyred early in the Church's initial fervor and persecutions while Philip who asks Jesus to show him the Father, goes on in the midst of persecution to preach to Gentiles and Jews, eventually being killed for bearing his share of the burden of the Gospel. They knew the intimate company of Jesus, ran from standing with him in the Garden, yet the gift of the Spirit made them courageous and out-spoken in their preaching. Jesus proclaimed that if we believe in him, we will do the same works that he did—and both Philip and James proved him true to his word. We too are called to believe, to obey and to know the Father in Jesus' word and works. And we too, must prove Jesus true to his Word, by doing the works that Jesus has begun in the world. We are to bear our share of the burden of the Gospel and to preach Jesus' word and do His works in our day.

❋ The readings speak of these 2 men, first James who was one of the witnesses to the resurrection (though we do not have any written account of that, except in Acts) and Paul's writings. But the importance in each man's life (as in our own) is believing in the Word of the Scripture, the gospel passed onto us. We hand on what we receive: the life, death and resurrection of Jesus. This is what we stake our lives and deaths on. In the gospel Philip seeks to know the Father and yet he does not understand Jesus' words—if we see Jesus, the Word made flesh, then we see God the Father. The mystery of the Trinity—the dwelling as one of Father, Son and Spirit, and our initiation into the Trinity is what our life is. It is what sustains us and makes us holy, whether we are apostles, disciples, preachers/ teachers/workers, husbands and wives, parents, students, single/ widowed/divorced—we are all coming to the Father through Jesus' Word.

May 14

MATTHIAS, apostle

FIRST READING   Acts 1:15–17, 20–26
Responsorial Psalm   Ps 113:1–2, 3–4, 5–6, 7–8
GOSPEL   Jn 15:9–17

❋ We are told that the greatest love is to give one's life for one's friends and we are the friends of God when we give our lives in obedience to Jesus' Word of life. In this giving we are freed from fear and know deep abiding joy. In obedience we learn to know the Father as Jesus did, but we must remember it is Jesus who chooses us and sends us out to bear fruit in the world. Matthias, the apostle who replaces Judas the betrayer dies a martyr as do all the disciples except John who dies in exile writing love letters to his beloved children, dying of love. We are chosen by God, baptized and anointed in the Spirit and sent out to lay down our lives, to love our enemies and make them all friends and to bring the Word of life to all we encounter. This is the only commandment and it covers everything we do with our lives.

✹ When the apostles number only eleven they choose another who is a witness to the resurrection. They pray and draw lots between the two and Matthias is chosen to replace Judas. He completes the number twelve though we know nothing else of him. Perhaps it is the process that is most instructive and crucial: It is God who reads the hearts of men and makes known who is to be a leader. Who and how should our leaders be nominated? We should pray and choose by lot—what a difference there would be in who was chosen and how the Church moved in the world.

Again Jesus keeps telling us that everything is love—as the Father has loved him, he loves us! And if we obey his word/commands that we will live in that love, now and forever and we will know the joy of Jesus who obeys. We are called to love unto death, call everyone beloved, treat all as friends because that is the love we have known from God.

May 31

VISITATION OF THE BLESSED VIRGIN MARY

FIRST READING   Zep 3:14–18a (or Rom 12:9–16)
Responsorial Psalm   Is 12:2–3, 4bcd, 5–6
GOSPEL   Lk 1:39–56

✹ Here in late spring, we spring forward to the secret ways of God coming to earth in the Incarnation and moving into the world that all will celebrate seven months from now. Mary has been visited by Gabriel and said Yes and is pregnant with the Word of God made flesh. Now she goes to visit her cousin Elizabeth needing protection as a single, unmarried woman in a society that would have stoned her and her child to death. She needs Elizabeth's sanctuary and knowledge and will be one of her midwives when she births John. She greets Elizabeth: Shalom, Peace be with you! And the sound of the word of God stirs John into life and stirs Elizabeth to prophecy and blessing of Mary. The Word is moving out into the world and the poor, the cursed, the remnant of believers even among Israel are the only ones to pick up on its presence growing in Mary. Mary is blessed by Elizabeth and she in turn blesses God. The Word is seeded in us in baptism and we are to go forth to greet others with the Peace that grows with us and to confirm one another in obedience as Elizabeth confirms Mary in her becoming a disciple of the Word.

The Word is in the world and Mary travels to see Elizabeth for sanctuary and refuge. Her prayer would be that of the whole people crying out for joy that God is with them and there is no need to fear anymore. "God is within you, Yahweh, saving warrior. He will jump for joy on seeing you, for he has revived his love." This is what is happening with Elizabeth and John the prophets of the earlier covenant and Mary the prophet of the new covenant that is the person/word Jesus the Lord. We rejoice for our God is within us. We are the Body of Christ in the world.

Our God has come and it is cause for joy and gladness, an end to fear and to be renewed in God's love. God comes to Zion, the city of Jerusalem described as 'O daughter of Zion' a title given to Mary who bears a mighty savior in the midst of the people. It is the savior that is the cause for rejoicing: for Mary, for Elizabeth and John and for all of us who seek to bring the Word into our world.

Paul's letter is a litany of commands about how we are to live. If all of us, the beloved children of God, could do only a few of them, the world would know that our savior has come to us, our God dwells with us and there is great cause for rejoicing. We are to live in hope, in joy, in love, in resistance, clinging to the good, looking to the needs of others, offering hospitality, bless our persecutors and be compassionate with all, and stay close to the lowly (the meek, the nonviolent). These are all the characteristics of Elizabeth and John as well as Jesus and Mary's visit to one another. We must learn how to meet and embrace each other, bringing the Word, sharing the peace/resurrection proclamation and confirming and inspiring each other, to sing the praises of God and all that God has done and is doing and will always do for all creation and all that he has made and called to be his own children.

also May 31

IMMACULATE HEART OF MARY

FIRST READING   Is 61:9–11
Responsorial Psalm   1 S 2:1, 4–5, 6–7, 8
GOSPEL   Lk 2:41–51

✺ This is Mary's prayer, but it is the prayer of her people, who have waited long for hope, for justice and for the One who would bring peace and freedom to them. And it is the prayer of prophets, of the poor and those who still cry out for justice and who seek a voice in a world that is deaf to their needs and hopes. Mary sings of joy, of exultation and of God's goodness to those who are faithful to the promises of the covenant. And she sings of God, the Holy One who remembers his people and who will continue to do amazing things for them, and for her in this child to be born who will be a revolutionary presence in the world. He will sear peoples' hearts and reveal their pride, speaking the truth. He will feed the hungry and send those who are filled with greed and the world and their own plans away and he will lift up those bowed down under slavery and oppression and reverse the order of the world, bringing God's justice to earth. Mary is caught up in God and as we pray, we too, must disappear into the glory of God, and do his will.

✺ In the days after Pentecost we celebrate deep mysteries of our God that are to sustain us all through Ordinary Time. Today we look at the love of God for us in Jesus' Spirit and Body. It has been there since the beginning but we are slow to see, understand and accept it. We are children held in arms, taught to walk, held in human cords, bands of love like an infant held to a cheek in tenderness. God is overwhelmed with love for us and so gives us Jesus, the Holy One always present among us, love burning yet not consuming us. It is love given in life and in death and in resurrection life—no end to its depth, breadth. We dwell in the heart of our God, with Jesus crucified, risen and sent in his Spirit. We live in the Trinity.

✻ Isaiah's words proclaim Jesus, and all those who believe in the Word of the Lord—giving all of our souls reason to rejoice and exult in the goodness and justice of God. We are clothed with the robe of righteousness (baptismal garment) and we are all called as the nation (Church/kingdom) to be the cause of justice for all nations. The people of God in every generation has sung the praises of God—Isaiah, Hannah, Mary and so, must each of us who have accepted the Word of the Lord into our lives.

Mary, with all believers, had to learn the wisdom of God in her child, Jesus. And even after 12 years with Jesus, she still does not know that he is not her child first, but he is the child of God the Father/Yahweh the Holy One. She had to 'keep all these things in her heart/memory, pondering the Word'. The gospel begins after this line and this is the image of the heart of Mary—pondering always the Word of her child and seeing to understand the wisdom and goodness of God ever more profoundly.

JUNE

June 11

BARNABAS, apostle

FIRST READING   Acts 11:21b–26; 13:1–3
Responsorial Psalm   Ps 98:1, 2–3ab, 3cd–4, 5–6
GOSPEL   Mt 10:7–13

✻ This is the work of the disciples of Jesus, imitating Jesus himself: Go and proclaim that the kingdom of justice for all and peace is near—heal the sick, bring the dead back to life, cleanse the lepers and drive out demons. And do this as graciously as we have known the power of God in our own lives. It appears to be impossible! The works of mercy—provide medicine and health care for all, forgive, bring hope and a future for people and their children with jobs and housing, accept the outsider, the migrant and the stranger and prisoner welcoming them into a life with others and resist and help others to resist evil, violence and injustice that is accepted as norm in so many places. And for those called to be missionaries (we all are in some small ways) travel radically free, depending on others' hospitality, open to all and bringing peace to wherever you come. Barnabas was the man who vouched for Paul and stood with him, helping him to remain constant in his conversion. We are to look not only to ourselves but to aide others as well.

Barnabas is often thought to be the one who was not chosen when Matthias was the one to replace Judas. Yet we know that Barnabas is the one that vouched for Paul and helped him be accepted by the church and begin his ministry and is sent to Antioch to encourage the young church—and he is described as one that is filled with the Holy Spirit and faith. What a way to be remembered! They are first called 'Christians' and Barnabas reveals essentially what spurred the community to spread and mature, going out into the world with the Good News. He was a missionary, a companion, a servant, a preacher/teacher, a guide for Paul and a leader in the church.

He obeyed the words of Jesus, announcing the presence of the kingdom in their midst and gave in his day to day life, as gift, all that Jesus had shared with him and the disciples. He blessed and was a blessing. Can the same be said of our leaders, and all of us sent to bring the reign of God to earth today?

JULY

July 3

THOMAS, apostle

FIRST READING   Eph 2:19–22
Responsorial Psalm   Ps 117:1bc, 2
GOSPEL   Jn 20:24–29

In Jesus we are no longer strangers or aliens but citizens of God's household and saints. We are the foundation of hope in the world, the dwelling place of God. And Jesus calls us all to show forth to the world his presence, crucified and risen. And unlike Thomas we are to listen to one another's accounts of the resurrection so that we do not stifle the work of the Spirit in the world and make the Risen Lord return to call us to task for our personal lack of belief and demands. We are blessed because we believe and have not seen.

✳ We are intimate and close to God, brought so near by Jesus and those who came after him, prophets, apostles, other disciples. And we are built up into one household of God rising on the foundations they first laid. We are the dwelling place for God in the Spirit—do we keep that in mind? This is not a description of us individually but as a people, a church, the whole people of God. Can anyone tell?

Thomas, like the other apostles, betrayed Jesus. He is absent (some think because as a twin he was hiding under that alter-identity) when the Risen Lord comes and gifts them all with peace, with the power of the Spirit and sends them into the world to forgive and hold bound those that need it. And he refuses to believe any of them, articulating his own crude criteria for belief. And so he stifles the Spirit and stops the Good News from getting into the world. Jesus comes after him, holding him bound to his words and blessing all those who will follow (like us) who will believe the words of others who tell us of resurrection life.

MARY MAGDALENE

July 22

FIRST READING   Song 3:1–4b (or 2 Cor5:14–17)
Responsorial Psalm   Ps 63:2, 3–4, 5–6, 8–9
GOSPEL   Jn 20:1–2, 11–18

✳ Mary of the town of Magdala was one of the twelve women who had followed Jesus from the beginning of his ministry in Galilee. Whoever she was, she is in all the gospel accounts of the resurrection of one of the myrrh-bearing women who go to the tomb. In John's account she sees the empty tomb and assumes that Jesus' body has been stolen and she is bereft and beside herself with grief. She tells Peter and the beloved disciple about the tomb, but does not enter (baptism). She stands outside weeping. Even angels do not shock her into some sense that something is happening and that her obsession with Jesus' body is a dead-end. Even Jesus' voice and questioning of her doesn't register—she is intent on getting his dead body. Her attachment to what she knew of him before crucifixion and resurrection has blinded her to who Jesus really is. She only recognizes her own name in his mouth and is told not to cling to him—he is not her possession. He belongs only to his Father and her Father, to his God and her God—and that is what she is commanded to tell the disciples. Do we cling to our personal ideas of Jesus and miss who the Risen Lord truly is? Is Jesus telling us to let go of the past and believe in a future that we could not imagine?

The Song speaks of longing, of someone who is lost, wandering about, bereft of the one she love, but she cannot find him and so she cries out: "Have you seen him?… "and then she found him. This is the core of the story of Mary of Magdala looking for the body of Jesus on Easter morning. But she is intent on finding his body; she will settle for that; she does not for a moment know who he was or that he is alive. She searches in her grief. She cannot cling to her own relationship with Jesus but only learn that he belongs to God the Father and so does she belong to God the Father, with him. We cannot judge our relations with Jesus humanly. This is a new creation and we live no longer in old ways. We are to seek the Father with Jesus in the power of the Spirit of life.

July 25

JAMES, apostle

FIRST READING   2 Cor 4:7–15
Responsorial Psalm   Ps 126:1–2, 2–3, 4–5, 6
GOSPEL   Mt 20:20–28

Surprisingly many of the stories about individual apostles are not exactly what you'd want to be remembered for! Here James (and John) send their mother in to get Jesus to give them the best seats in the kingdom when he's king! And this happens just after Jesus has invited all of the disciples to walk with him on the road to the cross and share his rejection and suffering and they ignore him. He asks them if they can drink the cup and be baptized in the cross—they off-handedly say yes, not having a clue what they are getting into. And they do—after the Resurrection and the gifting of the Spirit's power, but they must first learn to be servants, the least bending before all others as Jesus does—and give their life for the ransom of many. James is the first to be martyred of the twelve, the brother of the Lord, but what made him holy was that he learned what true love is—to lay down your life so that others may believe and be strengthened to follow Jesus. Jesus is still inviting us to share intimacy with him—and his suffering with those who walk the way of the cross today.

✴ Jeremiah tries to get the attention of the people in a bizarre fashion, burying a loincloth, letting it rot in the ground and digging it up again and using it to describe Judah and Jerusalem. Hardly flattering! God wants his people to cling to him, but they tear themselves away from him. Jesus tells the parable of the mustard seed, tiniest of all that becomes a bush, a small tree that harbors and protects all the birds that no one cares about. And the story of yeast buried in dough that rises and feeds a multitude. We are to cling to God and be refuge for the lost and forgotten and feed the hungry. And we are to rejoice that we are given the wisdom hidden since creation!

✴ James, the brothers of John (the beloved) and a cousin of Jesus, was one of the early leaders of the church in Jerusalem and the first to be martyred by Herod. He is one of the sons of thunder, wanting one of the best seats in the kingdom. He held his treasure in a very earthen vessel that allowed the power of God to shine through. He knew the dying of Jesus and shared in his sufferings, believed in the resurrection of Jesus, and knew it in his own life. His life was to bring grace and glory to God.

We, like James and John, have been given to drink of the cup of salvation—the cup of the Eucharist that feeds us and we have been baptized in the death and resurrection of Jesus. But we have not drank much of the cup of suffering, of rejection and crucifixion because of the company and closeness that we share with Jesus, the Son of Man, who gave his life as ransom for the many and was servant to us all. We are invited—in our earthen vessels, to put our lives at the service of the Lord and those of the earth in most need. Can Jesus come to rely on us to share his cup and his suffering and his life?

July 26

JOACHIM and ANN, parents of Mary

FIRST READING   Sir 44:1, 10–15
Responsorial Psalm   Ps 32:1113–14, 17–18
GOSPEL   Mt 13:16–17

✺ This is one of Matthew's other beatitudes: blessed are you who see and you who hear what the prophets and the just ones longed for over the long generations of living on promises! And we find ourselves in that group of the blessed because we too have seen the works of God in Jesus, in the Eucharist, in the community, in the sacraments and the poor and we hear in our communities at liturgy and in base communities the Word of God among us. Do we long for these scriptures and stories, prayers and exhortations of how to live together, how to pray, how to forgive, how to live meekly (nonviolently) in a world of injustice and violence? Maybe we need to pray for the prophets' passion for God's will to be done on earth and God's word to be respected and integrated into our communities' lives and to pray for the just ones' dedication to obeying the Word in our own lives.

✺ A day to look backwards to our ancestors, those who went before us in faith and passed it onto us by their lives, devotion and instructions. All that we have comes from others who were gracious in passing it onto us. They are buried in peace, yet they live in us and we are to take the time to gather and tell of their wisdom and how they praised God with their lives. And first and foremost we are rooted, sourced and given birth to in Jesus the Word of God made flesh. Blest are we because we have seen and known what so many generations waited for and did not see or hear. Are we appreciative of our faith and heritage?

✺ These are the parents of Mary, the grandparents of Jesus. This feast was created, along with their names to give Jesus a heritage, a family, ancestors, like ordinary people. The readings reflect this: Sirach praises those who have passed on to their descendants their faith, their virtue and God's covenant with them. Honoring parents/grandparents that went before us in faith, and telling this stories, passing on their wisdom keeps the community alive and growing through the generations.

But we are blest by Jesus in the gospel, reminding us that our ancestors in faith, are not just or even primarily our families, but the prophets and holy men and women who went before us who longed to see what we see and wanted so much to hear the Word of God in Jesus but were not able to. What are we passing on to the generations that come after us, not only our own families, but the people who watch us and long to see the Word of God in our lives taking flesh so that they might belong to the family of Jesus?

July 29

MARTHA

FIRST READING   1 Jn 4:7–16
Responsorial Psalm   Ps 34:2–3, 4–5, 6–7, 8–9, 10–11
GOSPEL   Lk 10:38–42

How did the love of God appear among us? It appeared in the beloved Son Jesus who has loved us first, commanding us to love one another. No one has seen God but if we love, then God lives in us and God's love spreads freely among us. We are sent to declare that the Father has sent Jesus into the world to save the world. We have known this love of God in Jesus and we must live this love in the world for all to see. Martha after the death of her brother Lazarus runs out to meet Jesus. But she is hardly welcoming. Jesus assures her but she cannot fathom his words that "I AM the resurrection and the life." It takes a lifetime after baptism to begin to let ourselves be buried in that mystery and begin to know this God in Jesus as life and love.

Again, all the stories of the men and women disciples around Jesus are fraught with weakness, lack and humanness. Martha is the sister of Mary and Lazarus. Jesus returns and Lazarus has been in the tomb four days. Martha is angry, grieving and hurt. "Lord, if you had been here, my brother would not have died. But I know that whatever you ask from God, God will give you." There is no greeting—only words that sting with guilt. She wants him to give her back her brother. And she is told he will rise, but she doesn't want that—she wants what was—what he was. Jesus loves these three so much and yet they don't see who he is either! Jesus tells her who he is—it is the central line of John's gospel. "I am the resurrection; whoever believes in me, though he die, shall live. Whoever is alive by believing in me will never die. Do you believe?" She says Yes, but her answer betrays her—she calls him the Christ, the Son of God, who is coming into the world. She misses him entirely. She too only sees him in light of the Messiah and prophet (sons of God). But we are each and all asked that question: do we believe that Jesus is the Resurrection and life? And that changes everything forever. Resurrection begins in baptism and we practice all our lives until we die. And like Martha we spend our whole lives learning who Jesus truly is—and never know but a small piece of the mystery.

AUGUST

August 10
LAWRENCE, deacon and martyr

FIRST READING   2 Cor 9:6–10
Responsorial Psalm   Ps 112:1–2, 5–6, 7–8, 9
GOSPEL   Jn 12:24–26

We turn today to John's gospel, the gospel of the beloved disciple, the one who will lay down their life for the strengthening of the faith of the community. Jesus is speaking of himself and his own suffering and death, but he is also speaking of all those who will come after him in the way of the cross, and laying down their lives, buried in the earth so that life and faith, and the presence of those who have loved will live forever. The blood of martrys is the seed of Christians (Didache) and we celebrate Lawrence, a deacon who cared for the treasures of the church—the poor and refused to bow before the gods of Rome, dying and proclaiming the dignity and gift of love. If we are to serve Jesus, then we must lay down our lives daily in service, as practice, perhaps for the honor of laying down our lives literally in death. As we have lived, so we will die and rise with Jesus.

✳ Are we sparing or bountiful in what we sow/and so reap? And we are questioned not just as individuals but as communities of faith. Does God multiply his favors among us because we give to the poor even far away and we are known for our justice? What's our yield like in this time of the year? Jesus tells us we are grains of wheat, and we must be buried in order to bring forth a harvest to life eternal. Are we willing to lose our life and let go of our excess and share? Are we really following Jesus and serving God in others?

✳ Lawrence, a deacon cared for widows, orphans, slaves and the poorest of the Jerusalem church, which was the poorest of the churches. He gave bountifully and was good news to all the least of the people, the children of God in need and he gave everything, including his life so that they might have life abundantly both physically and spiritually. Lawrence became the grain of wheat, dying after serving his Lord—and all the people knew that where Lawrence the servant of God was, truly God was there with them too. And we are told that the Father honors him forever now. Are we deacons, servants of the Lord, caring for the least of our brothers and sisters, and loving our lives but losing it for the sake of others? Do we do anything that would cause the Father to honor us?

August 22

QUEENSHIP OF MARY

FIRST READING   Is 9:1–6
Responsorial Psalm   Ps 113:1–2, 3–4, 5–6, 7–8
GOSPEL   Lk 1:26–38

✳ Again we hear the story of the first disciple and believer in Luke's community, the model for all disciples of the Word made Flesh who dwells among us in Incarnation, in the Scriptures and in our lives by baptism, and in the people he has made his own on earth. Our God is Lord of history, not just Israel's but all peoples, all nations and all the earth. Our God is the fulfillment of all the hopes, the prophecies, the promises of the human race for millions of years. Our God is the Word made flesh among us forever. This presence is with us always in the Scriptures, in the Eucharist, in the Church, in the poor and in those who cry out for justice, who obey the Word that they have heard and seek the coming of God's will and God's kingdom on earth now. This is what we pray for in the Our Father and this is what Mary models as believer and disciple when she answers in the tradition of Moses, Isaiah, David and many others: "Behold, I am the servant of the Lord." This is our dignity, our calling and it is the way the kingdom of God comes to earth.

This is a feast of Mary, but as always the scriptures seek to tell us who her child is, the Word of God made flesh. The angel Gabriel proclaims that this child to be born, Jesus, "will be great, and shall rightly be called the Son of the Most High. The Lord God will give him the kingdom of David his ancestor; he will rule over the people of Jacob forever and his reign shall have no end." This is Jesus and the kingdom that he brings is the sanctuary of the poor, the lost, the forgiven and those who honor God, with the words that Mary speaks to Gabriel: "I am the handmaid of the Lord, let it be done to me according to your word." We too belong to this kingdom inheriting it all with Mary.

The child born of Mary is the child of light, the shattering of death, the presence of joy in living. It is the dawn of a new creation where there is no slavery or oppression, no hunger and want. There is no more war, for the child is the Peace of God, dwelling with us forever. His kingdom is one of justice, community, righteousness and zeal for the glory of the Lord. It is the Father's kingdom for all peoples, the beloved children of God.

If there is a queen of this kingdom, then she is the least of the least, poorest with the poor, nobody from nowhere, anonymous among the masses of the world's people who hunger for justice, seek peace, hope for their children's future, the basic necessities of life where people have what they need, where there is no war and the light of the world is the Son of Justice. We are all called to obey the Word of the Lord and let God's will be done in us—and lives as the royalty of God together.

The child born of Mary is the child of light, the shattering of death, the presence of joy in living. It is the dawn of a new creation where there is no slavery or oppression, no hunger and want. There is no more war, for the child is the Peace of God, dwelling with us forever. His kingdom is one of justice, community, righteousness and zeal for the glory of the Lord. It is the Father's kingdom for all peoples, the beloved children of God.

If there is a queen of this kingdom, then she is the least of the least, poorest with the poor, nobody from nowhere, anonymous among the masses of the world's people who hunger for justice, seek peace, hope for their children's future, and the basic necessities of life. People have what they need, there is no war and the light of the world is the Son of Justice. We are all called to obey the Word of the Lord and let God's will be done in us and we are to live as the royalty of God together.

BARTHOLOMEW, apostle

August 24

FIRST READING   Rev 21:9–14
Responsorial Psalm   Ps 145:10–11, 12–13, 17–18
GOSPEL   Jn 1:45–51

Today we hear the story of how the first apostles were called in John's gospel and the apostle we remember today isn't even mentioned—he is just among the others. And they are called, not by name in John's gospel (only Philip) but by others who are caught and then go after another, passing on what they have found. And they are all finding something a bit different—but none of them actually find Jesus. In this very first chapter he tells them and us that we know nothing of who he is and who we belong to—one day though we will see the Son of Man coming in glory for judgment over heaven and earth. He is the crucified One, the suffering servant and the judge of the nations, no matter what we think he might be for us. Like all the apostles we must spend our lives relearning and stretching our heart and minds so that we can know more of our God in Jesus.

We are given a glimpse of a vision and a wall surrounding a city, that is massive in splendor with the names of the 12 tribes of Israel written on it, and a foundation set of stones with the names of the 12 apostles of the Lamb. Bartholomew is one of those 12 and we know nothing about him, except that he was an apostle of "the Lamb." And we hear the story of the calling of others: Philip, Nathanael, and of course, our names. We are to be the followers of the Lamb of God, the Son of Man, suffering servant of God, crucified and Risen. Are we?

✶ We know nothing of Bartholomew except his name and so we hear of the calling of the apostles in John. Each one who sees Jesus, goes and finds another to tell about the discovery and bring him back as another follower. Who told Bartholomew? Did Jesus call him personally? How did he become part of the inner circle of twelve? How are we called? Who calls us? Who do we call to come and see, to meet Jesus? The vision of the city of God in Revelation describes what will be—the fullness of the kingdom that was entrusted to the apostles and now entrusted to us that we may bring it to earth. We are to be followers of the Lamb of God, the Crucified and Risen One who is the Savior of all the peoples of the World.

August 29

BEHEADING OF
JOHN THE BAPTIST, martyr

FIRST READING   Jer 1:17–19
Responsorial Psalm   Ps 171:1–2, 3–4, 5–6, 15, 17
GOSPEL   Mk 6:17–29

✶ John, the one who goes before the Lord's face has been arrested for telling the truth on a personal basis to the powerful: the king in his relationship with his brother's wife (he murdered his brother among many others). And he has called all the powerful of the earth to repentance and conversion. And Herod's new wife is intent on killing John since Herod is afraid of him, but won't kill him because of the people. John loses his head at a party, as a gift in return for a young woman's dance. He is beheaded and his disciples bury him, in grief and loss. This was the arrow hidden in the quiver of God, sent to the heart of his people. This was the light in the darkness, bringing hope for salvation, freedom and life. This is the fate of those whose lives cry out justice as surely as their words. It is the end of all the prophets, martyrs, Jesus himself. We do not abide gracefully with purity of truth and being seen for what we truly are. Do we ever go before the face of the Lord preparing his ways with conversion and truth telling?

✺ A description of the prophet John who must call the people, the king and the leaders to repentance, standing against them all, knowing they will all fight against him but they will not prevail. God will be with him to deliver him. But this is the telling of the imprisonment and beheading of John by Herod in collusion with Herodias and her daughter. John speaks the truth and the Lord God is with him, as he preaches, in jail and as he is beheaded. God is our refuge in life and in death. Our hope is in God from our mother's wombs to our burial places. Are we standing firm?

✺ The prophet John is a fortified city, a pillar of iron, a wall of brass against the whole land, calling everyone back— standing against the kings and priests and people. They will fight against you—and they did. He was murdered but God was with him always to deliver him in spite of death. John was faithful, calling the people to a baptism of repentance that led to the forgiveness of sins and many of the people came to him and turned from their lives of sin and injustice. But it was the religious, economic and political leadership that resisted him. And since he is a prophet he went after King Herod who had murdered his brother so that he could have his wife (she was definitely part of the murder and the marriage). He is imprisoned but Herod is afraid of the people and won't kill him. But he was more afraid of his new wife and of looking bad at a dinner party. And so he has John beheaded in a prison on the spur of a moment. He is the last and greatest prophet of the older testament who depended on God as his rock and prepared the way for Jesus. Do we stand up and tell people all that the Lord commands us?

BIRTH OF MARY

September 8

FIRST READING Mic 5:1–4a (or Rom 8:28–30)
Responsorial Psalm Ps 13:6ab, 6c
GOSPEL Mt 1:1–16, 18–23

A birthday remembrance that goes way way back beyond the actual birth of this woman who will give birth to the Savior. Because our meaning, even Mary's meaning does not lie in what we do, but whether or not we have done the one thing we were born to do: incarnate the Word in our flesh and bring the good news to the poor of our history and world. And this Jesus is born of a long line of sinners and holy men and women, matriarchs and patriarchs, prophets and psalm-singers, those who were faithful and enduring as they waited and those that betrayed every word out of the mouth of God. We are each born into this world, like Mary and we are born into the kingdom of our Father in our baptisms. We are born from a long line of folks. Mary's life, Mary's meaning was found in the Word made flesh, crucified and risen from the dead. It is the meaning of each of our lives.

Mary's birth is celebrated because the birth of her child gives her meaning. It is her child who will stand and feed his flock with the power of the Lord, with the name of God and God's name in Jesus is Peace. God transforms everything in the lives of those who love him, so that they become true images of the beloved Son of God. This describes both Mary and each of us. He is our elder brother and with Mary we are all the beloved daughters and sons of God, sharing in God's glory. We are all born to bring forth the Word of God in our lives and worlds.

We read always about Jesus on the days we honor Mary. It is her child and the Incarnation—God becoming flesh/human in the world; our hope, our salvation and our life. The child is born in Bethlehem, a place of no consequence that will bring forth a shepherd in the strength of God who will reach the ends of the earth and he shall be peace.

All things work together for God. God's Son is the first born of many brothers and sisters—we are all given birth in Jesus and given to God. Mary was given birth (by her parents like all of us) but it was her child, the Son of the Father who gave birth to her in the power of the Spirit, giving her back to the Father, as each of us is given over to God.

We are all called to give birth to the Word in our flesh and to celebrate our birthdays—born in the world, born into Christ and hidden in God in our baptisms and born into the Body of Christ, the Church. Happy Birthday to Mary and to us all.

September 15

OUR LADY OF SORROWS

FIRST READING   Heb 5:7–9
Responsorial Psalm   Ps 31:2 and 3b, 3cd–4, 5–6, 15–16, 20
GOSPEL   Jn 19:25–27 (or Lk 2:33–35)

These are the faithful ones, who stand at the end, the bitter end with their Lord and Master: there is 'his mother, his mother's sister Mary, who was the wife of Cleophas, and Mary of Magdala' and there is the beloved disciple—never named because it is supposed to be each one of us. At the ancient ritual of baptism, the one to be immersed in the waters knelt and was told: you are already saved, on your knees and under the sign of the cross. This is where we dwell, as believers, as the faithful and loving friends, brothers, sisters and mothers to our crucified and suffering servant Lord. This is Jesus' new family, birthed in his blood and water. It is the church and the church, the Body of Christ, all of us are to be found at the foot of the cross everywhere in the world, as silent witnesses to injustice, to pain that should never have happened and grieving for the horror and evil that we do to one another. There are four—where are we found?

This is the wonder of our God in Jesus. He prayed aloud and in tears and submitted to death as a human being, humbly believing that his prayer was heard. We too, follow in his way and learn obedience through suffering as all human beings do, as a result of our sin and compliance with evil, or at the hands of those who do evil or live in collusion with violence and injustice. And Mary, the mother of Jesus learned this obedience in suffering since she was bound so closely to her beloved child. We are all revealed as those who believe in the way we respond to suffering in our lives. What secrets do we lay bare in others by our being bound intimately to the Cross of Christ?

✹ Jesus is the one who suffered with us and for us, revealing how to be human in the face of pain and sorrow. All of us who are his followers must learn how to be odedient and how to remain faithful in the face of the violence, horror and misery that human beings inflict upon one another in sin.

Jesus dies broken, humiliated and tortured, through crucifixion, the legal and massively unjust form of capital punished used by the Romans on those that threatened their power. Jesus dies alone, except in John's gospel, where his mother, his mother's sister, Mary of Cleopas, Mary of Magdala and the disciple whom Jesus loved stand witness in his company, in silent sorrow and mourning. This is the beloved community. This is where all of us who are baptized are to be found—sorrowing with his mother and the others, at the foot of the cross where millions still are crucified. Where do we stand together in witness and solidarity?

September 21

MATTHEW, apostle and evangelist

FIRST READING   Eph 4:1–7, 11–13
Responsorial Psalm   Ps 19:2–3, 4–5
GOSPEL   Mt 9:9–13

✹ Here we meet Matthew, a man of many jobs, experiences and lives: a tax collector, though a minor official, with many friends, who likes parties and threw one for Jesus to meet them all, a man shunned by good religious people and leaders of the community, in collusion with the Romans, making a living off his neighbors' ill fortune, a public sinner who knew the touch and the look and the word of mercy from the Master's coming after him.

Jesus tells all those who scoffed at his choice of Matthew: "healthy people do not need a doctor, but sick people do. Go and find out what this means: "What I want is mercy, not sacrifice." I didn't come to call the righteous but sinners! And so Matthew becomes apostle, one of the twelve, disciple of the Master of Mercy, scribe and evangelist of the Word and all he writes is about what Mercy is, not sacrifice, spirit not only law, freedom and hope not only demands. How much have we learned from this man about the mercy of our God?

✻ Matthew, tax collector turned evangelist, bringer of Good News in word spoken and written; martyr, giving as his last word in service of the truth—his own life. That was his share of grace. What is ours? Who are we and what are we engaged in as a way of life? How do we need to turn so that we too are bringers of good news in word and deed? We are the sick that have been touched by water and word and bread. Do we live in gratitude with mercy and sacrifice on behalf of others now?

✻ Matthew is an evangelist, a prophet and a disciple among the twelve. We all share the same hope and the same call and so must make every effort to preserve unity among us. We must all strive to build up one another in knowledge of God's Son and to share the favor that has been given to us. Matthew's gospel emphasizes many of these exhortations because his community is being torn apart by persecution by the Romans and the Jews and they are struggling as Jewish and Gentile Christians to be one heart and mind in Christ.

Matthew was a tax collector. He stops taking from others to give to the state and the temple treasury. He begins to give mercy and healing/health of mind/soul/spirit that Jesus so graciously offered to him. What are we called to leave behind so that we can begin giving to each other?

September 29

MICHAEL, GABRIEL, and RAPHAEL, archangels

FIRST READING   Dn 7:9–10, 13–14 (or Rev 12:7–12ab)
Responsorial Psalm   Ps 138:1–2ab, 2cde–3, 4–5
GOSPEL   Jn 1:47–51

✻ This is the feast of the archangels, those who defend the honor of God, protect the poor and those who work for justice (Michael), accompany those who preach, teach and speak the Word (Gabriel), care for the sick, travelers, refugees, those in exile, in need of friendship, rescue, lovers, the blind, fishermen and teach all to pray (Raphael) and those who remind us to change, to be transformed, to die to ourselves, and stand with us at our death (Ariel). These are only a few of the great company that will come with the Son of Man when we returns in glory to judge the nations and to take possession of the earth and heavens as his dwelling place. Jesus is Lord of the universe, always more than anything we think he might be for us, for our family and friends, church, state or world. He is the Son of the Living God made flesh among us and is worshipped, served and obeyed by all those who are spirit. Our world is much larger than anything we can see—today we call on the archangels and spirits that serve our God to help us obey and know his glory too.

✻ War in heaven and those who honor God, and are obedient to God's Word triumph, while Satan, anyone and anything that hinders the Word of God and deceives the children of God is hurled down to earth. This is an epic story of good and evil and victory belongs to those who do good, who live and die without violence on earth, who are witnesses to the truth by martyrdom. It is given to those who love life, yet lay it down if necessary. They do not take lives just to proclaim their belief. War in heaven is different than war on earth and though there are those driven out, nobody dies in the name of religion or God. We are not alone in our struggle: creatures of light serve with us, they honor God and will be a part of the judgment upon the earth, as they were once judged. They serve the Son of Man—do we?

✻ The angels of God, pure spirits/light/power stand always before the throne/the face of God, in his presence worshipping and attending to God in his holiness and truth. They serve the Ancient One (Father) and the Son of Man doing his will in heaven and on earth. They are more 'at home' in the Spirit and presence of God, though they are also bound to us here on earth in obedience to the will of God.

They themselves have struggled to obey and they know that those who did not obey among their own now are upon the earth. But we have been given power, dominion, authority and the testimony and Word of God to stand against them and they do not have power over us. Even if we must die, we are given the power of the Son of Man to aide us, along with the angels' protection/witness in our lives. Jesus sees Nathanael coming towards him (each of us) but he has seen him under the fig tree. We also have been seen by God since we were conceived. Our God knows us intimately—the good and what needs to be transformed. But like Nathanael and all the disciples, we are reminded that our personal relationships with Jesus, even our relationships in community are not all that is—the angels of heaven and all that God has made are one, and called to be one in worshipping The Son of Man.

OCTOBER

October 2
GUARDIAN ANGELS

FIRST READING   Ex 23:20–23
Responsorial Psalm   Ps 91:1–2, 3–4ab, 4c–6, 10–11
GOSPEL   Mt 18:1–5, 10

The angels have accompanied the people of God since the beginning, guarding us, bringing us to the place God prepares for us. We are to reverence and listen to the angels and offer no defiance against them. God's name is in the angel. Angel means "messenger of God," both a spirit of God's power and grace, and the Scripture, the Word of God, the presence of the Name of God in Jesus among us. Who or what are we listening to? The children are all those without power in this world: the poor, outcast, sinners, those who disobey the law, slaves, servants, outsiders, and the sick—these are the greatest and first in the kingdom of God. We are to be angels to them and all of us have an angel that guards us and implores us to take heed and obey God's work.

An angel goes before the people into freedom/the desert and they are to attend to his voice as he guards them on the way. They were not to rebel. He would not forgive them, yet God's authority resides in him. Some think this angel, this messenger of God is not just an angel but Moses who has been sent to lead the people to freedom and the land.

Yet each person has an angel, especially those who have no power/authority/rights in our world to defend and guard themselves from harm, sometimes from us. An angel can be a person, but most often an angel means a message from God and more importantly the message from God is always the Word of God, the scriptures. We are attended by angels, but the Word of the Lord is our companion, our safety and refuge and our source of strength, grace and truth.

October 7
OUR LADY OF THE ROSARY

FIRST READING   Job 42:1–3, 5–6
Responsorial Psalm   Ps 119:66, 71, 75, 91, 125, 130
GOSPEL   Lk 10:17–24

We find ourselves in the upper room waiting with the disciples, some women, including Mary, the mother of Jesus and his brothers, in obedience to Jesus, praying constantly. The Spirit will come upon them and give birth to the Church. This experience is an echo of the experience of each individual, like Mary when the Spirit is sent upon her and all of us and the power of the Most High overshadows us and the Holy Child to be born in us is called the Son of God. We walk with Mary, as a disciple of The Word, obeying God's word to us, living in obedience, living in the Spirit, hidden with Christ in God.

October 18
LUKE, evangelist

FIRST READING   2 Tim 4:10–17b
Responsorial Psalm   Ps 145:10–11, 12–13, 17–18
GOSPEL   Lk 10:1–9

✦ Jesus appoints seventy-two as his disciples and sends them out two by two ahead of him to prepare the way. He sends them forth with prayers for more laborers for the harvest, with courage and an exhortation to resist power and violence without doing evil or harm to anyone. They are to travel lightly, without money or clothing that would allow them to make it on their own—they are to rely on the hospitality of God that is now in the world, in the person of Jesus and the kingdom of God. They are to bring Peace to all those upon whom God's favor rests. They are to eat what is offered and in exchange bring healing, hope and the good news of God to all who will be open to them. This is the vocation of Luke, the disciple, evangelist and for all who are to be missionaries, teachers, preachers, healers, those who forgive, comfort, bring hope and live with those who are still waiting for the Word of the Lord to come to them in those who believe in Jesus. Do we pray for disciples, who go out two by two and who bring the presence of Jesus to those still waiting for his company and Word?

✦ Paul tells Timothy that Luke has stayed faithfully with him, in preaching the Gospel and in the work of evangelizing— bringing others to belief by modeling and living what is spoken and exhorted. And Luke is one of those who went forth, no staff in hand, no purse, extra clothing, no sandals, proclaiming by their radical poverty and intense devotion to the Good News, in their own person, that the kingdom of God is in the world among us. Like the Lamb of God they go fearlessly, without protection, in twos, to prepare the way of the Lord, to go before his face. Do we remember that we too are called to go before the face of the Lord, preparing for the Word in our lives?

October 28

SIMON and JUDE, apostles

FIRST READING   Eph 2:19–22
Responsorial Psalm   Ps 19:2–3, 4–5
GOSPEL   Lk 6:12–16

✦ Jesus prays all through the night in the hills and then calls his own by name to him. Simon and Jude are chosen among the twelve. We know that Simon was called a zealot—one who was passionate about the coming of the messiah and the kingdom of God in justice for the people. Whether he belonged to the Zealot party (that was sometimes violent in attacking the Romans, engaged in subversive activities) or not, he is remembered for his strength in wanting God's kingdom to come into the world. And then there is Jude, the son of James—really Judas, the same as the one who betrayed Jesus but this one remained faithful. Both died martyrs deaths after they came in the power of the Spirit to know the courage of the cross and allegiance to Jesus. Not much else is known about them except that they were from the beginning two of those who brought the good news to the poor. We too by our baptisms and confirmation have been called by name to walk with Jesus and to share the good news to the poor. Jesus has prayed for our faithfulness, our freedom and our obedience. Let us remember whose company we belong to and pray for one another.

☀ In Jesus we are no longer aliens, we are saints and citizens of the kingdom of God's peace and justice, which knows no borders. We are a refuge and building that is secure on its foundations from the beginning, with Christ as a cornerstone. We grow together in God and God dwells in us in the Spirit. Jesus chose 12 from among his companions to lay the foundation in the Spirit and most of them cemented the stones with their blood as witness to Jesus' Word. But their work, and ours now, is to work to make the foundation sure: with hope preached and the weak and the sick tended and cared for and to make sure the whole world knows sanctuary in God here upon the earth, now.

NOVEMBER

PRESENTATION OF MARY

November 21

FIRST READING   Zec 2:14–178
Responsorial Psalm   Dn 3:52, 53, 54, 55, 56
GOSPEL   Mt 12:46–50

ANDREW, apostle

FIRST READING   Rom 10:9–18
Responsorial Psalm   Ps 19:8, 9, 10, 11
GOSPEL   Mt 4:18–22

❊ Jesus catches sight of Andrew and his brother Simon casting their nets into the sea and summons him to follow him. He catches him in his daily work and family and lays claim to him forever. Andrew leaves and goes off in the company of others who have been called, a new family casting their nets widely in the world, snaring the sick, the paralyzed, the dranged and all who suffer in a net of healing and hope. Who do we spend our lives catching off guard and snaring in the net of God's embrace? Who will you catch today?

❊ We are to believe, to confess Jesus as Lord of all life. We are saved but we must preach this gospel and we must be a part of those who send others forth to preach this life. Have we heard and professed our belief? Can anyone tell? Andrew was called, with his brother Simon and his friends and together they became the company of believers. We too are called, to leave our concentration on what we are doing, and to serve, to follow and to put all at the service of God's project of justice, the care of the poor, and peace upon the earth—all found in the Word of Christ, in scripture and in the Body. This is confession and belief in fact.

❊ Andrew preached Jesus the Lord—crucified and risen from the dead, and that belonging to all nations and peoples. He went forth and brought this good news of Jesus to the poor and to all those who would listen. He was a missionary, a preacher, a fisherman, a brother and a believer himself. He began early, leaving everything, his boats and livelihood, to follow Jesus when he was called together with his brother Simon. He was called within his family, his work and his nation, to leave it all for larger horizons and countries and inner worlds he could never imagine—into the company of Jesus, the Word, the Christ. We are each called this way to follow, to preach and to be the good news we proclaim—to our families, in our jobs, in our countries. And yet we are to be aware of the world that waits for our word, our risking, and our reaching out beyond our small personal lives. If we call on the name of the Lord, we must also confess with our lives that Jesus is Lord.

DECEMBER

December 12

OUR LADY OF GUADALUPE

FIRST READING	Zec 2:14–17 (or Rev 11:19; 12:1–6, 10)
Responsorial Psalm	Jdt 13:18bcde, 19
GOSPEL	Lk 1:26–38 (or Lk 1:39–47)

Sing and rejoice O daughter of Zion, I am about to come! I shall dwell among you! Today is the feast of the poor indigenous woman who stands with her feet on the earth with music and abundant life all around her. As angels came to shepherds who came to her, she is the angel and the shepherd that comes to her poor children with words of hope to ponder and to let seep deep into our hearts. This child that she carries under her heart will be joy for all peoples and will dwell with the poor with special devotion and tenderness. She who is mother to Jesus the Poor One so she is mother to all those who suffer and struggle to live. She and her child, the Holy One of God, and Joseph dwell with us all days. Rejoice and sing!

Our Lady of Guadalupe is the patroness of the Americas, standing on the bridge between the two Americas, drawing all peoples to her unborn Son of Justice. She and her child will dwell among the people. Keep still in his presence! Mary brings the Word of God to Elizabeth's child who hears the presence of Justice and Peace and leaps for joy, and the Spirit springs upon them. Blessed are all those who hear, believe and set out in haste to bring the Word into their world. Do our lands reflect their presence dwelling upon us?

✻ The readings are of wisdom, whom God made first and who is close beside him always, bringing God delight, playing in the world, and bringing delight to humans. An apt description of the woman of Guadalupe, who brought the child who is Wisdom to the world, accompanied by the sound of music, flowers, light and joy. She is the patroness of the Americas, the one who sought to bring together the victims and the conqueror by standing with the victims and calling them to rejoice for she is their mother first. She brings God's presence and dwelling place to the indigenous peoples. The incarnation, the birth of Jesus, born of a woman brings true justice to all peoples, in spite of believers' destruction and evil. God seeks to make his dwelling place with all peoples—not just the ones his followers choose as worthy.

The 'annunciation' is really the Incarnation—God becomes flesh in the womb of Mary at her submission and word of acceptance, just as God's word becomes part of our flesh at our baptisms and acceptance of the Word of God. And the 'visitation' is really Mary's confirmation by Elizabeth—the exchange of the Spirit between believers that culminates in the shout of joy in praise of God for liberation and freedom given to the lowly (those without violence), the poor, the hungry and those without power on earth. This is Guadalupe's message to the oppressed. If we call ourselves children of Nuestra Senora La Virgen de Guadalupe is it our message?